NATURE
designed a
forest as an
experiment in
unpredictability;
we are trying to
design a regulated
forest. Nature designed
a forest over a landscape;
we are trying to design a
forest on each hectare. Nature
designed a forest with diversity;
we are trying to design a forest with
simplistic uniformity. Nature designed
a forest of interrelated processes; we are
trying to design a forest based on isolated
products. Nature designed a forest in which
all elements are neutral; we are trying to design
a forest in which we perceive some elements to be
good and others bad. Nature designed a forest to be
a flexible, timeless continuum of species; we are
trying to design a forest to be a rigid, time-constrained
monoculture. Nature designed a forest of long-term
absolutes. Nature designed a forest to be self-sustaining and
self-repairing; we are designing a forest to require increasing
external subsidies—fertilizers, herbicides, and pesticides.
Nature designed forests of the Pacific Northwest to live 500
to 1,200 years; we are designing a forest that may live 100 years.
Nature designed Pacific Northwest forests to be unique in the
world, with twenty-five species of conifers, the longest lived and the
largest of their genera anywhere; we are designing a forest that is largely a
single-species on a short rotation. Everything we humans have been doing
to the forest is an attempt to push nature to a higher sustained yield. We
fail to recognize, however, that we must have a sustainable forest before we can
have a sustainable yield (harvest). In other words, we cannot have a sustainable
yield until we have a sustainable forest. We must have a sustainable forest to have a
sustainable yield; we must
have a sustainable yield
to have a sustainable
industry; we must have
a sustainable industry
to have a sustainable
economy; we must have a
sustainable economy to
have a sustainable society.

Chris Maser

Lines from "Logging"

The ancient forests of China logged
      and the hills slipped into the Yellow Sea.
Squared beams, log dogs,
      on a tamped-earth still.
San Francisco 2 X 4s
      were the woods around Seattle:
Someone killed and someone built, a house,
      a forest, wrecked or raised
All America hung on a hook
      & burned by men, in their own praise.

Snow on fresh stumps and brush-piles.
The generator starts and rumbles
      in the frosty dawn
I wake from bitter dreams,
Rise and build a fire,
Pull on and lace the stiff cold boots
Eat huge flapjacks by a gloomy Swede
In splintery cookhouse light
      grab my tin pisspot hat
Ride off to the show in a crummy-truck
And start the Cat.

"Pines grasp the clouds with iron claws
like dragons rising from sleep"
250,000 board-feet a day
If both Cats keep working
& nobody gets hurt

—Gary Snyder

Clearcut : the tragedy of industrial forestry / edited by Bill Devall.
     p.   cm.
     Includes bibliographical references.
     ISBN 0-87156-494-7
     1. Clearcutting—Environmental aspects—United States.
     2. Clearcutting—Environmental aspects—Canada.   3. Forest ecology—
United States.   4. Forest ecology—Canada. I.   Devall, Bill, 1938-.
SD387.C58C53   1994
333.75′137′097—dc20   93-35989
                                                   CIP

Published by Sierra Club Books and Earth Island Press, San Francisco, California.
Design by Tamotsu Yagi/DelRae Roth.

Grateful acknowledgment is made to the following for permission to reprint copyrighted material:

Gordon Robinson, *The Forest and the Trees*, 1988, used with permission from
Island Press, Washington, D.C. and Covelo, California.

Random House, Inc. for permission to reprint an excerpt from the poem "The Tower Beyond Tragedy" by Robinson Jeffers
from *The Selected Poetry of Robinson Jeffers*. Copyright 1925 and renewed 1953 by Robinson Jeffers.
Reprinted by permission of Random House, Inc.

Cedric Wright, *Words of the Earth*, 1960, used with permission from the Sierra Club, San Francisco, California.

Portions of "Policy in the Woods" from *Ghost Bears*, 1992, by R. Edward Grumbine, used with permission of Island Press,
Washington, D.C. and Covelo, California.

"Escape" by D. H. Lawrence, from THE COMPLETE POEMS OF D. H. LAWRENCE by D. H. Lawrence, Edited by V. de Sola
Pinto & F. W. Roberts. Copyright © 1964, 1971 by Angelo Ravagli and C. M. Weekley, Executors of the Estate of Frieda Lawrence
Ravagli. Used by permission of Viking Penguin, a division of Penguin Books USA Inc.

Printed and bound in Japan.

DEDICATION

This book is in memory of the plantlife, birds, insects, animals, and indigenous cultures
that have been driven to extinction by the greed and delusion
of human arrogance. All of us in the Industrial Growth Society must take the responsibility
for this condition and make it our duty to halt the continuation
of economic and social structures that perpetuate this "death of birth."
We must try to visualize extinction and learn
to understand accurately how certain patterns of human behavior lead to the
extinction of species. We *do* have the ability to enrich,
not impoverish, our lives and the planet wherein we dwell. We pray and hope
for the continuing evolution of forest ecosystems.
We work for realistic, ecological, sustainable interpenetration of humans and forest
ecosystems, living by ecological terms rather than economic terms.

CLEA

THE TRAGEDY OF IN

EDITED BY BILL DEVALL

RCUT

DUSTRIAL FORESTRY

SIERRA CLUB BOOKS / EARTH ISLAND PRESS

TABLE OF CONTENTS

Trygve Steen

Collectively, the photographs in this book provide a portrait of the great forests of North America as they cling
to life at the end of the twentieth century. They reveal that the forests of North America are suffering from a massive, human-caused,
catastrophic event—an epidemic of massive clearcutting.

INTRODUCTION

BILL DEVALL

The photos in this book reveal one aspect of our increasingly devastated Earth: the clearcutting of the forests of North America. From Prince William Sound in Alaska to the red hills of Georgia, from Nova Scotia to the high mountains of New Mexico, the industrial, extractive logging industry, encouraged and subsidized by federal and provincial governments, has stripped ancient trees from the soil through the timber extractive process called clearcutting—either leaving regions deforested or creating tree plantations that do not resemble natural forests.

In the United States, at least once in each generation during this century, there has been a great public debate over forest policy. The first debate, during the administration of Theodore Roosevelt, pitted John Muir, founder of the Sierra Club, and his followers against Gifford Pinchot, first head of the U.S. Forest Service. Muir argued that national forests should be a buffer between wild nature and encroaching industrial civilization. Pinchot, arguing from a utilitarian, resource development philosophy, stated that national forests should primarily provide a continuous supply of wood and water for economic development to serve an ever-increasing human population. Pinchot and his followers won that debate. Forests on public as well as private lands have been managed primarily for economic development including timber supply, water development, mining, grazing, and oil and gas development.

We are now engaged in another debate on forest policy both in Canada and the U.S. With the rise of regional trade agreements such as the North American Free Trade Agreement (NAFTA) and increasing penetration of transnational corporations into forested regions of Chile, Southeast Asia, and Russia, the current debate over forest policy in North America has worldwide implications. The integrity of all remaining primary forest ecosystems, as well as forested regions that were previously logged and are recovering some of their wild qualities, hangs in the balance.

When John Muir argued for the protection of forested regions at the close of the nineteenth century, the great primeval forests of California and the Pacific Northwest were still largely intact. Loggers were cutting the ancient redwood forests of California, but it sometimes took a crew of loggers up to a week to cut down a single old-growth redwood tree with a crosscut saw. Muir saw the beginning of commercial logging in the redwoods of the Sierra Nevada in the 1880s. Since then the industrial model of forestry has spread across North America at an ever-accelerating pace. It took over a hundred years to log the nearly two million acres of primeval coastal redwood forests in California. But the most massive and destructive clearcutting has occurred since about 1950 with the widespread use of chainsaws and tractors.

Forests are expressions of soil, water, climate—and time. Forests have evolved over hundreds, thousands, and millions of years. Each forest, and each stand of trees within a forest, has a unique history of natural catastrophic events including fires, floods, droughts, and earthquakes. Over time, these events create a mosaic of patterns across forested landscapes, expressed in biological terms as natural biodiversity.

To understand how quickly the massive forests of North America have been clearcut by axe, and during the past fifty years by chainsaw, we need to understand this human-caused catastrophe in a large time frame. In his book, *The Great American Forest* (1965), naturalist Rutherford Platt cites evidence that a "modern" oaklike tree was growing in the forests of Maryland 70 million years ago.

"If we consider that oaklike tree as a cornerstone, it establishes a date on the geologic calendar for the coming of age of the summer-green forest that spread from the Atlantic Coast to the Mississippi Valley. By subtracting from 70 million the twenty thousand years since early Stone Age people were hunting prehistoric animals where white cliffs of ice glittered on the northern horizons, we know that the forest [of North America] waited 69,980,000 years for people to come to live in it. This is the awe-inspiring time dimension of the [North] American forest. Through time, beyond human intellect to comprehend, our oaks, elms, and maples with their company of shrubs and vines were scattering their seeds, thrusting up their trunks, flaunting their flowers, and creating a lively, beautiful blanket of wildness. That was how long they were the dominant life on this continent—with no relation at all to human lives."

During the last fifty years—since the advent of the chainsaw, tractor, and logging truck, forests have been clearcut from steep mountain slopes in California, Oregon, Washington, and British Columbia. Forests in Alberta, Minnesota, California, and several other regions of North America are being clearcut and fed as fiber into pulp mills or converted into "waferboards."

Collectively, the photographs in this book provide a portrait of the great forests of North America as they cling to life at the end of the twentieth century. They reveal that the forests of North America are suffering from a massive, human-caused, catastrophic event—an epidemic of massive clearcutting.

These disturbing views of the forests were taken by a new generation of landscape photographers. An older generation of landscape photographers, including Ansel Adams, Eliot Porter, and others dating back to the nineteenth century, are familiar to many people through exhibit-format books. Adams, Porter, and their colleagues documented the great wild places from the Brooks Range of Alaska to the mountains of California and the Grand Canyon. They sought beauty in wildness and they found beauty in grand vistas. With their beautiful photographs, they inspired millions of people to take action to protect the last remaining wild areas.

The present generation of landscape photographers came to their task with a different sensibility. They were raised and educated with an ecological awareness of Nature's processes. They understand the ecological realities of CFCs, holes in the ozone layer, industrial pollution, acid rain, herbicide and pesticide poisoning, and nuclear waste. They are witness to vast changes across North America—from the disappearance of natural landscapes under urban sprawl to the destruction of forest landscapes by clearcutting. These photographers do not bring pretty or charming pictures to grace the pages of this book. They bring neither a romantic nor sentimental aesthetic to their documentary photos. Indeed, it is extremely difficult to maintain a romantic or sentimental approach to Nature while sitting in the middle of a large clearcut.

Aldo Leopold, ecologist and author of *A Sand County Almanac*, once wrote that to be trained as an ecologist was "to live alone in a world of wounds." Many people in the present generation have been trained in ecology, and many thousands more have developed ecological sensibilities on their own accord, and together they live among these wounds. The photos in this book reveal the landscape of forests behind what logging industry public relations officers euphemistically call "beauty strips"—thin borders of trees left standing along "scenic highways" and "scenic waterways" to hide the devastation of massive clearcuts.

The photographs herein are of course two-dimensional representations. They provide the reader with only a partial sense of what it is like to visit the site of a recent massive clearcut.

Ecofeminists frequently use the term *rape* when comparing the domination of women and violence against women as parallel to the domination and exploitation of Nature. Only an extremely insensitive person or one simply in denial could fail to sense the invasion, the violation, and the unnecessary—even violent—intrusion into the forest through massive clearcutting. *Rape* is an appropriate comparison to make—these forests have been seized and taken away by force, and they have been despoiled.

Another, equally appropriate term used in reference to massive clearcutting is *warfare*. Indeed, massive clearcuts look like bombed-out war zones. This analogy rings true, from the fundamental philosophical approach of the logging industry to the final results on the field of battle. The industry has openly declared its intent to clear Nature's forests and transform them into tree plantations. This endeavor is classically characterized as "man against Nature" wherein humans invade and "conquer." This open conflict is also expressed in hostility toward people who attempt to intervene on Nature's behalf. But in defeating Nature and wreaking havoc on natural ecosystems and processes, industrial loggers are also defeating themselves—it is a war that over the long term cannot be won. Industrial forestry allows a few people to reap short-term profits, but this war on the forests is foreclosing our long-term prospects for sustainability and biodiversity.

Furthermore, the underlying philosophical assumptions about human relationship with forest ecosystems is warped by industrial foresters who argue that tree plantations are "factories in the field" producing raw materials for our expanding economy through "scientific management" for "highest yield." Historian Carolyn Merchant, in her book *The Death of Nature*, persuasively argues that our contemporary alienation from the forest—indeed from Nature—emerged from a political battle waged in the seventeenth century in European philosophy. That battle, she argues, was between those who viewed Nature as a "machine" and supporters of "vitalist" philosophy that held that Nature has intrinsic values not explicable by the laws of chemistry and physics alone. The mechanistic perspective on Nature became dominant in Western society, congruent with the rise of industrial capitalism, and forests were exploited, manipulated, and managed primarily as sources of

raw materials for the expanding economy rather than appreciated for their intrinsic value or the value they give to any human society by providing fresh water, wildlife habitat, and aesthetic and spiritual sanctuary.

The photos of clearcuts shown in this book reveal the "shadow" side of the logging industry. This is the dark side that these huge corporations, and the government agencies with whom they conspire, conceal behind symbols such as Smokey the Bear and slogans such as "Trees are America's renewable resource." In Humboldt County, California, the logging industry attempts to co-opt the anger that many citizens feel when they see massive clearcutting by proclaiming that "Everyday is Earth Day for Pacific Lumber Company." The logging industry attempts to convince the public that it has reformed its ways by claiming, "We plant two trees for every tree we cut," without acknowledging that there is a difference between seedlings and mature trees and that a forest is a complex expression of the soil and water. Natural forests provide continuous fresh water, renewal of soils, habitat for wildlife, and self-regenerating forest communities. Monoculture or tree plantation forestry can never duplicate natural, primary forests.

THE ESSAYS

The essays in this book reveal historical, social, cultural, and ecological contexts to explain this massive, recent epidemic of clearcutting. The authors come from a new generation of scientists, philosophers, and social activists who have an ecologically based understanding of forests and forestry—based upon the new field of conservation biology and on ancient wisdom traditions—including the wisdom of traditional Native Americans, Buddhism, and Celtic reverance for sacred groves.

Many of these authors are motivated by the search for what Alan Drengson calls *ecosophy*. Drengson is a philosopher by training and a supporter of the deep long-range ecology movement. He appeals to our conscience as informed citizens and challenges us to make a commitment: "If each of us personally had to destroy the individual beings wiped out by the destruction of forest communities, we would refuse to do it.... Inaction over forest destruction must be partly a result of the success of public relations and other efforts to conceal the reality and consequences of destructive practices, which we tacitly support, even if only indirectly through various forms of economic activity." Turning ancient giant elders into chips and destroying forest communities so as to manufacture paper tissue is crazy. There are alternative sources of fiber that do not involve such destruction. There are alternative forestry practices that do not interfere with evolutionary processes of natural forests, that leave forest communities intact. There are practices that can help to restore natural forests. There are thoughtful, preserving ways to live. Certainly, if fully informed, we each would morally and spiritually support only practices that are nonviolent and let other beings be, practices that respect and honor them, that treasure and add to richness and diversity. And as we become informed, what level of commitment to saving and serving natural forests are we willing to make? With respect to jobs, saving natural forests will create more work than leveling them does.

As a philosopher, Alan Drengson is concerned with our alienation from and loss of meaningful experience with the forest that occurred as a result of historical processes. Drengson encourages us to increase our "capacity to perceive moral and spiritual realities, to be fully receptive to the world, to be open to learning from each being." We can make such progress he explains, by listening to and cultivating our *deep ecological self* through meditation, for example, which can be practiced by everyone through simple breathing exercises.

The new generation of forest ecologists, represented in this book by Reed Noss, Herb Hammond, Chris Maser, and Ed Grumbine, have made a rigorous and thorough examination of the patterns that condition one's thoughts and actions concerning forests. They have transcended the narrow anthropocentric model of silviculture taught in most "forestry schools" and have immersed themselves in the process of the evolving forest system. Their emotional, personal, ecological investigation of forests is intellectually informed by their studies of evolutionary biology, conservation biology, ecosystems analysis, and forest ecology.

They understand, as Reed Noss says, that "biodiversity is a central concept in modern conservation, but many people misunderstand or misrepresent what it means. Having co-opted the term 'sustainability' for their own purposes in many cases, pro-development forces try hard to convince the public that logging will do wonderful things for biodiversity. These bastardizations of the concept must be nipped in the bud."

These ecologists follow in the footsteps of John Muir, Aldo Leopold, Richard Saint Barbe-Baker, Arthur O. Baker, and Rachel Carson, who all warned of the peril of following the industrial-technological paradigm. Indeed in their book *Dynamic Biology*, published in 1938, Arthur O. Baker and Lewis Mills warned that our primary forests were rapidly disappearing and appealed to all citizens to protect virgin forests. They presented a map of the original forest cover of the U.S. (the lower 48 states) and the "virgin forests today"(1938). "Certainly," they concluded, "the reduction indicated [only 20 percent of virgin forests remained in 1938] proves that something must be done, and done soon, if we are to save what is left." In 1993 less than 10 percent of the ancient forests in the Pacific Northwest region of the U.S. remain.

The essays in this book address several crucial questions. How do we approach forest-watershed ecosystems in our scientific studies, in our emotions, our experience? Is sustainable forestry possible? What does restoration of damaged ecosystems mean? What forest policy would protect the intrinsic value and integrity of forested regions and provide some products from forests?

In his essay "A Sustainable Forest Is a Diverse and Natural Forest," Reed Noss examines the critical qualities that make a forest sustainable and healthy: *biodiversity* and *naturalness*. He provides us with an understanding of biodiversity at several levels of biological organization: genetic diversity, species diversity, community/ ecosystem diversity, and landscape diversity. Naturalness, a quality that resists quantification, remains a critical characteristic of a healthy and diverse forest nonetheless. *A tree farm*, explains Noss, "is hardly a *forest*.... A forest differs from a tree farm in being naturally regenerated and essentially self-regulating." Noss suggests a long-term strategy for promoting native biodiversity, naturalness, and sustainability across a regional landscape—a strategy in which he makes a case for preserving 50 percent of the region as true wilderness, while the remainder is managed for multiple use through practices that closely mimic natural processes.

Herb Hammond explores the historical roots of clearcutting and he unearths the ecological and economic flaws in the assumptions made by industrial foresters. As with Noss and others, he cautions us to be aware of misleading jargon created by the logging industry as euphemisms for massive clearcutting and similar destructive logging practices that do not sustain a forest. Hammond gets to the point when he states, "clearcutting is deforestation."

Hammond exposes four *Ecological Fallacies* used by industrial foresters to justify clearcutting: that clearcutting mimics natural disturbances; that clearcutting will rid the world of "cellulose cemeteries" found in natural old-growth forests; that

reforestation following clearcutting provides healthy future forests; and that the ecological effects of clearcutting are confined to the cutover area.

On the economic side of the forest management equation, Hammond draws an important distinction between forests and forest-based economies: "Forests are natural, self-sustaining systems. Forests can exist and persist without humans. Forest-based economies, on the other hand, are artificial systems—human ideas that cannot exist without forests." Hammond lays out four *economic fallacies:* that clearcutting is the most economically efficient way of cutting and growing trees; that clearcutting provides sustainable employment; that clearcutting rids us of valueless, decadent wood; and that clearcutting is necessary to compete in the global economy. Hammond concludes that "Good ecology is good economics."

Chris Maser, forest ecologist and author, says that "as we liquidate the ancient forests, we are redesigning the forests of the future. In fact, we are redesigning the entire world, and we are simultaneously throwing away Nature's blueprint." Maser concludes that "we must have a sustainable forest before we can have a sustainable yield.... We must have a sustainable yield to have a sustainable industry; we must have a sustainable industry to have a sustainable economy; we must have a sustainable economy to have a sustainable society." In other words, we need to reorder our priorities. In order to have any sustainable jobs from products drawn from a forest we need a new paradigm of culture. Ecologists who have studied the ancient forest ecosystems of the Pacific Northwest advise us to be humble. Forest ecologists are beginning to understand some of the complexity of forest ecosystems. However, they warn that ancient forest ecosystems cannot be recreated by human interventions and perhaps cannot be fully understood by scientists.

Mitch Lansky writes from the perspective of a historian and observer of industrial forestry in Maine. Although many critics correctly address the mismanagement of publicly owned forests in the United States and Canada, Lansky warns that privatization and "free market" economics is not a better solution when corporate giants rule the forest. In the 1970s the logging industry in Maine was required to leave "beauty strips" along roads and waterways. These buffer strips, he says, "do not help protect the forest—they preserve only the *illusion* of a forest. To step beyond the beauty strip is to step into a world of distorted metaphors and distorted logic."

Felice Pace, a community activist in rural, northern California, has witnessed the "timber wars" between loggers and environmentalists. Pace writes sympathetically of the plight of loggers and their families in small communities. In his exploration of the sociology and politics of these small "one mill towns," Pace says that "we must understand not only the timber workers, but also the local business owners and mid-level managers of timber corporations. Local mill owners and the mid-level executives, who manage the holdings of transnational corporations, constitute the power elite of the so-called timber-dependent communities of the rural West."

Pace explains in dollars and cents the reason why local school boards and county government officials in tax-poor rural communities will support and lobby hard to maintain unsustainable cutting rates on public forests. "Their support is virtually guaranteed by the system that provides funding from timber harvest revenues which are generated by logging on federal lands within their boundaries." This economic incentive combined with the social and political characteristics of timber-dependent communities has assured, until now, unwavering support for the logging industry until the last available old-growth forests are clearcut.

Pace recounts social changes in timber-dependent communities with the influx of "urban refugees" in the 1970s and the growth of the rural grassroots forest reform movement in response to industrial forest management practices such as herbicide spraying and clearcutting. With the ancient forests of the Pacific Northwest whittled down to the final 5 to 15 percent, and with the intensity of the "timber wars" increasing, Pace describes the inner community conflicts and the logging industry backlash in the form of "grassroots" industry support groups aligned with the Wise Use movement of the rural American West and the Share movement in Canada.

Pace quotes the writer and historian of the American West, Wallace Stegner, who believed that "within a generation or two," Westerners will "work out some sort of compromise between what must be done to earn a living and what must be done to restore health to the earth, air, and water." But before such a compromise can be reached, we need both an ecologically realistic understanding of the state of the forests of North America and some principles guiding our vision of the future.

Dave Foreman in "The Big Woods and Ecological Wilderness Recovery" renders an appraisal of wilderness preservation efforts in an historical context, and he provides a vision of ecological wilderness recovery based on principles of conservation biology applied to great regional ecosystems throughout North America. "We have not simply turned trees into lumber," Foreman says, "we have destroyed a complex, stable, ancient community. In the space of a century, we have wrought a holocaust in the wilderness. And we continue."

Foreman proceeds to assess opportunities for wilderness recovery in the major forest regions of the United States. He asserts, "The opportunity for such restoration will never be better than it is today.... All that is lacking is enough popular demand to force the necessary political will. Now is the time for conservationists in [the United States and Canada] to envision real wilderness, with its full complement of native species.... If conservationists do not act swiftly, however, the opportunity will be lost."

Colleen McCrory, winner of the Goldman Award for distinguished grassroots activism in North America, and an experienced commentator on forest policy in Canada, concludes that Canada is the "Brazil of the North." Behind a facade of "green proclamations," provincial governments in Canada have written long-term agreements with huge corporations allowing them to create some of the most massive clearcuts anywhere on Earth.

In his essay "Cutting Down Canada," Jim Cooperman provides a wake-up call for Canadians and U.S. citizens. He explains that while Canada encompasses nearly 10 percent of the world's forests, "a lush and wild image of this landscape would be a green illusion—the ancient forests are vanishing." Cooperman summarizes the state of Canada's eight major forest regions and the social policies that are rapidly leading to deforestation region by region and province by province. He describes how people of First Nations, forest ecologists, and environmentalists are working together to develop a vision of forest and community sustainability in many regions of Canada. He calls on Canadians to make a commitment to sustainability.

Sustainability must somehow be translated into forest policy and practices. Ed Grumbine, author of *Ghost Bears: Exploring the Biodiversity Crisis*, in his essay "Policy in the Woods" provides us with a brief historical account of U.S. forest policy and management. He states that we can reform forest policy in the U.S. by moving away from the Forest Service's concept of *sustained yield* management, which does not sustain forest ecosystems, and adopting concepts of *sustainable ecosystems* and *sustainable landscapes* that do.

Grumbine suggests that we first adopt a working definition for *ecological integrity*, proposed by biologist Jim Karr as "the capability of supporting and maintaining a balanced, integrated, adaptive community of organisms having a species composition and functional organization comparable to that of the natural habitat of the region."

On this foundation, Grumbine proposes principles for an "ecological forest policy platform": a moratorium on the logging of ancient forests; ecosystem-based research; a biodiversity protection network with a web of connecting corridors; restoration of damaged lands; and creation of an ecosystem-based native forestry industry.

Grumbine calls for support and training of ecologically enlightened forest managers to practice ecosystem-based forestry. "Multiple use," he says, "is based on economic rather than ecological goals: its ideology is pre-ecological and therefore inappropriate to address today's forestry problems."

Ecologist Chris Maser points out the fact that ecologically enlightened forest managers are not being trained through the standard curriculum in forestry colleges in North America. Maser examines the root causes of problems stemming from the forestry profession. "Traditional forestry," he explains, "is exploitation of the economic value of trees.... If the twentieth-century exploitation of forests is to be replaced by a healing of forests in the twenty-first century, forestry as a profession must be founded on documented ecological truth."

Maser provides a stinging critique of the forestry profession by unveiling the dogma through which the logging industry dominates and manipulates the profession of forestry and its institutes of learning. He challenges the colleges to "lead the profession of forestry toward a new vision, one that harmonizes human culture and Nature's forest beyond the dogma of traditional forestry and the economics of commodity extraction. This can best be done by helping students realize their dreams of finding a nurturing philosophy of life within the profession, as trustees of forest health and productivity."

"The twenty-first-century forester," according to Maser, "must be a bridge between the ecology of the forest in relation to the dynamics of the landscape and the cultural necessities and human values of society. Tomorrow's forester is the guardian of both the forest and the future's options, because when all is said and done, the great and only gift we can give our children is the right of choice and something of value from which to choose."

THE DEEP, LONG-RANGE ECOLOGY MOVEMENT

Proposals for new ecosystem-based forest policies and ecological training for forest workers are emerging from the work of conservation biologists, from the voices of traditional, indigenous peoples in forested regions, and from contemporary philosophers and social activists. This movement is sometimes referred to as the *radical ecology* movement. The word *radical* is entirely appropriate in that this movement is based upon fundamental principles, marked by a considerable departure from the traditional, and tending toward making extreme changes in existing views, habits, conditions, and institutions. The word *ecology* originates from the Greek word *oikos* pertaining to *the logic and reason of the household, habitat, and environment;* that branch of science concerned with the interrelationships of organisms and their environments. Radical ecology puts ecological principles first. With respect to *economy*— another term of Greek origin pertaining to *management of the household, habitat, environment*—radical ecologists for forest practices reform insist that management be based on ecological principles (i.e., operating within the logic of the forest).

Another term characterizing this movement promoting radical ecology is *deep culture*—providing common ground for discussion and action for people from all ethnic traditions, gender orientations, religious traditions, and social classes. In deep culture, the definition of community is extended and inclusive—including the soil, water, forests, and creatures of the forests. In the context of deep culture, more and more people are asking how they can discover their *sense of place*. They seek to dwell sustainably in their bioregion, while considering the seventh generation in the future—as is the traditional practice of many First Nations—not only of humans but all beings who dwell therein. A growing number of people recognize the wisdom and practicality in Henry David Thoreau's statement made in the middle of the nineteenth century: "In wildness is the preservation of the world."

Consumers of products derived from forest ecosystems are beginning to stir, to ask questions related to their consumption of wood and forest products. Where is this wood coming from? Is it coming from rainforests or from the remaining ancient temperate forests? Do I need this product or do I merely think I need it because of my habits or my addiction to consumption? Are there ecologically sound ways of producing this product? Can the paper I use be more easily derived from some plant other than trees?

More and more people, including forest activists, forest practitioners, consumers, and other members of the community, are taking a stand for their own integrity as part of the integrity of natural systems. The photos in this book show the deforestation caused by massive clearcutting. The names of places where groups of people and their supporters took a stand for the integrity of forest systems, resisting the advancing armies of industrial loggers, will be recorded by historians in the twenty-first century as part of the turning tide toward deep culture: *Carmanah Valley* on the west coast of Vancouver Island, British Columbia; *Cathedral Forest* on Pyramid Creek, Middle Fork Santiam River, Oregon; *Bald Mountain* in Siskiyou National Forest, Oregon; the *high country* in the *Siskiyou Mountains* of northern California; *Headwaters Forest* in the Salmon and Lawrence Creeks of Humboldt County, California; the *Albion River*, Mendocino County, California; *Sand Bench* in southern Colorado; *Shawnee National Forest*, Illinois; *Hoosier National Forest*, Ohio; *Monongahela National Forest*, West Virginia; the *Northeastern forests* of the U.S.; the forested "island in the sky" on top of *Mount Graham*, Arizona.

Each of these names calls up stories yet to be fully recorded by historians, stories of broad and deep identification with place, stories of political oppression by powerful corporations and government bureaucracies, stories of suffering and determination by groups of people who "took their stand" that the forests might stand. As a result, at least some fragments of forests that give sanctuary to threatened and endangered species—fragments that may someday become core areas for a broader biodiversity protection network—may survive intact in the emerging Age of Ecology.

One of those stories tells of a small group who took a stand for the Cathedral Forest in the Santiam watershed in the Cascade mountain range of Oregon. *The Cathedral Forest Wilderness Declaration* is an example of the clarity of expression that is found in people of place in all bioregions of North America:

"We believe that all things are connected; that whatever we do to the Earth, we do to ourselves. If we destroy our remaining wild places, we will ultimately destroy our identity with the Earth: wilderness has values for humankind which no scientist can synthesize, no economist can price, and no technological distraction can replace.

"We believe that we should protect in perpetuity these wild places, not only for our own sake, but for the sake of the plants and animals and for the good of the sustain-

ing Earth. The forests, like us, are living things: wilderness should exist intact solely for its own sake; no human justification, rationale, or excuse is needed.

"We perceive the Earth is dying. We pledge ourselves to turning this process around, to stopping the destruction, so that the Earth can become alive, clean, and healthy once again.

"We call on the United States government to preserve the forests of the Pacific Northwest as some of the many irreplaceable treasures of our great continent.

"On behalf of all citizens of the Earth community, we declare the Oregon Cathedral Forest—all that which remains of Oregon's old-growth ecosystem—an inviolable wilderness for all time."

TOWARD SUSTAINABLE FORESTS AND SUSTAINABLE CULTURE

Growing from the search for deep culture and with an awareness that forestry has much to do with sense of place, a new generation of forest practitioners is beginning to reflect on making a living, "a right livelihood" in Buddhist terms, through a *bioregional practice*. This movement is called *community forestry*, *ecosystem-based forestry*, *natural selection ecoforestry*, *wholistic forest practice*, and *sustainable forestry*. The concluding essays in this book reflect some, but certainly not all, of the expressions of the emerging practice of right livelihood deep in the forest.

In his *Wholistic Forest Use: An Ecosystem-based Approach to Timber Management*, Herb Hammond says that "our plans and activities in the forest, from the largest landscape to the smallest patch, must reflect [ecosystem-based ecological principles].... Wholistic forest use represents a different set of ethics, values, or worldview when compared to conventional timber management.... Fewer trees are cut down with wholistic timber management than with conventional practices. However, approximately the same number of timber-oriented jobs may be created...." A key concept for this wholistic system of management is *zoning* forested landscapes for large protected reserves, with protection of sensitive landscape features and cross-valley corridors, and with timber management zones operated with ecologically responsible practices. Hammond asserts that "the time has come to make large protected reserves, protected landscape networks, and ecologically responsible forest use the norm."

Orville Camp, who dwells in southern Oregon and harvests products from his own forest on a sustainable basis, discusses his approach in his essay "Natural Selection Ecoforestry." He describes his understanding of what a *forest* is, and he examines the meanings of *forestry* and *agriculture*. Camp provides us with a list of ten Forest Ecosystem Management Goals. He describes his natural selection ecoforestry concepts as "producing results far superior to any conventional forest management program" and as "a high-quality solution to the world's forest management crisis."

As consumers, forest activists, students of forest ecosystems, forest practitioners, and generally speaking, as supporters of the deep, long-range ecology movement, more and more people are joining in a great cultural transformation. The question is: will this cultural change and forest policy change occur before more irreversible and massive loss of biodiversity occurs on this continent? Nobel Prize–winning scientists, traditional elders from First Nations, philosophers and poets speaking from the great wisdom traditions of the Earth, as well as all citizens who have moved beyond denial and are awakened to the condition of the Earth understand that current dominant practices by humans have put us on a collision course with Nature. Lester

Brown of the Worldwatch Institute, and editor of the annual *State of the World Report*, calls the 1990s a *turnaround decade;* unless contemporary society radically changes its current dominant approach to forests—summarized in this book as "industrial forestry"—thresholds will be crossed that will lead to the inevitable and immense loss of biodiversity, and, indeed, of life-support systems for the Earth.

We see in this book, at least in outline, the vision and the power emerging from deep culture and radical ecology in the wounded forests of North America. Massive clearcutting is far more "radical" (in a negative extremist connotation of that word) than the benign approach to sustainable forest communities advocated herein. This vision is expressed in *The Wildland Project*, which is fostering a North American wildness recovery process. This vision is expressed in *The Cathedral Forest Wilderness Declaration*. This vision is expressed by poet-philosopher-bioregionalist Gary Snyder. Snyder understands the *ancient wisdom* of First Nations of North America, and supports the emerging deep, long-range ecology movement. In his poem "For All" he calls upon all residents of North America to acknowledge a new pledge of allegiance to each of the bioregions on this continent.

For All

Ah to be alive
on a mid-September morn
fording a stream
barefoot, pants rolled up
holding boots, pack on
sunshine, ice in the shallows, northern rockies

Rustle and shimmer of icy creek waters
stones turn underfoot, small and hard as toes
cold nose dripping
singing inside
creek music, heart music, smell of sun on gravel

I pledge allegiance

I pledge allegiance to the soil
of Turtle Island

and to the beings who thereon dwell
one ecosystem
in diversity
under the sun

with joyful interpenetration for all

—Gary Snyder

Garth Lenz

What you see herein is the tip of the iceberg.

Daniel Dancer

We are not now headed toward sustainable forestry, because we are training plantation managers, not foresters. A forester manages a forest. We are liquidating our forests and replacing them with short-rotation plantations. Everything nature has done in designing forests adds to diversity, complexity, and stability through time. We decrease diversity, complexity, and stability by redesigning forests into plantations.

SUSTAINABLE FORESTRY

CHRIS MASER

As we liquidate the ancient forests, we are redesigning the forests of the future. In fact, we are redesigning the entire world, and we are simultaneously throwing away Nature's blueprint.

Nature designed a forest as an experiment in unpredictability; we are trying to design a regulated forest.
Nature designed a forest over a landscape; we are trying to design a forest on each hectare.
Nature designed a forest with diversity; we are trying to design a forest with simplistic uniformity.
Nature designed a forest of interrelated processes; we are trying to design a forest based on isolated products.
Nature designed a forest in which all elements are neutral; we are trying to design a forest in which we perceive some elements to be good and others bad.
Nature designed a forest to be a flexible, timeless continuum of species; we are trying to design a forest to be a rigid, time-constrained monoculture.
Nature designed a forest of long-term trends; we are trying to design a forest of short-term absolutes.
Nature designed a forest to be self-sustaining and self-repairing; we are designing a forest to require increasing external subsidies—fertilizers, herbicides, and pesticides.
Nature designed forests of the Pacific Northwest to live 500 to 1,200 years; we are designing a forest that may live 100 years.
Nature designed Pacific Northwest forests to be unique in the world, with twenty-five species of conifers, the longest lived and the largest of their genera anywhere; we are designing a forest that is largely a single species on a short rotation.

Everything we humans have been doing to the forest is an attempt to push Nature to a higher sustained yield. We fail to recognize, however, that we must have a sustainable forest *before* we can have a sustainable yield (harvest). In other words, we cannot have a sustainable yield until we have a sustainable forest. We must have a sustainable forest to have a sustainable yield; we must have a sustainable yield to have a sustainable industry; we must have a sustainable industry to have a sustainable economy; we must have a sustainable economy to have a sustainable society.

Put another way, we must first practice sound *bio-economics* (the economics of maintaining a healthy forest), before we can practice sound *industrio-economics* (the economics of maintaining a healthy forest industry), and before we can practice sound *socio-economics* (the economics of maintaining a healthy society). And it all begins with a solid foundation—a sustainable forest.

We are not now headed toward sustainable forestry, because we are training plantation managers, not foresters. A forester manages a forest. We are liquidating our forests and replacing them with short-rotation plantations. Everything Nature has done in designing forests adds to diversity, complexity, and stability through time. We decrease diversity, complexity, and stability by redesigning forests into plantations.

We must learn to reinvest part of Nature's capital, such as large merchantable logs and large snags, in the maintenance of forest health, so that our mills will have, in perpetuity, a sustainable harvest of timber from fertile, healthy, stable soils, clean water, clean air, and clear sunlight. To *reinvest* means to give up some of the short-term profits to ensure the long-term sustainability of the forest for future generations. Fertilization and planting trees are not reinvestments. They are investments in the next commercial stand; they are investments in a product, not a reinvestment in maintaining the health of a process. We do not reinvest, because we do not see the forest—only the product, the tree. We do not reinvest, because we ignore the cornerstones of forestry—soil, water, air, sunlight, and biodiversity. If we continue to ignore the fact that the cornerstones of forestry are variables whose health must be accounted for in our economic endeavors, we will surely destroy the forests of the world for future generations.

We need to maintain ancient forests because they are the only living laboratories we have through which we and the future may be able to learn how to create sustainable forests—something no one in the world has so far accomplished. As a living laboratory, ancient forests serve four vital functions.

First, they are our link to the past, to the historical forest. The historical view tells us what the present is built on, and the past combined with the present, in turn, tells us what the future may be projected on. To lose the ancient forests is to cast ourselves adrift in a sea of almost total uncertainty with respect to the potential sustainability of future forests. We must remember that knowledge is only in past tense; learning is only in present tense; and prediction is only in future tense. To have sustainable forests, we need to be able to know, to learn, and to predict. Without ancient forests, we eliminate learning, limit our knowledge, and greatly diminish our ability to predict.

Second, we did not design the forest, so we do not have a blueprint, parts catalog, or maintenance manual with which to understand and repair it. Nor do we have a service department in which the necessary repairs can be made. Therefore, how can we afford to liquidate the ancient forest that acts as a blueprint, parts catalog, maintenance manual, and service station—our only hope of understanding the potential sustainability of a redesigned, plantation-forest complex?

Third, we are playing "genetic roulette" with the forests of the future through genetic selection for mass wood fiber production in plantation management. What if our genetic simplifications run amok, as they so often have around the world? Maintenance of ancient forests is thus imperative, because they contain the entire genetic code and a full complement of vital processes for living, healthy, adaptable forests. We can help them by maintaining as much biological diversity as possible, which in turn will make our forests as resilient as possible. Resiliency, which equates to adaptability, will allow the plant and animal communities the greatest opportunity to adapt to new and changing environmental conditions.

Fourth, we must maintain intact segments of the ancient forest from which we can learn to make the necessary adjustments, in both our thinking and our subsequent course of management, to help assure the sustainability of the future's plantation-forest complex. If we choose not to deal with the heart of the ancient forest issue— sustainable forests—we will find that reality is more subtle than our understanding of it, and unknowingly, our "good intentions" will likely give bad results.

Although there are many valid reasons to save ancient forests, there is only one reason that I know of for liquidating them—short-term economics. Economics, however, is the common language, the common objective that drives Western civilization; is it not wise, therefore, to carefully consider whether saving substantial amounts of well-distributed ancient forests is a necessary part of the equation for maintaining a solvent forest industry?

I have often heard that "we can't afford to save ancient forests, they are too valuable and too many jobs are at stake." I submit, however, that we must be exceedingly cautious that economic judgment does not isolate us from the evidence that without sustainable forests we won't have a sustainable forest industry. Therefore, if we liquidate the ancient forests—our living laboratories—and our plantations fail, as plantations are failing over much of the world, industry will be the bathwater thrown out with the baby.

As we liquidate the ancient forests of the world, for whatever "rational" reason, we are, as a global society, simultaneously destroying our historical roots and grossly impairing our spiritual well-being. What we are doing to the forests is but a mirror reflection of the mentality with which we treat ourselves and one another. All we have in this world as human beings is one another—here, now, this moment. And when everything is said and done in our frantic drive for short-term economic gains, if we have lost sight of one another, we will find that we have nothing of value after all.

The Trees of Siberia

The trees of Siberia
know when the axe falls in Oregon.
    Gone now the sacred druidic oaks,
    the Schwarzewald, the cypress

All trees touch
forming a single vegetal mat,
a circumglobal
circuit-board
of the intertwining roots of oak and aspen,
manzanita and redwood—
or linked at great distance by the designs of mycorrhizal lace.
    Gone the southern hardwoods.
    Gone the unbroken mantle
    of tropical rainforest.
All trees standing
know the pain of the trees
that fall to the saw.
Information chemically coded
is passed through flesh of soil,
or transmitted through subtle electrical surges
pulsing down fungal filaments
one plant to another,
one forest to the next.

The trees of Siberia
know when the axe falls in Oregon.
    Gone the solemn council of elder firs
    Gone the botanical lessons
    of perseverance and place.

—Lone Wolf Circles

Garth Lenz

Forests can teach us only if we are prepared to learn by being open to them. Openness means attentive awareness to place.

REMEMBERING THE MORAL AND SPIRITUAL DIMENSIONS OF FORESTS

ALAN DRENGSON

MEETING ELDERS

In the spring of 1991, seven of us went to visit Merv Wilkinson in Wildwood Forest on Vancouver Island, B.C., Canada. Wildwood Farm contains some of the oldest trees on Vancouver Island, trees that were already thirteen hundred years old when Columbus landed on Turtle Island, the land that Europeans called America. Wildwood still looks like an ancient, natural forest, even though Wilkinson has been taking wood out of it for fifty years.

This forest provides a sharp contrast to the clearcuts and plantations in parcels surrounding his land. The forested parcels wherein Wilkinson dwells have a diversity of species and ages, and a wild feel to them.

In contrast, industrial forestry is based on the same approach as conventional agriculture that relies on heavy machinery, fossil fuels, and petrochemicals. In industrial forestry humans strive to control and manage all factors that impede or enhance forest productivity. Production must keep up with demand, and the faith is that this will happen efficiently in a competitive, monetarized, market economy. In only four and one-half decades since my school days in Shelton, Washington, timber-based communities of the Pacific Northwest, from northern California to southern Alaska, have either all but disappeared, or have suffered a steep decline in prospects.

MODERN INDUSTRIAL SOCIETY: COMMUNITY AND PLACE

Modern industrial society, with its waves of technological revolution, is between three and four hundred years old, even though it has more ancient roots. It is a society that has tried consciously to break with its ancestral traditions, so as to control Nature and humans through science and technology. Mass education and mass production were made for each other. A civilization based on the idea that humans can master and control Nature for human ends is unique in the history of culture. Modern industrial techniques and models have been applied to almost everything, with large spiritual and environmental costs. Industrial civilization has selectively eliminated deeper values and rich sources of meaning, while destroying large areas of the beautiful and bountiful natural world.

Many people are beginning to understand what an enormous moral and spiritual blunder it is to cut down such trees. Here I use the word *blunder*, rather than *sin* or *evil*, because it is hard to imagine anyone cutting or causing to have cut down such beings if they understood all that they were destroying.

The temperate and tropical forests are among the most complex and biologically diverse areas on the Earth. Industrial forestry destroys almost all of this complexity and genetic diversity. When the forest is completely gone, only a two-dimensional plane remains, the third dimension of depth and height is lost as is the fourth dimension, time—as accumulated learning. This learning, which took centuries

to accumulate and is unique to that one location on Earth, is gone *forever*. The increasing diversity and richness of the natural forest is swept away by "harvesting" practices based on the time scale of quarterly reports.

When we try to list the diversity of *values* we find in natural forest communities, we find that the list grows as our understanding deepens. Their multiplicity of values can be approached under the following, not exhaustive, list of categories: life support, natural history, species diversity, spiritual, moral, aesthetic, scientific, productive, utilitarian, recreational, personal and community growth, and nonhuman intrinsic values of the forest as a whole. Each of these categories has a large number of values falling under it, and we discover new ones as time goes by.

Let us consider just some of the values in the "productive" category. For this purpose let us compare the forest ecosystem to a factory. Imagine a town that has some good, efficient, clean, production facilities that supply goods vitally needed by humans. Some wags come to town who manage to convince people that they would be better-off if they would dismantle the factories and sell them to outsiders. So the townspeople do this, and while dismantling the plants they are busy and making money. After the last part is shipped, however, they realize they have nothing left to do. They no longer can earn a living from their past employment. Only those who have lost their temporal perspective could be convinced that such short-term gains are better than the long-term ones that would have been provided by the lost production facilities.

It is difficult to grasp the long time span and complexity of natural forest communities, unless one spends time living in them over a forty to fifty year period. After several decades we might appreciate how little we know. What we *do* know is humbling. Who would have dreamed even a few years ago that the largest single living being, and oldest discovered so far, is not a tree, but a mycelium, living in symbiosis with tree and other plant roots? Who could have said how interdependent trees and fungi are? Or who would have thought that in a natural forest trees exchange information that helps them to control bug infestations? And what of the role of forests in creating atmosphere, modifying climate, and controlling floods? The Earth's forests are integral to the vast dance of life.

Forests can teach us only if we are prepared to learn by being open to them. Openness means attentive awareness to place. One time on a hike I stopped on a ridge, in a forest of tall trees that were moving together with the wind. I was alone at the time because I had moved far ahead of my party. I just stopped walking and stood quietly in the forest; before I knew it I was swaying with the trees in the wind. I became one with the forest and had a clear sense of connectedness with its will. This just happened spontaneously. Some traditions have spiritual disciplines called tree meditations. Through them one can become aware of the worlds within worlds in which the forests dwell. A forest is not just a stand of isolated trees. Although each tree is an individual, it is also part of the forest. Its forest in turn is part of larger biogeoclimatic processes that are evolving through time.

As biodiversity and richness increase, value and meaning increase. In current scientific theories, evolution moves toward complexity, differentiation, and symbiosis, toward greater richness and diversity. Each evolving form of life is dwelling in these natural processes and adds to the sum total of values realized. Moreover, these create new possibilities that build on accumulated ecological wisdom (*ecosophy*). In contrast, the practice of modern industrial forestry, based on the petrochemical agricultural model, does just the opposite. It reduces all values to the lowest common denominator—monetary considerations. It reduces the possibilities for meaning. It undermines significant relationships and community.

MODERN INDUSTRIAL SOCIETY: COMMUNITY AND KNOWLEDGE

Natural forests and sustainable, symbiotic human communities greatly increase the range for meaningful and valuable relationships. By being members of a community, we are able to create and maintain relationships that realize more values and greater meaning than we each can realize alone. When we explore the ecology of the human *self* and natural communities, we realize how interdependent we are. The industrial model assumes that each part can be isolated and defined independent of everything else. But no individual can be isolated in this way and realize meaning and value, let alone survive. All that each of us is, is shared by everything else that is.

If each of us personally had to destroy the individual beings wiped out by the destruction of forest communities, we would refuse to do it. Few of us would kill birds and animals, or pull up wildflowers. On the contrary, most of us will go to great lengths to rescue a trapped kitten or duck. Inaction over forest destruction must be partly a result of the success of public relations and other efforts to conceal the reality and consequences of destructive practices, that we tacitly support, even if only indirectly through various forms of economic activity.

The division of labor and specialization of knowledge that characterize industrial society reflect a top-down hierarchy of power and control. Knowledge is pursued for profit and power. Under these circumstances it becomes a commodity. Knowledge of the world as a whole is thought impossible, and rewards are given to those with specialized expertise. Knowledge in industrial society is fragmented and placeless. Without larger vision of the whole it can be trivial or even dangerous. Thus, such knowledge is out of touch with an older wisdom.

Without comprehensive understanding, we tend to lead isolated lives as producers and consumers. Everything is subjugated to production and consumption. The values that clearly count in modern industrial society are those related to production, consumption, and profit. These are taken for granted, along with a narrow economic definition of progress—more is better. We each resent being treated as objects or units of production, but this is what the industrial model requires. This process of separation, isolation, and reduced capacity for perception of values, meanings, and a larger wisdom brings with it the terrible emptiness of being alienated from ourselves, each other, and Nature.

This loss of meaning, through loss of membership in the larger natural order that is committed to place, cannot be overcome by consuming and producing more things. These bring temporary relief, perhaps, as can the pursuit of less tangible rewards such as fame, fortune, and power. But few can attain these, and so personal pleasure and comfort become primary aims for which industrial society produces an array of goodies that are only substitutes for authentic connection and spontaneous experience of Nature. In this manufactured "virtual reality," experience becomes an artifact, the programmed production of media and functionaries.

We hunger to leave the technosphere and enter the real world of living time, to escape the unit-based, clock-measured time.

The ancient forests are witnesses to the folly of the short-term, narrow pursuits that grip us with addictive power. When we sit in the forests, with the ancient elders bearing witness to centuries, we can be taken out of this narrow, functional mind. We have for a moment escaped the mind control of the industrial ego that applies its forms of manipulation to everything in order to avoid facing its own shadow, that which it denies but which nonetheless defines it. Perception of the forest becomes more complete the more the reins of control are released, and the more the forest is respected for itself. The less we attempt to control it and our own experience, the more we will learn from the revelations of the natural forests.

MEANING, TRADITION, AND PRIMAL STORIES

Many wisdom traditions have specific ceremonial rituals that facilitate opening to spontaneous experiences of Nature. Listening, watching, smelling, tasting, feeling— these suggest an activity—I refer to as an active opening or receptiveness to the natural world. In some primal cultures this is approached through shamanic journeying and vision quests. Shamanic journeying helps to facilitate *spontaneous* encounters with the spiritual powers of Nature. That these encounters must be spontaneous is underscored by warnings against trying to capture a guardian spirit. A guardian spirit must choose to show itself to you three times before you can ask its help, for if it has shown itself three times, it has most likely chosen to help. If the quester, on a vision quest, tries to grab or control it, or flaunt it, it will be lost. It might even become an enemy.

Michael Harner, a contemporary teacher of shamanic rituals, coined the term *core shamanism* to refer to the central spiritual practices and main philosophical elements shared by different shamanic traditions worldwide. From firsthand study and participation in different traditions, Harner distilled the essential, cross-cultural elements of core shamanism. These seem to arise from our basic humanity and its deep interconnections with the natural world. The paleolithic shaman is deep within the consciousness of each of us. Forests show us this, and they also show us that they too are in the larger conscious stream of Nature. In this stream there are many manifestations of grandparents and elders.

Together we can help one another to realize the sin of destroying whole forests. I use the word *sin* here in the spiritual rather than religious sense. The spiritual transcends religion. Ideally, religions are cultural creations aimed at facilitating the holy life, a life of spiritual purification and harmony with creation. To fully appreciate this realization and remind ourselves of it is very difficult. We must realize our place spiritually. This comes through humility and nonviolence, through recognizing our own ignorance. We then can wonder at the mystery of the natural forests. How can we tell all of the stories of the many lives that the forest communities encompass, with their diverse and rich ways of life, and with their larger webs of connections to the world as a whole? We need all of the arts, skills, and imagination at our disposal to portray and celebrate them.

Richness in narrative details can help us come down from abstract concepts to the concrete reality of the primal natural forests. We leave cleverly manufactured human abstractions so as to return to our whole, original, spontaneous experience in which there are no fixed boundaries between self and others. Professor Arne Naess, who coined the term *deep, long-range ecology movement*, uses the term *ecological self* to refer to broad and deep identification beyond our ego and physical bodies. In the broadest identification, our *ecological self* is intertwined with all beings. We can explore this *ecological self* by means of expanding our personal commitment. In doing so we enlarge our capacity for sharing and caring. We can then explore our many interconnections, if only through breathing.

Philosophers and transpersonal psychologists such as Theodore Roszak and Warwick Fox convincingly argue that all persons have the capacity to perceive moral and spiritual realities, to be fully receptive to the world, to be open to learning from each being. Whether we do so depends on our willingness to remove the barriers we ourselves continually reinforce. These are both cultural and personal. At our core, however, we are all still natural beings, for what is visible is only the culturally self-conscious tip of the deeper ecological consciousness. The deep *ecological self* speaks or resurfaces, stands out and comes forth, during moments of spontaneous experience, such as we have tried to portray here through our stories. These stories work only if they help us to remember who and what we are.

In the Gaia hypothesis the central image is that the Earth is a living being made up of myriads of other living beings. There is life within life, within life, within life. Each of us is a community of living beings, and each community of living beings is part of a larger community of communities. A community is the smallest ecological whole, or perhaps we should say the smallest comprehensible whole about which we can tell multi-generational stories. It holds all of the other individual stories together through time, generation after generation. Language (or communication) is interdependent with community. With community (and communication) vast new possibilities open up. Community is not just a physical location, but space enlarged by shared moral, spiritual, and other relationships and activities. It makes communion possible. The root of the words *community* and *communion* is the same.

In human communities meaningful stories are held together by the elders; they are the continuity the group has with its past, just as children are with the future. They define a community's relationships to time. The community's wisdom is fully embodied in them. Even though an elder might be silent, his or her mere presence speaks eloquently of the community's traditions. The accumulated wisdom of the elders prepares the community for facing extreme conditions, and weathering storms and trials. How the elders are treated reveals the community's spiritual condition.

In human life we seek values and meaning. We judge ourselves in the values by which we try to live. We all want meaningful lives, rich with a diversity of values. However we define values, we know that there is a range of acceptable, nonviolent values, by which we can live meaningful lives in harmony with other beings. This wide range of values consistent with sustainability allows for great diversity in human cultures. This diversity increases richness, whereas too much cultural homogenization is impoverishing; everything becomes general and there are too few centers. This is central to the wisdom of bioregionalism—culture should reflect the unique attributes of dwelling over generations in specific places and regions that make sense as ecological wholes.

In a human community, shared commitment to a core of values is necessary if we are to live together. What or whoever we share our lives with, nurtures or is nurtured by us, cares for, supports, or depends on us, requires our respect and care. In spiritual traditions from Buddhist to Native American, becoming aware of our life-worlds, and of the networks of communities to which we belong, is crucial to maturing out of a narrow self-focused preoccupation. In all of these traditions the central, core values are those that make community possible. Maturity is measured by how far one moves from an egocentric focus to commitment to the integrity of the community, and to realizing the larger Self through it. Here is a story from Native American traditions that helps bring this out:

An elder and a young warrior journeyed together to the high alpine world. While camped there, the elder asked the warrior late one afternoon if he yet knew who he was. The warrior replied that he did. He said, "I am Diving Hawk, head of the bear clan, and I have counted many coups against my enemies." The elder sat quietly during the warrior's brief speech. After a long silence, he stood up and gestured to the meadows and flowers, and then to the forests and mountains, as he said, "Until you realize that you are the flowers and meadows, and the forests and mountains around us, you will not know who you are."

When men and women make commitments equal to the task of saving and caring for the elders—the ancient forests—that remain, they learn from them. When our practices harmonize with the way of the natural forests, elders who remain alive will speak to us, if we listen with an open heart. Practices that exemplify sustainability will lead to sustainable human communities that depend on self-sustaining natural forest ecosystems.

Gary Braasch

Clearcutting thus reflects our trust in ordered, linear human institutions—political, economic, social, scientific, and educational. We think quite naturally today of the forest as "ours," as "jobs," as a "resource" to exploit and redesign. Even schools of forest science do not escape this human-centered trap. The fallen trees that give life to a new forest are called "debris." Forests are "log supply centers."

CLEARCUTTING: ECOLOGICAL AND ECONOMIC FLAWS

HERB HAMMOND

Clearcutting is the most efficient, the most ecologically damaging, and (in the short term) the most cost-effective method of converting trees to logs and forests to nonforest human uses such as pastureland, cropland, townsites, and tree plantations. Simply put, clearcutting is deforestation. For the purposes of this essay, I consider clearcutting to be any form of timber removal that does not leave a fully functioning forest after logging is completed.

Technically, clearcutting means cutting every tree on the site and removing those trees considered to be merchantable to a mill. Other logging systems, lumped under the general category of *partial cutting*, cut and remove only selected trees and leave the rest standing. But in practical terms, many systems of partial cutting currently in use are simply variations on conventional clearcutting.

Seed tree cuts, for example, leave a scattered number of large trees on the site to provide a portion of the regeneration needs. *Shelterwood cuts* remove all of the merchantable trees in two cuts. *Green tree retention* removes the highest-quality, most readily merchantable trees, leaving behind mostly poor-quality understory trees. This cutting system reduces not only the future economic value of the forest, but also the tree species and individual trees that would provide the most desirable seed for regenerating the site. Other terms that are variations of clearcutting include *patch cuts* and *overstory removal*.

Partial cutting systems do exist that protect the forest and ensure that a fully functioning forest remains after logging. Therefore, in the face of growing public and scientific criticism, the timber industry has developed some confusing and misleading jargon to describe its cutting systems that are essentially clearcutting in disguise. Before you accept any term describing a timber cutting system, go out and look at the forest. As veteran forester Gordon Robinson said (1988):

"Anyone can identify destructive forest practices. You don't have to be a professional forester to recognize bad forestry any more than you need to be a doctor to recognize ill health. If logging looks bad, it is bad. If a forest appears to be mismanaged, it is mismanaged."

Understood mainly as a simple, efficient method of timber extraction, clearcutting has dominated human relationships with the forest in North America, beginning with the era of European settlement and accelerating with each new wave of technological development. This seemed to work fine as long as we had low levels of population, low levels of consumption, and low levels of pollution. If the timber industry fouled up one forest, there was always another forest somewhere else.

We were wrong. As a result of this philosophy—and our activities (we are now clearcutting more than 90 percent of the land logged in much of the world), our technology (we clearcut as much as ten times faster than just twenty years ago), and our indifference to the testimony of the forest itself—we are now facing serious and growing problems in forest ecosystems and in human economies. The decisions that we made in the past regarding timber are now affecting all forest uses: air, water, carbon storage, climate modification, wilderness, public recreation, tourism, fish, wildlife, and the long-term timber supply itself. The problem that transcends all of these is the exponential loss of biological diversity—the genetics, the species, the communities, and the landscapes that form the basis for life—for sustaining Earth as we know it. As a result of clearcutting in the forest, this basis for life is now disappearing at a rate several thousand times average rates of natural extinction. When we clearcut the forest, we are like the frog drinking up the pond in which he lives.

This essay will trace the history of clearcutting and examine the flaws in the ecological and economic rationales behind clearcutting.

THE HISTORICAL ROOTS OF CLEARCUTTING

Destruction of forests to obtain fuelwood, building timber, and other wood products, as well as to create grazing land, has occurred for millennia in some parts of the world. Cedar trees once cloaked the now parched hills of Lebanon. As trees in the lands surrounding the Mediterranean Sea were steadily cut, often through methods similar to clearcutting, forests were converted to arid, inhospitable, and treeless regions. The trees were no longer there to pull water from deep within the earth, to humidify the atmosphere, and to protect the environment from drying winds and the heat of the sun. Desertification resulted.

The practice of large-scale clearcutting was imported to North America by European settlers in the seventeenth century. For many thousands of years, most of the indigenous nations on this continent practiced a philosophy of protection (first) and use (second) of the forest. In scientific terms, we recognize that their use of the forest was ecologically responsible—meaning that it kept all the parts. Their demands on the forest were not extravagant and their population was in balance with the forest where they lived. The indigenous peoples of North America respected the forest as a physical, emotional, and spiritual source. As a part of the forest, they were sustained.

This is not to say that the white newcomers did not depend on the forest; like humans everywhere they needed its abundant water, clean air, building materials, fuel, and food. But they kept their distance. People of European descent who now control forests in North America, indeed much of the forests of the world, depend on the forest as much as any other humans, but they have never considered themselves a part of it. These people do not understand that what we do to the forest, we do to ourselves.

The European and subsequent North American estrangement from the forest—a precondition to the broad-scale adoption of clearcutting—is an outgrowth of an intense debate that took place about four hundred years ago regarding the earthly role of human beings. On one side of that debate were those who thought that humans were meant to be part of the forest, part of the grasslands, part of the wetlands, part of the streams, rivers, oceans—part of the Earth. On the other side of the debate were those who believed that humans were meant to dominate Nature. We know by now which side won (and we are beginning to understand the price of that victory). I want to emphasize that this was a political debate, not one based on the science of the day. Politics, not science, has shaped humans' domineering relationship with the forest around the world.

The dominant view that forest ecosystems can be made into "fiber factories" through application of "industrial forestry" and "scientific management" created the illusion that we can force ecosystems to produce more timber through practices such as clearcutting, planting genetically improved seedlings, fertilizing these seedlings, and destroying any "undesirable" species that might compete with these seedlings for the light, water, and nutrients necessary to grow timber.

The dominant view does not recognize that our lack of concern for whole forest ecosystem functioning has led to applications of technology that threaten the survival of the forest, indeed threaten the survival of ourselves and the Earth we are part of. The misapplication of technology has also led to scientific rationales for such ludicrous goals as perpetual economic growth based on ever-increasing production of resources from finite forests and limited forest processes.

Clearcutting thus reflects our trust in ordered, linear human institutions—political, economic, social, scientific, and educational. We think quite naturally today of the forest as "ours," as "jobs," as a "resource" to exploit and redesign. Even schools of forest science do not escape this human-centered trap. The fallen trees that give life to a new forest are called "debris." Forests are "log supply centers."

Most of the politicians we elect, the scientists we educate, the foresters we train, and the managers we appoint to make decisions about forests have a timber bias. They confuse the forest with one commodity that can come from the forest—trees. Policies, laws, research, planning, prescriptions, and even philosophies of forest use are centered around trees for timber. Trees are considered products, not living beings.

It has taken us a long time to understand the profound impacts of this timber bias. We believed that our experts understood the forest. We trusted that our government leaders were acting in the best interests of all when the timber industry was given so much power throughout the world. We believed that scientists and foresters could recreate "forests" as uniform rows of a single or a few species of trees called plantations. We depended on industry managers to make responsible decisions, both to protect jobs and to conserve our common resources.

In response to our abdication of interest and common sense, the timber industry has generated its own self-serving version of "forest science" and "forest economics." In the following parts of this essay, I will examine the major Ecological and Economic Fallacies that are still used to justify clearcutting around the world.

THE ECOLOGICAL FALLACIES OF CLEARCUTTING

Government, the timber industry, agencies in the U.S. and Canada, and many foresters offer a variety of "scientific" rationales to support the claim that forests are ecologically suited to clearcutting. These claims are used to justify the clearcutting of forests around the world. We will look in detail below at the four major Ecological Fallacies, and contrast these to Ecological Realities.

Ecological Fallacy #1: Clearcutting mimics natural disturbances.

Ecological Reality: No natural disturbance—wind, fire, flood, or insect—ever cuts all the trees, loads them on a truck, and hauls them to a mill.

The cutting and removal of even one tree is an unnatural event. I'm not suggesting that we stop logging, but I am suggesting that we stop defending tree removal as a natural process. Perhaps this small measure of humility will help foresters and other timber managers rethink their ecologically indefensible support of clearcutting. The following four arguments expose the major differences between natural disturbances and clearcutting:

1. *Natural disturbances may kill trees, but they leave the bodies on the site.* Natural disturbances leave behind vital structures in the form of snags, fallen trees on the land, and fallen trees in water courses—the biological legacies passed from one forest to the next. These dead trees, or bodies, are responsible for vital functions including the maintenance of critical fish and wildlife habitat, storage and filtration of water, and maintenance of soil fertility. Clearcutting, in contrast, "removes the bodies," thereby eliminating the source of snags and fallen trees from the site. By creating a significantly warmer microclimate, clearcutting also hastens the breakdown and loss of organic material left on the site. This depletes the soil of nutrients and contributes to the concentration of greenhouse gases. Slash burning, a common post-harvest treatment following clearcutting, further reduces the natural supply of woody material on the surface of the ground and in the soil.

Jerry Franklin (1992) summarizes the significance of "leaving the bodies on the site":

"[T]he effects of clearcutting are not ecologically comparable to the effects of most natural disturbances, including wildfire. Levels of biological legacies are typically high following natural disturbances, leading to rapid redevelopment of compositionally, structurally, and functionally complex ecosystems. Traditional approaches to clearcutting purposely eliminate most of the structural and most of the compositional legacy in the interest of efficient wood production."

2. *Natural disturbances seldom kill all of the trees.* Fire, wind, disease, and insects all leave significant numbers of trees alive in a forest following the disturbance. Most natural disturbances skip around the forest stand or landscape, creating an unpredictable mosaic of different conditions. The most frequent natural disturbances are low-intensity changes involving the death of a few individual trees or small groups of trees. Even in cases of hot, stand-replacing wildfires, individuals and groups of trees remain alive. These remnant stands in naturally disturbed areas provide critical animal habitat; supply genetic reservoirs for plants, animals, and microorganisms; and modify microclimates to facilitate forest regeneration. Natural disturbances thus diversify and perpetuate forests.

In contrast, clearcuts kill all or virtually all living trees—and many other species—in predictable, consistent ways. Clearcuts simplify and stress forests, result in immediate deforestation, and may result in long-term loss of forests.

3. *Major natural disturbances such as wildfires and insect outbreaks are infrequent.* Natural forest stands in temperate rainforests frequently exceed 500 years in age, and interior forest stands are commonly more than 200 years old. Evidence indicates that in temperate rainforests, large-scale disturbances are separated by many hundreds, perhaps thousands of years. Even within drier interior forests, which have the reputation of being propagated by fire, major forest-replacing wildfires occur in cycles of more than 200 years. Clearcut logging, on the other hand, is

planned to occur on 60- to 100-year cycles.

4. *Natural disturbances do not create severe soil damage.* With the possible (and slow-moving) exception of glaciation, no natural event other than a landslide is capable of changing productive soil to a sterile rock pile. Naturally occurring landslides are infrequent and extend over very small parts of the landscape. But severe soil damage is common in clearcuts—the result of scraping, gouging, and compaction by heavy equipment used for road building and removal of logs (i.e., skidding and yarding). Soil also suffers long-term degradation from clearcutting when the sources of future fallen trees are removed; when vital plants such as alder and fireweed, which replace soil nutrients after disturbances, are restricted by timber management techniques; and when important microorganism communities such as mycorrhizal fungi, which transfer water and nutrients from the soil to tree roots, are disrupted or destroyed.

Clearcuts are planned on short, regular cycles and dominate forest landscapes. Landslides that originate from clearcuts and cause severe soil damage occur from twenty to two hundred times more frequently than those in undisturbed forest areas. Many of the landslides associated with clearcut logging result from the concentration of water along roads, skid roads, and other logging features. By concentrating water instead of maintaining the naturally dispersed downslope pattern of water movement through the soil, sensitive areas become saturated with water, resulting in the mass movement of soil, trees, and other plants that we call a landslide.

Ecological Fallacy #2: Clearcutting will rid the world of "cellulose cemeteries" found in natural old-growth forests.

Ecological Reality: Old trees are critical forest structures linking today's forest to the forest of the future.

If a forest is to continue functioning as a forest, it must contain old trees—both living and dead. These large old structures carry out unique functions in the forest web. They are virtually forest communities unto themselves, living in mutually beneficial relationships with smaller organisms of the forest network. For example, epiphytic (aerial) plants, usually mosses and lichens, colonize live old crowns, where some gather atmospheric nitrogen that is eventually returned to the forest soil. Many insects that live in old trees prey on other insects that eat young trees and other plants. Small mammals, such as tree voles and squirrels, depend upon the large accumulations of organic matter in the crowns of individual old-growth trees for food and shelter. When these mammals descend to the forest floor, they move seeds and spores from place to place in the forest.

Because of their extensive root systems, trees have the unusual ability to stand upright, sometimes for a century or more, after they die. Standing dead trees—called snags—provide habitat for cavity-nesting birds and bats, which help balance insect populations. As the snag softens and crumbles, it provides for a new group of animals such as martens and owls. Many of these animals prefer large old snags that require centuries of tree growth—structures that are missing in the managed forest.

When a snag finally falls, its usefulness to the forest community does not end. If anything, it becomes even more valuable. A fallen tree is literally soil for the future. Bark beetles, wood borers, and fungi invade the tree, bringing with them nitrogen-fixing bacteria. Like a giant sponge, the decaying wood holds water, slowly releasing moisture and nutrients to the forest. Even in a small watershed, billions of tons of decaying wood are the main purifier of water. This is why the older the forest, the higher the quality of water it provides.

While the slow transformation from tree to soil is occurring on the microscopic level, the fallen tree body itself plays large-scale functions, maintaining the stability of forest slopes, acting as a collection point for water and nutrients, and continuing to create vital animal habitat. Trees that fall into or across water bodies shape the stream channel by serving as dams, thus slowing the erosive capacity of the stream and creating pools or riffles. Large fallen trees provide critical spawning and rearing habitats for fish, and sites for aquatic plants and insects needed for fish food.

From seedling to soil, old trees are essential links in the forest framework. Their journey may take from 500 to more than 2,000 years. Continuous clearcut cropping of trees on short cycles (60- to 100-year rotations) eliminates future sources of large old trees, large snags, and large fallen trees. For a period of time, the forest will continue to function, albeit in a degraded state, because of the enrichment of the forest by large old trees over many previous millennia. But as this biological legacy is exhausted, the forest itself will be lost.

The healthiest forest is Nature's design. To suggest that human modification of the forest, particularly the aggressive modification that accompanies clearcutting, can improve upon Nature's design is the height of human arrogance. This arrogance may well be our undoing.

Ecological Fallacy #3: Reforestation following clearcutting provides healthy future forests.

Ecological Reality: We can plant trees, but we cannot plant a forest.

It's easy to see the flaw in this ecological fallacy simply by remembering what a forest is. A forest is an interconnected web that focuses on sustaining the whole, not on the production of any one part or commodity. Trees are critical structural members of a forest framework; however, they are only a small portion of the structure needed for a fully functioning forest.

Sweden is often presented as a model of "sustainable" timber management. Clearcutting followed by timber plantations is the forest management system of choice in Sweden. But changes in the Swedish forest, brought about largely by timber management, have resulted in the loss of more than 200 species of plants and animals, with another 800 species considered rare or declining. In Finland's boreal forest, 805 species of plants and animals are endangered from the clearcutting of old forests (Olsson et al. 1992).

German foresters have encountered excessive windthrow in plantations as old as 170 years. Notwithstanding their maturity, these planted trees did not exhibit natural root form. Many foresters and forest ecologists believe that the only way to develop a natural root form is through germination of a seed on the soil. Naturally developed roots carefully but persistently wind around rocks, avoid areas with too little air, and seek out plentiful sources of moisture, nutrients, and beneficial microorganisms. The seedling becomes a part of the local environment as a result of natural design rather than human desire, thereby developing more resistance to natural disturbances.

Another interesting observation about natural germination of seeds compared to plantation management is that germination occurs randomly without spacing, while tree plantations have regular spacing between both individual trees and rows of trees. Natural germination and subsequent tree growth depend upon micro-site patches of nutrients, water, and microorganisms. These are not uniformly distributed throughout the forest floor. In the long term, human attempts to bring order to this perfectly functioning system are not only inefficient, but futile. The best tree planters are diverse old trees left after logging to provide seed for and to nurture the new forest. The trees in such a forest will have the best defenses against blowdown and "pests."

By explaining the weaknesses and failures of tree plantations, I am by no means suggesting we should stop planting trees. Planted trees can be used to assist Nature in the diverse process of restoring a degraded forest, in working with the forest to heal inappropriate human modifications. In contrast, clearcutting and tree plantations simplify the forest in an attempt to remake the forest on a technological basis rather than on an ecological foundation. These efforts are taking place in a biological system that we do not understand, in a climate undergoing dramatic change, where the only other long-term monoculture experiment (agriculture) has encountered severe problems with this approach.

High-quality water is one aspect of a forest that cannot be replaced by planting trees. Clearcutting, road building, and burning of logging slash change the way water works in a forest. Natural water systems within the forest are broken, and water is concentrated. Roads and skid roads catch and concentrate rain and snowmelt in ditches and on road surfaces. The forest canopy is no longer there to intercept and redirect precipitation. Clearcuts and young forests accumulate about 30 percent more snow and rain than uncut forests, particularly old-growth forests. Because there is no shade in a clearcut, snowpacks melt at least 30 percent faster in a clearcut than under a full or partial canopy (Gray 1974, Norse 1990). Thus, more rapid spring runoff occurs in clearcut areas than in forested areas.

In a fully functioning forest, water moves in a dispersed manner down the slope. In a clearcut, it moves along the path of the road, across the slope, until it finds an outlet—a culvert, a bridge, or a weak spot where it can erode its way to freedom down the slope. This often results in loss of fertile topsoil, siltation of water supplies, and reduced timber productivity.

Ecological Fallacy #4: The ecological effects of clearcutting are confined to the limited area cut at any one time.

Ecological Reality: The forest is connected in time and space across stands, valleys, landscapes, continents—Earth.

Conventional timber management is founded on the human tendency to relate to forests as stands of trees. Timber management techniques assume that each stand is an independent, self-contained unit. Perceiving the forest in this small-scale way is a human tendency, arising, I think, because of our small size relative to trees. But when we focus on stands, we are not seeing the forest in its entirety—we literally cannot see the forest for the trees. What we are missing is the forest landscape.

When I use the word landscape, I don't mean pretty scenery. Rather, I'm talking about landscape in the sense used by landscape ecologists—a repeating yet only partially predictable pattern of stands of trees and other ecosystem types across large areas—5,000, 10,000, 50,000 hectares and beyond. A forest landscape is an interconnected, interdependent spatial mosaic of smaller forest units. These units are called stands if you are a forester, ecosystem types if you are an ecologist, and habitat patches or simply patches if you are a landscape ecologist.

Landscape ecology, which looks at the big picture of Earth's forests, tells us that every forest patch or ecosystem type is connected to other forest patches by the movement or flow of water, energy, nutrients, plants, and animals across the landscape. Humans tend to think that plants and nutrients don't move. Yet animals that eat plants carry them from place to place by spreading their seeds; seeds float and are carried from place to place by water courses from small trickles to large rivers; and nutrients are dissolved in soil water moving through the ground and within every water body.

The forest landscape is the framework within which interconnected and interdependent forest patches function. Forest uses that damage the connections in a landscape will damage the functioning of individual forest patches. Damaged forest patches and forest landscapes impair the functioning of the Earth.

The spatial arrangement of the forest landscape changes over time. Changes can be as small as the death of a single tree and as large as a stand-replacing fire. These changes serve to maintain and renew forest composition and structures necessary for a fully functioning forest landscape. A tree falls and begins to build soil for the next generation. A forest fire kills some trees in a stand, leaving their bodies on the site, but spares others, resulting in a mixture of light and shade supporting a renewed community of diverse ages, species, and characteristics.

In contrast, large-scale, human-induced changes to the landscape—changes such as clearcutting, slash burning, tree planting, and brush control—remove vital forest structures, simplify ecosystem composition, break landscape connections, and disrupt the functioning of the forest landscape.

When a forest is disrupted by a checkerboard of clearcuts, large areas of contiguous or interior forest habitat are transformed into a number of isolated forest habitats— forest "islands" separated by clearcuts, logging roads, highways, and other human-created disturbances.

Nowhere is fragmentation more obvious or critical than in riparian ecosystems. Forests adjacent to creeks, rivers, lakes, and wetlands are part of riparian chains, forming a network that connects the forest across the landscape. Logging a riparian forest is like taking links out of a chain—things tend to fall apart.

Removal of even a small patch of riparian forest by clearcutting or other means can close an important connecting corridor. The seasonal movements of mammals such as marten, grizzly bear, and caribou can be seriously interrupted by logging riparian forests.

Intact riparian zones are also extremely important sources, and storage sites, for nutrients and energy. In most forests, a significant amount of the nutrients moving down a forested hillside in the soil are below the reach of plant roots. These nutrients are collected and stored by luxuriant vegetation in the riparian zone. Large amounts of energy from sunlight are also stored through photosynthesis in these lush plant communities.

Think of the riparian forest as Nature's battery and voltage regulator. The large trees and dense, diverse vegetation are the energy/nutrient storage cells in the battery. The humid, cool climate of the riparian ecosystem regulates the dispersal of this energy to the surrounding forest and water systems. Without an intact, healthy riparian ecosystem, energy overloads damage the system and little energy is stored for tomorrow's use.

As forest fragmentation spreads with clearcutting across the landscape, parks and preserves will not be immune. When the landscapes around these protected areas are clearcut, reserves tend to become fragile forest fragments. Landscape conservation should not be viewed as a luxury, but as a necessity. Without a healthy forest landscape, the various parts—timber cutting lands, reserves, recreation and tourism areas, human communities, and riparian ecosystems—will eventually succumb to the stresses created by fragmentation.

Fragmention of a forest with logging roads and clearcuts is like climbing a rope with a few broken strands—more strands are likely to fray and snap and you never know when the stress load will cause the rope to break. Similarly, we continue to break the strands of forest landscapes without understanding how they "hang together," how each part contributes to the whole. We are left with no idea how many strands we have severed, what order the strands belong in, or what the strands were made of.

Thanks to the science of landscape ecology, we do know that the damaging effects of clearcutting are felt far from the logging site, whether or not we can see the damage.

THE ECONOMIC FALLACIES OF CLEARCUTTING

In considering the economics of clearcutting, we must remember that both natural forests and contemporary economies are highly complex systems. To understand the relationship between forests and economies, I think we first need to talk about the differences between forests and economies.

A forest may be defined as an interconnected web of producers, consumers, and recyclers connected in time and space. Components of this web include plants, animals, microorganisms, soil, climate, and landscape.

Remarkably, we can define an economy with the same words: an interconnected web of producers, consumers, and recyclers connected in time and space. Components of this web include governments, corporations, shareholders, markets (local, national, and international), credit unions and banks, labor unions, social institutions (hospitals, schools, transportation), consumers, agriculture, small business, and resources. To this basic definition, however, we must add one further element in order to distinguish forests from forest-based economies. Forests are natural, self-sustaining systems. Forests can exist and persist without humans. Forest-based economies, on the other hand, are artificial systems—human ideas that cannot exist without forests.

To put it very bluntly, forests are not the same thing as "money in the bank." We convert forests into money only if we choose to think of them in that way—and we do so at our peril. Healthy forests can cope with and survive the natural effects of wildfires, insects, root diseases, decay, and death. But forests are not designed to cope with ecologically inappropriate profit-taking activities that designate one isolated part of the forest web—the trees—as a commodity and consider other parts as competition, pests, litter, waste, and debris.

Economic Fallacy #1: Clearcutting is the most economically efficient way of cutting and growing trees.

Economic Reality: Clearcutting considers only short-term timber economics, not long-term forest economics.

If we consider only the costs of planning a clearcut, building the roads, cutting the trees, and hauling them to the mill, then clearcutting is obviously cheaper and more efficient than ecologically responsible systems of timber management. But this method of calculating "costs" hides or ignores many long-term costs that must eventually be paid. Thus, the conventional cost of clearcutting does not reflect the actual cost of timber production.

For example, in contrast to various ecologically responsible partial cutting systems, clearcutting, especially in large blocks, almost always involves extensive tree planting. Associated with tree planting are costs of preparing the site (slash or shrub removal to reduce the cost of planting and improve the results). Since one of the goals of clearcutting is to grow merchantable crops of wood fiber in as short a period of time as possible, thinning young trees to increase their growth rate is another hidden cost of clearcut systems. All of these activities—site preparation, tree planting, and thinning—are frequently subsidized by federal, state, or provincial governments, so that citizens, rather than timber companies, bear the cost.

Road construction is designed on the same short-term, least-cost principles as clearcut logging itself. As a result, high maintenance costs and often reconstruction costs are frequently incurred when roads are used in the future. Also, timber companies are not normally held responsible for damages when "cost-efficient" methods of road construction result, months or years later, in slope failures, landslides, siltation of water courses, and damage to domestic and agricultural water supplies.

In my experience, the hidden or additional timber production costs involved with most clearcut operations mean that clearcutting actually costs somewhere between 30 and 100 percent more than ecologically responsible partial cutting where roads are constructed to high standards.

The conventional cost of clearcutting does not reflect the actual cost of forest restoration or rehabilitation. Soil degradation due to compaction, scraping, gouging, and erosion can result in rehabilitation costs of more than $1,500 per hectare (Utzig and Walmsley 1988). In many cases, soil cannot be rehabilitated or restored by any means, no matter how much money is spent.

The conventional cost of clearcutting also does not reflect the actual *social* cost. Water degradation forces rural people to relocate and forces urban people to spend millions of dollars treating their water to meet safe drinking standards. The loss of biological diversity and the associated loss of wilderness threaten our very survival and result in fewer opportunities for economic diversity in the future. Clearcut logging forecloses on forest uses, from tourism and public recreation to mushroom picking and berry gathering. When forest uses are carried out in an ecologically responsible manner, they provide readily sustainable employment and revenues year after year—as long as the forest is there. In other words, the social costs that government and the timber industry ignore today are simply postponed to future generations.

Other consequences of clearcutting such as fragmentation of forest landscapes, siltation of water supplies, loss of animal and plant species, and loss of entire forest communities cannot be valued in dollars. These ecological costs associated with clearcutting, however, do not result from ecologically responsible timber extraction. Disregard of these unpriced ecological costs ignores a truth: what we do to the forest we do to ourselves.

The short-term timber economics of clearcutting values timber and devalues forests. If we valued forests for all that they provide (air, water, wood, spirituality, food, shelter), if we valued the future, if we valued diverse, stable human economies and societies—we would not clearcut.

Economic Fallacy #2: Clearcutting provides sustainable, expanding employment.

Economic Reality: The evolution of clearcutting has resulted in the loss of employment and the loss of dignified, meaningful work.

One reason offered consistently by government and the timber industry to justify high clearcutting rates has been employment: jobs from the forest fuel all aspects of the economy. Meanwhile, the timber industry has simultaneously pursued a policy of replacing high-cost workers with lower-cost technology whenever possible. The goal, of course, is higher profits for the corporations. The unwelcome result is fewer jobs for workers in the timber industry.

Clearcutting jobs are based on forest destruction. As mechanization increases the "productivity" of each worker in a clearcutting operation, forest workers must destroy more and more forest day by day in order to meet their "needs." Consider this: to be economically viable, a mechanized logging operation needs to log more than ten times the timber to employ twice the number of workers as a horse logging operation. Put another way, nearly two logging truck loads per day are needed to employ each person in a mechanized operation, while less than one-third of a load is needed each day to provide a job for a horse logger.

It matters for jobs how timber is cut in the forest. Labor-intensive approaches, such as horse logging and appropriate use of small machines, cut fewer trees to create each job. This also means that more money stays in the local community. Both the forest and the people close to the forest benefit.

If we see that our real job is an ecologically responsible life, then meaningful work that protects and maintains the integrity of both forests and people will emerge as the new direction for forest use. This will require a major turnaround for our society, from an unsustainable (and overpopulated), consumption-based, throwaway economy toward a sustainable conservation-based recycling economy.

Economic Fallacy #3: Clearcutting rids us of valueless, decadent wood.

Economic Reality: Clearcutting of old-growth forests around the world removes the highest-quality, highest-volume, highest-valued wood from healthy forest ecosystems that have functioned successfully for millennia without human intervention.

Old-growth and many other forests unmodified by logging are often viewed by foresters and timber managers as "decadent" or "unhealthy"—in need of logging—before they topple over. Decadent or unhealthy trees, timber managers explain, are rotting faster than they are growing, thereby "wasting" forest space. The Forest Service in British Columbia refers to old-growth as "the aging forest," where "decay overtakes . . . growth and the volume of timber begins to decline" (British Columbia Ministry of Forests 1990). But this position is not supported by science. According to Dr. Jerry Franklin (1984), plant ecologist and one of the foremost experts on old-growth forests, "It appears that many old-growth forests manage to maintain wood levels or actually increase them. . . . It is logical to conclude that old forests tend to be stable in terms of their biomass or board foot accumulation. Foresters have long recognized the basic stability of wood accumulations in old-growth forests. Hence the expression, 'storing wood on the stump.'"

If old-growth forests are not rotting faster than they are growing, what about the wood quality? Thirty years ago I grew up in a cabinet-making business in Oregon. Any of us who manufactured wood products could tell the difference immediately between old-growth and second-growth softwoods. Old wood was clear, soft, fine-grained (from slow-growing trees), and strong. It was easy to plane and shape, glued easily, and held nails and screws well. Whether we wanted a beam to hold heavy loads or an ornate knob for a drawer, old-growth wood worked, and worked well. Second-growth obtained from previously clearcut areas was the opposite—knotty, hard, coarse-grained (from fast-growing trees), and weak. It was fussy to plane and

shape, gluing was unpredictable, and it did not hold nails and screws as well as old-growth. We questioned its ability to handle structural loads and knew that its coarse grain made it a poor choice for fine woodworking.

Science has recently caught up with these practical understandings. An analysis carried out by FORINTEK, a cooperative government and industry research organization in British Columbia, confirmed that second-growth Douglas-fir had low structural strength. The study also described problems with warping and workability, and explained that virtually no high-grade lumber could be milled from short-rotation second-growth trees without pruning.

The real blow with second-growth timber, however, was found in its value. Through economic analysis, FORINTEK indicated that second-growth Douglas-fir trees grown on average or better tree-growing sites need to reach an age of ninety years and be pruned to increase wood quality in order to have positive dollar value (Kellogg 1989).

The difference in wood quality, and correspondingly in wood value, between old-growth and second-growth is largely due to the length of fibers that make up the wood. Most of the wood fibers in old-growth conifers are long. In contrast, second-growth fibers are predominantly short. Longer fibers provide greater strength and better workability.

This is true for pulp as well as lumber. The highest-quality, strongest paper made from wood comes from long-fiber, old-growth coniferous wood. The FORINTEK report indicates that the yield of some grades of pulp declines in second-growth wood.

Long-fiber wood, termed mature wood, is not formed on the trunk of the tree until branches die (natural pruning). As long as wood is produced around green or living branches, juvenile or short-fiber wood is formed. Old-growth trees contain about 80 percent mature wood, while sixty-year-old second-growth is made up of about 50 percent juvenile wood (Kellogg 1989). Thus, second-growth short rotation timber monocultures that follow clearcutting are growing low-value, marginally useful wood.

The timber industry would like us to believe that clearcutting old-growth forests is a service to society. The real economic benefits, the industry claims, will come in the future, from managed, productive second-growth timber monocultures. But this has never been the case. Decadence is a convenient and unfounded rationalization for converting high-quality old-growth forests into high profits as quickly as possible.

Economic Fallacy #4: Clearcutting is necessary to compete in the global economy.

Economic Reality: Powerful transnational timber interests impose their short-term economic objectives on local communities, resulting in degraded local forests and degraded local communities.

For the handful of transnational corporations that are able to operate at home and abroad with little or no control by national and regional governments, clearcutting ensures "cheap resources" that can be taken in massive amounts by least-cost means; transported for processing to any place that has ready workers and benevolent terms; and then sold (sometimes to the people who gave up the resources in the first place) for the highest price the market will bear. This is called the "global economy."

Over this issue, the futures of workers, communities, and corporations finally converge. Healthy global economies are sustained by healthy community economies, and not the other way around. The long-term formula for this relationship can be constructive or destructive.

If communities are stripped of their forests through clearcutting with little compensation; if workers are laid off by the hundreds at one mill due to overcutting while capital pours into a new mill someplace else; and if small, local, innovative businesses are starved for raw materials while these same materials are freely exported by large corporations to global markets, then communities are being manipulated for someone else's benefit. The effect of the global market on communities in this situation is destructive.

On the other hand, if communities control the forest; if communities can make decisions that provide their workers with meaningful and stable employment; and if small community-based businesses have equal access to the forest, then communities are making their best possible contribution from the village economy to the global economy. In this situation, the effect of the global market on communities and the effect of communities on the global market is constructive.

Even if ecologically appropriate partial cutting results in higher short-term logging costs, high-quality timber will still retain its niche in the global market. Careful stewardship of remaining old-growth forests and cultivation of high-quality wood on longer growing cycles or rotations will assure a supply of high-quality wood that will always find a buyer, regardless of price. The economic law of scarcity applies to high-quality products such as fine-grained, clear, mature wood. If it costs more to produce it, the market will pay. If these additional costs mean stable communities and protected forests, then the money will be well spent.

CONCLUSION

When examined in a wholistic way, clearcutting makes neither ecological nor economic sense.

Ecologically, clearcutting causes irreparable damage to biological diversity—the foundation of life. We cannot see this damage because much of it is too small to see (destruction of soil microorganisms), and too subtle to see (interception of precipitation by large old trees). As well, some of the negative effects of clearcutting require many years to see because the biological legacies of millennia of old forests (large snags and fallen trees) can require centuries to wear out through clearcutting and short-cycle timber cropping. Yet the damage is inevitable because clearcutting does not maintain the composition and structures necessary to maintain fully functioning forests at any scale—from microscopic soil communities to the global forest.

The economics of clearcutting are little more than the economics of short-term greed. Workers, human communities, and the forest are all degraded so that a privileged, powerful few may benefit. As with the ecological problems of clearcutting, we must often look beyond today, tomorrow, and next year to the time of future generations for the economic problems to become plainly evident. The real economics of clearcutting are clouded by political manipulation that makes clearcutting appear to be the best economic choice for employment, corporate revenues, and government tax bases. But when examined closely, these illusions crumble.

The economic viability of clearcutting is rapidly declining, even in the world of short-term timber economics. When subjected even to the conventional economic analysis that ignores the environmental costs, and even the costs of regeneration, many of the stands being clearcut today do not pay. Why? Because many of the forests that remain unlogged today are found on terrain where road building is

expensive; they contain mainly low-volume trees; and they are a long distance from processing plants. These forests are logged through a variety of subsidies whose cost to society is higher taxes, lower employment, and once again, degraded forests.

To escape the ecological and economic fallacies of clearcutting, society must see forests as something more than logs standing upright. We must make decisions about the forest in the forest. We must make decisions about forest economics in the communities affected, with all interests sharing in the decision making.

Good ecology is good economics. Good ecology requires that we protect all the parts of the forest. Clearcutting throws away ecological parts while it ignores economic realities required to maintain future forests and the societies that depend on the forest.

Take a walk in the forest. The ecology necessary for its functioning is all there. Take a walk in a clearcut or a second-growth fiber farm. The ecology necessary for a forest to function is missing some critical parts. Without a healthy ecosystem, there is no economy, no society.

REFERENCES

British Columbia Ministry of Forests. 1990. *Forest management in British Columbia*. Victoria.

Franklin, J. F. 1984. Characteristics of old-growth Douglas-fir forests. In *New forests: Forests for a changing world*. Proceedings of the 1983 Society of American Foresters Convention, Portland, OR. Bethesda, MD: Society of American Foresters.

Gray, H. L. 1974. Snow accumulation and snowmelt as influenced by a small clearing in a lodgepole pine forest. *Water Resources Research* 10(2).

Kellogg, R. M., ed. 1989. Second growth Douglas-fir: Its management and conversion for value. *Report from Douglas-fir task force*, FORINTEK. B.C. Special Pub. No. SP-32. Vancouver, B.C.: FORINTEK Canada Corp.

Norse, E. A. 1990. *Ancient forests of the Pacific Northwest*. Covelo, CA: Island Press.

Olsson, R., S. Hagvar, and J. Kinnunen. 1992. Forests and forestry in Scandinavia: A status report. *Taiga News: Newsletter on Boreal Forests*, No. 2 (July): 4-5.

Robinson, Gordon. 1988. *The forest and the trees: A guide to excellent forestry*. Washington, D.C.: Island Press.

Utzig, A. and M. Walmsley. 1988. *Evaluation of soil degradation as a factor affecting forest productivity in British Columbia: a problem analysis. Phase I*. Prepared for the Canadian Forestry Service, Victoria, B.C. FRDA Report 025.

Daniel Dancer

The gloomy record of human subjugation of Nature does not provide much hope that we can suddenly
turn around and start managing forests and other lands in a truly sustainable way. But we have little choice but to try.
We are truly on the brink of a catastrophe.

A SUSTAINABLE FOREST
IS A DIVERSE AND NATURAL FOREST

REED F. NOSS

The environmental optimists have found their buzzword: *sustainability*. All that is needed to make forestry, agriculture, or economic development projects palatable to many people is to dress them in the cloak of sustainability. Do those who so sanguinely embrace this concept have any idea of what sustainability means ecologically? How do we tell when a forest is sustainable, and how does this differ from the exploitation of that forest being sustainable? What qualities make a forest sustainable?

I will address some of these questions in this essay, though I will not be so bold as to provide definitive answers. One thing we know is that forests can be sustainable under natural conditions. Indeed, forests have sustained themselves for over 350 million years with no help from humans. This is not to say they have stayed the same; in fact, they have never sat still. The "Coal Age" forests of *Calamites*, *Lepidodendron*, *Sigillaria*, and other ancestors of today's diminutive clubmosses, spikemosses, and horsetails, gave way to forests of tree ferns and gymnosperms, including the cycads, ginkgos, and conifers. Then came the angiosperms and forests composed of broadleaf, hardwood trees. The blend of species composing the forest in any region shifts endlessly. The "ancient" Douglas fir forests of the Pacific Northwest are actually quite young, having existed for only 5,000 years (Brubaker 1988), even though the other tree species that compose these forests have been around much longer. The Big Woods vegetation of Minnesota, described as the regional climax, developed only about 300 years ago with the onset of the Little Ice Age and a reduction in natural fire frequency (Grimm 1984). Then, after only a century and a half of existence, all but a few scattered patches of the Big Woods were rapidly replaced by farm fields.

The major factor affecting forest distribution and composition is climate. Climate change has been continuous, as far as we know, since the world began, although more rapid at some times than at others. As climate changes, each species responds individually according to its unique physiological tolerances and dispersal capacities. Forest communities are not organisms, for their organs (species) are largely interchangeable and, from a functional standpoint, are often redundant. Close associations between species, for instance parasites and their hosts, certainly occur, but these obligatory symbioses are the exception rather than the rule. For the most part, populations of species come together and then drift apart over time. Some get left in the dust, but new species evolve while old ones go extinct. Or so it has been for ages.

Some people argue that, because change is natural, the massive changes in forest cover and structure occurring today as a result of human activity are nothing to be alarmed about. These people are wrong. Although forests have always changed at many spatial and temporal scales, from individual treefalls to whole regions being bulldozed by mile-high glaciers, globally they have been remarkably persistent. The broad ecotones that separate forests from grasslands and deserts have shifted back and forth across continents over the centuries, but over the long expanse of time such changes are like the rhythms of a giant tide. Only in the last millennium has the ebb of forests been incessant and increasingly global in extent. Most alarming, the loss of forests to the axe and saw is occurring at an ever-faster rate. What replaces forest today is habitat for few living things besides domesticated plants and animals, and weeds. Deforestation and forest conversion are of crisis proportions.

In this essay, I discuss some qualities that make a forest sustainable and healthy, in hope that human society can find the wisdom to allow these qualities to endure. A *forest*, as the term is used in this essay, is a naturally occurring ecosystem distinct from a tree farm. We can characterize a forest at various scales, from a relatively homogeneous stand that occurs on a few acres, to a landscape or watershed covering thousands of acres, to a regional ecosystem comprising many different plant and animal communities. The critical qualities of sustainable forests at all of these scales are *biodiversity* and *naturalness*. These concepts are notoriously ambiguous and imprecise, but better indicators of forest sustainability have not been found.

BIODIVERSITY

Biodiversity is a central concept in modern conservation, but many people misunderstand or misrepresent what it means. Having co-opted the term *sustainability* for their own purposes in many cases, pro-development forces try hard to convince the public that logging will do wonderful things for biodiversity. These bastardizations of the concept must be nipped in the bud.

Biodiversity is a slippery concept, difficult to capture in a definition. A widely cited report defines biodiversity as "the variety and variability among living organisms and the ecological complexes in which they occur" (Office of Technology Assessment 1987). A still simpler definition, "the variety of life and its processes," was adopted as the summary definition by the Keystone Center National Policy Dialogue on Biological Diversity (Keystone Center 1991). What do these definitions tell us? Mostly, they tell us that we must move quickly beyond definitions if we wish to apply the biodiversity concept fruitfully to real conservation problems.

One of the most significant aspects of the biodiversity concept, what distinguishes it from traditional wildlife and endangered species issues, is that it is explicitly hierarchical (Noss 1990a). Biodiversity exists at several levels of biological organization and at each of these levels it may be threatened by human activities. Four commonly recognized levels of biological organization, and biodiversity, are *genetic*, *population-species*, *community-ecosystem*, and *landscape*. These various manifestations of diversity must be perpetuated in forests everywhere, not just in the high-diversity tropics. If our goal is to maintain global biodiversity, each type of ecosystem in every region must be permitted to follow its natural course. Humans may be part of this course, but directing it to our purposes at the expense of other creatures is neither ethical nor ecologically prudent.

GENETIC DIVERSITY

Species differ from one another, and individuals within species vary, in large part because they have unique combinations of genes. Genetic change leads to evolutionary change as individuals, populations, and species adapt to different situations and pass on their altered traits to offspring. Thus, genetic diversity is fundamental to the continually unfolding variety of life.

Conservation goals at the genetic level include maintaining genetic variation within and among populations of species and assuring that processes such as genetic differentiation and gene flow are relatively balanced. Without genetic variation, populations are less adaptable and their extinction is more probable. Small populations isolated from others of the same species by habitat fragmentation are more likely to diverge genetically, but at the same time they are more likely to suffer from inbreeding depression caused by mating between close relatives, which may result in reduced fertility and other problems (Frankel and Soulé 1981). Small, isolated populations also are subject to random loss of genetic variation, known as genetic drift, restricting their ability to adapt to changing circumstances.

Commercially important forest tree species, such as Douglas fir and loblolly pine, are better understood genetically than most other organisms. Trees tend to have more genetic variation than other plants, primarily because they are more highly outcrossing (as opposed to self-pollinating). For most species, the within-population component of genetic diversity appears to be greater than the differences between populations (Ledig 1986). Some of the genetic diversity within tree populations occurs within single individuals: different branches of the same tree may differ genetically because of somatic mutations arising spontaneously in different meristems (Gill and Halverson 1984). Because trees live a long time—if we let them—those mutations have time to accumulate and trees become genetically heterogeneous. This finding suggests that genetic impoverishment may be an unsuspected negative consequence of short rotations.

Genetic and additional within-species diversity of trees and other organisms have repercussions for community ecology. For example, various populations, individuals, or clones of a single plant species may differ in their production of secondary compounds used in defense against herbivores. These differences, in turn, may affect the abundance and diversity of herbivores in the community and of the predators that feed on them. In addition to genetic variation, individual organisms in a population differ ecologically due to phenotypic plasticity (such as the ability of plants to adjust their architecture and rate of photosynthesis to light levels), developmental stage (for example, caterpillars vs. moths, and saplings vs. canopy trees), sexual identity, and other effects (Wayne and Bazzaz 1991).

SPECIES DIVERSITY

The species level of biodiversity is probably what most people think of when they hear the term *biodiversity*. Although in some ways species diversity is the best-known aspect of biodiversity, we should bear in mind that the vast majority of species in the world are still unknown. Of an estimated 10 to 100 million species on Earth, we have named only about 1.4 million (Ehrlich and Wilson 1991). Many invertebrates, bacteria, and other organisms remain to be discovered, even in the United States. Hundreds of invertebrate species and perhaps thousands of species of bacteria can be found in one square meter of soil in an old-growth temperate forest (Lattin 1990, Wilson 1992).

At the species level, a common conservation goal is to promote maximum species richness. This goal is certainly appropriate at a global scale, but at smaller scales it is problematic because exotic and weedy species may compose much of that diversity. Management for diversity at a local scale, an example being habitat manipulation that intersperses several successional stages within a small area, may benefit opportunistic species (blackberries and brown-headed cowbirds come to mind) at the expense of sensitive species that require forest interior habitat.

Single-species management, particularly game management, has contributed to many conservation problems. For instance, wildlife managers have traditionally advocated forest harvest patterns that maximize fragmentation of the landscape because most deer and other game species are edge species. But we now know that while fragmentation may often benefit deer and other game species, it does not contribute to native biological diversity (Noss 1983). Forest fragmentation has benefited deer so much in the upper Midwest that several conifer species—the Canada yew, eastern hemlock, and arbor vitae—are barely regenerating in many areas due to overbrowsing (Alverson et al. 1988).

Species-level management is still necessary in many cases. Certain kinds of species warrant special management emphasis because their protection will conserve more than themselves. *Keystone species*, which play pivotal roles in their ecosystems and upon which a large part of the community depends, are especially important in this regard (Noss 1991a). Woodpeckers, because they excavate cavities that are later used by many other animals, can be considered keystone species. Woodpeckers and other cavity nesters usually decline with the conversion of natural forests to tree farms. Major declines of ecologically pivotal species are more important ecologically than the loss of the last few individuals of species that play lesser roles.

Other categories of species that deserve extra conservation attention include *umbrellas* and *flagships* (Noss 1991a). Some animals have large area requirements, so that if we maintain enough habitat for them, many other species will be carried under this umbrella of protection. Umbrella species are often charismatic megavertebrates, so they also function as flagships or symbols for major conservation efforts. The grizzly bear, for example, is a potent symbol for wilderness preservation. If we protect and restore 40 million acres of wilderness for grizzlies in the northern Rocky Mountains, we can rest assured that most (though not necessarily all) other species native to the region will be in good shape. No umbrella is complete—some endemic species have very small ranges that will not be captured even in an ideal reserve network for a wide-ranging species.

Species that are particularly vulnerable to human activity often need to be managed individually, at least until their habitats can be protected by an ecosystem-level approach. Otherwise, biodiversity will continue to diminish with each extinction. Conservation must focus on species and habitats most threatened by human activities (Diamond 1976). Although we might accept the egalitarian notion that all species are ultimately equal, at any given place and time some species thrive on human activity and others suffer. Society has an obligation to protect the latter. Familiar examples of species extremely vulnerable to human activity are the northern spotted owl, threatened by logging of old-growth forests in the Pacific Northwest (Thomas et al. 1990), and the red-cockaded woodpecker, threatened by loss of old forests in the Southeast (Jackson 1971).

COMMUNITY OR ECOSYSTEM DIVERSITY

A growing number of ecologists claim that conservation is most efficient when focused directly on the community or ecosystem. I generally agree, but argue that community-level conservation should complement, not replace, species-level management. The Nature Conservancy estimates that its *coarse filter* of community inventory and protection can take care of perhaps 90 percent of species without having to consider each species individually (Noss 1987). Species that fall through the pores of the coarse filter, such as large predators that use many habitats, and narrow endemics that are restricted to a few examples of a given community type, can be captured by a *fine filter* of rare species conservation. The most ambitious coarse filter conservation project in the United States today is the Gap Analysis project of the U.S. Fish and Wildlife Service (Scott et al. 1991). This project uses vegetation types and vertebrate species distributions as surrogates of biodiversity, and seeks to identify vegetation types and species that are inadequately protected in each region.

Practicing conservation at the ecosystem level also demands attention to ecological processes. The processes that are most crucial for ecological health vary from ecosystem to ecosystem, but in forests, some of the most important processes to consider are fire and other natural disturbances, hydrological cycles, plant-herbivore interactions, predation (including control of herbivorous insects), mycorrhizal interactions, and soil building. All of these processes affect biodiversity at several levels and they must be maintained within normal limits of variation if native bio-diversity is to persist. Clearcutting, plantation silviculture, and other intensive forest management practices ultimately fail because the perpetuation of ecological processes in the long term is not an objective.

LANDSCAPE DIVERSITY

Landscape diversity—the pattern of habitats and communities across a large land area—can be considered a higher-level expression of biodiversity. Landscape patterns are ecologically functional. Many animal populations regularly use more than one habitat type to meet their life history needs; they cannot be protected through management of different communities in isolation. For example, Rocky Mountain elk use low elevation forests and openings in winter but alpine and subalpine forests and meadows on their summer range. Also, adjacent habitats affect each other in many ways, including microclimatic effects, such as penetration of wind and sun into forests from their edges, and transfer of nutrients and propagules (seeds and spores) between habitats.

Species richness varies along environmental gradients in the landscape. The most commonly studied gradient is elevation. In the Western Cascades of Oregon, the number of species of amphibians, reptiles, and mammals declines sharply with increasing elevation (Harris 1984). This represents a problem for conservation, because generally speaking, the low-elevation, high-diversity sites are private lands; mid-elevation sites are commodity-production public lands; and large protected areas (such as designated wilderness) occupy the high-elevation, lowest-diversity sites. This biased pattern of habitat protection, the "rock and ice" phenomenon, occurs almost everywhere in the western U.S. (Davis 1988, Foreman and Wolke 1989, Noss 1990b). Conservation programs must strive to maintain natural ecosystems across all environmental gradients, from the highest to the lowest, and wettest to driest sites, and representing the full spectrum of substrates and topoclimates.

The landscape scale is where we can best see the diversifying effects of disturbance. Natural disturbances typically create patches of various sizes scattered across the landscape. Different seral stages of regenerating forest are often used by different sets of species (Pickett and White 1985). The complexity of disturbance regimes is only beginning to be appreciated. For example, most forest fires are mosaic burns, being underburns in some areas, crown burns in others, with some patches untouched. Recovery after fire varies with fire intensity (sometimes the soil may be

"sterilized" and succession is slow), seed sources, weather, and other factors. Variability in disturbance regimes is responsible for much of the habitat diversity we find in forests. Generally speaking, the more diverse the habitat, the more species can coexist, so long as certain habitat types are large or interconnected enough to maintain viable populations of species associated with them.

The native species in a region have adapted, through evolution, to a particular disturbance regime. If we alter that regime radically, such as replacing wildfires by clearcuts, we can expect that many species will not be able to adjust rapidly enough to avoid extinction. The patchwork created by clearcutting differs from the mosaic created by fire or windthrow in some fundamental ways, such as having less dead wood and other structure within patches, greater contrast between patches, more intense edge effects (which threaten biodiversity in many ways), and the presence of roads and vehicles (Franklin and Forman 1987, Noss in press). Fragmentation, because it breaks up large forests into smaller and eventually isolated patches, reduces population size for species with large area requirements and thereby makes them more vulnerable to extinction (Wilcove et al. 1986). Clearcutting and road building are also the major threats to aquatic ecosystem integrity and survival of fish populations in forest landscapes, particularly where slopes are steep and soils unstable (Swanson et al. 1990).

Forest conservation in recent years has become more sophisticated with the realization, on the part of many activists, that whole forest landscapes are worth protecting, and not just for aesthetic or recreational reasons. Not only must the "crown jewels" or stands of big trees be saved, but entire functioning landscapes must be maintained. We learn in studying landscape ecology that context is at least as important as content (Noss and Harris 1986). Small reserves that may be set aside for their content—for example, to represent plant community types or save magnificent stands of old growth—are heavily affected by their context when the surrounding landscape is altered radically. Natural fire regimes, metapopulation dynamics (interactions between spatially distinct populations), migratory corridors for large animals, and watershed protection are all ecological functions that can be perpetuated only at the landscape and regional scales.

NATURALNESS

Biodiversity alone may be insufficient as a criterion for management of forests at a regional or local scale. Biodiversity is often difficult to measure or consider in a broader context; furthermore, we do not know much about it. We need a buffer for our ignorance; I suggest the best buffer is naturalness. As a criterion for land conservation, naturalness has lost favor in scientific circles because it is difficult to quantify. Science, after all, progresses largely by quantification. This is a limitation of science, but not a fault. Numbers do mean something and, practically speaking, there is nothing like good data (maps, statistics, figures, and graphs) to make a convincing case for conservation to many audiences. It is difficult to produce statistics and graphs to show how natural an area is. But this does not mean that naturalness is unimportant.

What is a natural forest? How might it serve as a buffer for our ignorance about sustainable forest management? To answer these questions, we must first appreciate the difference between a sustainable forest and sustainable forestry (Noss in press). Sustainability advocates chatter a great deal about sustainable forestry, but very little has been said about how to sustain forests. Forestry, as a profession, has been mostly concerned with silviculture, the primary aim of which is the "continuous production of wood" (Toumey 1947). A tree farm managed intelligently on the basis of ecological principles may be able to provide wood products continuously (in terms of human generations) and therefore would qualify as a bona fide example of sustainable forestry. But a tree farm is hardly a forest.

A forest differs from a tree farm in being naturally regenerated and essentially self-regulating. Although ecological restoration may someday be able to produce forests from planted trees, it is too early to count on this. Natural forests are probably always more diverse in total species, structures, and processes than plantations in the same region. Although natural forests are dynamic, their component species have evolved over millions of years and their ecological and evolutionary processes have been in operation even longer. It is hubris to think that humans have learned to duplicate these processes in the few centuries that we have been practicing intensive forestry, or the few years over which we have even thought about sustainability.

Naturalness is a relative concept, of course. Some naturally regenerated forests have been exploited for a long time, or are small and surrounded by civilization. On the other hand, some large, multi-species plantations may appear fairly natural. Size and accessibility to humans are among the most important factors determining the naturalness of a forest. Thus, a natural forest is generally a wild forest. A large, unroaded forest is more likely to have maintained its primitive characteristics than smaller, accessible forests that may be heavily influenced by outside forces. Nature reserve managers commonly say that the smaller the reserve, the more management is necessary to maintain the qualities for which the reserve was set aside (Pyle 1980, White and Bratton 1980, Noss 1983).

The contribution of wildness to naturalness and sustainability of forest ecosystems can be appreciated by envisioning a regional landscape composed of many different habitats, ranging from true wilderness through various levels of exploitation, from light single-tree selection to clearcutting. Such a landscape is diverse and serves many utilitarian and non-utilitarian functions. Even if we accept that even-aged plantation silviculture has a place in this landscape, the case for protecting large areas as wild forest is strong. What are the values of maintaining wildness in such a landscape? In a recent essay (Noss 1991c), I noted four *primary values of big wilderness* (cf. Foreman and Wolke 1989). These values are:

1. *Scientific.* Everything we do in land management is an experiment. Whether we know it or not, we are testing hypotheses about the response of a system (e.g., a forested watershed) to a particular management regime. We may try a variety of harvest methods, harvest patterns, means of access, site preparation techniques, tree species and genotypes for planting, regeneration strategies, pest and brush control methods, and rotation lengths. If we are intelligent, we measure the effects of these various experimental treatments on the ecosystem, as well as on wood production. But our experimental design is valid only if treatments are properly replicated and comparable *control areas* exist that receive no or very light treatment (Hurlbert 1984). Because our forestry experiments are conducted at a landscape scale, often over tens or hundreds of thousands of acres, we need control areas that also encompass entire landscapes.

What do we call these landscape-sized, strictly protected benchmarks against which we measure the effects of management experiments? Wilderness! Aldo Leopold recognized this function of wilderness over fifty years ago. Wilderness, he wrote, is essential to the "science of land health" because it offers a "base-datum of normality, a picture of how healthy land maintains itself as an organism" (Leopold 1941). Without huge wild areas in every region and ecosystem type, our land management experiments are uncontrolled and dangerous.

2. *Biological and Ecological.* Wilderness has much to contribute to biodiversity conservation (Noss 1990b, 1992). A large wild area, or better yet, a network of connected wild areas, might contain viable populations of virtually all species native to a region, including large carnivores. These and other species most sensitive to human activity may persist only in large, wild areas with limited human access. For species with more modest area requirements or less vulnerability to people, multiple demes (genetic populations) or metapopulations may be maintained in a single Big Wilderness. Big Wilderness also offers the best opportunity to maintain complete environmental gradients, disturbance-recovery patch dynamics, and other expressions of biodiversity at the landscape scale.

3. *A Source of Humility.* Many wilderness advocates are thrilled to be able to explore areas where they are not the top dog, where there are animals bigger and meaner than they are. But exposing oneself to danger in wilderness is not just thrill seeking; it is an opportunity to be profoundly humbled. Forest managers, who tend to hold their manipulative abilities in high regard, could stand a healthy dose of humility. Mosquitoes, freezing temperatures, lightning, floods, venomous snakes, cliffs, and other sources of danger and discomfort might do much to encourage a more cautious and respectful approach to land management. Perhaps all forest managers should be required to spend part of their time in such humbling environments.

4. *Intrinsic.* I have saved the most important value for last. "Wilderness," Ed Abbey wrote, "needs no defense, only more defenders." Wilderness predates us, made us what we are, and defines us still. It can and will go on without us. If we have value, then all living things and the places in which they live have value for their own sakes.

If we lose wilderness from our hypothetical landscape, as we have in most landscapes across North America and the world, these four values are severely diminished. We might try to practice sustainable forestry in such a landscape, but there would be no blueprint from which to proceed, no benchmarks for measuring our success. We would have lost sensitive animals, such as wolves and grizzlies, and many other species that we know little about. We would have lost opportunities for solitude and contemplation. Given these losses, we could hardly call any forest that remains "sustainable."

It will take a lot of convincing for many forest managers to appreciate the values of wild, natural forests. These managers are beginning to think about biodiversity, thanks to the popularity of the concept and a multitude of workshops and conferences, but they often disassociate diversity and wildness. The wilderness idea has been so firmly captured by recreational and aesthetic interests that the potential contributions of wilderness to biological conservation have been virtually ignored. Only recently have federal agencies and professional societies, such as the Society of American Foresters, begun to examine the nonrecreational values of wilderness (Reed 1990). Wildness and biodiversity should be seen as complementary, in the sense that (1) the wilderness protection movement could be strengthened by evaluating the contribution of wilderness protection to biodiversity conservation goals, such as ecosystem representation (Davis 1988); and (2) a conservation strategy that includes protection of large wild areas is more likely to be successful in maintaining the full scope of native biodiversity (Noss 1990b).

Although naturalness suffers from vagueness of definition, there are ways in which it can be measured. Anderson (1991) proposed three criteria for assessing the relative naturalness of an area: (1) the amount of cultural energy required to maintain the system in its present state; (2) the extent to which the system would change if humans were removed from the scene; and (3) the proportion of the fauna and flora composed of native versus non-native species. Forests that can take care of themselves, that would change little if we left them alone, and that are made up of native species are more natural—and, I submit, more sustainable—than humanized forests. Managing forest landscapes to maintain their natural qualities will also make them more sustainable (Noss in press).

What can we do to make our forest landscapes more natural and sustainable? As suggested above, size and human access are crucial considerations. Large wild areas are better able to encompass natural disturbance regimes and the shifting mosaic of recovering forest patches across the landscape (Pickett and Thompson 1978). Some scientists estimate that, in order to maintain a fairly stable spectrum of successional stages and habitats for species, a landscape would have to be at least fifty times the size of the average stand-replacing disturbance (Shugart and West 1981, Shugart and Seagle 1985). As an example, forest types that regularly experience fires 1 million acres in size (such as boreal spruce and lodgepole pine in the northern Rocky Mountains) would have to be maintained in blocks of at least 50 million acres in order to maintain a relatively stable distribution of seral stages. By other measures, however, areas as small as 2.5 million acres may show stability (Romme and Despain 1990), and a steady state may not be the natural condition for some ecosystem types (Baker 1989). In any case, forests that are small relative to the scale of disturbance are likely to experience radical fluctuations in the proportions of seral stages, which in turn threaten populations that depend on certain stages. Many nature reserves are smaller than the area likely to be disturbed by a single wildfire or windstorm, and therefore are quite vulnerable to loss of habitat diversity and species.

Human access also must be controlled in order to maintain naturalness. Socially, this is not a popular idea, as people like to use forests for many purposes. But a truly natural forest would contain populations of all species native to the region, including those that are vulnerable to human activities. Research has shown that road densities as low as 0.8 or 0.9 miles per square mile may make habitat unsuitable for wolves or black bear (e.g., Brody 1984, Thiel 1985, Mech et al. 1988), but that areas with higher road density may be inhabited if adjacent to large roadless areas (Mech 1989). In these cases, the roads themselves pose little danger to the animals, but roads bring people with guns and traps. In other cases, roads are important direct sources of mortality from collisions (Harris and Gallagher 1989). Roads also affect naturalness by serving as corridors for the invasion of exotic species, including forest pests and pathogens. In the Northwest, Port Orford cedar root rot fungus, black-stain root disease fungus, spotted knapweed, and the gypsy moth are all known to disperse and invade natural habitats via roads and vehicles (Schowalter 1988). A roaded landscape is not a natural or a sustainable landscape; thus, I consider road closures a necessary step in healing abused landscapes. Selection forestry that requires frequent entries, and road densities usually as high or higher than in even-age management, may be no more sustainable than clearcutting.

CONCLUSION

The strategy I suggest for promoting native biodiversity, naturalness, and sustainability in a regional landscape is essentially twofold: (1) maintain a large portion of the region as true wilderness, and (2) manage the rest of the region for multiple uses, but through use of management practices that closely mimic natural processes. The question of how much of each region to maintain as wilderness must be asked for each region individually; obviously, more of Alaska can be maintained as wilderness than in the case of Illinois. I am among those who have suggested (Noss 1991c) that at least 50 percent of the United States as a whole be maintained as wilderness.

The 50 percent recommendation, also the "compromise" position of Dave Foreman,

is based on a rough guess of how much of an average region must be strictly protected in order to support viable populations of all native species, including large carnivores, and to have at least one area big enough to allow a natural disturbance regime to function without human intervention. Other authors, using different criteria, have come to similar conclusions about the proportion of a region that should remain natural (e.g., Odum and Odum 1972, for south Florida). In order to restore native biodiversity, predators, other species, and fire should be reintroduced to landscapes where they have been extirpated. These are the central goals of the Wildlands Project (see Noss 1992, Foreman, this volume).

The other half of the strategy, sustainable management for multiple uses, may be even more challenging. As noted above, all management is an experiment; so far, most land management experiments have been dismal failures. Multiple use, as interpreted by agencies such as the U.S. Forest Service and Bureau of Land Management, has not worked (Grumbine 1990). The only success stories in real multiple-use conservation are a handful of indigenous peoples who have somehow been able to coexist with their environments for long periods without impoverishing them. Some indigenous cultures have even contributed to the biodiversity of their regions (Posey 1990), suggesting that humans have the potential to act as a keystone species in the most positive sense. The beaver provides a good model of how humans could contribute to native biodiversity by creating habitats used by many different species (Johnston and Naiman 1987). In general, however, human cultures have been causing extinctions for at least 50,000 years, prompting biologist Jared Diamond to nickname our species "Man, the exterminator" (Diamond 1982). Extinction rates have been rising for several centuries and exponentially over the last few decades, in concert with human population (Ehrlich and Wilson 1991).

The gloomy record of human subjugation of Nature does not provide much hope that we can suddenly turn around and start managing forests and other lands in a truly sustainable way. But we have little choice but to try. We are truly on the brink of a catastrophe. In such a situation, radical change (or, looking at it another way, true conservatism) is the only hope for survival. Do not misunderstand: the Earth will survive and Nature will endure, no matter what we do. Humans are not all that powerful. Ecosystems can be greatly impoverished and still function, in the sense of capturing energy and cycling nutrients. They can certainly get along without human beings and other large mammals. The question is whether this massive impoverishment is ethical and in the best interests of our species and all other living things. A preferable attitude toward Nature is one of respect and compassion.

The topic of precisely how to manage forests sustainably for multiple uses is beyond the scope of this essay. Promising experiments include natural selection forestry; retention harvests that maintain snags, dead and down material, and many live trees on site ("New Forestry"); aggregation of harvest units; minimization of road building; corridor retention; prescribed fire; and many other practices. But none of these experiments has a prayer of succeeding without drastic declines in wood harvested and total amount of land in production. Legislation that replaces even-age management with selection forestry will not sustain forests if timber targets remain high. Hence, any advance toward sustainable forestry will depend on a precipitous drop in the worldwide demand for wood products. Coupled with decreasing production and consumption, a serious, global restoration effort is needed to repair ecosystems damaged by past management (Noss in press). It is time to put people to work repairing forests rather than destroying forests. And where it is not too late, now may be our last chance to set aside forests large and wild enough to sustain themselves.

REFERENCES

Alverson, W. S., D. M. Waller, and S. L. Solheim. 1988. Forests too deer: Edge effects in northern Wisconsin. *Conservation Biology* 2:348–58.

Anderson, J. E. 1991. A conceptual framework for evaluating and quantifying naturalness. *Conservation Biology* 5:347–52.

Baker, W. L. 1989. Landscape ecology and nature reserve design in the Boundary Waters Canoe Area, Minnesota. *Ecology* 70:23–35.

Brody, A. J. 1984. Habitat use by Black Bears in relation to forest management in Pisgah National Forest, North Carolina. M.S. Thesis. University of Tennessee, Knoxville.

Brubaker, L. B. 1988. Vegetation history and anticipating future vegetation change. In *Ecosystem management for parks and wilderness*, ed. J. K. Agee and D. R. Johnson, 41–61. Seattle: University of Washington Press.

Davis, G. D. 1988. Preservation of natural diversity: The role of ecosystem representation within wilderness. Paper presented at National Wilderness Colloquium, in January at Tampa, Florida.

Diamond, J. M. 1976. Island biogeography and conservation: Strategy and limitations. *Science* 193:1027–29.

———. 1982. Man the exterminator. *Nature* 298:787–89.

Ehrlich, P. R., and E.O. Wilson. 1991. Biodiversity studies: Science and policy. *Science* 253:758–62.

Foreman, D., and J. Wolke. 1989. *The big outside*. Tucson: Ned Ludd Books.

Frankel, O. H., and M. E. Soulé. 1981. *Conservation and evolution*. Cambridge: Cambridge University Press.

Franklin, J. F., and R. T. T. Forman. 1987. Creating landscape patterns by cutting: Ecological consequences and principles. *Landscape Ecology* 1:5–18.

Gill, D. E., and T. G. Halverson. 1984. Fitness variation among branches within trees. In *Evolutionary Ecology: The Twenty-third Symposium of the British Ecological Society*, ed. B. Shorrocks, 105–116. Oxford: Blackwell Scientific Publications.

Grimm, E.C. 1984. Fire and other factors controlling the Big Woods vegetation of Minnesota in the mid-nineteenth century. *Ecological Monographs* 54:291–311.

Grumbine, R. E. 1990. Viable populations, reserve size, and federal lands management: A critique. *Conservation Biology* 4:127–34.

Harris, L. D. 1984. *The fragmented forest*. Chicago: University of Chicago Press.

Harris, L. D., and P. B. Gallagher. 1989. New initiatives for wildlife conservation: The need for movement corridors. In *Preserving communities and corridors*, ed. G. Mackintosh, 11–34. Washington, D.C.: Defenders of Wildlife.

Hurlbert, S. H. 1984. Pseudoreplication and the design of ecological field experiments. *Ecological Monographs* 54:187–211.

Jackson, J. A. 1971. The evolution, taxonomy, distribution, past populations, and current status of the red-cockaded woodpecker. In *The ecology and management of the red-cockaded woodpecker*, ed. R. L. Thompson, 4–29. Tallahassee, FL: Bureau of Fish and Wildlife and Tall Timbers Research Station.

Johnston, C. A., and R. J. Naiman. 1987. Boundary dynamics at the aquatic-terrestrial interface: The influence of beaver and geomorphology. *Landscape Ecology* 1:47–57.

Keystone Center, The. 1991. *Final Consensus Report of the Keystone policy dialogue on biological diversity on federal lands*. Keystone, CO: The Keystone Center.

Lattin, J. D. 1990. Arthropod diversity in Northwest old-growth forests. *Wings* 15(2): 7–10.

Ledig, F. T. 1986. Heterozygosity, heterosis, and fitness in outbreeding plants. In *Conservation biology: The science of scarcity and diversity*, ed. M.E. Soulé, 77–104. Sunderland, MA: Sinauer Associates.

Leopold, A. 1941. Wilderness as a land laboratory. *Living Wilderness* 6(July): 3.

Mech, L. D. 1989. Wolf population survival in an area of high road density. *American Midland Naturalist* 121:387–89.

Mech, L. D., S. H. Fritts, G. L. Radde, and W. J. Paul. 1988. Wolf distribution and road density in Minnesota. *Wildlife Society Bulletin* 16:85–87.

Noss, R. F. 1983. A regional landscape approach to maintain diversity. *BioScience* 33:700–6.

———. 1987. From plant communities to landscapes in conservation inventories: A look at The Nature Conservancy (U.S.A.). *Biological Conservation* 41:11–37.

———. 1990a. Indicators for monitoring biodiversity: A hierarchical approach. *Conservation Biology* 4:355–64.

———. 1990b. What can wilderness do for biodiversity? In *Preparing to manage wilderness in the twenty-first century: Proceedings of the conference*, ed. P. C. Reed, 49–61. Southeastern Forest Experiment Station, Asheville, NC: USDA Forest Service.

———. 1991a. From endangered species to biodiversity. In *Balancing on the brink of extinction: The Endangered Species Act and lessons for the future*, ed. K. A. Kohm, 227–46. Washington, D.C.: Island Press.

———. 1991b. A Native Ecosystems Act (concept paper). *Wild Earth* 1(1): 24.

———. 1991c. Sustainability and wilderness. *Conservation Biology* 5:120–22.

———. 1992. The wildlands project: Land conservation strategy. *Wild Earth* (Special Issue): 10–25.

———. (In press). Sustainable forestry or sustainable forests? In *Defining Sustainable Forestry*, ed. J. T. Olson. Washington, D.C.: Island Press.

Noss, R. F., and L. D. Harris. 1986. Nodes, networks, and MUMs: Preserving diversity at all scales. *Environmental Management* 10:299–309.

Odum, E. P., and H. T. Odum. 1972. Natural areas as necessary components of man's total environment. *Proceedings North American Wildlife and Natural Resources Conference* 37:178–89.

Office of Technology Assessment. 1987. *Technologies to maintain biological diversity*. Washington, D.C.: U.S. Government Printing Office.

Pickett, S. T. A., and J. N. Thompson. 1978. Patch dynamics and the design of nature reserves. *Biological Conservation* 13:27–37.

Pickett, S. T. A., and P. S. White. 1985. *The ecology of natural disturbance and patch dynamics*. Orlando, FL: Academic Press.

Posey, D. A. 1990. The science of the Mebengokre. *Orion* 9(3): 16–23.

Pyle, R. M. 1980. Management of nature reserves. In *Conservation biology: An evolutionary-ecological perspective*, ed. M. E. Soulé and B. A. Wilcox, 319–27. Sunderland, MA: Sinauer Associates.

Reed, P. C., ed. 1990. *Preparing to manage wilderness in the twenty-first century: Proceedings of the conference.* Southeastern Forest Experiment Station, Asheville, NC: USDA Forest Service.

Romme, W. H., and D. G. Despain. 1990. Effects of spatial scale on fire history and landscape dynamics in Yellowstone National Park. Paper presented at Fifth Annual Landscape Ecology Symposium: The Role of Landscape Ecology in Public-Policy Making and Land-use Management, 21 March, Oxford, Ohio.

Schowalter, T. D. 1988. Forest pest management: A synopsis. *Northwest Environmental Journal* 4:313–18.

Scott, J. M., B. Csuti, K. Smith, J. E. Estes, and S. Caicco. 1991. Gap analysis of species richness and vegetation cover: An integrated biodiversity conservation strategy. In *Balancing on the brink of extinction: The Endangered Species Act and lessons for the future,* ed. K. Kohm, 282–97. Washington, D.C.: Island Press.

Shugart, H. H., and S. W. Seagle. 1985. Modeling forest landscapes and the role of disturbance in ecosystems and communities. In *The ecology of natural disturbance and patch dynamics,* ed. S. T. A. Pickett and P. S. White, 353–68. Orlando, FL: Academic Press.

Shugart, H. H., and D. C. West. 1981. Long-term dynamics of forest ecosystems. *American Scientist* 69:647–52.

Swanson, F. J., J. F. Franklin, and J. R. Sedell. 1990. Landscape patterns, disturbance, and management in the Pacific Northwest, U.S.A. In *Changing landscapes: An ecological perspective,* ed. I. S. Zonneveld and R. T. T. Forman, 191–213. New York: Springer-Verlag.

Thiel, R. P. 1985. Relationship between road densities and wolf habitat suitability in Wisconsin. *American Midland Naturalist* 113:404–7.

Thomas, J. W., E. D. Forsman, J. B. Lint, E. C. Meslow, B. R. Noon, and J. Verner. 1990. *A conservation strategy for the northern spotted owl.* Portland, OR: USDA Forest Service, USDI Bureau of Land Management, USDI Fish and Wildlife Service, and USDI National Park Service.

Toumey, J. W. 1947. *Foundations of silviculture, upon an ecological basis.* 2d ed. New York: John Wiley & Sons.

Wayne, P. M., and F. A. Bazzaz. 1991. Assessing diversity in plant communities: The importance of within-species variation. *Trends in Ecology and Evolution* 6:400–404.

White, P. S., and S. P. Bratton. 1980. After preservation: Philosophical and practical problems of change. *Biological Conservation* 18:241–55.

Wilcove, D. S., C. H. McLellan, and A. P. Dobson. 1986. Habitat fragmentation in the temperate zone. In *Conservation Biology: The science of scarcity and diversity,* ed. M. E. Soulé, 237–56. Sunderland, MA: Sinauer Associates.

Wilson, E. O. 1992. Keynote address. Defining Sustainable Forestry Workshop, The Wilderness Society, World Resources Institute, and American Forestry Association, 13 January, Washington, D.C.

Barry Tessman

Big timber generally has local political support as well as the support of educational institutions and boards of education. Support is virtually guaranteed by the system that provides funding to schools and local governments from timber harvest revenues that are generated by logging on federal lands within their boundaries.

CULTURAL CLEARCUTS: THE SOCIOLOGY OF TIMBER COMMUNITIES IN THE PACIFIC NORTHWEST

FELICE PACE

Clearcuts are ugly. People who see them, even children, know instinctively that they are wrong, an outrage, a sacrilege. Yet, in the face of thirty years of negative public reaction, in spite of legal challenges, restrictive legislative language, and mountains of bad press, the United States and Canadian governments and the timber industry continue clearcutting public and private forests. Why?

The answer lies in the imperatives of modern Western capitalism, the mind-set of foresters taught to impose an industrial agricultural model onto forest ecosystems, and the sociology of communities whose economies are dominated by logging and the production of wood products. Factors favoring liquidation of forests for short-term profit include excessively high interest rates and a corporate culture that emphasizes the short-term bottom line over long-term economic health and social responsibility.

Large timber corporations have traditionally provided substantial funding for the nations' forestry schools and, until recently, the curriculum of these institutions has reflected industry's desire for foresters who will manage public and private forests in a manner compatible with corporate priorities. Consequently, most industry and government foresters think of the forest as a "crop" to be "planted," "cultivated," and "harvested." The industrial agriculture model also serves a major goal of post–World War II public policy. Clearcutting facilitates flooding timber markets with cheap logs from public lands. This has meant inexpensive lumber, a factor that helped fuel the post–World War II housing boom and every economic "recovery" in the postwar era, 1945–1990.

Economic and public policy decisions have implications for communities and for the people who make up those communities. Managing forests like cornfields with a public policy of low *stumpage* (log) prices has necessitated development of communities in which extracting timber and processing it into cheap lumber for housing dominate. This is the classic formula for a colony and, as in all modern colonies, the economic imperative favors the dominance of transnational corporations. So it was that during the 1950s and 1960s when a myriad of small locally owned lumber mills in the forested West were replaced by relatively few large mills operated by corporations that rank among the largest, most powerful, and most profitable in the world.

In the small Northern California valley in which I write, six sawmills operated as late as the 1950s. In 1992 no mills operate here. Siskiyou County, in which the valley is located, is roughly the size of Connecticut. Its population is about forty-four thousand. Of the logs cut in this county in 1988, 66 percent were processed elsewhere, mainly in the urban centers to the north, south, and west (calculation from data in Anderson and Olson 1991; and Siskiyou County Assessors Office 1991). Logs are transported hundreds of miles to coastal ports where they are either exported or replace exported logs in coastal mills.

When Euro-Americans first encountered the vast forests of the Pacific Northwest they were inspired with awe and dread. Working for months to fell, burn, and clear a small patch of forest, the early settlers could not conceive a limit to the forests. This perspective was the milk on which their children and grandchildren cut their teeth, happily cutting away at the forest without thought that it could someday be exhausted. The settlers who came west, of course, had seen native forests cleared and tamed. The vast white pine, spruce, and hardwood forests of New England and the mid-Atlantic states had been virtually eliminated by the time the pioneers moved west. The great softwood forests of the North Central states, Michigan and Minnesota, were obliterated in a single generation by loggers who were rootless, itinerant laborers with no connection to place. It was the logging of these forests that built Chicago and the railroads west and that created the culture of the timber industry, a mentality to get it all now and then move on.

When George Weyerhaeuser sold out in Minnesota and moved his operation west, he entered forests too vast to be eliminated by a single generation of loggers. And so, there developed in the West settled towns of loggers and mill workers whose fathers and grandfathers had worked "in the woods" or "down at the mill." Some of these settlements, like Pacific Lumber's Scotia near U.S. Route 101 in the redwoods, began as company towns in which a paternalistic capitalist founder owned not only the mill and forest but even the stores and the very homes of the workers. Most remaining company towns were sold off in the 1980s and early 1990s, victims of a U.S. government financial policy that undervalued their assets. Those "undervalued assets" were old-growth trees growing in forests that were ancient when Columbus landed in the West Indies. These are the last remnants in private hands of forests that the early loggers thought would last forever. These remnant ancient forests are being clearcut in order to pay off corporate takeovers and finance new raids on other productive, but "undervalued" companies.

The old timber towns of the Northwest and British Columbia produced a particular society and, like all societies, a mythology to support it. *Sometimes a Great Notion*, the Ken Kesey novel later made into a Hollywood film, expresses in moving prose both the reality and the mythology of this society. The mythology stresses rugged individualism, tough-as-nails manhood, and male-dominated family values. In timber town mythology the danger and difficulty of work in the mill or in the woods was transformed into challenge, excitement, and nobility. Young men eagerly followed their fathers into this work and the women stood by their men through good times and bad.

Next to mining, work in the timber industry is the most hazardous occupation in the United States; injuries in the woods and in the mills often result in loss of limb, lifetime disabilities, or death. Hazardous work and low concern for worker safety are usually fertile ground for labor organizers. In the rural Northwest, however, timber town mythology made labor organizing difficult. The Wobblies (International Workers of the World) organized the transient workers of the timber camps with some success, but failed to organize successfully in the towns. Even the mainstream Industrial Wood Workers never achieved in the Pacific Northwest what groups like the United Auto Workers, United Mine Workers, and other unions achieved for workers in other industries and regions.

Industrial consolidation, which industry trade groups and resource economists began noting in the 1960s, accelerated during the 1970s and 1980s. This completed the transformation of the timber industry from paternalistic to modern industrial capitalism. The industry emerged well prepared to take advantage of the weakness of organized labor. The recession of the early 1980s provided the opportunity for management either to win major concessions from the workers or to eliminate the union entirely.

The maintenance of timber country social mythology required denial of the changes taking place in the woods and in the workplace as well as the causes. Loggers and mill workers through the 1980s continued to ignore the mounting evidence pointing to overcutting, automation, and unmitigated corporate greed as the predominant causes of chronically high unemployment in timber communities. They also denied the decline of native species of plants and animals associated with pristine forests. The cultural imperative called for scapegoats, and corporate propaganda astutely provided them. Workers were encouraged to blame their problems, and the problems of their communities, on government overregulation and environmental preservation. The most virulent anger of timber workers, however, is reserved for the minority who live in timber communities and question the dominant myths and the practices of the timber industry. Anger and resentment is likewise directed toward the very creatures of the forests that have come to symbolize and focus what timber and mill workers most fear and least want to admit—their powerlessness and vulnerability. The timber industry promotes the image of the noble logger put out of work by a useless owl. In this way, the industry masks its leading role in wreaking widespread ecological damage and fostering unsustainable communities that are overdependent on timber extraction.

Threatened forest creatures like the Northern spotted owl, and rural forest activists, have become the "enemies" of timber-industry-dependent families and businesses, while anti-environmental politicians and timber industry executives are their "heroes."

To understand timber communities we must understand not only the timber workers, but also the local business owners and mid-level managers of timber corporations. Local mill owners and the mid-level executives who manage the holdings of transnational corporations constitute the power elite of the so-called timber-dependent communities of the rural West. These men and their wives sit on the boards of all significant social institutions—schools, banks, hospitals, service clubs. They supply the largest contributions to local political campaigns and they sometimes boast how they have ordered or engineered the removal of politicians who have strayed from wholehearted support for timber interests. One must be liked by the power elite in order to advance socially, economically, and politically in these communities. It is no surprise that small business people overwhelmingly support the interests of big timber.

Big timber generally has local political support as well as the support of educational institutions and boards of education. Support is virtually guaranteed by the system that provides funding to schools and local governments from timber harvest revenues that are generated by logging on federal lands within their boundaries.

Public lands are not subject to property taxes. To compensate for the loss of prop-

erty tax revenue, counties receive $0.75 per acre of federal land—or $0.10 per acre plus 25 percent of the gross revenues generated by logging, grazing, and other revenue-generating activities on these lands. Receipts from the sale of timber constitute the bulk of federal revenues generated on Pacific Northwest national forests. Because per-acre payments are low, timber receipts typically far exceed per-acre payments. Consequently these federal receipts are an important revenue source for timber-dependent counties, tied directly to the amount of federal timber sold and cut. Laws reserving these funds for local schools and roads guarantee that most school and county government officials in tax-poor rural communities will lobby long and hard to maintain unsustainable cutting rates on public forests.

The economic, social, and political dominance of the timber industry in western forest communities went unchallenged for many years. The major environmental groups, content with the growth of urban support for their agenda, ignored rural opposition. Government forest managers either met their assigned "timber targets" or were quickly transferred to boring desk jobs in Washington, D.C. Contract loggers—those proprietors of small companies that actually do most of the logging—and a few forward-looking foresters began to recognize that cutting levels were far exceeding regrowth and that many clearcuts were not properly regenerating. Those who spoke out, however, were promptly blacklisted. Some of the foresters went to work for environmental groups, but the contract loggers had no avenue of escape. Recognizing their vulnerability, most concerned foresters and contract loggers will not speak publicly against cutting rates that they know cannot be sustained.

In the 1960s, increasing numbers of urban dwellers began visiting public forests. The visitors came to escape the pressures of urban life, to enjoy the forested mountains and rivers, and to seek renewal. Assaulted by the ugliness of clearcuts, forest visitors began to pressure major environmental groups for action. The resulting reform movement culminated in the *Monongahela* decision, a federal court order that temporarily blocked clearcutting on national forests. The court ban provided the context for congressional debate on federal forest management culminating in 1976 with passage of the National Forest Management Act (NFMA). The act stated that clearcutting could be used on national forests only when it is the "optimum method" to achieve "multiple-use goals established for a given area"—and only after assessment of environmental impacts (The Wilderness Society et al. 1983). The major environmental groups heralded the NFMA as holding "great potential for better and more balanced management of public forests." Many environmentalists who had worked on the act, however, express deep disappointment in its contents. The NFMA gives the Forest Service broad discretion in managing public forests. Environmentalists had hoped for a congressional ban on clearcutting and other similar methods (e.g., seed tree removal, shelterwood removal). Instead, Congress issued broad guidelines. As a result, clearcutting became even more dominant on the nation's public forests after 1976 than it had been before the *Monongahela* decision.

The 1970s heralded the beginning of another trend, however, that was to prove the greatest challenge yet to big timber's dominance of public forests and western timber communities. Early in the 1970s retirees, back-to-the-landers, and other "urban refugees" began moving to rural communities. Many "landed" in timber country. They built homes, settled in, and began looking around. They did not like what they saw—forests mowed down, burned, sprayed with herbicides, and replanted with alien species of "super trees." These realities conflicted with the image of pristine forests that had drawn them to the country. The newcomers found support from a number of "old-timers," often including tradition-minded Native Americans. The outrage led them first to question and later to challenge forest management practices and the assumptions on which these practices are based. Those who valued the forests for their noncommodity values—clean water, native vegetation, wildlife, and spiritual inspiration—banded together and began working for forest management reform.

The reformers' (newcomers, old-timers, and traditional Native Americans) first major battle in rural western forests concerned aerial spraying of herbicides. Clearcuts were sprayed by the industry to clear the ground for planting conifer seedlings, and then again to "release" the young conifer trees from the "competition" of hardwoods, grasses, and other unwanted "weeds." These "weeds" included native plants traditionally used by Native Americans for food, medicine, basketry, and spiritual purposes. Moreover, the sprays in use were toxic agents, including components of the infamous Agent Orange, a defoliant that was used during the Vietnam War to destroy crops and forests and that had poisoned Vietnamese peasants and soldiers, including some U.S. soldiers. Sprayed in steep mountain country by helicopters, the herbicides routinely drifted into the mountain streams that supplied water for local residents who soon began observing increased rates of sickness, miscarriage, and birth defects.

The "Herbicide Wars" of the 1970s taught the reformers how to effectively utilize administrative appeals, lawsuits, and direct action to challenge public land management decisions. They also motivated activists to ask broader questions about why government land managers were so intent on maintaining what were obviously dangerous and ineffective practices. What activists learned was that spraying was used as one of a constellation of practices to justify increased timber cutting on national forests. Government foresters, with support from professors at industry-supported forestry schools, argued that herbicide and other "treatments" would increase growth rates for conifers in replanted clearcuts. These "tree plantations" would consequently be ready for harvest more quickly—meaning that native forests could be liquidated now at accelerated rates.

Armed with a new understanding of legal requirements and administrative procedures, the reformers began to challenge a broad range of forest management practices. As more and more timber sales were challenged, the timber industry reacted. The industry attempted to use its political influence to exempt clearcutting and other destructive logging practices from administrative appeals and court challenges. In Canada the industry was successful in insulating itself from administrative and judicial review—once a timber concession is awarded there is no mechanism for appeal and no access to court review. In the United States, Congress has, for the most part, reaffirmed the right of citizens to challenge federal land management decisions. In specific instances, however, federal timber sales or classes of sales have been exempted from administrative and judicial challenge. Access for U.S. citizens to review logging plans for private lands varies from state to state. Generally there are no mechanisms for administrative appeals but court challenges are possible under state and federal environmental laws.

At the local level the timber industry relies on its political and social dominance to promote clearcutting and oppose forest protection. At the behest of the power elites, local politicians and business people have organized timber industry support groups with titles that mimic those of grassroots environmental groups. Industry support groups like KARE (Klamath Alliance for Resources and the Environment) and SHARE (Shasta Alliance for Resources and the Environment) follow the lead of timber industry lobbying associations.

Despite local industry opposition, however, the rural, grassroots forest reform movement continued to gain strength. During the 1980s major environmental groups like the Sierra Club and The Wilderness Society recognized that a new force for public land management reform was in motion and they moved to ally with it. Functional coalitions of grassroots and national environmental groups fueled challenges to a new generation of federal land management planning documents. Appeals and lawsuits were pursued jointly by these groups. Local knowledge of forest conditions combined synergistically with national legal and political resources to constitute an unprecedented challenge to the timber industry's dominance of federal forest management practices. These activities culminated in the late 1980s with formation of the Ancient Forest Alliance in an effort to end, once and for all, the liquidation of the remaining native forests on public lands in California, Oregon, and Washington.

Thus the future of our public forests, and especially the fate of the 5 to 15 percent of Northwest ancient forests that have not yet been logged, came to issue between two powerful political coalitions, both of which have critical constituencies in rural timber communities. At the local, rural level not only the fate of the remaining uncut forests is at issue but also the balance of social and political power. In these forest communities the power elites, firmly allied to the giant timber corporations, stand for maintenance of the status quo, while the reformers stand for change. Each group marshals its forces, uses its symbols, and manipulates the statistics in hopes of influencing public opinion and gaining local support from many rural folk who, until recently, have been uninvolved in these decisions that will have a profound influence on the future of their communities.

On the timber side, the power elites and their supporters emphasize "owls vs. jobs." Timber industry supporters point out that the economies of these rural communities are dominated by the timber industry and that government had "promised" that all the ancient forests would be made available to keep the loggers and the lumber mills well supplied with cheap logs. Industry supporters claim that "putting owls ahead of families" is antisocial and inhumane.

Grassroots reformers counter that it is massive overcutting, automation of the mills, export of unprocessed logs, and the failure of clearcutting and other "intensive" forest management techniques that threaten both the logger and the forest ecosystem. They emphasize that overdependence on timber, while it has created huge profits for the timber corporations, has never fueled prosperity in timber country. They point to unemployment rates that exceed 10 percent in some timber communities even during housing (lumber) booms and that rise to over 20 percent during recessions, when the demand for lumber plummets and federal timber sales fail to garner bids.

Reformers point out the need to diversify local economies, and they emphasize the importance of forest and watershed protection for communities to sustain jobs. In recent years the cumulative impacts of clearcutting on native Pacific salmon became apparent. Unemployed commercial fishermen joined the reformers in pointing out that liquidation of the ancient forests has imperiled salmon and the communities that depend on salmon (California Advisory Committee 1988; and, Oregon Rivers Council 1992).

Reformers further point out that the dominant transnational corporations have removed the capital of these communities—their old-growth logs—and have returned little in new investment, preferring instead to locate modern new mills out of the region or out of the country. They emphasize that these corporations continue to export logs from extensive corporate holdings that are the most productive of all Northwest timberlands. By processing at home the one-in-four logs that are being exported, timber industry employment could be maintained at current levels while simultaneously preserving all remaining native ancient forests (Anderson and Olson 1991, pp. 55–62).

The struggle for political and social power in West Coast forest communities in the late 1980s and early 1990s parallels and is part of a larger struggle concerning management of all public lands in western North America. There are signs that the struggle is coming to a head not only in forest communities but elsewhere as well. The rural power elites call into the fray their longtime allies in agriculture and mining. For generations they have cultivated the belief that current practices, however destructive, are environmentally sound. They accuse environmental groups of hiding their true agenda—the "lock-up" of public lands throughout the West for the exclusive use of an elite group of backpackers. "You are the true environmentalists," they tell the loggers, the ranchers, and miners. They play on the image of the hard-working western family man at the mercy of socialist government regulators and antisocial preservationists. This attitude has ignited support across the rural West for the so-called Wise Use Movement.

By manipulating the powerful ideology of private property rights, by invoking the constitution, projecting current unsustainable and environmentally damaging practices as sacred "custom and culture," and by utilizing grassroots organizing techniques borrowed from the toolbox of environmental organizations, a host of Wise Use organizations have been taking aim at the environmental victories of the 1970s and 1980s. Among their goals are dismantling the federal Endangered Species Act, repeal of regulations protecting wetlands, curtailment of grazing management reform, and maintenance of unrestricted corporate access to public timber, energy, and minerals. Wise Use groups are funded by big timber, mining, and oil interests. They draw on rural political and community support and intimidate public land managers into backing off from reform and stewardship responsibilities and relaxing in the cozy relationships of the past.

Major environmental groups are organizing to respond to the Wise Use challenge. Their efforts at public education are making available to the general public the true agendas and financing of the movement. It is rural grassroots environmental organizations, however, who are challenging the assumptions of the Wise Use groups on their home turf—the rural West. By relentlessly pointing out who funds these groups and who determines their agenda, grassroots rural activists utilize Wise Use extremism to mobilize those rural families who have remained uninvolved and uncommitted. The excesses of Wise Use organizations and the lack of support in reality for their assertions provide the environmental movement with an opportunity to reclaim the concept of balance that has been owned by the despoilers of western lands, including forests, rivers, wetlands, deserts, and the coast. Thus the Wise Use Movement could unwittingly serve as the straw that breaks the political and social dominance of rural western power elites who serve the interests of the giant transnational extractive corporations.

The war of words, statistics, and symbols rages on. Forest management, private and public, has become one of the top environmental issues of our times—with clear-cutting the symbol of the struggle. The fallout from this political power struggle over reforms that are long overdue lands squarely on the timber-dependent communities. The timber wars have polarized these communities, whose timber workers are being cut out of work and are falling on hard times.

Timber workers, who are totally dependent on the industry, rank among the most oppressed workers in the U.S. today. Like many of the most oppressed, they identify with the oppressors and look to them for answers. Most have adopted the view that they must oppose any change, lest "the preservationists" succeed in destroying the timber economy. These workers are afraid, as well they should be, that their jobs will disappear. They desperately hope to hold on until the house is paid off and they can retire. Most timber industry workers no longer assume that their children will

be able to follow them into the woods or the mill. They are afraid their children will be forced to move away to find work or else face life on the welfare rolls.

Rural reformers in timber country are also subject to oppression. The wife of a grassroots reform leader is denied a teaching job because the wife of the local lumber mill owner sits on the school board. Late at night loggers appear in front of the home of a leader after a timber boss tells them they won't work that winter because the grassroots organization won a lawsuit blocking several timber sales. A car bomb cripples an activist; another's tires are slashed. Letters to the editor keep the social pressure on, identifying grassroots environmental leaders as unpatriotic and uncaring, and inviting social ostracism. The children of a reform leader are taunted at school by the children of loggers who have been told that the reformer is trying to destroy their family's livelihood.

Vindictive social behavior is not unexpected or uncommon in small communities. The reformers are challenging an established order, a power elite that has had its way in these communities, and in the forests which surround them, for three generations. Change is in the air now in timber country, but the needed changes will not come easy. As in all times and places, those who hold power will not easily relinquish that power. So the struggle that has begun will continue, probably for some time to come. The people of rural timber communities are being pressured to take sides, to declare their allegiance to the status quo, or to stand up for change—for the timber industry and its unsustainable practices, or for what little remains of the once vast ancient forests. On that future day when the conflict is resolved, there will be many wounds to heal. As in the forests, healing in the communities will take time, perhaps generations.

Author and longtime western resident Wallace Stegner suggested that Euro-Americans in the rural West have failed to develop a stable culture. The shallow social attitudes that substitute for culture have served the purpose of those who would continue to despoil the West in the name of narrow greed and unrestrained self-interest. Still, Stegner saw signs that an "indigenous, recognizable culture" was emerging in the West and, at eighty-seven years of age, he cherished hope for the future.

Stegner believed that "within a generation or two" westerners would "work out some sort of compromise between what must be done to earn a living and what must be done to restore health to the earth, air, and water." (Stegner, 1992.) His hope is shared by a growing number of those who have lived through the forest conflicts of the 1960s, 1970s, 1980s, and now into the 1990s. Stegner recognized that the required synthesis must be cultural at heart; that people, their institutions, and communities are integral to a solution. He asserted that the synthesis would be evident on the physical, as well as on the cultural landscape.

The stark contrast between integral, ancient forest and the fragmented landscape of clearcut areas is painfully evident whenever one flies over, drives through, or walks about the forested lands of western North America. Physical polarization in the forest and cultural polarization in our forest communities are two faces of the same social disease. Natural diversity within *forest* communities is compatible with economic diversity within *human* communities. Both are essential aspects of a healthy western landscape.

The clearcut stands as a dominant symbol of the anti-culture of the Euro-American West. The move to end clearcutting, and with that to truly reform management of our forests, stands as a light at a crossroads on the road to true culture. Let it shine.

REFERENCES

Anderson, H. Michael, and Jeffrey T. Olson. 1991. *Federal forests and the economic base of the Pacific Northwest.* Washington, D.C.: The Wilderness Society.

California Advisory Committee on Salmon and Steelhead Trout. 1988. Restoring the balance. *Annual Report.* Sacramento, California.

Oregon Rivers Council, Inc. 1992. The economic imperative of protecting riverine habitat of the Pacific Northwest. *Research Report no. 5.* Eugene, Oregon.

Siskiyou County Assessors Office, 1991, unpublished data.

Stegner, Wallace. 1992. *Where the bluebird sings to the lemonade springs.* New York: Random House.

The Wilderness Society et al. 1983. *National Forest planning: A conservationist's guide.* 2d ed. 60–67. Washington, D.C.: The Wilderness Society.

Terry Livingstone

Stepping beyond the beauty strip of an illusory forest reveals a stark reality shielded by industrial myths. What we see is the result of inverted priorities. The forest is expected to adjust to the demands of an ever-growing economy rather than the economy to adjust to the constraints of a sustainable forest ecosystem. The damage inflicted is not just to the forest; it is also to the communities of people who rely on the forest. What you see is actually worse than it looks.

MYTHS OF THE BENIGN INDUSTRIAL CLEARCUT

MITCH LANSKY

To those who canoe on Maine's northern rivers or lakes, the surrounding trees appear to be part of the "immeasurable forest" that Henry David Thoreau observed from the heights of Mount Katahdin over a century ago. Today, one can paddle down the same stretches of the Allagash that Thoreau explored and still see no roads, powerlines, or other signs of development. One can still watch a majestic moose dipping its head underwater to pull up succulent water weeds or hear the haunting cry of a loon echoing across a still pond at sunset.

An observer in an airplane, however, would see that the forests around the Allagash and many other lakes and rivers in northern Maine are mere strips of trees only a few hundred feet wide. Surrounding these buffer zones are clearcuts that stretch on to the horizon. The forest in Maine is not a wilderness—it is what the forest products industry calls a "working forest."

Through the 1980s, nearly half of the cuts reported to the state were clearcuts. In 1989 alone, clearcutting in Maine reportedly reached an all-time high of about 145,000 acres (and these reports are conservative estimates). In contrast to the western United States, very little of the forestland in Maine is owned by the federal government (less than 1 percent). We therefore cannot blame corrupt federal bureaucracies with below-cost sales for the massive clearcuts that have left some townships nearly devoid of mature forest. Most of the clearcuts reported in the state have been done on private land in response to incentives from the "free market."

The largest market for trees in northern Maine is the pulp mills. The trees most favored by these mills are red spruce and balsam fir, species that have long fibers ideal for making strong paper. Absentee-based, transnational paper companies own most of the region where spruce and fir is abundant. They also do most of the clearcutting.

Although Maine is a relatively small state, its eight million acres of industry-owned forestland is the largest concentration of industrial forest acreage in the U.S.—far more than the five million acres of industrial forestland found in second-place Oregon.

These companies call their domain the "industrial forest." Names have power. They influence how we perceive and relate to that which is named. An industrial forest is perceived as a resource that can and should be efficiently exploited. Other values, such as hiking, canoeing, hunting, or fishing, exist by the good graces of the landowners who inform us they are managing their working forests for "multiple uses." In an industrial forest we should be grateful that any wildlife survives, that any forest is worth looking at, or that any river is unpolluted and free flowing, since these are not primary considerations.

In Maine's industrial forest, most of the roads are private. The region has such a low population that there are almost no local governments—the state regulates the affairs of the townships.

Minimal state forest regulations have helped to shape the forest into the image that one can view from above. When regulations were first imposed in the 1970s, the major restriction to clearcutting was a requirement to buffer water bodies. Loggers called these mandatory buffers around water bodies, and the voluntary ones along roads, "beauty strips." While these buffer strips may help protect water quality and scenic views, they do not help protect the forest—they preserve only the illusion of a forest.

To step beyond the beauty strip is to step into a world of distorted metaphors, and distorted logic. If what you see looks degraded and ugly, the fault (according to corporate spokespersons) lies with your vision rather than their companies' management. Once you learn the proper attitude, it should all look acceptable, if not admirable.

Industrial foresters maintain that, by some happy coincidence, whatever they do to the forest to benefit their company just happens to also benefit the forest, wildlife, local communities, and society in general. Industrial foresters invoke an elaborate array of myths to justify their management actions as both beneficial and necessary.

These myths are less the propaganda of a formal conspiracy than the tenets of a shared belief system. Many of those who state the industrial arguments sincerely believe them to be true. The appearance of verity of these forestry myths is reinforced by their harmony with the dominant beliefs of our economic/political system.

The myths employed by industrial foresters in Maine to excuse their clearcuts are similar to those used in other forested regions of the country, or even the world, regardless of forest types (see Herb Hammond's essay in this volume, "Clearcutting: Ecological and Economic Flaws"). The results of massive clearcutting—bare, rutted soil and acres of stumps—are also similar.

Industrial myths dominate forestry discussions in academia, the media, and the legislature. Indeed, these myths are often codified into law. Because the myths of industrial forestry tend to be so widely accepted as reality, they are one of the most serious barriers to forestry reform. The first step in forestry reform, therefore, is to identify and refute myths of industrial forestry that support forest destruction.

The second step in forestry reform is acceptance of the fact that sustainable forestry depends on sustainable natural forests. Because the concept of sustainability of natural forest ecosystems is a relatively new idea, ecologists do not know how much biomass humans can remove from any specific forest without harming important ecosystem processes. Ecologists do know that sustainability is not the same as *productivity* or *sustained yield* as these concepts are used by industrial foresters.

The time horizon for the owner of an industrial forestry mill, which lasts for a few decades, is not the same as for forests, which last for centuries.

When challenged as to the sustainability of cutting on their ownership, industrial foresters proudly point out the ample regeneration. Indeed, they often do not use the word *clearcutting*, but rather refer to their activities as *regenerating* a forest. It is easy to get the impression from talking to enthusiastic foresters that their management goal is to produce seedlings rather than mature trees.

Replacing a mature forest over a wide area with seedlings, however, does not sustain wildlife, timber quality, or recreation. It also does not sustain local mills. Industrial foresters respond that although they are cutting a certain volume every year, they are also growing a certain volume every year, and the cut is balanced by growth.

With clearcutting, the growth that balances the cut is somewhere else. The cut-equals-growth formula can excuse the cutting of an entire township as long as an equal volume is growing in other townships. But such heavy cutting in one area could be devastating to both the forest and local communities.

Unless it specifies species and quality, the formula can also excuse balancing a cut of high-value timber with the growth of low-value biomass. And the formula does not account for what grows back after the cut. The new growth may be quite different in productivity, quality, species ratios, and wildlife from the previous forest.

Unlike public foresters, industrial foresters in Maine are under no obligation to prove that they are cutting their lands in a sustainable manner, but they all claim to do so anyway. That leads the shocked observer of a massive clearcut to ask how it is possible to sustain a forest by removing it?

What paper companies most want to sustain is their mills. Though the companies in Maine have hundreds of thousands or even millions of acres, they generally purchase half or more of their wood supply from other landowners, and even from other countries. The flattening of a township or two, therefore, has little effect on a sustainable supply to the mill—especially when one considers that the supply need only be "sustainable" as long as the mill is operating.

When industrial foresters talk about "productivity," they are usually referring to productivity of timber extraction rather than productivity of soil, wildlife, stream quality, or beauty. Because of concerns that the cut already exceeds growth for many species and timber grades, industrial foresters have argued that by clearcutting they are doing the future a favor—the best way to increase stand productivity for the future is to cut all the trees down now.

Unfortunately, a simple clearcut-and-run operation is not very productive for even marketable fiber. Clearcuts, which are severe disturbances, tend to be followed by growth adapted to catastrophe (e.g., brush, pioneer hardwoods, and stump sprouts). Often stands have areas that are deficient of commercially valuable trees or so crowded that it may take seventy-five or more years before the trees reach a merchantable size. Waiting long enough for the trees to get big enough to cut means losing a sizable volume of shorter-lived and suppressed trees to mortality.

Through the use of herbicides, and through planting and thinning, industrial foresters can weed out undesirable species, concentrate growth on desirable species, and space the trees so that they reach marketable diameters much sooner. When foresters claim to be increasing productivity through this *intensive management*, they are comparing their softwood fiber yields to that obtainable over the same time period with clearcuts followed by no management. They are not comparing yields to the site's potential, or to yields that might be obtainable with other management systems, such as selection. And they ignore the yield of hardwoods.

Because timberland investments are subject to a compound interest rate that increases faster than the trees grow, companies have an incentive to cut timber stands on as short a rotation as possible. Industrial foresters sometimes boast that they will be able, with intensive management techniques, to have rotations as short as thirty-five or forty years—as if the shorter the rotation, the more productive the "forest."

Short rotations, however, do not increase productivity—even of fiber. At a given site, the peak of average growth per acre per year of an even-aged stand will be the same regardless of the spacing of trees. This peak is reached sooner, however, at denser spacing. While wider spacing, from either planting or thinning, means wider-diameter trees sooner, it also means the peak of productivity is reached *later*. Cutting widely spaced trees on short rotations, therefore, means *lowering* potential productivity.

Productivity is also lowered when trees die prematurely from insects or disease. As foresters simplify stand structure to favor only desired species, they also simplify the checks and balances of predators and parasites. With a higher concentration of food, but less controls, outbreaks can be more devastating.

Clearcutting on short rotation can lower site productivity by compacting the soil, blasting soil microlife with heat and dryness, and leaching nutrients with rain. Large volumes of nutrients and organic matter are removed with the trees, but not enough time is allowed for the soil to recover to preharvest conditions. Future rotations will have diminishing yields.

The major purpose of intensive management (which in Maine is only done on a fraction of sites that are clearcut), is not so much to increase yields later as to justify overcutting now.

The public is led to assume that trees grown in assembly line rows have higher quality than wild trees growing in unmanaged disorder. While companies may boast that their forests are "tree farms" and their trees are "crops" that they periodically "harvest," the reality in Maine is that very little wood volume that is "harvested" comes from stands which were cultivated in any way. Companies are reaping what they did not sow.

If they did intensive management on a wide scale, however, it would not lead to higher-quality trees. Spacing trees for cutting on short rotations often results in highly tapered trees with a high proportion of crown to height. Lumber from such trees has low density and low strength, is knotty, and tends to warp. The wood is also inferior for paper because it has a high content of extractives (which must be removed at a cost of energy and pollution), and it has shorter fibers (which means lower strength).

If you manage the regeneration intensively for pulpwood in Maine, it leads to losses, not gains, at current wood values and discount rates. Perhaps this is why planting and precommercial thinning were done in Maine on only a small fraction of clearcuts during the 1980s.

Indeed the early stand investments for planting, spraying, and thinning become profitable only with subsidies. In regions where such management is more common, the subsidies come from government. In Maine, to some extent, the subsidies come from the mills. Most such management is done on industrial, rather than nonindustrial landholdings. Nonindustrial landowners have realized that it is cheaper to avoid such costs by doing partial cuts and relying on natural regeneration. The most economical way to grow fiber is on existing trees.

The paper companies, however, are vertically integrated—most of their profit comes from making paper, not from growing trees. Only the company accountants know what the pulpwood is really worth to the mills.

Paper companies can keep the price for wood they purchase from nonindustrial landowners artificially low. They can, for example, flood the market with wood from their own lands. They can also avoid price competition with other mills in the state for purchased pulpwood. Though this is in the best interest of the mills, it is not in the best interest of woodlot owners—it is also illegal, so it must be done informally. Because the companies are reducing costs for purchased pulpwood, they can therefore afford to spend some money on a few thousand acres a year of their own land to create the appearance of management.

In the last few years, even some of the paper companies in Maine have scaled back on their clearcutting. A prime reason is economic—they do not want to unnecessarily hold early-stand management costs over decades. They usually have much better places to put their investment dollars.

Why do they clearcut?

If it is not highly profitable to manage the result of clearcuts, then why would a corporation that is in business to be profitable bother to clearcut? There are in fact many reasons why corporations might clearcut, but most of them have little to do with silviculture.

In Maine, much of the heaviest clearcutting coincided with a spruce budworm outbreak. The companies claimed to be salvaging or pre-salvaging trees. Apparently, after they mastered the technique it turned into a bad habit. They started salvaging stands that were neither dead nor threatened. Indeed, some of the heaviest cutting occurred after the outbreak had ended.

There are other reasons, therefore, besides salvage. The companies may, for example, be able to take the funds from forest liquidation and place them in investments that get higher returns than growing trees. Or the companies may have timberland that is undervalued, making them ripe for a leveraged buyout. Cutting the timber not only raises revenue, but lowers the value of the forest. To the extent that the companies do get subsidies or tax breaks for early-stand management, they get all the revenues from the clearcut, and the public pays for part of the management costs—a very good deal.

One of the more compelling reasons for clearcutting in Maine is to eliminate jobs. This reason may seem shocking to those who are used to the idea of loggers set against environmentalists. Certainly the corporate landowners encourage such an opposition, because it takes attention away from themselves.

In the last half of the 1980s, there was a 30 percent loss in logging jobs in Maine. This was not due to land removed for wilderness or habitat for spotted owls. Maine has no spotted owls, and designated wilderness takes up only 1.5 percent of the forestland. Job loss was also not due to a slump in logging or even a decline in clearcutting due to environmental interference. Indeed, logging and clearcutting reached a peak in 1989. And there was no spruce budworm outbreak to use as an excuse for this clearcutting. These job losses were primarily a result of mechanization.

Logging is one of the highest-risk occupations in the nation. The hazards of logging have been made even worse by paying loggers by piece rate to remove trees as fast as possible—rather than by wage to manage a forest as well as possible. The companies, who want production more than they want healthy forests, have kept wood prices low enough so that loggers on a piece rate cannot afford the time to take care.

During the 1980s, even with better-designed chainsaws and safety equipment, an average of five loggers per year were killed in the Maine woods. Loggers don't retire; they get permanently disabled. Workers' compensation costs for employers can be more than 50 percent of the logger's wage. Almost all of the big corporate landowners have washed their hands of responsibility for worker safety by claiming that the loggers who cut on their lands are "independent" contractors who must handle their own insurance.

Large contractors, to avoid insurance costs, have purchased machines that can cut in an hour what it would take a worker with a chainsaw to cut in a day. The machines have to be run full time to keep up payments. Forest management tends to be designed around the needs of the machines, rather than the needs of the forest. And the needs of the machines tend to be clear-cut.

CONCLUSION

The industrial landowners in Maine are not clearcutting their forests to improve productivity, benefit wildlife, or create jobs. They are not in business to be social or environmental reformers; they are in business for profit and growth. Social and ecological considerations are only pursued to the extent that they do not interfere with these primary economic goals.

Unfortunately, these corporate priorities have become state, national, and even global priorities. "To regulate a general system," wrote anthropologist Roy Rappoport, "such as society or a forest in accordance with the narrow purposes of one of its sub-systems, such as a business firm or an industry, or even industry as a whole, is to narrow the range of conditions under which the general system can survive."

Stepping beyond the beauty strip of an illusory forest reveals a stark reality shielded by industrial myths. What we see is the result of inverted priorities. The forest is expected to adjust to the demands of an ever-growing economy rather than the economy adjust to the constraints of a sustainable forest ecosystem. The damage inflicted is not just to the forest; it is also to the communities of people who rely on the forest. What you see is actually worse than it looks.

For full documentation of the statements in this chapter, see *Beyond the Beauty Strip: Penetrating the Myths of the Industrial Forest*, 1993, published by Tilbury House, Publishers, 132 Water Street, Gardiner, Maine 04345.

TREE FARMS ARE NOT *FORESTS*

Trees planted in rows by industrial foresters do not make a forest. They make "tree farms" or "tree plantations." Industrial foresters took literally their own rhetoric that "growing trees is just like growing corn." Indeed, driven by their rule of discounting the future and maximizing yield, and profit, in the present, industrial foresters would prefer that trees were an annual crop.

On a "tree farm" or "tree plantation" industrial foresters replace complex forests composed of many species interacting with each other directly and indirectly over time with one or a few species of trees.

Industrial foresters frequently plant "exotic" species of trees—species not native to the region. These species are selected for their "rapid growth potential."

Sometimes industrial foresters make mistakes. For example, redwood trees, native to the north coastal region of California, were introduced on some plantations in England fifty years ago. By the early 1990s, foresters were discovering that these redwoods produced poorer-quality wood than native oaks. Restoration ecologists advocated removal of the "exotic" redwoods and regeneration of native, slower-growing oaks.

When tree farms are introduced in small areas, such as a "Christmas tree farm," consisting of a few acres of trees selected for their appeal to the "Christmas market," it has little effect on the native species of the bioregion. When tens of thousands of acres of native forest are clearcut or deliberately burned, and replaced with single-species tree plantations of an exotic species, a whole watershed or habitat for native wildlife might be liquidated.

Some nations officially count tree plantations as part of their "forest cover."

Forest ecologists have criticized the widespread introduction of tree plantations for several reasons. Due to their lack of diversity, single-species plantations are much more susceptible to damage from natural forest processes, such as wind, fire, insects, and disease, than native forests are. They may also be more susceptible to global changes, such as climatic change and acid deposition. For example, an old-growth forest, with trees of varying heights and frequent canopy gaps and openings, does not provide the continuous, uniform fuels that facilitate rapid fire-spread or destructive crown fires. In contrast, an even-aged plantation of young trees offers many closely spaced branches and a relatively level, dense, single-canopy layer. A fire can easily climb to the top, find a continuous, uniform fuel source, and become an all-consuming crown fire.

Insect populations often increase dramatically in plantations simply because tree-eating insects are well-fed and safe there. In addition, numerous roads and vehicles facilitate access for insects and disease organisms to invade nearby plantation areas. In contrast, insects traveling through complex, old-growth forests must cope not only with unpredictable or widely spaced food supplies, but also with healthy populations of insect-eating predators. Replacing huge areas of native forests with a tree plantation consisting of a "genetically enhanced" species of exotic trees, managed by eliminating "competing species" by aerial spraying of herbicides and pesticides, and "harvesting" with labor-saving machinery, such as a feller-buncher, is the fullest expression of the industrial forestry mentality. The entire landscape of the forest is domesticated, managed for narrow goals of profit, efficiency, and production of fiber for the market.

As the president of one large industrial forestry corporation said, "the consumer won't know the difference if the product came from a natural forest or a fiber plantation."

We are not now headed toward sustainable forestry, because we are training plantation managers, not foresters. A forester manages a forest. We are liquidating our forests and replacing them with short-rotation plantations. Everything nature has done in designing forests adds to diversity, complexity, and stability through time. We decrease diversity, complexity, and stability by redesigning forests into plantations.

We must learn to reinvest part of nature's capital, such as large merchantable logs and large snags, in the maintenance of forest health, so that our mills will have, in perpetuity, a sustainable harvest of timber from fertile, healthy, stable soils, clean water, clean air, and clear sunlight. To *reinvest* means to give up some of the short-term profits to ensure the long-term sustainability of the forest for future generations. Fertilization and planting trees are not reinvestments. They are investments in the next commercial stand; they are investments in a product, not a reinvestment in maintaining the health of a process. We do not reinvest, because we do not see the forest—only the product, the tree. We do not reinvest, because we ignore the cornerstones of forestry—soil, water, air, sunlight, and biodiversity. If we continue to ignore the fact that the cornerstones of forestry are variables whose health must be accounted for in our economic endeavors, we will surely destroy the forests of the world for future generations.

—Excerpt from Chris Maser's "Sustainable Forestry"

Top, left to right: Trygve Steen, Barry Tessman. Middle, left to right: Alex MacLean, Judy Johnson. Bottom, left to right: David Hiser, Bill Ellzey.

THE TECHNOCRATIC SYSTEM IN INDUSTRIAL FORESTRY

Industrial foresters attempt to apply principles of industrial management developed for production of such products as automobiles to what they call the "working forest." These principles include ever-increasing efficiency, lower labor costs (frequently translated to mean replacing humans by machines), destroying craftsmanship and sense of community by hierarchical management, and attempts to constantly increase "worker productivity."

The widespread use of chainsaws in logging after World War II illustrates many of these principles. With a chainsaw, one man can cut down many more trees per day than a crew of men could cut down in a week with crosscut saws.

Current vanguard industrial forestry is replacing men with chainsaws with feller-bunchers. One of these machines, operated by one man, can snip off trees, pull the logs together and lift them onto trucks for transport to the mills.

After World War II, large bulldozers were introduced on a large-scale basis into forests of the Pacific Northwest. With these bulldozers, logging roads could more quickly be built on steep mountain terrain. Road building in previously roadless areas allowed more rapid exploitation of old-growth timber on fragile mountain slopes.

In the mills, worker productivity was increased by elimination of tasks such as sorting and stacking timber of different sizes. Operations of fully automated mills can be directed by a few employees in a "command station."

Time is considered a "cost" by industrial foresters. They want to plant "genetically superior" seedling trees that will grow faster than naturally reproducing forests. Foresters want to eliminate "competing species." For example, in some regions of California, when conifer trees are planted after clearcutting, the open areas are prime habitat for deciduous trees such as alders. Conifers will tend to grow through this canopy of trees and the deciduous trees will not live as long as the conifers. In order to give the commercially valuable conifers an earlier advantage over alders, industrial foresters like to aerially spray forests with herbicides that kill or defoliate the broadleaf trees. Aerial spraying of forests with herbicides was perfected during the 1960s in the war in Vietnam. The U.S. Air Force sprayed Agent Orange (a toxic concoction including 2-4-D) over an estimated one million acres of forest in Vietnam. After learning of this practice, critics invented the term *ecocide* to refer to the systematic destruction of a natural landscape for a limited or narrow goal—victory over the enemy.

Aerial spraying of forests in Vietnam with Agent Orange was justified as "denying cover to the enemy."

When defoliants are aerially sprayed on "industrial forests" the practice is justified as "enhancing forest productivity," which means allowing the industrial forester to "harvest" commercially valuable trees in less time (time is money).

In the minds of industrial foresters, it is logical to replace complex, natural forests with tree plantations, and to use cloning and genetic engineering to "design" trees to fit specifications of forest engineers.

The introduction of ever more "efficient" technologies to increase growth, harvest faster, or to inhibit competition from "tree crops" has been a natural consequence of the industrial and mechanistic world view. This thinking was a product and outgrowth of the Cartesian logic of the Enlightenment. Modern civilization continues to fall into the trap of reducing nature to a system resembling a machine rather than a flowing, interacting organic web so complex that it is incomprehensible and unpredictable. These technologies always tend toward one principal end—speed; speed in converting the world of Nature to the culture of human beings. The objective is to increase production, as well as the speed at which a corporation or forest harvester can process wood. This competition to deliver wood to market fails to recognize that natural systems operate with their own time frames and cycles. These natural cycles are totally independent from and oblivious to the abstractions of economics, time and motion studies, labor-saving devices and so forth. The ecological truths are lost and "economic truths" are substituted. In terms of the costs of restoration and social upheaval, the entire economic rationale becomes absurd. Often (in human time frames) the renewability of damaged ecosystems is impossible.

Unless human beings, endowed as they so arrogantly profess, begin using their powers of intelligence, and turn radically toward an organic model and away from the technological/mechanistic view, we will continue to blunder forward with more of the same destructive behavior that we see manifested in clearcutting and industrial forestry. The mentality that we see time and again throughout industrial forestry runs deep in our culture. Its failure is easily ascertained by looking at the photographs in this book.

Certainly we can see—just on an economic level—that the destruction of our forests by ever more efficient technologies is not in our best interest. We need *fewer* labor-saving devices and many more labor-intensive forestry practices. Just as in agriculture and its failed "green revolution," forestry's failed "industrial revolution" needs more "eyes to the acre," more astute, careful foresters in the woods, working gently with the forest, not against it.

Photos: Top row, left to right; Trygve Steen, Randy Stoltman. Middle row, left to right; Garth Lenz, Trygve Steen. Bottom row, left to right; Voscar, Gary Braasch.

Barbara Molin

As the seemingly never-ending spiral of human consumption increases, so does the impact on the remaining
natural forest ecosystems. Certainly a reduction in timber cutting to sustainable levels must parallel a global effort to reduce
consumption and make ecologically sane lifestyle changes in the developed countries.

CUTTING DOWN CANADA

JIM COOPERMAN

Canada is a forested nation encompassing nearly 10 percent of the world's forests. There are eight major forest regions within Canada that together provide a great diversity of trees, plants, and animals.

Nearly 50 percent of Canada's land mass is forestland, but a lush and wild image of this landscape would be a green illusion—the ancient forests are vanishing. In eastern Canada, most of the ancient pine forests were logged off in the 1800s and replaced with early successional forests. In central Canada, the boreal forests are suffering an onslaught to feed new pulp mills. In British Columbia (B.C.), which provides nearly half of Canada's timber output, clearcuts fragment nearly every commercially viable forested valley. Most of the remaining coastal old-growth in B.C. is slated to be logged in the next two to three decades.

Prior to 1960, before clearcutting became the dominant forestry practice, selection of the largest and best trees for logging—a practice known as *high-grading*—left a legacy of degraded forests. For the past thirty years the forests throughout Canada have been clearcut at an alarming rate. Despite this sad history, Canada still contains the largest concentration of intact temperate and boreal forests on the North American continent. Canada presents a challenge to conservationists who seek protection and wise management of these remaining natural ecosystems.

Eighty percent of Canada's forests are owned and managed by the provinces. In 1990, the federal government increased its role in forest management through the appointment of a minister of forests who is in charge of Forestry Canada. This federal agency is responsible for research, policy development, public relations, and promotion of international markets. Forestry Canada is a partner with provincial forest ministries through Forest Resource Development Agreements (FRDAs) that have been in place since 1983.

Nearly two billion dollars ($500 million in B.C. alone) have been channelled through FRDAs to "reforest" the *not satisfactorily restocked* (NSR) lands that have not recovered from past logging or wildfires. The most recent Forestry Canada statistics reveal that despite the expanded tree-planting program, the area of land "not growing commercial species 10 years after harvesting" has continued to increase. When this area is combined with the loss from fires and insects it totals over four million hectares of new NSR land in the last ten years.

Government inventories claim that nearly half of Canada's forest land base contains mature forests. But many of these mature and old-growth forests have been seriously fragmented by a multitude of clearcuts. The truth about Canada's growing timber shortage has become apparent with mills closing and logging trucks hauling smaller logs. When viewed from an airplane, the forest landscape resembles a patchwork quilt with numerous threadbare sections.

Paradoxically, as the cutting increased, the employment level decreased due to mech-

anization that benefits both Canada's "competitiveness in the world marketplace" and private corporate profits. Canada produces fewer jobs per volume of wood cut than any other industrialized country. Canada spends far less on research and development. There are only about one-fourth the number of foresters employed in Canada in comparison with the U.S. and Scandinavian countries.

Transnational corporations and governments have clearcut vast forested areas for short-term profit, leaving damaged and polluted water courses, loss of wildlife habitat, and eroded hillsides. Nearly 10 percent of Canada's once-productive forestland has been so devastated that it is unable to reproduce any sort of merchantable timber at all. Aboriginal people in Canada face disruptions to their lifestyle similar to those of the Amazon Indians. Canada's boreal forest is almost equal in size to the Amazon rainforest and nearly every tree is destined to become pulp. It is no wonder that Canada is called the "Brazil of the North."

The following tour of each province and territory provides a brief digest on the state of Canada's forests.

BRITISH COLUMBIA

British Columbia contains one-fifth of Canada's forested land base and nearly one-half of the country's timber volume. There is probably more temperate forest wilderness remaining in B.C. than anywhere else in North America. Within this mountainous province is a rich tapestry of diverse forest ecosystems that range from magnificent, ancient temperate rainforests to stunted high-elevation stands of spruce, to ponderosa pine growing within dry interior grasslands. Forest ecologists have identified fourteen major biogeoclimatic zones within B.C., each of which is further divided into many subzones according to variations in temperature, moisture, and geographical features.

Despite this recognized ecosystem diversity, the same logging system, clearcutting, is used (over 90 percent of the time) in every area except the drybelt country. Since 1987, logging companies and the forest service have been required to return each logged site to a free-growing state where the planted or naturally regenerated trees are taller than the competing vegetation. Up to 20 percent of each site, however, is allowed to be permanently scarred and compacted with landings and skid trails that may never grow a forest again. A 1988 government study of soil degradation concluded that the annual loss of forest productivity to the B.C. economy is approximately $80 million per year, a cost that is increasing $10 million further every year.

The vast majority of B.C.'s productive forests, including areas under First Nations' land claims, were long ago signed over in tenure agreements to private industry. In 1991, the major corporations controlled nearly 85 percent of B.C.'s "annual allowable cut" (AAC).

In the early 1950s, a forest minister (an elected official) landed in jail after a kickback scandal erupted over the awarding of a large tree farm license on Vancouver Island. But this scandal was minor when compared to how the government has allowed companies to devastate forested hillsides and watersheds, waste millions of cubic meters of wood, and cheat on their stumpage payments.

The cut in B.C. has been steadily climbing. Half of all the timber cut in the public forests since 1911 has been cut in the last 19 years. The annual cut increased to 78 million cubic meters in 1991, well above the estimated long-range sustained yield of 60 million cubic meters. In 1991, the Ministry of Forests released a report that revealed that the forest inventory was inaccurate and that the annual allowable cut was too high. Since the report was released, the AAC has been reduced in some areas and a major effort is underway to complete new analyses.

Nowhere in Canada is the battle to preserve ancient forests more intense and more crucial than on Vancouver Island, where the remaining ancient temperate rainforest is one of the natural wonders of the world. Majestic, moss-laden, thousand-year-old Sitka spruce, western red-cedar, and western hemlock provide cover for a myriad of plant and animal species. These forests have been the site of tense confrontations between forest advocates, loggers, government, and industry. If governmental reform initiatives fail, there is potential for more sit-ins, arrests, blockades, court cases, and rallies to protect valleys and watersheds like Clayoquot Sound, the Walbran, and the Tsitika. As of September, 1993, over 700 people had been arrested for blocking a logging road at the entrance to Clayoquot Sound.

After a major conservation campaign, the B.C. government divided the Carmanah Valley in half, making the lower section a park. A logging plan is being considered for the upper watershed, which could result in erosion, creek siltation, and damage to the lower valley's giant forests, including Canada's tallest tree (95 meters, 312 feet). The Western Canada Wilderness Committee has constructed a research station in the top of one giant Sitka spruce tree in the upper Carmanah, where studies are being conducted on the many species of plants, insects, and birds that live in these high canopies. Already, 50 new species have been discovered.

The Sierra Club of Western Canada and the Seattle-based Wilderness Society have completed the first stage of an ancient forest inventory of Vancouver Island using computerized geographic information systems and satellite imagery. The inventory found that less than half of the ancient forest that existed in 1954 is still standing today, and that only one-fourth remains in the southern half of the island. Of the ninety watersheds greater than 5,000 hectares, only five are unlogged, and only two are currently protected in a park. At the current rate of logging, all unprotected, old growth forests on southern Vancouver Island will be logged by the year 2003.

Watershed protection is a major concern of B.C. citizens. Vancouver residents occasionally must cope with dirty tap water during the frequent rainy spells, and Victoria water quality has been steadily deteriorating. Logging roads and clearcuts have compromised the once pristine Vancouver and Victoria watersheds. While hundreds of landslides have dumped tons of sedimentation into the reservoirs from clearcuts and roads, the "experts" continue to deny that logging has damaged the watersheds. Vancouver is now considering installation of a half-billion dollar filtration system—a system whose costs are not covered by the profits from logging. Under current B.C. laws, there is no legislated protection for drinking water and no one can be held responsible if water supplies are adversely impacted.

In B.C.'s interior, watershed logging has impacted not only water supply and water quality. A few years ago, after heavy spring rains, a mud slide buried three people and a house near Kelowna. An old clearcut and skid trails were identified by the forest service as "contributing factors." In the Kootenays a similar slide covered a highway a few hours before a school bus full of children was scheduled to pass the area. Eighty-three local residents were arrested after they blockaded the construction of a logging road in one of their watersheds. The road has since been completed, but the area is temporarily deferred from logging to allow for local, shared decision making facilitated by a new Land-Use Commission.

In 1991, a new provincial government was elected with promises to double the number of parks and legislate a stronger forest practices act. They established a new Commission on Resources and Environment (CORE) with a mandate to design a land-use strategy for B.C. and organize and facilitate negotiation processes in local and regional areas where there has been the greatest conflict. However, the government's decision to log most of Clayoquot Sound and its reluctance to reform the tenure system have now jeopardized the legitimacy of CORE. Despite a flurry of government processes that seem designed to keep groups talking while the logging proceeds, land-use decisions are still based on short-term economics and will continue to be made by Cabinet behind closed doors. If Clayoquot Sound can't be protected with all the public support then there isn't much hope for other forested areas.

The largest intact temperate rainforest in the world, the 400,000 hectare Kitlope Valley on the west coast of B.C., remains unlogged. Preservation of this valley is possible—it is currently deferred under the old-growth strategy and is being studied by the Ministries of Parks and Forests. The Kitlope is also claimed as traditional territory by the Haisla people and may thus one day be a combined native heritage and greater ecosystem reserve that will protect forever this prime habitat for grizzly bear, the endangered marbled murrelet, the native salmon, and hundreds of other species of plants and animals. In 1992, the 40,000-hectare Kutzeymateen Valley northeast of Prince Rupert, home to the largest known concentration of grizzly bears on the B.C. coast, was declared to be permanently protected by the provincial government.

Logging threatens other mainland coastal wilderness valleys that few people know anything about. Recent explorations have revealed that these magnificent valleys may well be the last ecologically exceptional coastal watersheds still intact. Logging is planned despite the fact that access to these areas is fraught with monumental engineering and environmental costs.

A major impediment to reforming the tenure system is the precedent for timber companies to receive financial compensation when a portion of their tenure area is removed to create a park. When the South Moresby National Park was formed, Doman Industries received $30 million, despite the fact that the tree farm license (TFL) was awarded at no cost to the original licensee. Proposed legislation may allow the establishment of new parks without major compensation costs to B.C. taxpayers. Recent amendments to the province's forest management legislation strengthen monitoring of TFL forest practices, and improve the ministry's and the public's ability to obtain information from TFL holders.

The B.C. government's pledge to double the province's parkland is now being implemented through the Protected Areas Strategy. The goal is to protect viable, representative examples of the natural diversity of the province. Although the initially proposed new park areas are predominantely "rock and ice," studies are underway to identify areas that best represent both ecosystem biodiversity and recreational opportunities. An amendment to the Forest Act now allows the government to reduce the AAC and suspend logging and road building in the study areas. The question remains whether the government will respond to the conservation concerns of the public, or bow to the increased pressure from industry and timber workers to continue cutting the remaining few untouched valleys.

ALBERTA

The government of Alberta has given pulp-and-paper corporations the cutting rights to 221,000 square kilometers of its boreal forest, an area almost the size of Great Britain. In total, almost $5 billion of new pulp mill developments—some of the largest in the world—have been built in northern Alberta. No independent environmental impact studies have been done on these forest management plans. The two largest Forest Management Agreements (FMAs)—which allow access to the timber for twenty years with an option for another twenty years—were awarded to firms controlled by Japanese interests: Daishowa and ALPAC (Mitsubishi and Honshu Paper). The Alberta government has given huge subsidies to encourage these mega-developments with nearly a half billion dollars in loan guarantees and millions more for roads, rail lines, and other infrastructure—in return Alberta will receive only minuscule stumpage royalties.

The profits will end up in Japan; a stand of sixteen aspen trees fifty feet tall will fetch Alberta $.90; when converted to pulp they are then worth $590; and as paper they are worth up to $1,250 (1993 prices). The companies can borrow money using their FMAs as collateral and then invest it elsewhere. The government proudly points to job creation but the few jobs available in the hi-tech pulp production facilities and timber harvesting are costing the government a few hundred thousand dollars each! In addition to being an economic boondoggle, these FMAs will create an ecological disaster.

The fragile boreal forest ecosystem is made up of nearly 50 percent aspen trees, once considered a "weed" species, but now valued for its superior pulp fiber. It is a slow-growing forest with little precipitation and thin soils and a mere ninety-day growing season. Twelve or more distinct forest types, each with a unique mix of species and conditions, are found within the boreal region. Many of the plant species are rare or endangered, including the yellow Indian tansy and the cypripedium orchid. Over the ages the boreal forest has renewed itself in an unbroken cycle of fires and succession that scientists have just begun to study. The boreal forest is the least understood of any forest type in North America. Foresters are ignorant about how to reproduce mixed-species stands; how fungi and microorganisms interact with animals and trees; which songbirds eat which insects; and what the impact will be from the massive clearcutting already taking place.

In a global context, the boreal forest is worth more to the planet as an ecosystem than as pulp and paper. The boreal forest conserves the soil and water, and is second only to tropical forests in its capacity to store carbon as a protection against global warming. A 1977 study of the effect of clearcut logging on stream flows in the Hinton, Alberta, area found a 27 percent increase in water yield during spring run-off, and peak storm-flow increases of 150 to 200 percent. The boreal forest is like a giant sponge that when clearcut will flood rivers that flow into the Northwest Territories and the Yukon. Already, 24,000 acres along the Keg River have been saturated because of clearcutting by Canfor, near High Level, Alberta.

Recent scientific studies (*Science* magazine, vol. 247) indicate that the bulk of carbon dioxide created by the burning of fossil fuels is absorbed not by the world's oceans, as was once thought, but by the plants and trees in the northern hemisphere. New information suggests that *temperate zone forests* may be the greatest carbon

sinks on the planet. Conversion of these natural boreal forests to tree plantations will significantly reduce this capacity and consequently accelerate the carbon dioxide loading in our atmosphere.

Destruction of the boreal forest ecosystem also impacts heavily on the First Nations people. The northern Cree, Dene, and Metis have historically depended on the forests for their livelihood. Forests surrounding the small Indian reserves in northern Alberta are the source of game, fish, berries, herbs, and spiritual values that sustain the native people's culture. Many native people leave their reserves each spring to live in forest camps, and return in late fall with a full harvest. The thousands of kilometers of roads and clearcuts will destroy their traditional territories and turn a once proud forest people into "environmental refugees," not unlike what is happening to Brazil's Indians in the Amazon. A Cree elder summarized the problem when he said:

"This you must know: this land, these forests and waters, are not just resources to be harvested and managed. They were given to us to take care of and treat with respect, the way our grandfathers have always done. We are responsible for taking care of Mother Earth because she takes care of us. These pulp mills will take those things away from them. The land won't be the same after they take away the trees. This destruction weighs heavily on us, like a war. You don't need a war to destroy a native person, just take away the bush, just take away the trees. That will destroy us. The money will be all that is left."

The forests and the native people are not all that is threatened. The pulp mills have already begun poisoning the northern river systems. Thousands of tons of toxic waste is being dumped into the northern rivers each day. Rivers like the Great MacKenzie are being turned into chemical sewers for pulp mill discharge. Already fish are contaminated and, according to the federal government, "constitute a threat to human health" for people who regularly eat these fish. New pulp mills had been built before the results of studies were completed.

The planned destruction of Alberta's boreal forest is proceeding amidst much controversy. Environmental groups have fought the decisions with demonstrations, media attacks, public conferences, and court challenges. Most of the mills have been built, and the clearcutting proceeds, the effluent continues to pour into the rivers, and native people's traditional livelihoods are being ruined. The Forest Management Agreements make no provision for parks, wilderness, fish and wildlife habitat, old-growth forests, biological diversity, watershed management, Indian land claims, subsistence fishing, hunting, and trapping, or much of anything other than wood chip production. The woodland caribou and hundreds of songbird species are rapidly losing their habitat as the natural forest is clearcut. Any set-asides for "other uses" of the forest of more than 3 percent will result in compensation to the companies. Additional set-asides are unlikely, since the Alberta forestry department is already underfunded. According to a government report, leaked in 1991, "The Alberta Forestry Service will be unable to monitor and enforce the environmental standards promised . . . to its citizens." Backed into a corner, Alberta environmental groups have called for an international boycott of Procter and Gamble, Diashowa, and Mitsubishi.

SASKATCHEWAN

Most of Saskatchewan forests are committed to sawmills and pulp-and-paper operations under Forest Management License Agreements. The remainder of the province's productive forest lands were turned over to two out-of-province pulp-and-paper companies. These long-term leases were negotiated by the government and companies in secret, with no public input. As part of these agreements, the provincial government offered subsidies to these companies in the form of grants, loans, low stumpage rates, and road building. In one operation, the government spent nearly one million dollars for each of the four hundred jobs created in the woods and at the mill!

The subarctic and northern boreal subregions occupy the northern one-third of Saskatchewan. Largely wilderness, these areas are dominated by black spruce, white spruce, and jack pine. Intermixed with these species are balsam, tamarack, aspen, and white birch.

Mismanagement of the Saskatchewan forests is evident, and some mills have closed due to lack of an adequate timber supply. At present, over one million hectares of cutover land is classified as NSR (not sufficiently restocked), with little available information on its condition. Forest managers claim that clearcutting mixed-wood forests mimics the natural forest fires that normally sweep through boreal forests. Critics, however, point out the potential ecological damage from the short rotations that convert mixed-wood stands to hardwoods and prevent old-growth forests from redeveloping. Other criticisms come from tree planters who doubt the claims of success in replanting. Hunters and wildlife experts tell of reduced animal populations due to the increased road access. Traplines have been cutover. Lakes not classified as "fisheries" are clearcut right to their edge without even a token buffer strip, and barren land that looks like desert sand after clearcut logging takes place tells us that Saskatchewan's boreal forests may well be one of the most fragile ecosystems in the world.

Native communities are adamantly against the continued assault on the boreal forests, because it destroys their traditional lifestyles. Tensions reached the boiling point during the summer of 1992 in northern Saskatchewan when thirty-one elders and supporters were arrested for blockading a logging road. As of the summer of 1993, this blockade has been the longest in Canadian history. The protesters have established a training center at the site to teach their young people the traditional way of life and to strengthen their solidarity. Traditional native elders called Protectors of Mother Earth are calling for an end to clearcutting and are pushing for joint control of the region's natural resources.

Only a minuscule 3 percent of Saskatchewan is protected in parks and other reserves. Representatives from both government and citizen organizations have been working on a committee to develop a protected area strategy. The committee's objectives include increased public awareness and citizen participation, and an inventory and mapping of endangered areas for preservation.

MANITOBA

Manitoba's boreal forests, two-thirds of which are coniferous, stretch across the center of the province. The boreal forest's natural cycle begins with fire, and goes through a succession of brush and deciduous growth to reintroduction of spruce, pine, and fir until another fire sweeps through the mature trees. Estimating the province's timber supply has always been difficult, because the annual loss to forest fires is roughly two and one-half times the annual timber harvest. In 1989, 68 million cubic meters of wood were lost to forest fires, while 1.7 million were cut. These massive fires occurred in remote forests where many of the trees are small and stunted.

Over two-thirds of Manitoba's annual cut is for pulpwood to feed the province's two pulp mills. Official policy requires that all publicly owned "productive" forest be managed for the production of wood fiber. Most of the logging has been concentrated in the regions close to these mills. Manitoba has one of the worst records in

Canada for regenerating its cutover forestland—as of 1990, over half remained as NSR. Increased investment in silviculture through federal-provincial funding agreements is beginning to reduce this backlog.

Manitoba can claim the dubious distinction of having awarded by far the largest forest management license in Canada, and possibly in the world, to one company. The agreement with REPAP Industries includes management of 108,000 square kilometers of boreal forestland, an area the size of Ohio, which comprises nearly 20 percent of the province's land mass and 40 percent of its productive forest land. In the first five years, the AAC would increase from 600,000 cubic meters a year to a shocking 3.4 million cubic meters, and thousands of miles of new roads would open up the remote north. This agreement was tied to a major expansion of the existing pulp mill that would quadruple its output and the area logged. Manitoba environmentalists mobilized to protest the agreement and now, thanks to economics, the project is on hold. REPAP is as yet unable to undertake the required expansion.

In 1992, Manitoba's Clean Environment Commission made a bold recommendation to protect Nopiming Provincial Park from logging, and recommended further that similar protection be extended to *all* provincial parks. The commission's review of the Abitibi-Price operating plan also recommended that the government amend its forest policy to conform with "sustainable development" principles, and that protection be extended along a canoe route corridor on the Manigotogan River. Unfortunately, these recommendations were overturned two months later when the government awarded Abitibi-Price a new license that allows them to continue cutting in Nopiming Park and along the Manigotogan River.

In Manitoba the parks are wide open to logging and mining. A network of logging roads has compromised the wilderness character of these parklands. A mere 0.6 percent of the province's land base is protected from development. Although most of Manitoba's northern region and the Canadian Shield lake country has remained free of logging, it is now committed to development. The province has adopted the World Wildlife Fund's Endangered Spaces goal of protecting 12 percent of its land base, but there appears to be a shortage of political will to achieve this goal.

ONTARIO

Located in the southernmost tip of Canada, the deciduous forest region now occupies only 1 percent of the province's productive forestland. Over 90 percent of the original hardwood forest has been converted to farms and urban development. The remnants of the once diverse beech, walnut, oak, and maple forests are increasingly fragmented by the expanding urban centers of southern Ontario. Most of the few remaining natural forests are in private hands and are being logged unsustainably for short-term profit. A recently proposed amendment to the Trees Act may enable municipalities to pass bylaws to restrict tree cutting in urban areas.

The Great Lakes-St. Lawrence forest region occupies about one-fourth of Ontario's productive forestland. Once coveted for schooner masts, the white pine climax forests have been virtually eliminated. Only seven areas have been identified by the provincial government that contain over 500 hectares of old-growth white pine. The future of these remaining stands was left unresolved while a government-appointed Old-Growth Committee attempts to develop a conservation strategy.

One of Canada's few remaining great old-growth red pine and white pine wilderness areas, the Temagami region, was the scene of many confrontations in the 1980s. The government appointed native and non-native representatives to the Wendaban Stewardship Authority (WSA) in May 1991 to address forest and land-use issues.

The WSA was given "authority" over four townships in the heart of the Temagami old-growth area and the communities and conservation groups are waiting for the outcome of this citizen committee. The first phase of the authority's Forest Steward-ship Plan includes a forest inventory of the area to serve as the basis for proper forest management. The Wendaban Stewardship Authority is only one of numerous co-management initiatives for forests inhabited by native peoples across the province.

Currently, 5.5 percent of the province's land base is designated as "parks" and "wilderness reserves." But logging continues within one park and adjacent to others. The Missinaibi Waterway Park has been reduced to a wilderness facade, with massive clearcutting that extends even into the narrow 122-meter buffer currently provided. Logging roads and bridges crisscross the waterway, further degrading the area's disappearing wilderness.

Most of the province's boreal forest region is held by transnational corporations under the long-term leases known as Forest Management Agreements (FMAs). In 1980, the majority of these leases were held by only eight corporations and were located adjacent to their pulp-and-paper mills. This distribution of forest wealth has not changed appreciably in the past decade. Ontario's boreal forest has been system-atically logged since the 1920s when mills were built in the north to convert the long fibers of the spruce trees into pulp and paper. The largest clearcut in Canada may well be located in northern Ontario on land that was leased to Spruce Falls Power and Paper, formerly a subsidiary of Kimberley-Clark, a supplier to *The New York Times*. The size of this vast tract of connected clearcuts was determined from satellite photos to be equivalent to half the size of Prince Edward Island, some 2,693 square kilometers (269,300 hectares). There is some softwood forest regeneration in this enormous clearcut, but much of the area is in early successional poplar. This massive cut has affected soil productivity, water flow and quality, and wildlife habitat.

Communities throughout northern Ontario are beginning to pay the price for forest mismanagement. Several pulp mills, the economic engines of most northern towns, are closing down. These mills have depleted their readily accessible mature coni-fers. With declining corporate profits, transnational corporations move their assets to more lucrative sectors of their investment portfolios such as real estate or tropical forest extraction. Many of the remaining pulp mills are now using a larger compo-nent of the second-growth poplar stands closer to the mill sites.

The Ontario government has launched a program to promote sustainable forestry. One initiative is the Old-Growth Committee mentioned earlier. Another initiative increases research into silvicultural alternatives, and incorporates a reduction of pesticide use. A Forest Policy Panel has also been appointed to develop and recom-mend a comprehensive framework to guide forest policy development, with citizen involvement. Individual and group forest advocates hope that their efforts will not be overshadowed by the continued lobbying of the wealthy forest industry. As another initiative, four community forest pilot projects have been established. These communities will eventually be given control over forestlands that for the most part have already been extensively logged.

QUEBEC

Logging in Quebec began with the colonization of North America in the mid- to late 1600s. At that time logging was taking place in the hardwood forests along the province's major waterways—the St. Lawrence, the Ottawa, and the St. Maurice rivers. The purpose of the logging activity was twofold: to create new farmland; and, after 1763, to supply Great Britain with raw material (primarily white pine) for the construction of navy and cargo vessels.

With the advent of steel in naval construction and the development of the pulp industry, a shift took place in the wood industry in Quebec. Between the late 1800s and early 1900s Quebec became a major exporter of pulp to the United States and Great Britain.

As in many other jurisdictions, the most productive forestlands were converted to agricultural use. Because of overcutting in the immediate areas of the mills, the wood products industry had to go ever-greater distances to find wood to fill its always growing needs.

At the end of the nineteenth century, large tracts of land were lent or given to pulp, lumber, and railroad companies. "Cut-and-run" was the order of the day. Quebec later allocated its forests to companies under a system of forest concessions. Some concerns about the possibilities of exhaustion of the resources started to grow before the mid-1900s, but no action was taken for forest regeneration.

The province began to regenerate the NSR areas in the mid-1960s and assumed responsibility for all the forest regeneration projects on Crown land. Many of the areas logged from the early 1900s to the late 1960s have regenerated only marginally.

The threat of a wood shortage became more evident with a large spruce budworm infestation. Large areas, primarily in eastern Quebec, were sprayed with insec-ticides. Environmental and community groups strongly opposed the spraying and were able to obtain first a five-year moratorium and then a total ban on chemical insecticide spraying. Since then, the government has switched to the bacteriological agent *Btk*, and spraying has nearly been eliminated. The government's position toward the use of *Btk* aerial spraying for spruce budworm continues to be one of continued use as long as the survival of large pieces of forest are at risk and in need of protection. Herbicide spraying is continuing despite public protest.

In 1987, the province of Quebec enacted new forest management policies under the *loi sur les forets* (Forestry Act), which shifted more responsibility to the forest users. These changes revoked the previous twenty-year leases and replaced them with vol-ume agreements for specified areas. These supply and management contracts are referred to as CAAFs—*contrats d'approvisionnement et d'amenagement forestier*. These CAAFs run for twenty-five years with five-year renewal terms.

Over the next five years, plans call for 200,000-300,000 hectares of forest to be clearcut annually. The industry is reaching further and further into the northern hinterland for its wood supply. Timber cutting of the southern fringe of the James Bay region alone is eliminating 60,000 hectares of forest a year. Since silvicultural and regeneration practices are new to forestry in Quebec, most of the forest planta-tions are still too young to be harvested.

Quebec's conservation record is abysmal. Only 0.4 percent of the province's land base is protected in parks and ecological reserves, the lowest percentage of any province in Canada. The provincial wildlife management areas have only minimal protection, with clearcut logging allowed. Although eighteen new park reserves and eleven new ecological reserves were established in 1992, most of the province's natural regions remain without protected areas. There is little hope for preservation of wild forests in Quebec, since few such areas remain.

NEW BRUNSWICK

If forest policies are not improved, Canada's future forests may resemble the industrial forests that dominate the New Brunswick landscape. Although they are often naturally regenerated, these "fiber farms" are a far cry from the once diverse and unique, natural Acadian forests that existed for thousands of years. The lack of biological diversity in these forests makes them ideal breeding grounds for disease and insect infestations. They are even-aged stands of trees destined for pulp, unsuitable for many of the animals and birds that had evolved to thrive there. So far, an attempt by conservation groups to protect one of the last natural forests in the Christmas Mountain region has been unsuccessful.

During the settlement period of nearly three hundred years, almost all of the forest had been cut down at least once—much of it has now been logged several times over. There is virtually no ancient forest left standing except in a few small areas that are not well defined or protected. Less than 1 percent of the province is currently protected in national and provincial parks and ecological reserves.

Forest management is largely controlled by the provincial government and six large corporations. Ownership of the land base is almost equally divided between the province and private landowners. The forest industry holds long-term leases to almost all of the Crown land, and they own outright 20 percent of the private land. Neither the companies nor the forests are being sustained, and some pulp mills have been importing wood from the U.S. and Quebec.

The remaining 30 percent of New Brunswick's forest lands are managed by over 30,000 woodlot owners, who must compete for markets with the large companies. The number of woodlot owners is decreasing as corporations continue to buy out these small holdings. The powerful, family-run Irving Corporation has been purchasing every available woodlot that comes up for sale, including forestland in Maine.

The stewardship of the private woodlots has not been much better than on Crown or company forests, but because the forestry practices have been less intensive, these forests are less disturbed. In fact, half of the private woodlots are not being logged, which means there are still some forests where alternative, sustainable practices could be tried.

Logging has increased dramatically in the last forty years. The wood products industry plans "to systematically convert the natural forests to managed forests" across the entire province. Yet, Forestry Canada and the provincial Department of Natural Resources now admit that there will be a shortage in the near future. While forest managers point to the crisis looming in the wood products industry, the real crisis is happening in the forest. Pulp plantations are composed of only five conifer species (there are twenty-seven other native tree species) that will be logged on short rotation schedules of less than sixty years. This intensive management requires continual infusions of pesticides, herbicides, and biological agents. Large-scale clearcutting often involves *whole-tree harvesting* where monster-sized machines remove the entire tree, including the roots and branches, resulting in long-term site degradation.

New Brunswick forests have sustained forty years of pesticide use, the longest sustained chemical intervention in any forest ecosystem in the world. The early phase of this program began with DDT and progressed through a range of other general systemic nerve toxins to today's avian killer, *fenitrothion*. Future Forest Alliance groups in the Atlantic region are focusing national and international attention on New Brunswick's *fenitrothion* spruce budworm spray program. In 1988 Environment Canada determined the pesticide causes unacceptable adverse impacts on migratory songbirds, forest pollinators, and aquatic habitats. Spray programs during the last two decades have been responsible for the deaths of millions of songbirds in eastern Canada. Biological agents like *Btk* kill harmless caterpillars, thus further impacting bird populations. Continual pesticide spraying has also increased human health concerns.

For years, industry has held a stranglehold on forest management; even forestry information has been kept secret. Several years ago, conservation groups went to court under the Right-to-Information Act to obtain the government's evaluations of timber companies' management activities. Although the groups were unsuccessful, the provincial government finally reversed this policy due to public pressure. Continued public pressure has led to some changes in forest practices, but public participation in forest management is still nonexistent.

NOVA SCOTIA

With guns and imposed legalities, the forests of Nova Scotia were stolen from the MicMac, the region's indigenous people, by European settlers. Nova Scotia's forests are part of the Acadian forest, an ecosystem that extends across three provinces and a portion of the United States. While the dominant tree species are red spruce, balsam fir, maple, and yellow birch, there are about sixty other tree and shrub species in the province.

Nova Scotia has embraced a pulpwood forestry policy, seen as necessary to feed the province's pulp-and-paper industry. The once diverse mixed-wood forests have been simplified by industry to softwood plantations that are supposedly ready for cutting in thirty-five to forty-five years. Considerable government and industry money is spent to convince the public of the myth that Nova Scotia is a "showcase for reforestation and forest management." But the reality for anyone who walks through the clearcuts or who drives the logging roads—even the main highways— is wanton forest destruction. Through clearcutting, conversion to softwood plantations, and use of chemical and biological sprays, there has been a serious loss of biological diversity and an impoverishment of wildlife.

Nearly half of all forestland in Nova Scotia, 48 percent, is controlled by over 30,000 woodlot owners. Of the remaining forestland, 22 percent is in large private holdings, 27 percent is owned by the provincial government, and 3 percent by the federal government. The five pulp-and-paper companies are major polluters and legally discharge various toxins into the air, the sea, and various landfills. The pulp-and-paper industry has been investigated by the Green Web environmental research group, which publishes educational documents for activists. The big three transnational pulp-and-paper corporations, Stora (Sweden), Scott (U.S.) and Bowater (Canada), dominate distinct areas of the province with their economic power. They hold extensive long-term leases on provincially owned Crown land.

Woodlot owners have had their attempts to cooperatively organize over the years thwarted by government and corporate hostility, court challenges, and the formation of government-funded *Venture Groups* whose purpose is to supply cheap pulpwood to the mills. Stora Industries has managed to convince its largest private suppliers to take a price rollback for pulpwood supplied to the mill. When the Primary Forest Products Marketing Board attempted to revamp the bargaining negotiation process, they were undermined by the government. Prices are now negotiated by fragmented groups representing the interests of contractors and truckers with close ties to the mills.

The contemporary forest pesticide opposition in Nova Scotia grew out of the struggles against forest spraying in the 1970s. Today, the concerns have grown to encompass the use of biological control including bacteria (*Btk*) that pulpwood forest managers deem necessary for tree farm survival. The Nova Scotia Coalition for Alternatives to Pesticides (NSCAP) published a retrospective analysis of the economic and environmental impacts of the province's decision to not use chemical pesticides during the spruce budworm epidemic in the late 1970s on Cape Breton Island. The study shows that, contrary to industry propaganda, the "no-spray" decision has been economically beneficial. The only adverse environmental impacts to be documented resulted from poorly planned large-scale salvage operations.

Another NSCAP study revealed how industry and government wildlife research was designed to conceal the adverse impacts of herbicides on birds and small mammals.

There is no provincial strategy to ensure adequate protection of wild areas in Nova Scotia. Presently, less than 3 percent of the province is truly protected from resource extraction and industrial activity. Most of the last remnants of Acadian forest are in two national parks, but because there are no buffer zones, clearcutting takes place up to the park's boundaries.

The steep slopes and remote areas in the Cape Breton highland plateaus contain the last unprotected remnants of native old-growth hardwood forests. Environmental groups recently helped to delay the logging by Stora of an original Acadian hardwood forest on Cape Breton Island and are calling for the establishment of more wilderness conservation areas and a Nature Trust program.

PRINCE EDWARD ISLAND

The destruction that is occurring *now* in western Canada happened on Prince Edward Island (P.E.I.) in the 1700s and 1800s. Large stands of some of the finest yellow birch, sugar maple, white pine, beech, and red oak were cleared, and much of this wood was shipped to England. The lynx, bear, marten, and moose all were exterminated long ago as forests were slashed and burned and converted to farmland. Clearing peaked at about 80 percent of available land by the late 1800s. Today, about half of P.E.I.'s million acres is forested, and of this 93 percent is in private woodlots.

Much of this woodland is early successional forest, primarily white spruce, poplar, and red maple. Only a few small remnants of old-growth remain. Private landowners often practiced indifferent forestry, making small clearcuts for firewood or lumber without burning and using chemicals. Although past woodlot management was not good stewardship, it was not as harmful as present-day practices. In the 1980s, government subsidies encouraged contractors and landowners to purchase larger equipment and to clearcut, burn, replant, spray, and even worse, use whole-tree harvesting.

P.E.I. woodlands continue to be overcut. Since most of the stands are still young (forty to seventy years old), they have not yet succeeded into more shade-tolerant Acadian species. Fragmentation is a serious problem for wildlife, with only a few large blocks of continuous forest remaining as habitat. Increased public awareness in the last few years has prompted the government to begin planning for biodiversity by limiting clearcut sizes, decreasing herbicide use and slash burning, leaving trees for wildlife, and planting more diverse species. But plans are moving forward for a cogeneration power plant in Charlottetown that would be fueled by increased whole-tree harvesting and clearcutting.

NEWFOUNDLAND and LABRADOR

Much of the land surface of the island of Newfoundland is either not viable or only marginally viable as forest land. The tree line is at a very low altitude compared with other areas at a similar latitude, and much of the land surface is dominated by heath and bog. The treeless state of the southern Maritime Barrens ecoregion is due

in part to the clearing of forests by early settlers. The forests that did not regenerate reverted to heath. Because of the harsh climate, the trees grow very slowly and forest regeneration is difficult at best, and impossible on steep slopes and shallow soils. Close to 10 percent of cutover areas are permanently lost as forestland due to bulldozer disturbance, and an additional 14 percent suffers from moderate to heavy disturbance.

Two pulp-and-paper companies, Abitibi-Price and Kruger, account for most of the commercial timber use on the island, and they control through long-term leases and outright ownership the majority of the forestland. Because of the rigid timber ownership structure, forest utilization standards are deplorable. The pulp-and-paper industry is allowed to set its own standards, which allow large, high-quality sawlogs to be sent to the chipper for pulp. Meanwhile, the few struggling sawmills on the island are forced to make lumber from logs as small as five inches in diameter.

After a century of abusive logging practices and virtually no reforestation, the Newfoundland forest industry is in crisis. Past practices have included high-grading, cutting the most cheaply accessible trees, and more recently, cutting immature, second-growth trees in areas close to the mills. As the costs of obtaining wood fiber increased, Abitibi-Price began to encroach on coastal Crown forest areas, thus displacing local operators from their traditional logging areas. The original legislation prohibited the issuing of timber licenses within three miles of tidal waters to ensure adequate timber supplies for local communities. This policy was circumvented without public notification.

After laying waste to the island of Newfoundland, the pulp-and-paper industry is now looking toward the black spruce and balsam fir of Labrador. These forests are characterized by poor growth, patchy stands, fragile sites, and exceptionally long growing cycles. In the past, forestry operations have been marginal, with the bulk of the logs exported to European pulp mills. On Labrador there are huge stacks of logs abandoned by operators who went bankrupt.

Labrador is Innu Nation land that has never been ceded to any government by the original people, yet logging plans and operations have proceeded without any consideration of the their cultural needs. In September of 1991, the Innu Nation blockaded a logging road to prevent expansion of the forest road network. The Innu Nation released a report by an independent forest consultant who found that forest management practices had little or no regard for scientific forest management or other uses; that artificially regenerated sites, composed mainly of the non-indigenous species of jack pine and larch, were of questionable value; that the allowable annual cut was extremely high and unrealistic; that streams and water bodies were poorly protected; and that there was no consideration of traditional hunting and trapping grounds. The Innu people continued to blockade the roads, "to protect their hunting, fishing, and gathering way of life for generations to come."

Currently, only 1.8 percent of Newfoundland and Labrador is protected in parks and wilderness areas.

THE YUKON

The Yukon forests are a continuation of the great spruce and pine boreal forest. To date, these forests have contributed more to the economy through subsistence, trapping, and wilderness recreation activities than they have as a timber supply. Small bushmills and firewood cutting operations predominate in the Yukon. The only sizeable sawmill in the territory has been plagued by bankruptcy. Distance from markets, outdated machinery, and limited productivity due to climatic and soil conditions have contributed to a relatively benign neglect by the forest industry.

Forest resources are presently under the control of the Federal Department of Indian Affairs and Northern Development. This will change when comprehensive land claims are settled and administrative authority is devolved to the territorial government.

The only existing Timber Harvest Agreement (THA) in the Yukon is in the southeastern Llard River basin region, the site of some of the territory's best commercial forests. The AAC is presently set at 100,000 cubic meters of white spruce, black spruce, and lodgepole pine. The most valuable trees are the riparian white spruce, which range from 100 to 250 years old. According to this agreement, Kaska First Nation (backed by ITT Rayonier of the U.S.) may export half of its AAC as raw logs.

Raw log export provisions have been the subject of criticism from regional environmental groups, the town of Watson Lake, and community logging interests. Kaska and Rayonier argue that the high-quality logs can be exported quickly at a profit to accumulate capital to update the Watson Lake mill. A modernized specialty mill would then be able to process the domestic timber. Charges of high-grading are fueled by Rayonier's plans to phase out their participation in the project when they have made sufficient returns on their investment.

Insufficient data on northern boreal forest regeneration is a major concern. Past logging practices of the THA have left a legacy of NSR land. The harsh climate, thin soils, and slow-growing trees demand that sustainable forest use be extremely sensitive and appropriately scaled. Past clearcuts range from 40 to 300 hectares.

In the face of our ignorance of boreal forest ecology and the isolation of the regional economy, a number of community-based groups are urging a slow and conservative approach to forest management. They are recommending community control, small-scale, cooperative ventures, with attention to Yukon markets. There is concern that the Kaska/Rayonier deal will set an unfortunate precedent for the future. There is even greater concern that the Yukon may become a pulpwood supplier to southern mills. Such a massive scale of clearcutting necessary for pulpwood would have a devastating impact on the soils and waterways of the fragile Yukon.

The pressure on the Yukon forest will grow as timber supplies in northern B.C. are depleted. Despite signs that industrial forestry is drifting northward, there remains an exciting potential to initiate a truly sustainable small-scale forest industry that would contribute to stable communities. With wilderness tourism growing in significance, native land claims settled, and a growing understanding of alternative forest practices, the timber companies may soon find that they will have to truly share the northern forest.

NORTHWEST TERRITORIES

Although approximately one-sixth of the territory contains forests, most of the trees are small and stunted and have little commercial value. Only a few hundred hectares of forests are logged each year and very little information is available about forest practices in the Northwest Territories.

SUMMARY

The *Forestry Canada 1990 Report to Parliament* is littered with remarks such as: "In the short term, there is a lot of timber available for harvest now," and, "a case could be made for increasing current harvest levels." The document also appears to recognize the importance of other forest values: "More recently, ecosystem stability and biodiversity have been added to the list of forest management objectives." The report goes on to explain, "Having identified new objectives for its forests, Canada must now develop the language and other mechanisms necessary to incorporate them into forest planning and management processes."

Forestry Canada and the Canadian Council of Forest Ministers leapt into action with a new "Forest Strategy," for the Earth Summit, complete with all the "environmentally correct language." *Sustainable Forests, A Canadian Commitment* is full of glowing promises for wise, wholistic forest use, fair and effective public participation in planning, maintenance of healthy forest ecosystems, and conservation of natural diversity. The strategy's *Framework for Action* outlines how the government plans to deliver these promises. Although it seems like business as usual in the forests, forest managers are now at least speaking the right language. It is up to conservationists to maintain the pressure to see that those words are put into action.

Crucial to positive change is the need for accurate information that can be shared by all concerned parties. The methodology and tools exist today that can deliver this information. But in some provinces, current forest management data is either not available or nonexistent. The Wilderness Society and the Sierra Club have led the way with the use of G.I.S. (Geographic Information Service) and Landsat technology to produce accurate inventories of remaining ancient forests. If provincial forest ministries are unable to fulfill the commitment for new inventories based on all forest values as stated in the federal strategy, then environmental groups will have to raise the funds and conduct their own more detailed inventories to present the true state of the forests to the public.

The conflicts over the use of Canada's forests extend to efforts made to influence the minds of students, the Canadian public, even to the Europeans and Japanese who purchase many of Canada's forest products. Posters, publications, and videos produced by Canadian environmental groups have helped raise the awareness of issues for Canadians, as opinion polls indicate. The forest industry in B.C. has launched a multi-million dollar campaign to change the public's perception of forestry. Engineered by the same public relations firm that handled Union Carbide's Bhopal disaster and worked for Argentina's right-wing junta, the B.C. Forest Alliance masquerades as an environmental group and produces newsletters and slick TV shows. The federal and provincial governments and the forest industry have published clever propaganda for school curriculums. Fortunately, many teachers and students refuse to be affected by these insidious attempts at brainwashing.

If governments live up to their promises, future forest education materials will reflect a more balanced viewpoint and allow students to think critically about forest issues. The scenes shown in the media of massive clearcuts, pulp mill pollution and damaged streams, have helped to fuel the debate in Europe. Threats of boycotts now have government and industry running scared, but instead of lowering the cut significantly and protecting the environment, they fly to Europe to assure their customers that Canada is sustainably managing its forests.

The slogan "jobs versus the environment" is too often used to characterize the conflict between conservationists and the timber industry. Community organizations with hidden connections to industry such as Share the Forests have sprung up throughout Canada to lobby for the continuation of status-quo forest annihilation in order to protect the already diminishing wood industry jobs. By feeding the flames of conflict that the media thrives on, industry is continuing to drive a wedge between loggers and environmentalists.

But a new spirit of cooperation and consensus is emerging from within the imaginary battleground. Union representatives, First Nations leaders and environmentalists have sat down together and reached agreements on many issues that industry would prefer to remain contentious. In 1991, an agreement was signed in Victoria by five conservation groups, the IWA Canada (International Woodworkers of America), and a local of the Canadian Labour Congress. Termed the South Island Forest Accord, the document calls for changes in forest management that will protect some old-growth forest ecosystems, accurately inventory all forest values, tie forest tenure to job creation, involve greater community planning, improve logging practices, and resolve outstanding native land claims. Agreements have also been reached within the Tin Wis Coalition, an alliance of British Columbia unions, First Nations, and conservationists. The Tin Wis group has produced a proposed Forest Stewardship Act that, if implemented, would create greater fairness and ecologically sensible practices in B.C. forest management.

To date, the environmental movement has focused its attention on ecosystem protection and pollution abatement. While these campaigns are far from over, it's time to think ahead to the awesome task of repairing the damage done to countless watersheds and hillsides. In the U.S., hundreds of groups are restoring salmon streams and replanting diverse species of trees on cutover lands. Ecological rehabilitation will not only help to prevent erosion, but also help to restore both a sense of community and a spiritual connection of the individual with Nature. Restoration should not be regarded as an exercise in human mastery of Nature, for previous attempts have sometimes disrupted natural ecosystems. Instead, restoration should be considered an attempt to rehabilitate the processes of natural succession that occur in Nature's self-regulating ecosystems. Restoration must not be confused with plantation reforestation that will produce only fiber for future mills. Federal programs such as the Environmental Partner's Fund and Tree Plan Canada are available to provide funding for community restoration projects.

Throughout the last three centuries, Canada's forests have been exploited from east to west, and south to north. Diverse, natural forests have been converted to fiber farms to supply pulp and fiberboard industries. An increasing amount of forestland is becoming denuded of trees. Just as the misuse of our forests contributes to global environmental problems, so can global problems such as global warming and ozone depletion severely impact Canadian forests. As the seemingly never-ending spiral of human consumption increases, so does the impact on the remaining natural forest ecosystems. Certainly a reduction in timber cutting to sustainable levels must parallel a global effort to reduce consumption and make ecologically sane lifestyle changes in the developed countries.

To best summarize the situation in Canada, I will present a vision of what future forest management could be like if Canada maintains its commitment to sustainability. . . . *It took a few more years of unusually warm weather, ultraviolet radiation damage to crops and a significant rise in the ocean levels to convince government leaders that real changes were necessary. Carbon taxes were instituted, a reduction in the use of wood and paper products resulted from rising costs that reflected the true worth of forests to the planet, and recycling became mandatory. Forests became more valuable for their ability to absorb carbon than for industrial use. To supply the society's reduced need for paper products, marginal farmland was used to grow hemp, which out-produces trees by four to one. A major national effort was*

underway to both replant denuded landscapes and restore damaged forest ecosystems. Forest research was successfully re-directed to find better ways to both grow and log uneven aged forests. Clearcutting was restricted to small patch cutting that maintains the ecological integrity of the landscape. A system of large and small protected areas was established with wildlife corridors connecting them. As mills closed, workers found jobs in forest restoration, trail building and eco-tourism. Canadian value-added wood products became world famous and in much demand after First Nation carvers and designers added a creative and unique flair to the industry. As military spending shrank, funds were re-directed to environmental cleanup and ecosystem rehabilitation. Forest planning was directed by local, shared decision making boards with advice from ecologists and biologists. Canada became known again for its magnificent forests and global catastrophe was averted with the help from both new and old forest ecosystems. A dream? . . . . perhaps, but the alternatives could result in the loss of many species, including our own!

REFERENCES

Bourdages, Jean-Luc, and Jean-Pierre Amyot. [1984] 1992. *Canada's forests: No future without good management.* Revised. Parliamentary Library, Research Branch, Science & Technology Division.

Dufour, Jules. 1991. Toward sustainable development of Canada's forests. In *Resource Management and Development*, Ed. Bruce Mitchell. Oxford University Press.

Forestry Canada. 1990, 1991, and 1992. *Report to Parliament: The state of forestry in Canada.*

Hummel, Monte, ed. 1989. *Endangered spaces: The future for Canada's wilderness.* Key Porter Books, Ltd.

Nikiforuk, Andrew, and Ed Struzik. 1989. The great forest sell-off. *Globe and Mail Magazine, Report on Business* (November), Toronto, Ontario.

Pearce, Tony. 1990. *Cutting down Canada.* Unpublished manuscript.

Resource Futures International, and Institute for Research on Public Policy. 1991. Environmental Scan, prepared for Canadian Council of Ministers of the Environment.

Runyon, K. E. 1991. Canada's timber supply: Current status and outlook. Forestry Canada. *Information Report* E-X-45.

World Wildlife Fund. 1991 and 1992. *Endangered Spaces Progress Report.* Washington, D.C.: World Wildlife Fund.

The Future of Our Forests, Forest Resources Commission, British Columbia, Victoria, 1991

An Inventory of Watersheds in the Coastal Temperate Forests of British Columbia, by Keith Moore, Earthlife Canada Foundation and Ecotrust/Conservation International, 1991

ACKNOWLEDGEMENTS:

Co-Authors: Ontario, Lucie Lavoie; Prince Edward Island, Gary Schneider; Nova Scotia, Charlie Restino and David Orten; Quebec, Paul Senez; Yukon, Alan Young; Saskatchewan, Phil Wasson.

Contributors: New Brunswick, Charlie Restino, Marc Spence, David Orten; Saskatchewan, Sam Mark; Alberta, Jim Darwish, David Parker, Bob Cameron; Canada, Colleen McCrory; Quebec, Christian Wolfe, Alain Charest, Sylvie Trudel, Michel Goudreau, Jules Dufour; Manitoba, Harvey Williams, Hendrik Herfst.

C O L O R   P L A T E S

"ANYONE CAN IDENTIFY DESTRUCTIVE FOREST PRACTICES.
YOU DON'T HAVE TO BE A PROFESSIONAL FORESTER
TO RECOGNIZE BAD FORESTRY ANY MORE THAN YOU NEED TO BE
A DOCTOR TO RECOGNIZE ILL HEALTH.
IF LOGGING LOOKS BAD, IT IS BAD. IF A FOREST APPEARS TO BE
MISMANAGED, IT IS MISMANAGED."

—GORDON ROBINSON, HEAD FORESTER, SOUTHERN PACIFIC RAILROAD, 1939–1966,
CHIEF FORESTRY SPOKESMAN, SIERRA CLUB, 1966–1979.

BIOREGIONS AND PLACE

An exciting concept developing in environmental consciousness is *bioregion.* Stephanie Mills, a leading bioregional activist who dwells on the upper regions of Michigan, summarizes what bioregionalism means: "Bioregionalism is about growing a lifeway, rather than . . . reforming industrial civilization's present practices. . . . It seeks more thorough change. For humans again to participate in, rather than mine, earth's ecosystems, most of our lately accustomed ways—of thought, perception, society, tenure, and livelihood—will have to be radically reshaped toward sustainability. In dozens of particular places across the continent of North America (and doubtless elsewhere by other names) bioregionalism is conjuring those shapes. It aims at 'saving the whole by saving the parts.'" Peter Berg, another spokesperson of the bioregional movement, states that bioregionalism upholds the hope of learning to live more lightly on the Earth—of developing communities integrated with their local ecosystems. A compilation of readings on the practice of bioregional dwelling is found in *Home! A Bioregional Reader;* and in Kirkpatrick Sales' *Dwellers in the Land, A Bioregional Vision.*

Bioregions are soft places; that is, they are not hard political boundaries or artificial lines on a map. Names for bioregions arise from collective experience and awareness of people sharing the moods, feeling, rhythms of place. Frequently, but not always, bioregions are watersheds or parts of watersheds. Sometimes bioregionalists have eschewed names—frequently of Christian saints or explorers—given to their region by Europeans and have sought names from Native American experience and tradition. In the following caption material, the names of some provinces and states are preceded with a bioregional name. In some cases several provinces or states are included within a bioregion. In other cases, a province or state contains many natural bioregions. At this stage in the development of bioregional awareness, there are many areas where no name has emerged for a region, and for some other regions a consensus has not yet been reached on a bioregional name. The editors apologize to readers if we left out your name for your bioregion. For places without bioregional names in this book, we encourage readers to form a local group to explore your bioregion and develop a consensus on a bioregional name that fits the place wherein you dwell.
—The Editors

Top, left to right: Daniel Dancer, Doug Thron. Middle, left to right: Randy Stoltmann, Daniel Dancer, Herb Hammond. Bottom photos: Doug Thron.

THE SHAWNEE STORY

JAN WILDER-THOMAS

The Shawnee National Forest includes less than 1 percent of the state of Illinois. Less than two centuries ago, Illinois had over 13 million acres of mature hardwood forests. The rich diversity of plants and wildlife in these forests included more than 70 species of huge hardwood trees interspersed with barrens, savannahs, and meadows in a continuous cycle of growth, death, decay, and regrowth.

This mighty forest is now a fragmented patchwork of its former diversity. Vast bottomland hardwood swamps have been cleared and drained for corn and soybeans. In Shawnee National Forest only 300 acres of mature hardwoods remain. The Shawnee National Forest is only 4 percent of the four and a half million acres of regenerating woods in Illinois.

The U.S. Forest Service, stewards of Shawnee National Forest, have engaged in several "new forestry" practices that have further fragmented the forest during the past decade. The Forest Service in Shawnee National Forest, as well as other national forests, has engaged in below-cost timber sales. Below-cost sales occur when the cost of building logging roads and preparing logging plans exceeds the timber-sale receipts. In the Shawnee National Forest, an average of one million dollars a year has been lost on these ill-advised timber sales. Furthermore, the Forest Service has used what they call *gap phase dynamics* to further their objective of logging rather than protecting the integrity of ecosystems. Gap phase dynamics implies removing trees in smaller groups, supposedly between three-tenths to six-tenths of an acre. It also includes

cutting of trees larger than twelve inches in diameter between groups. As documented at the Whoopie Cat Mountain Wildlife Area, this new term is just another method of widespread forest canopy eradication. The Forest Service has issued five hardwood timber-sale decisions which will use *group selection* or *patch clearcutting* in the last old-growth (100- to 150-year-old trees) contiguous forest canopy in Illinois, thereby eliminating critical habitat for endangered species, as well as many opportunities for the recreationists to visit the remaining old-growth forests of southern Illinois.

Fragmentation of hardwood forests in the Ohio Valley threatens the neotropical migratory songbird population. These birds winter in Mexico and Central America but depend on the last big blocks of hardwood forests on public lands in the eastern United States as breeding sanctuaries. Fragmentation of these sanctuaries with logging roads and tree cutting allows predators and parasitic brown-headed cowbirds access to nests of songbirds. Studies in Illinois indicate a 72 percent songbird population decline during the last decade.

BEWARE OF TIMBER COMPANIES CLAIMING
THEY CAN NO LONGER CLEARCUT!

Clearcutting is the logging of all trees in an area over a short period of time. There is usually nothing left standing. Big Timber has invented many other terms that are just short of clearcutting, but have consequences close to those of clearcutting:

Seed-tree cutting—the logging of an area that leaves generally six to ten trees per acre, but could leave as few as one tree to drop seed "to generate a new crop."

Shelterwood cut—the logging of an area that leaves ten to twenty mature trees per acre in order to have a seed source. These trees are later cut and not left for wildlife habitat.

Nondeclining even-flow management—the maintenance of an established level of cutting. Every year the forest is entered and the same level is cut, never reduced. A reassessment based on scientific evidence is not considered as long as trees can be found to cut (i.e., cutting on Dead Pine National Forest should equal 300 million board feet per year because that's what we've been getting for the last five years).

Allowable cut effect—logging based on the trees that will be planted in the future, rather than on what is scientifically acceptable to maintain habitat today.

Wildlife study trails—large trails cut through groves without approved timber harvest plans, under the guise of studying the wildlife. In Headwaters Forest, which has the largest unprotected stand of ancient redwoods in northern California, a wildlife study trail is highway width in some places.

Group selection—the removal of trees in clearcut groups up to two acres in size. In some operations trees between the groups are also removed. These openings, when spread, for example, over several hundreds of acres of contiguous forest canopy, destroy the integrity of the forest ecosystem and jeopardize the survival of interior forest-dependent species. In some operations, the logger removes 30 percent of the forest cover and then returns within a few years to remove another 30 percent and then the remaining wood fiber a few years later.

Ecological restoration—as practiced by the USFS, is a guise to continue below-cost clearcutting thousands of acres of Shawnee loblolly pines, thereby destroying young, native hardwood saplings, the so-called beneficiaries of this management practice.

Under some definitions used to regulate logging on private lands, even if 70 percent of the trees are removed during one cutting, the operation is called a selective cut rather than a clearcut.

A L A S K A

KLUKWAN, INC., NATIVE CORPORATION LAND, LONG ISLAND
Photographer, Robert Glenn Ketchum, 1992

Long Island is about 14 miles long and 7 miles wide at its widest point. Mostly owned by Klukwan, Inc., a native corporation, it has been managed totally for short-term revenue extraction. Clearcut from nearly shore to shore, the island is virtually denuded and constitutes one of the largest contiguous clearcuts in Alaska.

Klukwan and other native corporations have recently cut virtually all of the timber on their own land. It is estimated that they have about one year's worth of timber remaining, after which they will face a very uncertain future.

The most extensive federal lands in southeastern Alaska are on the Tongass National Forest, which, at 17 million acres, is the largest national forest in America. Under the 1990 Tongass Timber Reform Act, Congress banned the excessive logging of large, ancient trees that are crucial to the health of the forest ecosystem, a practice known as "high-grading." The Forest Service, however, is still approving logging plans that allow high-grading because it relies on timber information that even its own experts have concluded is grossly inaccurate.

"Clearcuts are ugly. People who see them, even children, know instinctively that they are wrong, an outrage, a sacrilege. Yet, in the face of thirty years of negative public reaction, in spite of legal challenges, restrictive legislative language, and mountains of bad press, the United States and Canadian governments and the timber industry continue clearcutting public and private forests. Why?

"The answer lies in the imperatives of modern western capitalism, the mind-set of foresters taught to impose an industrial agricultural model onto forest ecosystems, and the sociology of communities whose economies are dominated by logging and the production of wood products. Factors favoring liquidation of forests for short-term profit include excessively high interest rates and a corporate culture that emphasizes the short-term bottom line over long-term economic health and social responsibility."
—Felice Pace, "Cultural Clearcuts: The Sociology of Timber Communities in the Pacific Northwest"

LONG SWATH OF CLEARCUT
NEAR NORTHWAY, ALASKA
Photographer, Galen Rowell, 1973

This photograph was taken by well-known landscape photographer Galen Rowell on a trip to Alaska in 1973. Not fully understanding the implications of clearcutting on forested ecosystems, Rowell and his companions were nonetheless amazed and angered at the oversized swath cut to build this road running hundreds of miles. They stopped their vehicle and took a posed shot of some of them trying to raise a fallen tree near the edge in imitation of the Marines raising the flag at Iwo Jima. This photograph later appeared in *Mountain Gazette*. In 1993, twenty years later, Rowell again drove north up the Stewart Cassier Highway toward Northway and was surprised at the incredible impact of industrial clearcutting that appeared along the edges and beyond.

These particular road cuts are excessively wide, creating clearcuts hundreds of miles long.

The trees are from the interior where the climate differs from the coastal forest. Its harsher, colder winters, warmer summers, lower precipitation, and permafrost all contribute to an extremely slow regeneration.

ALASKA

PRINCE WILLIAM SOUND, SHERIDAN MOUNTAIN
Photographer, Daniel Dancer, 1992

Images of the huge oil spill from the *Exxon Valdez* in Prince William Sound are shown around the world as an example of damage to marine environments from oil spills. In the 1990s, however, the greatest threat to Prince William Sound's coastline is from logging forests entrusted to some of Alaska's native corporations.

In order to clear title to land needed to build the Trans-Alaska pipeline from Alaska's North Slope to Prince William Sound, Congress passed, in 1971, the Alaska Native Claims Settlement Act (ANCSA), deeding indigenous peoples of Alaska "ownership" of their ancestral lands, but only through corporations set up for profit. This was perhaps the last and most significant act designed to destroy traditional native culture and values and assimilate native peoples into Western economic forms. Under ANCSA, native corporations along the south coast of Alaska selected the highest-volume old-growth forestlands for ownership primarily for potential timber value. Under ANCSA, these lands would not be subjected to most federal forestry laws.

In Prince William Sound and other parts of Alaska, where native corporations could not harvest timber at a profit, they were allowed by a bizarre congressional tax loophole from 1986 to 1989 to sell their losses to large, profitable corporations in the lower forty-eight states for use as tax breaks. This then encouraged most coastal native corporations to sell their forests to timber companies at rock bottom prices to create a loss, and so began the rapid destruction of the forest.

Through such economic and cultural assimilation, many native peoples lost touch with the very land that had sustained their culture over the centuries. And, in a boom/bust frenzy that has come to typify human exploitation of the Alaskan "frontier," the timber rush was on.
—Rick Steiner

KENAI PENINSULA, DOGFISH BAY ▶
Photographer, Daniel Dancer, 1992

A L A S K A

PRINCE WILLIAM SOUND, TWO MOON BAY
Photographer, Daniel Dancer, 1992

One of the most profound ironies in the history of Alaska occurred just as the timber rush started in earnest in Prince William Sound at Two Moon Bay, when in March 1989, the loaded supertanker *Exxon Valdez* slammed into Bligh Reef, only a few miles away, causing the most devastating oil spill in human history.

The irony of the intentional destruction of coastal forest lands superimposed on the accidental devastation caused by the spill was lost on no one. It was widely acknowledged that coastal deforestation would likely have a more profound, longer-lasting effect on the ecological integrity of the region than would the spill. The juxtaposition of the oil spill and the start of industrial logging in Prince William Sound brought to public attention the fact that the chronic, cumulative destruction over this century of the Pacific Northwest forest, of what had been the largest temperate rainforest on Earth, was more damaging over time than all the acute disturbances such as oil spills combined.

As a result of the spill, Exxon is paying about $1 billion over ten years to the state and federal governments to be used to aid recovery of the ecosystem. Because it will be virtually impossible to directly restore, rehabilitate, or replace most of the damaged resources, it is agreed that the most effective way to aid recovery of Prince William Sound is to prevent further degradation.
—Rick Steiner

A L A S K A

SHERIDAN GLACIER REGION
Photographer, Daniel Dancer, 1992

Immense areas were being clearcut in 1992 by Whitestone, logging for Eyak Native Corporation. Every tree is cut, but only about half the timber is sold. This method is called "high-grading," selecting only logs suitable for overseas export, leaving "imperfect" 500-year-old spruce and hemlock trees to rot.

The spruce-hemlock forests in Prince William Sound represent the northernmost temperate rainforests in the world. At 60° N latitude, the tree line drops to only 1000' elevation in many places and these forests form a very thin band—a living membrane of sorts—between the north coast of the Gulf of Alaska and the steep, glacier-capped coastal mountains.

Temperate rainforests generally occur in areas with a moderate maritime climate; they are limited to relatively narrow bands along coastal margins poleward of 45° N latitude. They cover an area of only 2-3 percent of what tropical rainforests cover, and because they produce high-quality wood, 60-80 percent of these ancient forests have been logged in the last part of this century. The temperate rainforest then is one of the rarest, most severely threatened forest-ecosystem types in the world.

ALASKA

SHERIDAN MOUNTAIN AND SHERIDAN GLACIER
Photographer, Daniel Dancer, 1992

The forest that was cut at the edge of the Sheridan Glacier was a primary forest. The glacier had only recently receded, gradually forming the first forest. The clearcut trees were between 90 and 100 years old.

One-quarter of a mile from the glacier, an old-growth forest containing 450-year-old trees was also clearcut. Old-growth temperate rainforests are in a dynamic equilibrium typified by a wide variety of age classes of trees and large numbers of dead and dying trees. They provide critical habitat for many coastal bird and mammal species, and pure, filtered water necessary for millions of spawning Pacific salmon.

At this latitude, with low solar insolation, long winters, and poor, unstable soils on steep slopes, forest regeneration is a slow process.
—Rick Steiner

B R I T I S H
C O L U M B I A

MT. PAXTON, VANCOUVER ISLAND
Photographer, Vicky Husband, 1989

Mt. Paxton is in northern Vancouver Island. The photo
was taken after clearcutting by International Forest
Products Ltd. (Interfor).

Mount Paxton was clearcut in the early to mid 1980s. A
rare remnant of a Douglas fir ecosystem was included in
the cut. While they were logging they lit a flash fire when
it was quite windy and the fire burnt the whole top of the
mountain. There was a fringe of trees along the bottom
which blew down because of high winds. Also at the bottom there were some burial caves. The name of the area
cut was Kyuquot, which means place of many winds.
—Sharon Chow, Sierra Club of Western Canada

"Nowhere in Canada is the battle to preserve ancient forests more intense and more crucial than on Vancouver
Island, where the remaining ancient temperate rainforest
is one of the natural wonders of the world."
—Jim Cooperman, "Cutting Down Canada"

BRITISH COLUMBIA

ESCALANTE REGION, NORTHERN BOUNDARY, CLAYOQUOT SOUND, VANCOUVER ISLAND
Photographer, Garth Lenz, 1992

This area was once a candidate for national park status. Instead, the Canadian federal government decided to confer park status on a narrow strip of coastal land in the Pacific Rim National Park; in so doing, they protected a mere fragment of the ancient temperate rainforest.

The lands in this photograph became victim to massive clearcutting.

In the Clayoquot Sound area there still remains the largest intact temperate rainforest on Vancouver Island. In April 1993, the government announced its decision to allow massive logging in the temperate rainforests in the Clayoquot Sound region.

The Escalante region of Vancouver Island represents the fate that has already befallen 20 percent of Clayoquot Sound.

BRITISH COLUMBIA

QUEEN CHARLOTTE ISLANDS, SKIDIGATE NARROWS
Photographer, Mark Hobson, 1993

Skidigate Narrows is the route to the west coast of Haida Gwaii (also called Queen Charlotte Islands). The channel is being logged by the multinational Fletcher Challenge. Clearcutting continues from the skyline to the shoreline because Tree Farm Licence #2 is running out of wood.

The channel separates Graham Island from Moresby Island, which is the entry point to Gwaii Haanas National Park Reserve.
—Sharon Chow, Sierra Club of Western Canada

"Unfortunately, a simple clearcut-and-run operation is not very productive for even marketable fiber. Clearcuts, which are severe disturbances, tend to be followed by growth adapted to catastrophe (e.g., brush, pioneer hardwoods, and stump sprouts). Often stands have areas that are deficient of commercially valuable trees or so crowded that it may take 75 or more years before the trees reach a merchantable size. Waiting long enough for the trees to get big enough to cut means losing a sizable volume of shorter-lived and suppressed trees to mortality.

"Through the use of herbicides, and through planting and thinning, industrial foresters can weed out undesirable species, concentrate growth on desirable species, and space the trees so that they reach marketable diameters much sooner. When foresters claim to be increasing productivity through this *intensive management*, they are comparing their softwood fiber yields to that obtainable over the same time period with clearcuts followed by no management. They are not comparing yields to the site's potential, or to yields that might be obtainable with other management systems, such as selection. And they ignore the yield of hardwoods."
—Mitch Lansky, "Myths of the Benign Industrial Clearcut"

BRITISH COLUMBIA

"Forest ecologists have identified fourteen major biogeoclimatic zones within B.C., each of which is further divided into many subzones according to variations in temperature, moisture, and geographical features.

"Despite this recognized ecosystem diversity, the same logging system, clearcutting, is used (over 90 percent of the time) in every area except the drybelt country. Since 1987, logging companies and the Forest Service have been required to return each logged site to a free-growing state where the planted or naturally regenerated trees are taller than the competing vegetation. Up to 20 percent of each site, however, is allowed to be permanently scarred and compacted with landings and skid trails that may never grow a forest again. A 1988 government study of soil degradation concluded that the annual loss of forest productivity to the B.C. economy is approximately $80 million per year, a cost that is increasing a further $10 million every year."
—Jim Cooperman, "Cutting Down Canada"

ALBERNI INLET, VANCOUVER ISLAND
Photographer, Gary Braasch, 1992

BRITISH COLUMBIA

NEAR UCLUELET, VANCOUVER ISLAND
Photographer, Mark Hobson, 1989

MacMillan Bloedel, the largest timber company in British Columbia, has clearcut extensively around Ucluelet, as well as southern, western, and northern Vancouver Island. This massive overcutting has led to enormous pressure by MacMillan Bloedel to cut the last remaining ancient forests in Clayoquot Sound, the Carmanah Valley, the Tsitika, and the Tahsish/Kwois.

The arrival of commercial logging to the island in the 1860s marked the beginning of perhaps the most rapid and dramatic ecological transformation the island has experienced in 10,000 years. After just 130 years of logging, Vancouver Island's ancient temperate rainforests have been reduced to a fraction of their original extent. Logging roads, clearcuts, and tree farms now dominate the island landscape.

Most of the island's best ancient forests—those found at lower elevations and on flat terrain—have already been logged. What ancient rainforest remains tends to be found at higher elevations, on steeper slopes, and in a landscape increasingly fragmented by logging and road building. Logging and road building in this rugged terrain with heavy rainfall often cause serious environmental problems—erosion, landslides, damage to fish-bearing streams, and soil degradation.

BRITISH COLUMBIA

BEFORE AND AFTER SHOT, NAHMINT VALLEY, VANCOUVER ISLAND
Photographer, Clinton Webb, 1989, 1991

The photo of the unlogged ancient forest in the Nahmint Valley was taken on a field trip in September 1989 after anonymous reports from a B.C. Forest Service employee of an unusually high-volume (2500 cubic meters per hectare) Douglas fir stand that was about to be logged. The densely spaced two-to-six-foot-diameter trees, pure Douglas fir stands in many places, were part of a rare forest. The stand, located in Tree Farm Licence #44 held by MacMillan Bloedel, Ltd., was already laced with newly built logging roads and was approved for cutting in 1990.

In March 1991, the photographer, Clinton Webb, paid another visit to Block 516 while gathering evidence for a court challenge by the Sierra Legal Defense Fund to stop logging and road building in the area. The second photo was taken on the same hillside in Block 516.

The court case resulted in a decision that placed some restrictions on the routine practice of logging companies obtaining approval to build roads to cut blocks that had not yet been assessed for nontimber values.

BEFORE

AFTER

BRITISH COLUMBIA

CARMANAH VALLEY, VANCOUVER ISLAND
Photographer, Vicky Husband, 1990

On Vancouver Island, giant Sitka spruce, western red cedar, and western hemlock provide cover for a myriad of plant and animal species.

Remaining ancient forests on the west side of Vancouver Island have been the site of tense confrontations between forest advocates who oppose logging and loggers and government officials who support the practices of the logging industry.

After a major campaign by citizen groups, the government of British Columbia divided the Carmanah Valley in half, making the lower section a park. Logging plans for the upper watershed can result in erosion, creek siltation, and damage to the giant forests of the lower valley.

Lines from "the earth"

when the animals come to us,
    asking for our help,
    will we know what they are saying?
when the plants speak to us
    in their delicate, beautiful language,
    will we be able to answer them?
when the planet herself
    sings to us in our dreams,
    will we be able to wake ourselves, and act?

—Gary Lawless

BRITISH
COLUMBIA

SOUTHERN VANCOUVER ISLAND
Photographer, Garth Lenz, 1989

This area has suffered the abuses of three large logging companies: British Columbia Forest Products (currently Fletcher Challenge of New Zealand), Canadian Pacific, and MacMillan Bloedel. This area constitutes approximately a 7000-hectare continuous clearcut. This size clearcut is completely legal in British Columbia, where there are no laws governing the size of clearcuts and where the Forest Act contains only guidelines as opposed to legally binding regulations.

CANADA—"BRAZIL OF THE NORTH"

A national and global crisis exists in Canada's forests. In Canada, one acre of forest is clearcut every 12 seconds. In Brazil, one acre is cut or burned every 9 seconds.

Industry and government critics of the "Brazil of the North" campaign argue that Canadian deforestation is different because the wood is utilized and the forests are replanted. There is also massive wood waste in the clearcutting of Canada's forest, but there are many other similarities. Consider the following:

Size of Canada: 9.9 million square kilometers
Size of Brazil: 8.5 million square kilometers

Percent of Canada covered by forest: 45%
Percent of Brazil covered by Amazon rainforest: 41%

Hectares of forest cleared in Canada in 1988: 1,021,619 (latest figures available; 1990 will be similar or higher)
Hectares of Brazilian Amazon cleared or burned in 1990: 1,382,000

Amount of productive Canadian forest that is now either barren or "not sufficiently restocked" after clearcutting: 10.3%
Amount of Brazilian rainforest that has disappeared: 12%

Estimated number of Indians & Metis in Canada's boreal forest: 100,000
Estimated number of Indians in the Amazonian forest: 170,000

Amount of forest officially protected in Canada: 2.6%
In Brazil: 9.4%

BRITISH COLUMBIA

CLAYOQUOT SOUND, BRITISH COLUMBIA
Photographer, Garth Lenz, 1992

The provincial government of British Columbia determines forest policy in the province. Recently a conflict of interest was exposed when it was revealed that the government, in April 1993, purchased $50 million of MacMillan Bloedel stock, making the B.C. government the largest known single shareholder of MacMillan Bloedel, which is both the biggest logging company in British Columbia and the company that stands to gain the most from the government's decision concerning Clayoquot Sound.

Over the years, many people have been arrested in B.C. trying to stop clearcut logging. Recent decisions by the provincial government to log the Clayoquot Sound region has again placed people in a difficult position. Only a large public outcry can help save Clayoquot Sound from clearcut logging.

WASHINGTON

CASCADIA BIOREGION:
UPPER SKOKOMISH RIVER DRAINAGE,
OLYMPIC NATIONAL FOREST
Photographer, Trygve Steen, 1990

This area was managed as the "Shelton Sustained Yield Unit" in a collaborative agreement between Simpson Forest Products Company and the U.S. Forest Service. The area was cut between 1973 and 1982. It is an outstanding example of the terrible destruction caused by pursuing the industrial forestry paradigm that calls for converting natural forest ecosystems into tree farms.

The overcutting represented here has contributed to extreme adjustments in cutting rates on Olympic National Forest. In the early 1980s, 400 million board feet of timber were cut annually from Olympic National Forest, 100 million by Simpson alone. A recent recommendation for a maximum allowable annual cut for the entire forest was 40 million board feet, just 10 percent of the peak level.

"Tom Foley and the timber industry are continuing their successful slaughter of America's last remaining Ancient Forests. The wishes of the American people, the entire environmental movement, the federal courts, a new 'green' cabinet, even the power of the president are no match for the entrenched interests of the timber industry as manifested in the congressional timber lobby and the U.S. Forest Service.

"Tom Foley is now the leading power broker, stealing billions from the American public and putting it in the pocket of his timber baron cronies. While other American industries are readjusting to a new era of economic efficiency and environmental protection, Tom Foley keeps billions of dollars of public subsidy flowing to support the outmoded, polluting, destructive and wasteful practices of the timber industry and the Forest Service for continued clearcutting of public forests.

"How much more will Foley be allowed to steal from the public coffers and future generations? Why are his congressional district and the timber industry immune from sharing in economic and environmental restructuring that is taking place across the U.S.?"
—Mark Winstein and Carl Ross, Co-Directors,
Save America's Forests

WASHINGTON

**CASCADIA BIOREGION:
MOUNT BAKER, SNOQUALMIE
NATIONAL FOREST**
Photographer, Elizabeth Feryl, 1990

Land ownership in the area photographed is a checker-board pattern of national forest and private forestland sections. Many of the private sections have their entire 640 acres fully clearcut. National forest sections are fragmented by clearcuts. The cumulative impacts from this pattern of ownership combined with clearcutting are severe, especially because of the loss of natural corridors. The entire landscape is reduced to biologically small refugia. Contrary to assertions of some industrial foresters, this pattern of clearcutting and fragmentation reduces opportunities for increasing diversity of species and species populations of those species dependent on old-growth forests or forests with old-growth characteristics. Clear-cutting and fragmentation provide more habitat for common widespread species such as deer.

"[Of the] original 19 million acres of old-growth in [Washington and Oregon], only 950,000 acres are now protected in wilderness areas or national parks, and another 1.3 million acres of quality old-growth remain unprotected on national forest lands. . . . Ancient forest experts in Oregon estimate that only 2 percent of Oregon's original old-growth is "saved" while another 3 percent remains in limbo. Before settlement by Euro-Americans, there were at least 1.5 million acres of low-elevation (below 2,000 ft. elevation) old-growth forest in western Washington, not including the Olympic Peninsula. Nearly all the low-elevation old-growth that remains in 1992 is on the Mt. Baker–Snoqualmie National Forest —where only 38,400 acres survive. Virtually none of this is designated wilderness.

"On first glance at a map showing [designated] wilderness areas and national parks, Washington does appear to be favored. Of the forty-eight coterminous states, it has the largest percentage of its land area in such protective classifications. Unfortunately, an ecological appraisal of Washington's parks and wildernesses shatters this pleasant illusion. . . . The alpine areas of Washington above timberline are well protected. The ecologically productive, diverse, and fragile old-growth forests at lower elevations are not."
—Dave Foreman, "The Big Woods and Ecological Wilderness Recovery"

WASHINGTON

**CASCADIA BIOREGION:
FROM WEST OF THE
GLACIER VIEW WILDERNESS
MOUNT RAINIER NATIONAL PARK
IN BACKGROUND**
Photographer, Trygve Steen, 1993

In the near portion of the photo, the steep clearcut area is private land in the headwaters of Busy Wild Creek. The fragmented intermediate cut area is administered by the Gifford Pinchot National Forest, and it shows cuts up to the Glacier View Wilderness boundary.

As one of the crown jewels of the U.S. National Park system, Mount Rainier National Park is in a setting of clearcuts. Clearcuts were made around the boundaries of the park. This is an example of a pattern found in many regions of Canada and the U.S. The clearcutting is done in an effort to prevent the expansion of existing parks and to maximize options for timber cutting. This effectively turns protected areas into biological islands, significantly raising the risk of extinction for many organisms that rely on the protected area for habitat.

"Clearcutting is the most dramatic demonstration of the squandering of the Earth's forest capital at the expense of future generations—an unethical form of indenturing our children."
—David Brower

WASHINGTON

CASCADIA BIOREGION: GIFFORD PINCHOT NATIONAL FOREST

Photographer, Trygve Steen, 1990

The extensive area of deforested land was mainly cut by International Paper, Longview Fibre, and Weyerhaeuser. In recent decades, unsustainable cutting rates on private land have resulted in increasing dependence on the national forests for timber. The small amount of remaining forest near the reservoir is on national forest and Washington State Department of Natural Resources lands. The area of forest in the left foreground, fragmented by clearcuts, is Gifford Pinchot National Forest.

The large area of intact forest to the upper left of the deforested area is the Siouxon drainage. The Siouxon watershed is of special significance, because it is one of the largest intact areas of natural, mature second-growth forest in the state of Washington. It is managed by both the Washington State Department of Natural Resources and the Gifford Pinchot National Forest. After a major fire in 1902, this forest contains pockets of old trees, large snags, and downed logs. This area is already developing significant old-growth characteristics and is habitat for the northern spotted owl. The features of a natural forest observable here in the Siouxon constitute an essential baseline for comparing natural forest processes to the consequences of management. The Siouxon will also become true old-growth forest much more quickly than more recently cutover lands.

WASHINGTON

**CASCADIA BIOREGION:
WEYERHAEUSER PRIVATE LANDS,
WEST OF MOUNT SAINT HELENS**
Photographer, Trygve Steen, 1992

The distant squares of forest are on Washington State Department of Natural Resources land. The remaining large area of deforested land is Weyerhaeuser's St. Helens Tree Farm. As more marginal forested areas are being cut, logging is done on increasingly steep slopes, and severe erosion damage has become more common. This image illustrates some of the dramatic adverse consequences of private efforts to convert natural forests into tree farms.

"...The groves are down
              cut down
Groves of Ahab, of Cybele
Pine trees, knobbed twigs
     thick cone and seed
        Cybele's tree this, sacred in groves
Pine of Seami, cedar of Haida
Cut down by the prophets of Israel
     the fairies of Athens
     the thugs of Rome
            both ancient and modern;
Cut down to make room for the suburbs
Bulldozed by Luther and Weyerhaeuser
Crosscut and chainsaw
     squareheads and finns
     high-lead and cat-skidding
Trees down
Creeks choked, trout killed, roads..."
—Gary Snyder, from "Logging"

O R E G O N

SISKIYOU BIOREGION
"BELLY OF THE BEAST"
Photographer, Elizabeth Feryl, 1992

While in the Port Orford, Oregon area, I'd heard of a slide along Bear Creek, so I decided to investigate. Nothing could have prepared me for the estimated 40,000 tons of mud, rock and logging slash that had been dumped on the road and littered the waterway. This "blow out," caused by the headwall of the drainage giving way, had also carved a swath through the hillside thirty feet deep, sixty feet across and a half mile long taking the drainage down to bedrock. We followed this carnage about a quarter mile to the "belly of the beast," the clearcut pictured here. Although the slide had not occurred until March of 1993, the logging took place approximately three years earlier, compliments of Moore, Mill & Lumber Co. of Bandon, Oregon. Prior to that, Moore, Mill & Lumber had closed its mill and exported the logs to Japan. The stumps nearest the creek are Port Orford Cedar, a species highly valued in Japan, and one that is currently threatened by a deadly fungus, *Phytophthora lateralis*, carried by logging trucks and spread along waterways. Because Port Orford Cedar is water tolerant, its roots anchored in creeks and streams, these trees help to stabilize drainages and steep hillsides in this coastal area thus protecting precious fish habitat and spawning grounds. The creek which blew out, now known as Disaster Creek, is a tributary to Bear Creek, a Class I sea-run cutthroat trout stream. Bear Creek empties into Bald Mountain Creek, a Class I steelhead spawning stream, which flows into Elk River—a Federal Wild and Scenic River, Oregon Scenic Waterway, and one of the most productive Chinook salmon rivers in the nation.
—Elizabeth Feryl

"Timber companies over the last decades have been 'strip mining' the Ancient Forests of the Northwest— stripping away billions of board feet annually from public taxpayer land at bargain basement prices. The devastating impacts of this cut-and-run timber company management policy are being felt throughout the commercial and recreational fishing industry."
—Pacific Coast Federation of Fishermen's Associations

O R E G O N

**CASCADIA BIOREGION:
MOUNT HOOD**
Photographer, Gary Braasch, 1989

This is an example of a fragmented forest landscape.

"In no other state can one man take the credit for destroying wilderness as single-handedly as Senator Mark Hatfield of Oregon. It is Hatfield, with his brick-wall arrogance; it is Hatfield, handmaiden to the timber industry; it is Hatfield, the dovish, liberal Republican, who has insured that the Forest Service will not be constrained from its chosen task of liquidating the last Oregon old growth. At every step of the political process, Mark Hatfield has used his legislative mastery and power of seniority to block protection of Wilderness *with trees in it*, to thwart restrictions on Forest Service roading and logging."
—Dave Foreman

"My unanticipated opportunity to draw a visual comparison between my picture of clearcuts at the headwaters of the Svetlaya River and those I see here in Oregon leaves me less shocked than some of the others on our Lighthawk flight. I have seen some other Oregon forests. It's true, not this time and not from an airplane, but as photographs in a newspaper. These pictures showed private forest lands in Oregon wiped clean by clearcuts. The areas resemble deserts. Huge ranges show no evidence of any forest rehabilitation work. This observation should force us, the Russians, who are now streaking forward to Capitalism, to give some very serious thought to the idea of private land holdings and private ownership of natural resources since the Oregon example speaks so well of how privatization of lands, especially of forest lands, can be a very dangerous matter."
—Anatoly Lebedev, Member of Congress,
Primorskii Region, Russian Far East

OREGON

**CASCADIA BIOREGION:
NOHORN CREEK WATERSHED,
BUREAU OF LAND MANAGEMENT
LANDS AND ESTACADA DISTRICT,
MT. HOOD NATIONAL FOREST**
Photographer, Trygve Steen, 1990

This clearcut on federal land is over the ridge from the famed Opal Creek area that is contiguous with the Bull of the Woods Wilderness. On two different occasions, in response to pressure from the logging industry, Oregon's congressional delegation removed the Opal Creek watershed from inclusion in Bull of the Woods Wilderness. Opal Creek contains an outstanding area of old-growth forest. The Opal Creek watershed remains under constant threat of clearcut logging like that shown in this photograph.

"Modern industrial society, with its waves of technological revolution, is between three and four hundred years old, even though it has more ancient roots. It is a society that has tried consciously to break with its ancestral traditions, so as to control Nature and humans through science and technology. Mass education and mass production were made for each other. A civilization based on the idea that humans can master and control Nature for human ends is unique in the history of culture. Modern industrial techniques and models have been applied to almost everything, with large spiritual and environmental costs. Industrial civilization has selectively eliminated deeper values and rich sources of meaning, while destroying large areas of the beautiful and bountiful natural world."
—Alan Drengson, "Remembering the Moral and Spiritual Dimensions of Forests"

OREGON

CASCADIA BIOREGION:
NEAR SWEET HOME, OREGON
Photographer, Gary Braasch, 1984, 1989, 1979, 1991

"If Oregon didn't have a gutsy statewide wilderness group like the Oregon Natural Resources Council, if hundreds of [people] hadn't blockaded bulldozers and chainsaws with their own bodies, politicians and the Forest Service would be even more effective in their service to the timber industry. Without swift enactment of comprehensive legislation to protect all remaining natural forests, without major cuts to the Forest Service road-building budget, without prohibition of below-cost timber sales, without strengthening the Endangered Species Act—without all of this, it is highly likely that the U.S. Forest Service will consume the remaining viable native forest ecosystems before the end of this century."
—Dave Foreman, "The Big Woods and Ecological Wilderness Recovery"

"Road construction is designed on the same short-term, least-cost principles as clearcut logging itself. As a result, high maintenance costs and often reconstruction costs are frequently incurred when roads are used in the future. Also, timber companies are not normally held responsible for damages when 'cost-efficient' methods of road construction result, months or years later, in slope failures, landslides, siltation of water courses, and damage to domestic and agricultural water supplies.

"In my experience, the hidden or additional timber production costs involved with most clearcut operations means that clearcutting actually costs somewhere between 30 and 100 percent more than ecologically responsible partial cutting where roads are constructed to high standards.

"The conventional cost of clearcutting also does not reflect the actual cost of forest restoration or rehabilitation. Soil degradation due to compaction, scraping, gouging, and erosion can result in rehabilitation costs of more than $1,500 per hectare. In many cases, soil cannot be rehabilitated or restored by any means, no matter how much money is spent."
—Herb Hammond, "Clearcutting: Ecological and Economic Flaws"

O R E G O N

CASCADIA BIOREGION: RIDGE, NORTH SIDE, MIDDLE SANTIAM WATERSHED, WEST OF WILLAMETTE NATIONAL FOREST
Photographer, Trygve Steen, 1990

The top right corner of this photograph shows fragmentation on the Willamette National Forest. In contrast, the ridge at the top left side of the photograph shows deforestation on the edge of a large block of lands owned by Weyerhaeuser Corporation.

The Weyerhaeuser holdings in this area total over 2,700 acres. Roading, yarding, and erosion damage on the steep hillsides in this watershed have been severe over the past several decades.

"We believe that all things are connected, that whatever we do to the Earth, we do to ourselves. If we destroy our remaining wild places, we will ultimately destroy our identity with the Earth; wilderness has values for human-kind which no scientist can synthesize, no economist can price, and no technological distraction can replace.

"We believe that we should protect in perpetuity these wild places, not only for our own sake, but for the sake of the plants and animals and for the good of sustaining the Earth. The forests, like us, are living things: wilderness should exist intact solely for its own sake; no human justification, rationale, or excuse is needed."
—Excerpt from "The Cathedral Forest Wilderness Declaration"

OREGON

CASCADIA BIOREGION: MT. JEFFERSON, WILLAMETTE NATIONAL FOREST
Photographer, Sandy Lonsdale, 1991

The Willamette National Forest, south and west of Mt. Jefferson, is the biggest timber producer in the National Forest system. Congressionally mandated rates of cut in the 1980s resulted in a fragmented and abused forest.

With 60 to 100 inches of annual precipitation, erosion from logging roads and clearcuts has removed topsoil and damaged aquatic habitat.

Besides clearcutting, salvage logging has been used by the Forest Service to further disrupt the natural changes in the forest. Using false "emergency" decrees, fire salvage sales are often rushed through planning processes with minimal environmental impact analyses. Salvage timber sales are often excluded from citizen appeals. Ancient forests of the Pacific Northwest evolved with fire, with many species adapted to or even dependent on fire for their natural health and regeneration. The thick bark and tall canopies of old-growth Douglas-fir trees, for example, enable them to survive all but the most severe burns. Salvage logging removes the survivors in burned forests, not the "victims" of fires. By salvaging timber, agencies such as the Forest Service have been scuttling the ecosystem, causing degradation to wildlife habitat, watersheds, and soils. Trees killed by fire are vital elements of the ecosystem and serve critical roles in the land's natural recovery. Fire-killed snags are essential habitat structure for threatened and endangered species such as the pileated woodpecker. Snags also provide important solar and wind protection for adjacent live trees and their natural regeneration. When snags fall into waterways or onto the ground, they provide habitat for fish, fungi, insects, rodents, and other mammals. Downed logs also help retain soil from eroding down steep slopes, and as they slowly rot, they add new organic matter and nutrients to the soil. As scientists continue to discover the multitude of ecological functions played by dead and downed trees, fire salvage logging has been revealed to be yet another smokescreen for wholesale timber extraction and industrial forest management.

O R E G O N

UMATILLA NATIONAL FOREST
Photographer, Trygve Steen, 1992

Except for the top left, which is the North Fork Umatilla Wilderness, this photo shows extensive fragmentation from clearcutting in eastern Oregon's mixed conifer forests. The pattern of clearcut fragmentation seen here is common on the national forests of eastern Oregon and Washington. It occurs because of national forest limitations on cut size coupled with the high rates of logging that have occurred in recent years. Clearcutting is especially unsuitable and damaging in this high and dry region.

O R E G O N

KLAMATH-SISKIYOU BIOREGION: PISTOL RIVER

Photographer, Daniel Dancer, 1990

The coast range of Oregon was one of the first targets of logging. Only remnant small stands of ancient trees remain in a few Oregon state parks in the coast range. Virtually no large areas of native, ancient forests remain on private or state forestlands. Clearcutting remains the method of choice for cutting the tree plantations that have replaced the original natural forest.

In southwestern Oregon and northern California, under U.S. Forest Service management, thousands of acres of the Klamath-Siskiyou forests have been clearcut. These complex, diverse forests continue to be replaced by brushfields. Many reforestation attempts have failed. Forest fragmentation is a major threat to the region's biological heritage.

The remaining roadless wildlands of the Klamath-Siskiyou are slated for major logging, road building, and mining. These practices threaten some of the most botan-ically diverse areas, free-flowing rivers, and wild fish runs in the region.

The Klamath-Siskiyou region contains the greatest con-centration of federally classified wild and scenic rivers in the United States. These rivers, including portions of the Rogue, Illinois, and Smith rivers, were named to the national system because of their outstanding water qual-ity, wild salmon and steelhead habitat, and recreational opportunities. Several more pristine rivers on federal lands in the region, endangered by mining and logging, are currently awaiting review for similar designation.

The Klamath-Siskiyou region is one of the few places in the U.S. Pacific Northwest where large-scale conservation of biological diversity is possible. Designated wilderness, current roadless wildlands, and wild and scenic river cor-ridors could be linked to create a biodiversity reserve of nearly a million acres.

In 1992, the International Union for the Conservation of Nature identified the Klamath-Siskiyou region as one of seven regions in North America critical for conservation, because of its "global botanical significance."

CALIFORNIA

KLAMATH-SISKIYOU BIOREGION: TURWAR CREEK, DEL NORTE COUNTY
Photographer, Trygve Steen, 1992

Extensive deforestation has occurred in both Turwar Creek and the adjacent Hunter Creek watersheds. Formerly part of Six Rivers National Forest, these lands were traded into private ownership in 1968 in exchange for private lands included in Redwood National Park. This exchange resulted in a net loss of old-growth redwood in federal management during the creation of Redwood National Park. Since then, deforestation has occurred on nearly all of the 14,000 acres containing old-growth redwood forest that were involved in this exchange.

Both Turwar and Hunter creeks flow into the Klamath River. High sediment delivery severely damages salmon spawning and rearing habitat by resulting in unstable spawning gravels, by inhibiting production of invertebrates that are food for juvenile salmon, and by keeping riparian zones from recovering, which contributes to high water temperatures that are unsuitable for salmon.

Scientists conclude there is a very real prospect of widespread extinction of Pacific salmon and steelhead stocks. The Klamath River, largest in northern California, has been characterized as "severely ecologically distressed."

CALIFORNIA

**KLAMATH-SISKIYOU BIOREGION:
HEADWATERS, HUMBOLDT COUNTY**
Photographer, Doug Thron, 1993

The Headwaters forest complex includes the only significant stands of ancient redwood forests in private
ownership. In 1993 these forestlands were controlled
by Maxxam Corporation, headed by Charles Hurwitz,
a Houston financier. After acquiring Pacific Lumber
Company in 1986 for about $900 million in a buy-out
financed largely with junk bonds handled by Drexel
Burnham Lambert, Maxxam has been in the center
of economic and environmental controversies. Citizen
groups have filed numerous lawsuits under state and
federal law to uphold the public interest in wildlife
habitat, protection of endangered species, water quality, and fisheries. Citizen groups have asked Congress
to establish a conservation and restoration reserve
on a portion of lands controlled by Pacific Lumber
Corporation.

CALIFORNIA

KLAMATH-SISKIYOU BIOREGION: SALMON RIVER, KLAMATH NATIONAL FOREST
Photographer, Trygve Steen, 1993

Studies commissioned by the U.S. Forest Service in the 1970s predicted that forestlands in Oregon and northwestern California were being depleted of merchantable timber and that drastic declines in timber yields from national forests would occur in the early 1990s. These studies were only based on timber supply and did not take into account efforts to protect habitat of endangered species or provide for the integrity of the forest and watershed systems or protection of spawning habitat for salmon and steelhead or the possibility of catastrophic forest fires.

This photo illustrates the added impact of salvage logging after a massive fire that occurred in 1987. While fires can be very damaging, what is left after a fire still has many values for the forest ecosystem. The dead trees provide a more gentle environment by shading the ground, decreasing wind, and allowing increased humidity. The larger trees also provide habitat as standing snags or as downed trees on the forest floor.

Salvage sales after fires typically remove all of the larger trees because of their commercial value and remove enough of the total number of dead trees to make the environment more severe. In addition, soils already stressed by the fire may be damaged by roads built to extract the timber.

CALIFORNIA

**LAST CHANCE CREEK,
PLUMAS NATIONAL FOREST**
Photographer, Jenny Hager, 1992

After fire and clearcutting, erosion gullies appeared in
Last Chance Creek, eastern Plumas National Forest.
These are sensitive soils. An unusual storm event scoured
the watershed and washed away massive amounts of
topsoil after logging.

Forest Service management ignored the constraints
of the natural world. The Forest Service should have
planned for a significant storm. It will take several
thousand years before this region will, under the best
circumstance, return to its original vegetated state
prior to logging approved by the Forest Service.
—Jenny Hager

CALIFORNIA

SHASTA BIOREGION: WEST SLOPES OF MT. SHASTA, SHASTA-TRINITY NATIONAL FOREST
Photographer, Trygve Steen, 1991

Mt. Shasta is a majestic landmark in northern California. When John Muir climbed Mt. Shasta in the nineteenth century he marveled at the stands of ancient red fir. Shasta-Trinity National Forest has allowed logging of red fir and has planted pine plantations on lower elevations.

The red fir have been cut to nearly tree line. An attempt was made to plant pine plantations at lower elevations. The large, nearly-bare areas were logged years ago. This extensive inability to regrow trees is a classic example of reforestation failure.

CALIFORNIA

CHEROKEE CREEK, TAHOE NATIONAL FOREST
Photographer, Jenny Hager, 1992

Tahoe National Forest has mixed ownership in a checkerboard fashion. The region was intensively logged on both public and private lands since the early 1890s. During the 1970s and 1980s, many of these lands were clearcut.

In the early 1990s, the only remaining old-growth stands are in steep canyons. The environmental community strongly opposed continued clearcutting.

Both representatives of the Forest Service and private industry have publicly admitted they made mistakes by overcutting and by using inappropriate post-harvest practices that led to soil damage. The forestlands were cut far in excess of sustainable rates.

"The conventional cost of clearcutting... does not reflect the actual social cost. Water degradation forces rural people to relocate and forces urban people to spend millions of dollars treating their water to safe drinking standards. The loss of biological diversity and the associated loss of wilderness threatens our very survival and results in fewer opportunities for economic diversity in the future. Clearcut logging forecloses on forest uses, from tourism and public recreation to mushroom picking and berry gathering. When forest uses are carried out in an ecologically responsible manner, they provide readily sustainable employment and revenues year after year—as long as the forest is there. In other words, the social costs that government and the timber industry ignore today are simply postponed to future generations."
—Herb Hammond, "Clearcutting: Ecological and Economic Flaws"

CALIFORNIA

**LAST CHANCE CREEK,
PLUMAS NATIONAL FOREST**
Photographer, Jenny Hager, 1992

Photographer Jenny Hager was shown this sight in California's great Sierra Nevada mountain range by local citizens who were seriously concerned with the management of public forests in the Plumas area. U.S. Forest Service district rangers often face pressure from logging company executives, local community members, and even congressional representatives to approve timber harvesting plans before they can be properly reviewed. Timber extraction in the mountains is complicated by

the slope of the land, where topsoil becomes vulnerable to heavy erosion after intensive logging. As seen here in Last Chance Creek, tons of soil, now without trees or undergrowth that help position this essential layer, slid from the heavily-logged hillsides after a single storm.

The fact that people, that is, citizens of the local community, the U.S. Forest Service, or even logging interests, will not be able to make a living from this area for many, many years provides a textbook example of the failure of such practices to be sustainable and stands as a foreboding testimony to the creek's name.

"We must learn to reinvest part of nature's capital, such as large merchantable logs and large snags, in the maintenance of forest health, so that our saw mills will have, in perpetuity, a sustainable harvest of timber from fertile, healthy, stable soils, clean water, clean air, and clear sunlight. To reinvest means to give up some of the short-term profits in order to ensure the long-term sustainability of the forests for future generations."
—Chris Maser, "Sustainable Forestry"

**TWO SEQUOIAS, REDWOOD CAMP,
SEQUOIA NATIONAL FOREST**
Photographer, Jenny Hager, 1992

The watersheds of the Sierra Nevada drain into the great Central Valley of California, one of the most productive agricultural areas in the world.

Soil loss is a major problem in the southern part of the Sierra Nevada range. After logging in the Sequoia National Forest, where the dry topsoil is easily turned over when walking through, hooves and appetites of grazing cattle further scour the land, discouraging undergrowth from returning.

"Only in the last millennium has the ebb of forests been incessant and increasingly global in extent. Most alarming, the loss of forests to the axe and saw is occurring at an ever faster rate. What replaces forest today is habitat for few living things besides domesticated plants and animals, and weeds. Deforestation and forest conversion are of crisis proportions."
—Reed Noss, "A Sustainable Forest is a Diverse and Natural Forest"

BRITISH COLUMBIA

SEVEN-STOREY CLEARCUT, MAMQUAM RIVER
Photographer, Randy Stoltmann, 1989

This is an example of "progressive clearcutting" where "separate" cut blocks adjacent to one another become one massive clearcut. This one is over six square miles in extent. This style of "progressive clearcutting" is being replaced by smaller "dispersed cutblocks," a practice that spreads smaller clearcuts across a larger area—thus fragmenting the forests even faster.

The "seven-storey clearcut" was created over a period of twenty years. Only patchy regrowth has occurred.

"The practice of forestry began with the idea that forests are perpetual producers of commodities. To capitalize on the harvest of such commodities as a way of life, there had to be a disciplined, economic rationale. The *soil-rent theory* became that rationale.

"The soil-rent theory—a classic, liberal, economic theory—is a planning tool devised by Johann Christian Hundeshagen in the early nineteenth century to maximize industrial profits. Since its unfortunate adoption by foresters, it has become the overriding objective for forestry worldwide. But the soil-rent theory is based on six flawed primary assumptions: (1) that the depth and fertility of the soil in which the forest grows is an ecological constant; (2) that the quality and quantity of the precipitation reaching the forest is an ecological constant; (3) that the quality of the air infusing the forest is an ecological constant; (4) that the amount and quality of solar energy available to the forest is an ecological constant; (5) that climatic stability is an ecological constant; and (6) that biodiversity is an ecological constant.

"By falsely assuming that all ecological variables are economic constants, one is misled to think that all one must do to have an economically sustainable tree farm is calculate the species of tree, the rate of growth, and the age of harvest that will give the highest rate of economic return in the shortest time for the amount of economic capital invested in a given site—the soil-rent theory.

"Traditional forestry is exploitation of the economic value of trees....If the twentieth-century exploitation of forests is to be replaced by a healing of forests in the twenty-first century, forestry as a profession must be founded on documented ecological truth."
—Chris Maser, "The Twenty-First–Century Forester"

BRITISH COLUMBIA

SOUTH CENTRAL MAINLAND COAST
Photographer, Herb Hammond, 1992

Extensive soil loss occurs within clearcuts themselves, not only from logging roads. Roads are progressively extended up the valleys and up the slopes to remove "lift after lift" of trees on the hillsides, until the forest is entirely gone. Overall habitat loss and ecosystem degradation occurs.

The logging industry likes to suggest that road-building activities are the cause of landslides, not clearcutting. Not only do clearcuts, particularly on steep wet slopes, result directly in landslide activity, but one can also argue that landslides that originate from roads are caused indirectly by clearcutting. The logging industry would not build roads into these areas were it not for the desire to clearcut timber.

—Herb Hammond

BRITISH COLUMBIA

BOWRON VALLEY NEAR PRINCE GEORGE
Photographer, Galen Rowell, 1992

"The Bowron Clearcut: Well, I haven't been to the moon, but I know that it takes a day to drive through this atrocity! The Bowron Clearcut covers an area of 1600 square kilometers! NO LIE. Standing on top of Two Sisters mountain near Bowron Lake Park looking north is very sobering. As far as your eye can see—is clearcut. In response to all of the public uproar [this cut created], the only action the Ministry of Forests and Industry has taken to soothe our anger and fear was to invent a slogan: 'What you are seeing, folks, is not the world's largest clearcut, it is the world's largest tree plantation!' What they fail to mention are the difficulties they are having with regeneration. I have talked to tree planters who have been sent back to the same sites for six years in a row—without success."
—Doug Radies and Ocean Hellman/Silver Moon Educational Projects

B R I T I S H
C O L U M B I A

NEAR MACKENZIE
Photographer, Garth Lenz, 1992

Despite election promises to reform and change the forest industry in British Columbia, the government's Forest Policy continues to be: "CUT—SLASH & BURN." More than half of Canada's timber production is clearcut in British Columbia. Now, the large multinational corporations have moved to the remote, northeastern part of the province; the BOREAL ZONE.

In Canada's sparsely populated northern regions the assault on its boreal forests has gone on largely undocumented. The Boreal is characterized by shallow soils and harsh climate: regeneration is much slower and more difficult. There are clearly major environmental implications to logging the northern Boreal. Unfortunately, by the time society finds out—it may be too late.
—Colleen McCrory, The Valhalla Society

"British Columbia contains one-fifth of Canada's forested land base and nearly one-half of the country's timber volume. There is probably more forest wilderness remaining in B.C. than anywhere else in North America. Within this mountainous province is a rich tapestry of diverse forest ecosystems that range from magnificent, ancient temperate rainforests to stunted high-elevation stands of spruce to ponderosa pine growing within dry interior grasslands."
—Jim Cooperman, "Cutting Down Canada"

BRITISH COLUMBIA

CHILCOTIN CARIBOU REGION
Photographer, Herb Hammond, 1989

This is a 600+ hectare clearcut. I like the image of the dead natural lodgepole pine in the foreground. This is the fate that awaits many planted or naturally regenerated trees in this harsh, cold, dry environment.

This area is a sub-boreal spruce ecosystem which consists of many stands of lodgepole pine and white spruce. The area has been extensively clearcut under the guise of mountain pine beetle "control." In reality, this type of clearcutting will only recreate a more serious beetle problem in the future due to homogenization of the landscape and forest stands. Mother Nature was going about diversification with random beetle activity throughout the landscape. This natural change would have resulted in a diversity of age classes, species composition, and overall landscape mosaics. This diversity would have provided stability for these dry, cold ecosystems. Instead, the timber industry is homogenizing the landscape in a way that degrades everything from water quality to animal habitat.
—Herb Hammond

BRITISH COLUMBIA

CARIBOU MOUNTAINS
Photographer, Doug Radies, 1991

High-elevation logging on the western slopes of the Caribou Mountains, in the central interior of British Columbia. Note that Weldwood of Canada Ltd. has cut right through slide chutes and just below tree line—prime habitat for grizzly and old-growth–dependent caribou.

"Virtually all of the headwaters of the Quesnel River watershed are scheduled for clearcut logging within the next five years. Never before has the overall health of the Quesnel system been so seriously threatened. In an attempt to feed overbuilt mills with a dwindling wood supply, logging companies are now moving into the steep upper reaches of the Quesnel watershed. Adding to this atrocity is the fact that logging in these remote areas is heavily subsidized by the people of British Columbia. The Ministry of Forests claims that the majority of the forested valleys are comprised of 'decadent' and 'overmature' cedar and hemlock. They claim that it is in the best interest of all British Columbians that these undesirable old growth forests are liquidated 'as quickly as possible' and replaced with young 'productive forest stands.' What they fail to mention is that the majority of the cedar and hemlock is burned or buried on site, while the high quality mountain spruce and fir is taken for stumpage rates as low as 25 cents per cubic meter."
—Ocean Hellman

ALBERTA

WOOD BUFFALO NATIONAL PARK
Photographer, Garth Lenz, 1992

The photographer, Garth Lenz, borrowed a boat from a native friend and went 30 miles down the Peace River photographing. "From the river one has no idea what lies behind the 10 to 15 meters of foliage along the banks. Only after climbing the banks and crossing the 'beauty strip' does one enter into the massive destruction crisscrossed with roads. A traveler on the Peace River would have a deluded sense of forest well-being," said Lenz.

The natives warned Lenz not to eat the fish from the river as the river is poisoned with dioxins from the Daishowa pulp mill upstream. This has highly impacted the native way of subsistence and made them dependent on expensive imported foodstuffs.

"What kind of future do we leave our children and grandchildren in this field of stumps and barren land?"
—Colleen McCrory, The Valhalla Society

ALBERTA

JAMES RIVER, WEST OF SUNDRE
Photographer, Gary Braasch, 1992

In spite of severe depletion and fragmentation of forest-lands like this, the Alberta government has no intention of slowing down. Billions of dollars of new pulp mills—some of the largest in the world—have locked Albertans into having their entire province stripped of trees. Two of the companies are Daishowa and Alberta Pacific. The land area of these two companies is over 100,000 square kilometers, or 15 percent of Alberta. This area is larger than the land areas of Nova Scotia, Prince Edward Island, Massachusetts, Delaware, Rhode Island, and Connecticut together. If these pulp decisions are not reversed, the consequence will be severe environmental damage for generations to come.

"When a forest is disrupted by a checkerboard of clear-cuts, large areas of contiguous or interior forest habitat are transformed into a number of isolated forest hab-itats—forest 'islands' separated by clearcuts, logging roads, highways, and other human-created disturbances.

"Nowhere is fragmentation more obvious or critical than in riparian ecosystems. Forests adjacent to creeks, rivers, lakes, and wetlands are part of riparian chains, forming a network that connects the forest across the landscape. Logging a riparian forest is like taking links out of a chain—things tend to fall apart."
—Herb Hammond, "Clearcutting: Ecological and Economic Flaws

ALBERTA

UPPER OLDMAN RIVER AREA, ROCKY MOUNTAINS
Photographer, Gary Braasch, 1992

"The government of Alberta has given pulp-and-paper corporations the cutting rights to 221,000 square kilometers of its boreal forest, an area almost the size of Great Britain. In total, almost $5 billion of new pulp mill developments—some of the largest in the world—have been built in northern Alberta. No independent environmental impact studies have been done on the forest management plans. The two largest Forest Management Agreements (FMAs)—which allow access to the timber for twenty years with an option for another twenty years—were awarded to firms controlled by Japanese interests, Diashowa and ALPAC (Mitsubishi and Honshu Paper). The Alberta government has given huge subsidies to encourage these mega-developments with nearly a half billion dollars in loan guarantees and millions more for roads, rail lines, and other infrastructure—in return Alberta will receive only minuscule stumpage royalties.

"The profits will end up in Japan; a stand of sixteen aspen trees fifty feet tall will fetch Alberta $.90; when converted to pulp they are then worth $590; and as paper they are worth up to $1,250 (1993 prices). The companies can borrow money using their FMAs as collateral and then invest it elsewhere. The government proudly points to job creation but the few jobs available in the high-tech pulp production facilities and timber harvesting are costing the government a few hundred thousand dollars each! In addition to being an economic boondoggle, these FMAs will create an ecological disaster."
—Jim Cooperman, "Cutting Down Canada"

WOOD BUFFALO NATIONAL PARK
Photographer, Garth Lenz, 1992

Wood Buffalo National Park is an area bordering Alberta and the Northwest Territories, an area larger than Switzerland and accessible by one dirt road. It is the second largest National Park in the world, designated a United Nations World Heritage. Few North Americans know that this National Park has become a patchwork of clearcuts. There has been logging in Wood Buffalo from the end of World War II until June 12, 1992: most of this old-growth boreal has already been cut.

In 1992 the Sierra Legal Defense Fund in conjunction with Canadian Parks and the Wilderness Society initiated a court action and stopped logging in Wood Buffalo National Park. The basis of the case was Section 4 of the National Parks Act, which states: ''The National Parks shall be maintained and made use of as to leave them unimpaired for the enjoyment of future generations.''
—Colleen McCrory, The Valhalla Society

SASKATCHEWAN

WIGGENS BAY CANOE LAKE
Photographer, Garth Lenz, 1992

Desertification from clearcut logging.

In a remote corner of northern Saskatchewan, 350 kilometers of north of Saskatoon, the Cree natives of this region have mounted the longest running blockade in Canadian history in an attempt to protect their traditional way of life. A way of life that is in conflict with the large scale clearcutting of these treaty lands as shown in this photograph. These lands are currently being cut by Mistik Management on behalf of Norsask Forest products.

In May of 1992 the Sakaw-Aski Aboriginal Elders council decided the only way they could protect their treaty lands was to mount a blockade. On July 1st of 1992 (Canada Day) the Canadian Government responded to this peaceful assertion of treaty rights by sending in a SWAT team of over 80 heavily armed RCMP officers. After surrounding the camp for three days and searching in vain for any sign of weapons, they arrested 29 elders and two pregnant women. Many of those arrested were led away handcuffed, with automatic weapons trained on them.

Cecilia Iron, a 72-year-old elder who was one of those arrested, reflects the aspirations of the protesters when she explains, "All I care about is saving something for the future generations. I don't care to have many things as long as I have a roof and a little food." Apparently even these modest aspirations are at odds with the goals of government and industry.
—Garth Lenz

"Mismanagement of the Saskatchewan forests is evident, and some mills have closed because of lack of an adequate timber supply. At present, over one million hectares of cutover land is classified as NSR (not sufficiently restocked), with little available information on its condition.

"Forest managers claim that clearcutting mixed-wood forests mimics the natural forest fires that sweep through boreal forests. Critics, however, point out the potential ecological damage from short rotations that convert mixed-wood stands to hardwoods and prevent old-growth forests from redeveloping."
—Jim Cooperman, "Cutting Down Canada"

MANITOBA

NOPOMING PROVINCIAL PARK
Photographer, Hendrik Herfst, 1992

Manitoba has one of the worst records in Canada for protecting its forest—less than 2% of its lands and waters are free from industrial development. Friends of Nopoming have been trying to stop clearcut logging in Nopoming Provincial Park but it is in its final stages of logging and some of the last remnants of old growth boreal in this region could soon be destroyed.

In the spring of 1989, the Manitoba government announced the expansion and sale of the largest forest management license ever granted in Canada: 108,000 km.—an area the size of Ohio. If this project goes ahead 40% of Manitoba's productive timber will be cut. The annual allowable cut would increase from 600,000 cu. metres to a shocking 3.4 million cu. metres of wood/year. Thousands of miles of new roads would be pushed into Manitoba's North. Lack of financing has temporarily put this project on hold. The combined expansions for Manitoba, Saskatchewan and Alberta equal well over 10 billion dollars worth of new mills (which could be built without the requirement of any Environmental Assessments). This project threatens the very existence of the Northern Boreal: North America's "great lung."
—Colleen McCrory, The Valhalla Society

GORDON COUSINS FOREST
Photographer, Barry Tessman, 1992

Originally one of Canada's most densely forested provinces, it has a long history of exploitation that has seen forests of white pine decimated in little more than a century. When the Ontario Ministry of Natural Resources looked for candidate wildernesss parks in southern Ontario, they were unable to find any wild land left except for two small tracts that were later dropped from the running—such is the devastation. There is very little original forest remaining in southern Ontario.

"Ontario's boreal forest has been systematically logged since the 1920s when mills were built in the north to convert the long fibers of the spruce trees into pulp and paper. The largest clearcut in Canada may well be located in northern Ontario on land that was leased to Spruce Falls Power and Paper, formerly a subsidiary of Kimberley-Clark, a supplier of *The New York Times*. The size of this vast tract of connected clearcuts was determined from satellite photos to be equivalent to half the size of Prince Edward Island, some 2,693 square kilometers (269,300 hectares). There is some softwood forest regeneration in this enormous clearcut, but much of the area is in early successional poplar. This massive cut has affected soil productivity, water flow and quality, and wildlife habitat.

"Communities throughout northern Ontario are beginning to pay the price for forest mismanagement. Several pulp mills, the economic engines of most northern towns, are closing down. These mills have depleted their readily accessible mature conifers. With declining corporate profits, transnational corporations move their assets to more lucrative sectors of their investment portfolios such as real estate or tropical forest extraction."
—Jim Cooperman, "Cutting Down Canada"

QUEBEC

LA VERENDRYE PROVINCIAL RESERVE
Photographer, Perry Beaton, 1992

"Quebec's transition of a natural forest to an industrial forest began in the mid 1600s and continues through to today. This long history of clearcut logging has given Quebec its notorious record of poor forestry management. In 1989, a forest official was quoted admitting that 'Quebec's forests are in such a pitiful state, we are facing shortages in many regions.'"
—Paul Senez and Michel Goudreau

THE ECONOMIC FALLACIES OF CLEARCUTTING

"Economic Fallacy #1: Clearcutting is the most economically efficient way of cutting and growing trees.

"Economic Reality: Clearcutting considers only short-term timber economics, not long-term forest economics. . . .

"Economic Fallacy #2: Clearcutting provides sustainable, expanding employment.

"Economic Reality: The evolution of clearcutting has resulted in the loss of employment and the loss of dignified, meaningful work. . . .

"Economic Fallacy #3: Clearcutting rids us of valueless, decadent wood.

"Economic Reality: Clearcutting of old-growth forests around the world removes the highest quality, highest volume, highest valued wood from healthy forest ecosystems that have functioned successfully for millennia without human intervention. . . .

"Economic Fallacy #4: Clearcutting is necessary to compete in the global economy.

"Economic Reality: Powerful transnational timber interests impose their short-term economic objectives on local communities, resulting in degraded local forests and degraded local communities."

—Herb Hammond, "Clearcutting: Ecological and Economic Flaws"

NEW BRUNSWICK

**NEAR FUNDY NATIONAL PARK,
NEW BRUNSWICK**
Photographer, John Cooper, 1992

"New Brunswick's Fundy National Park is a 20,700 hectare "island" surrounded by extensive forest. Logging
outside the park boundaries has degraded the quality
and reduced the extent of the aquatic habitats within
the park as a result of sedimentation and contamination
from insecticides and herbicides."
—Federal Government of Canada, State of the
Environment Report, 1991

"Forests have sustained themselves for over 350 million
years with no help from humans. This is not to say they
have stayed the same; in fact, they have never sat still.
Some people argue that, because change is natural, the
massive changes in forest cover and structure occurring
today as a result of human activity are nothing to be
alarmed about. These people are wrong.... Deforestation
and forest conversion are of crisis proportions."
—Reed Noss, "A Sustainable Forest Is a Diverse and
Natural Forest"

NEWFOUNDLAND

NEAR COOK'S BROOK, SOUTHWEST OF CORNERBROOK
Photographer, Barry Tessman, 1992

"After a century of abusive logging practices and virtually no reforestation, the Newfoundland forest industry is in crisis. Past practices have included high-grading, cutting the most cheaply accessible trees, and more recently, cutting immature, second-growth trees in areas close to the mills. As the costs of obtaining wood fiber increased, Abitibi-Price began to encroach on coastal Crown forest areas, thus displacing local operators from their traditional logging areas. The original legislation prohibited the issuing of timber licenses within three miles of tidal waters to ensure adequate timber supplies for local communities. This policy was circumvented without public notification.

"After laying waste to the island of Newfoundland, the pulp-and-paper industry is now looking toward the black spruce and balsam fir of Labrador. These forests are characterized by poor growth, patchy stands, fragile sites, and exceptionally long growing cycles. In the past, forestry operations have been marginal, with the bulk of the logs exported to European pulp mills. On Labrador there are huge stacks of logs abandoned by operators who went bankrupt.

"Labrador is Innu Nation land that has never been ceded to any government by the original people, yet logging plans and operations have proceeded without any consideration of their cultural needs. In September of 1991, the Innu Nation blockaded a logging road to prevent expansion of the forest road network. The Innu Nation released a report by an independent forest consultant who found that forest management practices had little or no regard for scientific forest management or other uses; that artificially regenerated sites, composed mainly of the non-indigenous species of jack pine and larch, were of questionable value; that the allowable annual cut was extremely high and unrealistic; that streams and water bodies were poorly protected; and that there was no consideration of traditional hunting and trapping grounds. The Innu people continued to blockade the roads, 'to protect their hunting, fishing, and gathering way of life for generations to come.'"
—Jim Cooperman, "Cutting Down Canada"

NOVA SCOTIA

CAPE BRETON
Photographer, Barry Tessman, 1992

On the Keppoch Plateau, an area of 19,200 acres, 90 percent of the area was clearcut. These areas have been converted to softwood plantations through artificial regeneration and extensive use of chemical herbicides.

On the Cape Breton Highlands Plateau, a region of 123,000 acres, 95 percent has been clearcut, most between 1976 and 1986.

Three large transnational pulp-and-paper companies control huge tracts of Nova Scotia land. Together they are responsible for converting Nova Scotia native forests into single-species fiber farms for pulp mills.

"Nova Scotia has embraced a pulpwood forestry policy, seen as necessary to feed the province's pulp-and-paper industry. The once diverse mixed-wood forests have been simplified by industry to softwood plantations that are supposedly ready for cutting in thirty-five to forty-five years. Considerable government and industry money is spent to convince the public of the myth that Nova Scotia is a 'showcase for reforestation and forest management.' But the reality for anyone who walks through the clear-cuts or drives the logging roads . . . is wanton forest destruction.

"Through clearcutting, conversion to softwood planta-tions, and use of chemical and biological sprays, there has been a serious loss of biological diversity and an impoverishment of wildlife."
—Jim Cooperman, "Cutting Down Canada"

M A I N E

APPALACHIAN HIGHLANDS BIOREGION: ALLAGASH WATERWAY
Photographer, John Cooper, 1992

I was completely unprepared to witness the extensive devastation of the Maine Northern Forest. Seen from the air, it was obvious that no long-term plan was ever implemented as every single tree was leveled, with the exception of the so-called 'beauty strips,' the 100 meters width of forest remaining next to the Allagash Waterway. It is insulting for paper companies that clearcut all but these narrow bits to believe that the impression of a 'wilderness' to vacationing canoeists justifies the thoughtless and complete wiping-out of a true wilderness. As seen from the air, the 'beauty strips' run the complete length of the Allagash...the visual equivalent of placing painted facades along the edge of the South Bronx. From the air, it was also quite easy to see the extensive erosion caused by clearcutting...over the Bay of Fundy in Canada we could see the soil run-off flowing directly into the Bay.

During the several days I spent in northern Maine, I tried to reach some of the clearcuts by land but discovered that access to almost all of northern Maine is controlled by the paper companies that own the land and access is restricted to their private road system. Thus it is not that easy to experience the devastation from the ground.
—John Cooper

Nearly one-third of the state of Maine is owned by large forest products corporations. From 1986 to 1991, they clearcut more than 1,000 square miles of the state's Northern Forest, an area equal in size to the state of Rhode Island.

The cougar, timber wolf, and caribou, all gone from Maine, are indirect victims of clearcut logging over many years. Logging roads gave hunters easy access to the animals and cutting big trees reduced the supply of lichen, the caribou's main diet.

While trees grow back after clearcutting, the *forest* does not return.

**APPALACHIAN HIGHLANDS BIOREGION:
MOUNT KATAHDIN,
BAXTER STATE PARK**
Photographer, Alex MacLean, 1989

"The largest market for trees in northern Maine is the pulp mills. The trees most favored by these mills are red spruce and balsam fir, species that have long fibers ideal for making strong paper.

"Although Maine is a relatively small state, its eight million acres of industry-owned forestland is the largest concentration of private forest acreage in the United States—far more than the five million acres of private forestland in second-place Oregon."
—Mitch Lansky, "Myths of the Benign Industrial Clearcut"

NORTHERN APPALACHIAN HIGHLANDS BIOREGION: SOUTH OF MOOSELOOKMEGUNTIC LAKE

Photographer, Alex MacLean, 1992

Much of the Maine woods is part of what the Canadians call the "Acadian forest"—a complex intersection of the boreal and northern hardwoods types. With the exception of balsam fir, the dominant softwoods in the Acadian type—red spruce, hemlock, white pine, and white cedar—are not true boreal species, but are near the northern ends of their ranges.

The pre-settlement Acadian forest consisted mostly of uneven-aged stands, dominated by shade-tolerant trees that could live for hundreds of years. Although small-scale disturbance from wind, frost, and insects was common, large-scale, catastrophic (stand-replacing) disturbance was relatively rare.

Such catastrophic disturbances are normally followed by early-successional pioneer species, such as aspen and white birch. If such occurrences were frequent, one would expect that vast areas of the state would be covered with aspen-birch stands. But early forest surveys in north-eastern Maine found very few such areas.

Modern clearcutters insist that they are merely imitating nature. They point to massive fires and spruce budworm outbreaks that devastated the forest in the nineteenth and twentieth centuries. Companies claim they are cutting the forest to save it from Nature—which would waste it, let it rot, rather than use it for necessary items like packaging, or advertising circulars. Protecting the forest from natural disturbances so that it can be more efficiently removed by a human disturbance (clearcutting) is called "conservation."

Historical evidence shows that fire and especially spruce budworm outbreaks increase in size, intensity, and frequency as a result of human interference in the forest ecosystem. Modern whole-tree clearcuts do not imitate "natural catastrophes" (even ones exacerbated by past logging practices); they surpass them.

The green, unlogged (or lightly logged) buffer strips of trees along rivers and lakes in Maine testify to the lie that companies have to clearcut the forest to save it.

M A I N E

NORTHERN APPALACHIAN HIGHLANDS BIOREGION: BEAUTY STRIP, EAST OF LINCOLN
Photographer, Alex MacLean, 1989

"Minimal state forest regulations have helped to shape the forest into the image that one can view from above. When regulations were first imposed in the 1970s, the major restriction to clearcutting was a requirement to buffer water bodies. Loggers called these mandatory buffers around water bodies, and the voluntary ones along roads, 'beauty strips.' While these buffer strips may help protect water quality and scenic views, they do not help protect the forest—they preserve only the illusion of a forest.

"To step beyond the beauty strip is to step into a world of distorted metaphors, and distorted logic. If what you see looks degraded and ugly, the fault (according to corporate spokespersons) lies with your vision rather than their companies' management. Once you learn the proper attitude, it should all look acceptable, if not admirable.

"Industrial foresters maintain that, by some happy coincidence, whatever they do to the forest to benefit their company just happens to also benefit the forest, wildlife, local communities, and society in general. Industrial foresters invoke an elaborate array of myths of justify their management actions as both beneficial and necessary."
—Mitch Lansky, "Myths of the Benign Industrial Clearcut"

NEW ENGLAND

NORTHERN APPALACHIAN HIGHLANDS BIOREGION: NORTHUMBERLAND TOWNSHIP, NEW HAMPSHIRE
Photographer, Alex MacLean, 1993

This photo *(top left)* of Northumberland Township in northern New Hampshire is one of dozens of clearcuts on private lands in this region. The rate of cutting has accelerated during the early 1990s.

MOOR RESERVOIR AREA, VERMONT, HYDRO-QUEBEC CROSSES CLEARCUT

Power lines eviscerate thousands of miles of wildlands *(photo, top right)*. This power line brings New England electricity generated by Hydro-Quebec from James Bay, nearly a thousand miles to the north. At the top of the photos (looking south) is the frozen Moore Reservoir, which drowned the wild stretch of the Connecticut River called Fifteen Mile Falls.

VICTORY BOG, VERMONT

Although Vermont is reputed to be progressive in environmental issues, huge clearcuts, such as this one near Miles Pond, are common in Vermont's beautiful— and still relatively wild—Northeast Kingdom *(lower left)*. There are no meaningful regulations to prohibit absentee multinationals or local contractors from liquidating hundreds and even thousands of acres of forestland. Some people have called for the creation of a Northeast Kingdom National Park to celebrate the rare beauty of this region.

WHITE MOUNTAIN NATIONAL FOREST

Since the Forest Service is limited to 30-acre clearcuts, they blessed this "opportunity area" to the east of Zealand Notch with 36 cuts *(photo, lower right)*. According to U.S. Forest Service "accounting" practices, their managing White Mountain National Forest lost taxpayers between $800,000 and $1 million last year while inflicting such fragmentation cuts. The Wilderness Society suggests that a more honest accounting system would show that the WMNF lost $1.4 million last year on its timber sales. Elimination of wasteful uses of wood fiber would more than compensate for the wood fiber cut on eastern public lands.

M O N T A N A

MID-CONTINENTAL ROCKIES BIOREGION: WEST OF KALISPELL

Photographer, George Wuerthner, 1990

"At one time Champion International Corporation was one of the largest owners of native forest in Montana. On over 800,000 acres of land, magnificent old growth forests of ponderosa pine, fir, and larch predominated. By the end of the 1980s, following a decade-long timber binge, assessors with the Montana State Department of Revenue estimated that only 1 percent of Champion lands were stocked with commercial timber over 8 inches in diameter. A forest fell, leaving stumps and new lines of unemployed workers."
—Alliance for the Wild Rockies

"A forest differs from a tree farm in being naturally regenerated and essentially self-regulating. Although ecological restoration may someday be able to produce forests from planted trees, it is too early to count on this. Natural forests are probably always more diverse in total species, structures, and processes than plantations in the same region. Although natural forests are dynamic, their component species have evolved over millions of years and their ecological and evolutionary processes have been in operation even longer. It is hubris to think that humans have learned to duplicate these processes in the few centuries that we have been practicing intensive forestry, or the few years over which we have even thought about sustainability."
—Reed Noss, "A Sustainable Forest Is a Diverse and Natural Forest"

M O N T A N A

BORDER: GLACIER NATIONAL PARK/
BLACKFEET INDIAN RESERVATION
Photographer, George Wuerthner, 1990

"Unscrupulous foresters with the Bureau of Indian Affairs convinced a cash-starved tribal business council to trade off a legacy for quick bucks. Traditional spiritual leaders within the Blackfeet Tribe spoke out strongly against the timber sales but were overruled by the tribal council. Decades later, the scars remain in this area, which is prime habitat for grizzly bear, gray wolf, and other large mammals that roam the area in and around Glacier National Park. The clearcut lands make the endangered animals more vulnerable to poaching."
—Alliance for the Wild Rockies

"The practice of large-scale clearcutting was imported to North America by European settlers in the seventeenth century. For many thousands of years, most of the indige-nous nations on this continent practiced a philosophy of protection (first) and use (second) of the forest. In scien-tific terms, we recognize that their use of the forest was ecologically responsible—meaning that it kept all the parts. Their demands on the forest were not extravagant and their population was in balance with the forest where they lived. The indigenous peoples of North America respected the forest as a physical, emotional, and spiri-tual source. As a part of the forest, they were sustained.

"This is not to say that the white newcomers did not depend on the forest; like humans everywhere they needed its abundant water, clean air, building materials, fuel, and food. But they kept their distance. People of European descent who now control forests in North America, indeed much of the forests of the world, depend on the forest as much as any other humans, but they have never considered themselves a part of it. These people do not understand that what we do to the forest, we do to ourselves."
—Herb Hammond, "Clearcutting: Ecological and Economic Flaws"

MONTANA

MID-CONTINENTAL ROCKIES BIOREGION: GOLD CREEK
Photographer, Mark Alan Wilson, 1991

"Champion Corporation and its predecessor, the Anaconda Copper Mining Company, had controlled...lands [in Montana] more or less for a century but had never logged them hard. Then in the late 1970s, change came. Champion, a timber giant with land and mills spread throughout the world, was pressed for capital to build mills in Michigan and Texas. Lumber prices were depressed. Buying logs from federal lands to supplement the supply from Champion's own lands, a long-standard practice, would eat into the profit margin. So would the use of environmentally sound but costlier logging methods. All this pushed toward a decision in Stamford, Connecticut, Champion's corporate headquarters, a decision that began to show on Montana's land in the late 1970s. Quietly the company decided it would no longer log its own lands only as fast as the lands could grow new trees. Instead, the company decided to log all of its lands as rapidly and cheaply as possible."
—Richard Manning, *Last Stand*

IDAHO

**MID-CONTINENTAL ROCKIES
BIOREGION:
TARGHEE NATIONAL FOREST**
Photographer, George Wuerthner, 1991

"During the 1980s timber cutting in all western states accelerated sharply. In Idaho, production rose a stunning 61 percent."

"Most of the cuts on the Targhee National Forest were justified to halt the spread of pine beetle which feed on lodgepole pine. Pine beetles are a natural part of the eco-system and run in periodic cycles. Logging has never halted an outbreak. Pine beetle infestations do not occur in a healthy forest, but when a forest is stressed—as in a drought. Pine beetles tend to attack even-age stands, so that when a 'crop' of trees is planted after clearcutting, it is likely that the infestation will reoccur.

"In Idaho, the timber industry, fighting hard for access to timber stands in roadless areas, is clearly alarmed about where its future timber will come from. An industry publication advises that: "While the timber industry and the Forest Service disagree on the amount of timber, which should be available from each national forest, there is no disagreement that timber must come from roadless areas. . . . We in the industry, along with the Forest Service, count on these roadless areas to meet our short term needs.

"Overcutting on privately owned commercial timber-land, industry leaders acknowledge, means the next privately owned crop of trees in the West won't be ready to harvest before 2000 at the earliest. . . . But it's curious that in almost all of the western states, regardless of who owns the privately held timberland or how much there is, the timber industry still looks to federal forestlands to supply ever-bigger volumes of saw timber."
—Grace Herndon, *Cut and Run*

WYOMING

NORTHERN ROCKIES BIOREGION: MEDICINE BOW NATIONAL FOREST
Photographer, Leila Stanfield, 1993

Extensive strip clearcutting beginning in the 1960s has cut the Medicine Bow National Forest into ribbons. The Forest Service continues to clearcut 2,000 acres a year from a forest already fragmented by 3,500 miles of roads.

Impacts have been severe. Numerous high-elevation spruce-fir stands have never regenerated, less than 10 percent of the designated old-growth (chopped into small patches) remains, and stream stability continues to decline. Suitable habitat for vulnerable interior species such as goshawks and pine martens is rare.

The Medicine Bow National Forest is the most badly fragmented forest in the Rocky Mountain region.

"Industrial myths dominate forestry discussions in academia, the media, and the legislature. Indeed, these myths are often codified into law. Because the fallacies of industrial forestry tend to be so widely accepted as reality, they are one of the most serious barriers to forestry reform. The first step in forestry reform, therefore, is to identify and refute fallacies of industrial forestry that support forest destruction.

"The second step in forestry reform is acceptance of the fact that sustainable forestry depends on sustainable natural forests. Because the concept of sustainability of natural forest ecosystems is a relatively new idea, ecologists do not know how much biomass humans can remove from any specific forest without harming important ecosystem processes. Ecologists do know that sustainability is not the same as *productivity* or *sustained yield* as these concepts are used by industrial foresters.

"The time horizon for the owner of an industrial forestry mill, which lasts for a few decades, is not the same as for forests, which last for centuries."
—Mitch Lansky, "Myths of the Benign Industrial Clearcut"

**NORTHERN ROCKIES BIOREGION:
BORDER OF YELLOWSTONE
NATIONAL PARK**
Photographer, George Wuerthner, 1991

The western border of Yellowstone National Park is defined by clearcuts on the Targhee National Forest, Idaho. This cutting border, which extends for miles, can even be seen in satellite images from space. Cutting has occurred in prime grizzly bear habitat.

These lands adjacent to Yellowstone National Park are a prime example of the lack of interagency cooperation that has fragmented ecosystems along bureaucratic lines. In a show of force to prove the Forest Service has a much different management emphasis than the preservation-oriented National Park Service, the district ranger in charge of this area ordered the forest be clearcut right to the park line. The pictures would later surface at congressional hearings chaired by former congressman John Seiberling, who denounced the lack of sensitivity for one of America's most valued treasures.

The Targhee National Forest has undergone one of the most extensive timber sale programs in the Northern Rockies. The Idaho Fish and Game Department formally appealed a timber sale in this area because of dramatic losses in big-game habitat. The deer and elk hunting seasons used to last for 45 days. Now they have been cut to only three days because of large-scale habitat degradation resulting from clearcutting large areas of forest.

COLORADO

SOUTHERN ROCKIES BIOREGION: HERMOSA CREEK SAN JUAN NATIONAL FOREST

Photographer, George Wuerthner, 1988

"The Rio Grande National Forest, on the east side of the Continental Divide in southern Colorado, shares common problems with the San Juan National Forest, its neighboring forest on the west side of the divide. Both bear scars of logging-gone-wrong in Englemann spruce and subalpine fir forests. Agency foresters shrug off these atrocities. Clearcutting, these foresters allow, turned out to be the wrong "prescription" for these slow-growing, high-altitude evergreens. Some clearcuts that went to timberline (10,000 ft. and higher) may never grow back, period. In other similarly inhospitable sites, 20 years after clearcutting, healthy seedlings are still hard to find despite repeated attempts at reforestation."
—Grace Herndon, *Cut and Run*

"We have not simply turned trees into lumber, we have destroyed a complex, stable, ancient community. In the space of a century, we have wrought a holocaust in the wilderness. And we continue."
—Dave Foreman

COLORADO

SOUTHERN ROCKIES BIOREGION: LONE CONE PEAK NEAR NORWOOD, SAN MIGUEL COUNTY

Photographer, Linde Waidhofer, 1992

Aspen clearcut on north-facing slopes. These aspen were cut to feed a waferboard plant operated by Louisiana-Pacific Corporation near Delta, Colorado. In recent years the Forest Service has been so eager to initiate aspen-logging programs in western Colorado that they have resorted to absurd fictions to sell these schemes to a doubting public—in one case claiming that clearcutting would increase water yields for agriculture by allowing more falling snow to reach the ground!

Louisiana-Pacific is widely regarded as one of the most cynical of all Big Timber operations. The EPA fined Louisiana-Pacific $11.1 million in May 1993 (the second largest environmental fine in U.S. history) for Clean Air Act violations at fourteen L-P wood product plants across the country. The fine, plus an additional $70 million of new anti-pollution devices the EPA has ordered installed, won't even dent the company's record profits. The bad faith, cynicism, and rapacious spirit of Louisiana-Pacific is evident in chairman Harry Merlo's infamous pronouncement: "We don't log to a 10-inch top, or an 8-inch top, or a 6-inch top. We log to infinity. Because we need it all. It's ours, it's out there and we want it all. Now."

COLORADO PLATEAU BIOREGION: HENRY MOUNTAINS
Photographer, Edgar Boyles, 1993

Coming over the mountains just west of Canyonlands National Park and seeing the destruction of the lower flanks of an entire range, the Henry Mountains of Utah, I was stunned, shocked, saddened all at once. Over the years, I had seen evidence of chaining in many western states, even on the North Rim of the Grand Canyon. But nothing had hit me like this sudden aerial revelation. So much destruction—generally carried out by the BLM in the name of 'range improvement.' Untold acres of slow-growing pinyon-juniper and other forests, perfectly adapted to their arid upland habitat, ripped out in the service of a scientifically discredited grazing policy, by a public agency, in our names. What would future generations say? Why had "we" done this? Why are "we" still doing this?
—Edgar Boyles

In the remote Henry Mountains of eastern Utah, bordering Canyonlands National Park, high arid forests have been butchered for the short-term benefit of one generation.

Southern Utah is one of the few places where chaining is still done on federal public land. Most federal land managers have abandoned this indefensible practice. The Bureau of Land Management has chained for at least thirty years, removing trees to plant crested wheat grass to create grazing areas for cattle. Two large bulldozers with a thick chain between them uproot pinyon forests.

COLORADO PLATEAU BIOREGION:
DIXIE NATIONAL FOREST
Photographer, Lori Mac, 1992

The Dixie National Forest is located on a high plateau of southern Utah. This complex bioregion of forests, deserts, and extensive rock formations supports a variety of plant and animal communities. Native species of conifers that evolved under formidable climatic conditions are an integral part of this ecosystem. These conifers host a diversity of plant and animal life ranging from microorganisms to peregrine falcons.

The geographic location of Dixie National Forest makes it extremely susceptible to desertification. As coniferous forests disappear through logging, the potential for impingement of old-world weedy species will grow.

The Dixie National Forest is scarred with 33-year-old clearcut strips that have not regenerated despite repeated plantings. The Forest Service has continued clearcutting under new pseudonyms.

The official plan for this forest requires 7 to 10 percent of the trees in each drainage area be preserved as old-growth. An inventory of old-growth would be needed to meet this requirement. At the beginning of 1993, no inventories of old-growth had been completed. Many Forest Service professionals working on the forest were reported to be concerned about this.

NEW MEXICO

COLORADO PLATEAU BIOREGION: JEMEZ MOUNTAINS
Photographer, Edgar Boyles, 1993

The archeologically rich, but heavily logged, mesa in the foreground of this photo was in private lands until the 1960s. It is currently included in Santa Fe National Forest. The Forest Service, in an effort to create an even-aged ponderosa pine tree farm, plowed large sections of the mesa and planted the rows of young trees seen in the photo. The plowing also destroyed dozens of priceless Anasazi ruins.

A court-ordered settlement in the mid-1980s forced the Forest Service to survey for archaeological sites before logging and required them to protect all identified sites.

In the distance can be seen other heavily logged mesa tops in the Jemez mountains of north-central New Mexico. The first aerial photos from the 1930s show that most of the Jemez mountains were roadless wildlands. In the early 1990s only a small and declining population of Mexican spotted owls are found in the forested canyons.
—Forest Guardians, Santa Fe

MICHIGAN

WHITE PINE TRILOGY
Photographer, Balthazar Korab, 1991, 1992, 1986

Photographer Balthazar Korab tells of his personal struggle to understand, and then articulate through his photography, the agony wrought by industrialism to his adopted home state of Michigan:

"The 'White Pine Trilogy' is the poignant statement around which my whole portfolio was developed. It tends to deal with man's ambiguous relation with nature. Its story in Michigan is dismal, while other examples from around the world tell sometimes about more balanced coexistence. In 1976 when working on an exhibit, 'Man's Presence in Michigan,' I discovered with shock that millions of acres of white pines covered the state when white men arrived in the mid 1800s and by 1910 all but a few acres were cut down, without any effort to replant. Only 49 acres of old growth exist today, preserved by accidental circumstances at Hartwick Pines State Park. Most of the later reforestations show pitiful, unimaginative monotony. These shown here were probably planted by some Youth Corps during the Depression. . . and today we listen to the inane debate of the politicians about the spotted owl versus jobs, while the clearcutting equipment is humming away. In a debate where nobody brings up the fact that when the white pines were gone the lumberjacks went on living by building cars."

MINNESOTA

**SUPERIOR UPLANDS BIOREGION:
CHIPPEWA NATIONAL FOREST**
Photographer, Judy Johnson, 1992

The employees of local logging companies, as well as
myself, have become victims of a forest policy that is
broken and needs fixing. That is the reason for my long
journey into the Minnesota forests.

I was a victim of the clearcuts in central Minnesota in
the 1940s-1950s era, and my father, who had a sawmill
for many years sawing Jack pine, often talked of his experience as a child at the turn of the century watching the
clearcuts of White pine. He often lamented how he hoped
it wouldn't happen again, but tragically, it is happening
again.

I know the richness of forest diversity, and I feel driven to
help save what is left, to pass it on to my grandchildren.
—Judy Johnson

The central hardwood forest extends roughly from the
Appalachians to the Great Plains, and from southern
Minnesota to northern Mississippi. This region is considered the most productive hardwood growing area in the
Northern Hemisphere. These hills and river valleys once
contained a great diversity of forest life extending from
the topsoil to the tree tops, including more than 70
species of huge hardwood trees interspersed with barrens, bogs, savannahs, and glades, in a continuous cycle
of growth, death, and decay.

This once-mighty forest is now little more than a fragmented patchwork of its former diverse glory. Vast
bottomland hardwood swamps have been cleared and
drained for corn and soybeans. High ground now grows
cities, highways, and fields where it once grew oak trees
ten feet across and a hundred feet tall.

Three species represent the central hardwood forest
region—the passenger pigeon, the wood bison, and the
American chestnut tree. The first is extinct, the second
has been eliminated from its former range and survives
elsewhere only as a hybrid, and the third barely clings to
life in isolated pockets.

Though only a few small remnants of native old-growth
forest still stand anywhere in the region, the soil remains
fertile and trees will grow again.

OHIO

OHIO VALLEY BIOREGION
Photographer, Daniel Dancer, 1992

The vast forest that once covered 95 percent of Ohio is now a tattered remnant scattered over only 30 percent of the state. With more than 335,000 private landowners and other private interests controlling 94 percent of these lands, the fate of the forests rests, to a large extent, on initiatives to convert private lands to sustainable forests.

Wayne National Forest is the only national forest in Ohio. Located in southern Ohio, it is a haphazard collection of forest islands in a rural and agricultural sea. Only 203,000 acres, 24 percent of the land within the Wayne National Forest, is publicly owned, and of that only 9 percent is set aside for non-timber uses. The rest is slated to be cut.

Besides encouraging clearcutting, Wayne National Forest is the only national forest east of the Mississippi River to allow strip mining, as most of the subsurface mineral domain is privately owned.

On private lands, cutting continues unabated. Heartwood, and other local organizations, have called for an end to logging on the Wayne National Forest. Only by protecting and connecting large core areas of contiguous forest will the viability of Ohio's forest ecosystems be assured.

WEST VIRGINIA

CENTRAL APPALACHIAN BIOREGION: MONONGAHELA NATIONAL FOREST
Photographer, George Wuerthner, 1990

Clearcutting in eastern national forests continues despite the fact that public forests make up only a small part of the land base and are among the only recreational lands available to the public in the East.

"In May 1973, the Izaac Walton League, along with the Sierra Club and others, filed suit to stop clearcutting in the Monongahela National Forest in West Virginia. Plaintiffs charged violation of the Organic Act of 1897 on three counts: that the Forest Service proposed to sell timber other than dead, mature, and large-growth trees, that it proposed to sell timber that was not marked and designated, and that it proposed to permit purchasers to cut trees in the national forests without removing them.

"[The judge in the Federal District Court] . . . agreed with the plaintiffs and permanently enjoined the Forest Service from allowing the cutting in the Monongahela National Forest of the following: (1) trees that are not dead, mature, or large growth; (2) trees that have not been previously marked; and (3) trees that will not be removed. . . .

"[The logging industry went to Congress for relief]. . . . After much debate, Congress finally passed the National Forest Management Act of 1976 (NFMA). That act legalizes all the objections environmentalists have to clearcutting and even-aged management in the national forests, that is, cutting far beyond sustained-yield capacity and managing the forests on short rotations as mere tree farms. It authorizes the Forest Service to depart from sustained yield under certain circumstances so that, in effect, industry is supported where private timber resources have been exhausted and the excessive cutting that had been taking place is legalized."
—Gordon Robinson, *The Forest and the Trees*

KENTUCKY

FLOYD COUNTY, PRIVATE LAND CLEARCUT
Photographer, Daniel Dancer, 1992

Bulldozing prepares the ground for planting a pine plantation.

Today forest covers only 49 percent of Kentucky's 25.3 million acres. Prior to European settlement, the state was estimated to have been more than 94 percent forested.

The Daniel Boone National Forest comprises only 4.89 percent of the current forestland in the state.

State and federal agencies boast that Kentucky's forests are recovering from past abuses. Despite rapid regrowth, Kentucky forests, public and private, face serious threats, including extensive clearcutting, high-grading, general oak decline, strip mining, and erosion.

Heartwood and other organizations demand an end to logging on Kentucky's public forests. Restoration and protection of the public land, combined with sustainable management of the state's private forestland, is necessary to counter the pressure from the logging industry and allow for the reestablishment of healthy and sustainable forest ecosystems.

TENNESSEE

HAMILTON COUNTY, PRIVATE LANDS
Photographer, Daniel Dancer, 1992

During one recent 12-month period, the Tennessee Valley Authority (TVA) received 17 requests for assistance in siting wood chip mills along the Tennessee River.

The chip mills would take hardwood trees and turn them into wood chips, then barge them down the Tennessee River and Tenn-Tom Waterway to supply increasing worldwide demand for paper products.

Each pulp mill requires a minimum of 10,000 acres of forestland per year to operate economically. A TVA environmental assessment states that if four mills southwest of Chattanooga were constructed, 1,353,000 acres of forest would be consumed over the next 20 years (approximately 51 percent of the forest cover in a 75-mile radius around Bridgeport, Tennessee).

Cumulative impacts from massive clearcutting include destruction of habitat necessary for many threatened and endangered species and species that prefer large undisturbed forestlands, including black bear, turkey, and many other bird species.

T E N N E S S E E

HAMILTON COUNTY, PRIVATE LANDS
Photographer, Daniel Dancer, 1992

The Foundation for Global Sustainability has tracked increasing requests for assistance by the TVA Division of Forest Resources for the siting of wood chip mills along the Tennessee River. It has been determined that Bowater, a pulp mill, is killing the river with a toxic effluent that contains the deadly chemical compound dioxin. The environmental group is appealing numerous chip mill applications to the Tennessee Valley Authority that would rapidly deforest this beautiful and highly touristed section of the state.

"The economics of clearcutting are little more than the economics of short-term greed. Workers, human communities, and the forest are all degraded so that a privileged, powerful few may benefit. As with the ecological problems of clearcutting, we must often look beyond today, tomorrow, and next year to the time of future generations for the economic problems to become plainly evident. The real economics of clearcutting are clouded by political manipulation that makes clearcutting appear to be the best economic choice for employment, corporate revenues, and government tax bases. But when examined closely, these illusions crumble."
—Herb Hammond, "Clearcutting: Ecological and Economic Flaws"

A R K A N S A S

OUACHITA HIGHLANDS BIOREGION: OUACHITA NATIONAL FOREST
Photographer, David Hiser, 1993

The Ouachita Watch League (OWL) has as one of its goals the protection of native biodiversity on public and private forestlands.

"Forest Service clearcutting has already drastically altered our native woods on approximately one-third of the Ouachita Forest land subject to logging. What was once a richly diverse community of many interdependent plant and animal species has been transformed into a single-species crop of commercially desirable pine trees. Logged-over areas are replanted with 'genetically improved' pines intended to grow fast and out-compete other species. Most hardwoods are killed with chemicals or struggle as mere sprouts from stumps.

"This pine farming results in inferior pine sawlogs lacking the strength and quality of trees grown more slowly. It increases the forest's susceptibility to insects and disease. It robs citizens of their natural heritage—the glorious oaks, beeches, hickory, and dogwoods that grace us with the seasonal changes that are the southern woodlands. Tourists usually flock to the Ouachita to enjoy brilliant fall foliage and spring blooms. Will they still journey here to witness a few patches of color in a monotonous green sea of pines?

"We believe the Forest Service should manage our public lands for all plant and animal species, preserving and restoring the forest's native diversity. Only then will the rich living communities of mixed hardwood-pine ecosystems remain intact for future generations."
—Ouachita Watch League

ARKANSAS

OUACHITA HIGHLANDS BIOREGION: OUACHITA NATIONAL FOREST
Photographer, David Hiser, 1993

Aerial view of clearcut near a major stream in Ouachita National Forest. Through efforts of the Ouachita Watch League (OWL) the Forest Service has had to increase the buffer zone of uncut trees next to perennial streams. Sedimentation from logging roads flowing into lakes and streams has been a problem in this area.

Below-cost timber sales in Arkansas's Ouachita National Forest was netted out, according to U.S. Treasury figures, at a loss of $476 per acre, but that wasn't as bad as the nearby Ozark St. Francis National Forest, which showed a $654 loss per acre, adding up to over $13 million in 1992 alone. And these examples of American taxpayers paying for the destruction of their own forests represent small losses compared to those of the huge forests in the West.

"Through clearcut logging and other forms of environmentally damaging even-aged timber management, the federal government has relentlessly created pine farms of 320,000 acres that we once proudly called woods in the South's oldest and largest national forest. That's 320,000 reasons why citizens should rise up together and say no to the Forest Service proposal to expand the butchery by 25% in ten short years, with no end in sight. We've needlessly lost forever 500 square miles of our natural heritage—one-third of the Ouachita's timber base—because a federal agency stubbornly insists on a particular logging method even though less damaging timber management methods are available, and we say enough's enough."
—Onachita Watch League

MISSISSIPPI

ITAWAMBA COUNTY, PRIVATE LANDS
Photographer, Daniel Dancer, 1992

This clearcut along an isolated backroad beside a small farm is indicative of a type of deforestation that has constantly crept across the country since settlers first began to cut the forests. To expand pasture or croplands the forest is gradually cut and eliminated until only riverside strips remain. In the Southeast, very few pockets of virgin hardwoods remain and most of those that do are in danger or being lost to expanding croplands. Judging by the immense size of the stumps and downed logs on this clearcut, it is likely that this was recently a rare tract of native hardwood forest. Standing on a giant stump to make this photograph I thought of similar scenes of wasted tropical rain forest fallen to the onslaught of slash and burn agriculture and colonization. It's been happening in the same manner yet on a larger scale right here in the U.S. for a long time.
—Daniel Dancer

"Some people argue that, because change is natural, the massive changes in forest cover and structure occurring today as a result of human activity are nothing to be alarmed about. These people are wrong. Although forests have always changed at many spatial and temporal scales, from individual treefalls to whole regions being bulldozed by mile-high glaciers, globally they have been remarkably persistent. The broad ecotones that separate forests from grasslands and deserts have shifted back and forth across continents over the centuries, but over the long expanse of time such changes are like the rhythms of a giant tide. Only in the last millennium has the ebb of forests been incessant and increasingly global in extent. Most alarming, the loss of forests to the axe and saw is occurring at an ever-faster rate. What replaces forest today is habitat for few living things besides domesticated plants and animals, and weeds. Deforestation and forest conversion are of crisis proportions."
—Reed Noss, "A Sustainable Forest Is a Diverse and Natural Forest"

DAVY CROCKETT NATIONAL FOREST
Photographer, Bill Ellzey, 1983

"Where 100 years ago large forests of mixed hardwoods and pines of many species and sizes covered most of East Texas, even-age logging (clearcuts and their deviants) has degraded and fragmented 16 million acres. At first, the loggers cut and ran. Most of the native species grew back. In 1936, the federal Forest Service purchased about 600,000 acres. That agency began to eliminate hardwoods, by burning more frequently than natural lightning fires, and by girdling and applying herbicides. The large industrial owners performed the same practices on millions of acres more. Within three decades, the Forest Service, corporations, and smaller owners clearcut, or seed-tree or shelterwood cut (two-stage clearcuts) stands of mixed pines and hardwoods, and began to replace them with loblolly or shortleaf pine. When the pine saplings were tall enough, the even-age managers burned the young hardwoods beneath them. The managers had replaced native biodiversity with pines, each of the same age as others in its field. And the burning continued.

"Some private owners declined. They practiced selection (not selective) management, removing scattered trees that are least likely to contribute to the health of the stand until the next logging. These owners preserved some native biodiversity.

"Many citizens rebelled further and persuaded Congress to pass a wilderness bill preserving 37,000 acres in five units from any logging at all—close to total native biodiversity in those small areas. Then several groups filed a suit to stop clear cutting in the four National Forests in Texas. On May 12, 1993 they succeeded in protecting the National Forests in east Texas from even-age management. With various exceptions, however, clearcutting continues on private lands in east Texas on at least half of the 12 million acres of commercial timberland."
—Ned Fritz, Forest Activist, Texas

T E X A S

PRIVATE LANDS NEAR NACOGDOCHES
Photographer, David Hiser, 1993

This 600 acre plot was clearcut in 1990. The owner's original intent was to make a cattle pasture. Instead, he took the money and bought a cattle ranch in New Mexico. It was half replanted in 1991. It is being converted from the native short leaf pine to faster-growing loblolly pine. The owner figures to harvest in 30-35 years. The local mills want timber 20 feet or less in size. Larger trees are now considered undesirable.
—David Hiser

"Clearcutting is the most efficient, the most ecologically damaging, and (in the short term) the most cost-effective method of converting trees to logs and forests to non-forest human uses such as pastureland, cropland, town-sites, and tree plantations. Simply put, clearcutting is deforestation. . . . Clearcutting [is] any form of timber removal that does not leave a fully functioning forest after logging is completed.

Technically, clearcutting means cutting every tree on the site and removing those trees considered to be merchant-able to a mill. Other logging systems, lumped under the general category of partial cutting, cut and remove only selected trees and leave the rest standing. But in prac-tical terms, many systems of partial cutting currently in use are simply variations on conventional clearcutting."
—Herb Hammond, "Clearcutting: Ecological and Economic Flaws"

NORTH CAROLINA

KATÚAH
NANTAHALA NATIONAL FOREST
Photographer, Terry Livingstone, 1992

These clearcut areas are in Nantahala National Forest, in the western part of North Carolina, near the Hiwassee Scenic River, less than 50 miles from the Great Smoky Mountains National Park.

"National Forests and Great Smoky Mountains National Park in the southern Appalachians form the largest block of federal land east of the Mississippi River—four million acres. This is the core for a major forested wilderness recovery area that could support the whole range of native species, including wolf, eastern panther, and elk.

"...The Forest Service has launched a blitzkrieg of logging and road building in these national forests to make up for decreasing timber extraction in Washington, Oregon, and northern California.

"...unless citizens throughout Canada and the U.S. wake up to the vision of living, natural forests as the key to healthy and prosperous sustainable communities, our legacy will be a wasteland of stumps. Our civilization will join civilizations and empires of the past, like those of the Middle East, Greece, Rome, and North Africa, who squandered their forest wealth for fast bucks from a quick cut.

"If we wake up from greed into humility, and protect the integrity of forest ecosystems of North America, we may avoid the fate of Ozymandias."
—Dave Foreman, "The Big Woods and Ecological Wilderness Recovery"

NORTH CAROLINA

KATÚAH
HARMON DEN BEAR SANCTUARY,
PISGAH NATIONAL FOREST
Photographer, Daniel Dancer, 1992

Biologists at the University of Tennessee have shown that cumulative effects of clearcutting and road building appear to cause bears to expand their home range beyond the protective boundaries of Harmon Den Bear Sanctuary. This increases the opportunity for hunters and poachers to reduce the number of bears to below the level necessary for population maintenance.

In the early 1900s, Pisgah National Forest became the home of scientific forestry under the direction of Gifford Pinchot. After 1945, huge road projects and clearcutting have dominated forest management practices in this forest.

A local group, Western North Carolina Alliance, is working to bring local involvement back into decisions about the management practices in this forest.

"The gloomy record of human subjugation of Nature does not provide much hope that we can suddenly turn around and start managing forests and other lands in a truly sustainable way. But we have little choice but to try. We are truly on the brink of a catastrophe. In such a situation, radical change (or, looking at it another way, true conservatism) is the only hope for survival. Do not misunderstand: the Earth will survive and Nature will endure, no matter what we do. Humans are not all that powerful. Ecosystems can be greatly impoverished and still function, in the sense of capturing energy and cycling nutrients. They can certainly get along without human beings and other large mammals. The question is whether this massive impoverishment is ethical and in the best interests of our species and all other living things. A preferable attitude toward Nature is one of respect and compassion."
—Reed Noss, "A Sustainable Forest Is a Diverse and Natural Forest"

ALABAMA

"ALABAMA BURNING"
Photographer, Daniel Dancer, 1992

Only fragments of Alabama's once-extensive hardwood forest remain as the state approaches completion in the conversion of its forests into monoculture pine plantations.

In Walker County in northeast Alabama I photographed a bulldozer clearing the remnants of a young hardwood forest, windrowing the downed trees into burn piles in preparation for planting pine seedlings. Bulldozers and herbicides ensure that the new "crop" of commercial trees are "released."

Witnessing the amount of active deforestation in Alabama was much worse than any experience I've had in the rainforests of Central America. Flying over Fayette County, I witnessed deforestation surpassing even the Pacific Northwest. The broad-leafed deciduous forests from the air look much like the tropical rainforests and the vast acres of burning, cutover lands made me think of Brazil. What we criticize Brazil for doing to its rainforests we have long been doing to forests in North America.
—Daniel Dancer

GEORGIA

This forest was probably cut in the fall of 1991 and burned in the fall of 1992. The burning of clearcut areas here is done by dropping napalm from helicopters.

This cut is located about one-half to one mile north of Highway 76 running east from Clayton, Georgia.

The cut borders the Chattooga wild and scenic river corridor and at one point comes to within a few hundred feet of the trail. A small stream next to this trail already showed signs of siltation from the cut's damage to the hill above it when this photo was taken.

**PANORAMA: CHATTAHOOCHEE
NATIONAL FOREST, TALLULAH
RANGER DISTRICT**
Photographer, Kathryn Kolb, 1992

MULTIPLY THE LANDSCAPES YOU HAVE JUST SEEN
BY A FACTOR OF SEVERAL THOUSAND
AND YOU WILL APPROXIMATE
THE DESTRUCTION WROUGHT BY INDUSTRIAL
FORESTRY ACROSS NORTH AMERICA.

The Deep Ecology Platform

1. The well-being and flourishing of human and nonhuman life on Earth have value in themselves (synonyms: inherent worth, intrinsic value, inherent value). These values are independent of the usefulness of the nonhuman world for human purposes.

2. Richness and diversity of life-forms contribute to the realization of these values and are also values in themselves.

3. Humans have no right to reduce this richness and diversity except to satisfy vital needs.

4. Present human interference with the nonhuman world is excessive, and the situation is rapidly worsening.

5. The flourishing of human life and cultures is compatible with a substantial decrease of the human population. The flourishing of nonhuman life requires such a decrease.

6. Policies must therefore be changed. The changes in policies affect basic economic, technological, and ideological structures. The resulting state of affairs will be deeply different from the present.

7. The ideological change is mainly that of appreciating life quality (dwelling in situations of inherent worth) rather than adhering to an increasingly higher standard of living. There will be a profound awareness of the difference between big and great.

8. Those who subscribe to the foregoing points have an obligation directly or indirectly to participate in the attempt to implement the necessary changes.

—Arne Naess and George Sessions

Randy Stoltmann

Although the existing situation is grim, there is some reason for hope. There is a powerful and growing grassroots involvement across Canada. Environmental groups and native groups in all regions of Canada are working for changes in all aspects of forest policy. Many conscientious scientists and civil servants want to help develop sustainable forestry.

CANADA—BRAZIL OF THE NORTH

COLLEEN McCRORY

Ninety percent of logging in Canada is clearcut logging. Clearcut logging continues to devastate the forests of Canada. The only difference between the ecological assault on the forests of Canada and the assault on the rainforests of the Amazon is a matter of degrees. In the Amazon region, one acre of forest is lost every nine seconds to logging and forest clearing. In Canada, one acre every twelve seconds is lost to logging or burning.

Global warming, erosion, loss of biological diversity, shattering of native cultures with ill-advised "economic development" projects (such as the James Bay project in Quebec), dwindling opportunities for developing sustainable communities—these are some of the impacts that Brazil and Canada share because of deforestation. Some of these impacts will affect people around the world.

The greatest difference between the forest policies of Brazil and Canada is that, in Brazil, the desperation of poverty and rapid population growth are the central driving factors in deforestation, whereas in Canada, the central cause of deforestation is the greed of multinational corporations, and their ability to dominate the public debate about forest policy because of their wealth and political influence. In only a few generations, large corporations, using more and more efficient technology, have had a devastating impact on forests and forest-based human communities of Canada. Provincial governments have willingly granted these corporations licenses to log vast areas of Canada's forests. Overwhelming scientific evidence clearly demonstrates that the timber industry and both the federal and provincial governments of Canada have displayed blatant disregard for the long-term ecological integrity of forests.

For example, on the west coast of Vancouver Island in British Columbia, some of the last stands of old-growth forest contain trees over a thousand years old. These ancient giants are majestic trees, their moss-laden branches reaching out from trunks so wide that several people must join hands to reach around the base. These guardians of the Earth put our lives in broader perspective, for European settlers have been in Canada only a few hundred years. These ancient trees are inheritors of untold secrets of a complex, evolving web of life that scientists have barely begun to understand. In 1993, the government of British Columbia decreed that ancient giants in the Clayoquot Sound region will be clearcut with chainsaws for voracious mills that will turn them into more newsprint, disposable diapers, and other disposable products that burden our already polluted cities.

While the coastal giants in British Columbia are exceptional in the awe they inspire, other types of forests in each of the provinces of Canada are equally important. Ten percent of the world's forested land is in Canada. As scientists learn more about the role that forests play in the well-being and very survival of life on Earth, the seriousness of Canada's responsibility is beginning to dawn on many people.

Although the logging industry is currently cutting at a rate far above sustainability, provincial governments in the early 1990s are allowing over $10 billion worth of additional pulp mill developments. Almost all of the forested land in some provinces has been signed over to multinational pulp-and-paper corporations in the form of long-term contracts. To feed these mega-mills, clearcut logging in Canada is expected to *double* over the next few years. Thousands of miles of new logging roads are planned. Many of these mega-mills are already under construction. They are being built despite the fact that there have been no studies done on the impact these projects will have on forest ecology and wildlife habitat or on the native or rural communities that will be severely affected.

These new pulp developments were the result of Forest Management Agreements (FMAs) between corporations and federal and provincial governments. These are legal contracts for trees and land that result in corporate control of what is, in reality, public land. Few people know the true extent to which the public interest has been sold on the marketplace, or the huge forces that have been set in motion toward the near total destruction of our forests. The expansions in the pulp industry link up with the Canada-US Free Trade Agreement (F.T.A.). Article 409 of the agreement states that with regard to natural resources, if Canada, for whatever reason, declares a shortage, the government cannot impose a restriction on exports to the United States. Once pulp exports to the United States increase, Canada will be obligated to maintain those levels—unless the Canadian government breaks the F.T.A.

The requirement to keep exporting pulp will rob Canada of potential jobs. The shift from lumber to pulp is putting many forest industry employees out of work. The pulp industry is termed *capital-intensive* rather than *labor-intensive*, meaning that machines and computers can replace the work of many men and women. Rather than creating value-added and secondary manufacturing jobs, Canada allows large-scale clearcutting and exports the raw pulp to other countries to be manufactured. In the view of multinational timber corporations, it is cost effective to liquidate large old-growth trees as soon as possible and then shift to pulp from boreal and sub-boreal forests, juvenile second-growth, hardwood forests, and scrub forests. Forestland that was previously seen as unprofitable to log is now deemed suitable fodder for pulp mills. Until now, these economically "marginal" forestlands have functioned as a major support system for the health of ecosystems. Birch, aspen, and cottonwood forests that still provide home for wildlife and aesthetic pleasure for outdoor recreationists of all ages are now on the chopping block.

The boreal zone in the north is characterized by shallow soils and harsh climate. Regeneration is slow and difficult. The logging industry expounds on the virtues of eliminating the "scrub forests" of the north and replacing them with tree plantations that have more commercial value. This, however, would be a disastrous experiment. The forest in the north is a "scrub forest" because that is what the growing conditions there will produce. These are forests that have survived and adapted to harsh conditions.

Sixty-five percent of the boreal forest region—comprising nearly 100 percent of the most productive boreal forest—has been committed to logging. The provincial governments of Alberta, Manitoba, Quebec, and Saskatchewan virtually gave away public boreal forests with little or no public review of the wood supply or the ecological impacts to the forest. Across the northern boreal, native people who have lived in the forest in a very traditional way now face thousands of miles of new road systems, clearcut logging, loss of important wildlife habitat, polluted river and lake systems, and dramatic changes to a traditional life closely connected to the land.

Simultaneously, wildlands in Canada are disappearing rapidly. Protected areas in Canada fall far below the 12 percent recommended by the United Nations' Brundtland Report on Sustainable Development, which was adopted by the federal government in Canada as a goal for Canadian policy. Only 0.4 percent of Quebec's land base is in protected reserves. Less than 2 percent of Manitoba is in parks. Only 2.5 percent of Nova Scotia has been preserved. Ontario and British Columbia have each set aside about 5.5 percent of their land base.

In British Columbia, where the greatest expressions of forest occur in the temperate rainforests of Vancouver Island, multinational logging corporations have liquidated most of the commercially valuable old-growth forests. Now, with new technology, automated mills, and consolidation in the industry, rural timber-based communities are seeing mill closures, lay-offs, and bitter struggles to maintain essential social services. In some provinces, including British Columbia, industry-funded organizations such as the ''share'' groups are blaming environmental groups for the forest crisis. This is a desperate attempt by multinational corporations to dominate public opinion as they have dominated the forests.

In some rural, forest-based communities, workers in the forest products industry, environmental activists, and members of native bands are angry and frustrated, and a sense of hopelessness lingers in the air. Concerned citizens look to their governments for leadership to solve the crisis in their communities and learn that governments act to serve the interests of the corporations that are robbing communities of a sustainable economy.

Richard St. Barbe-Baker, one of the world's most respected foresters, said that the fate of nations will always be determined by the degree of their harmony with the laws of Nature. Clearly every human being has the capacity to learn these laws and how to live in harmony with them, and thus to be part of the movement *for* the Earth instead of against it. Every human being has the capacity for broad, deep identification with the forests that Arne Naess and other philosophers of the deep, long-range ecology movement persuasively argue is the basis for protection of the integrity of Nature.

If allowed to continue, the liquidation policy that governments in Canada are practicing on remaining old-growth forests will surely mean the extinction of many wildlife and forest species over the next two decades and will deter citizens from developing sustainable bioregional communities. If the integrity of forestlands of Canada is to be maintained, bold action must be taken soon.

Although the existing situation is grim, there is some reason for hope. There is a powerful and growing grassroots involvement across Canada. Environmental groups and native groups in all regions of Canada are working for changes in all aspects of forest policy.

In the early 1990s a powerful grassroots network of forest activists, called Canada's Future Forest Alliance, was formed from citizens' groups in communities across Canada. Canada's Future Forest Alliance asks that the provincial and federal governments of Canada take immediate action to restructure the forest industry so that government forest policy and practices reflect principles of ecological responsibility, ecosystem integrity, and biological diversity. Equally important are justice for native peoples through aboriginal rights, treaty rights, and land claims. Forest tenures should be revised to conform with land-claim agreements. Increased interest in sustainable forestry as expounded by Herb Hammond and Orville Camp in essays in this book, and by the Ecoforestry Institute and Silva Foundation, indicates that many private forestland owners want to practice a land ethic on their own lands.

Unfortunately, time is running out for citizens who want forest policy based on sustainable forests. The failure of provincial and federal politicans in Canada to be adequately responsive to the need for fundamental changes in forest policy and practices has forced some forest activist groups to turn to other nations and to the United Nations for help. International pressure is necessary to expose Canadian politicans who have collaborated in the betrayal of the public trust. The United Nations Charter for Nature, passed by the United Nations General Assembly in 1982, calls for all nations to protect the integrity of Nature.

International pressure is also needed to change the behavior of multinational logging corporations. Nongovernmental organizations, appalled by corporate irresponsibility, formulated a statement of principles for corporate behavior after the disastrous 1989 Exxon oil spill off the coast of Alaska. These are called the *Valdez Principles*, after the place in Prince William Sound where the oil spill occurred. The Valdez Principles call for corporations to protect the biosphere, engage in sustainable use of natural resources, reduce waste, market safe products, provide compensation for damages caused by corporate activities, disclose risks, and provide an annual assessment of their environmental record. The Coalition for Environmentally Responsible Economics (CERES), which formulated the Valdez principles, asked corporate leaders to endorse these guidelines. Forest activists throughout Canada and the United States are waiting for logging corporations to endorse these principles and to prove, by their behavior, that they are following them.

Unlike the United States, Canada has no Endangered Species Act. Forest policy, under the jurisdiction of provincial governments, has been written to allow the large multinationals to clearcut.

Corporate and government behavior, however, will only be changed by pressure from concerned citizens. Those who are seeking to save wildlands, biodiversity, and old-growth forests and to establish sustainable forestry policies and practices cannot give up. When a land ethic becomes official government policy in Canada, it will be because of their efforts.

Lines from "The Tower Beyond Tragedy"

I entered the life of the brown forest,

And the great life of the ancient peaks, the patience of stone,

I felt the changes in the veins

In the throat of the mountain,
      …and I was the stream

Draining the mountain wood; and I the stag drinking;
      and I was the stars,

Boiling with light, wandering alone, each one the lord of his own
      summit;
      and I was the darkness

Outside the stars, I included them, they were a part of me.
      I was mankind also, a moving lichen

On the cheek of the round stone…they have not made words for it,
      to go behind things, beyond hours and ages,

And be all things in all time, in their returns and passages,
      in the motionless and timeless center,

In the white of the fire…how can I express the excellence
      I have found, that has no color but clearness;

No honey but ecstasy; neither wrought nor remembered;
      no undertone nor silver second murmur

That rings in love's voice…

—Robinson Jeffers

Gary Braasch

Unless citizens throughout Canada and the U.S. wake up to the vision of living, natural forests as the key
to healthy and prosperous sustainable communities, our legacy will be a wasteland of stumps. Our civilization will join
civilizations and empires of the past, like those of the Middle East, Greece, Rome, and North Africa,
who squandered their forest wealth for fast bucks from a quick cut.

THE BIG WOODS
AND ECOLOGICAL WILDERNESS RECOVERY

DAVE FOREMAN

One hundred and forty years ago, when their wagons came to a welcome halt after traversing half the continent on the Oregon Trail, the pioneers were greeted by the grandest coniferous forest on Earth. Stretching from California's Big Sur coast south of Monterey Bay to Glacier Bay in Alaska, over two dozen species of pine, cedar, spruce, fir, hemlock, and other conifers grew; some to heights of three hundred feet and ages of a thousand or more years. These were not just large individual trees, however. They were bound together as a *forest*, a single, interlocked entity—a community. The web of mycorrhizal fungi in the Pacific Northwest forest floor, aided by red-backed voles, northern flying squirrels, and northern spotted owls, tied the trees together into a whole far greater than the sum of individual trees. This old-growth forest, this *ancient forest*, watered by the fog and plentiful rain of the Pacific Ocean, created—with the sodden reservoir of water trapped in fallen trees, thick duff, and moss—its own climate beneath the overstory. The coastal forest was a graceful interpenetration of land and sea, with salmon and steelhead as much members of the community as black bear and Pacific salamander, with the marbled murrelet, an ocean bird, nesting in the crowns of the tallest trees, with seals and sea lions hauling themselves out where the big woods came down to the sea.

This forest flowed east to the crest of the Cascades. Douglas-fir, hemlock, spruce, cedar, and fir exchanged dominance in the forest according to distance from the sea, proximity to watercourses, elevation, and elapsed time since previous disturbance events such as forest fires. It was a forest from the Pacific Ocean to the heights of the Cascades such as shall not be seen again for a thousand years.

Witnessing the wealth of this forest, its awesome grandeur and silence, its powerful, constant recycling of life, should have been a humbling experience, drawing the settlers into a new relationship with the land. Instead, it was merely an inducement to greed.

During the late 1800s, the best of these forests passed into the ownership of large logging companies, as the timber frontier moved from the North Woods of Minnesota and Michigan to the Pacific Northwest. By the end of World War II, most of the old-growth forests on corporate land had been sacked, and the timber industry turned its eyes toward the remaining giants—on the national forests. The Forest Service, long eager to open its holdings to the timber industry, readily complied with industry wishes. Tens of thousands of miles of road were bulldozed on the national forests, clearcuts spread like mange through the Coast Range and the lower elevations of the Cascades, streams turned brown with silt, and profits from the dismemberment of the titans flowed into the pockets of timber company stockholders.

The ancient forests of Oregon and Washington, west of the Cascade crest, contained 19 million acres of pure old-growth before logging on an industrial scale began in about 1860. In addition, mixed in with these huge old-growth forests were younger stands in varying stages of succession—results of fire, disease outbreaks, and other natural disturbances. Of that original 19 million acres of old-growth in the two

states, only 950,000 acres are now protected in wilderness areas or national parks, and another 1.3 million acres of quality old-growth remain unprotected on national forest lands, according to The Wilderness Society. Ancient forest experts in Oregon estimate that only 2 percent of Oregon's original old-growth is "saved" while another 3 percent remains in limbo. Before settlement by Euro-Americans, there were at least 1.5 million acres of low-elevation (below 2,000 ft. elevation) old-growth forest in western Washington, not including the Olympic Peninsula. Nearly all the low-elevation old-growth that remains in 1992 is on the Mt. Baker–Snoqualmie National Forest—where only 38,400 acres survive. Virtually none of this is designated wilderness. The Wilderness Society, in their publication *Ancient Forests of the Mt. Baker-Snoqualmie National Forest*, reports that there are 298,300 acres of all types of old-growth on the forest, but only 102,700 acres are protected in wilderness or research natural areas.

Loggers and politicians scoff at these figures and point instead to the map of the state of Washington. On first glance at a map showing wilderness areas and national parks, Washington does appear to be favored. Of the forty-eight coterminous states, it has the largest percentage of its land area in such protective classifications. Unfortunately, an ecological appraisal of Washington's parks and wildernesses shatters this pleasant illusion. Olympic, North Cascades, and Mt. Rainier national parks, and Mt. Baker, Pasayten, Glacier Peak, Alpine Lakes, William O. Douglas, and other wilderness areas are mostly higher-elevation rocks and ice. The alpine areas of Washington above timberline are well protected. The ecologically productive, diverse, and fragile old-growth forests at lower elevations are not.

The tracts of ancient forest protected in the national parks and designated wilderness areas of Washington, Oregon, and northern California are isolated patches of what was once continuous temperate rainforest for nearly two thousand miles along the Pacific Coast. Each of the remaining large roadless areas in Washington, Oregon, and northern California represents a core of alpine wilderness fringed with disjunct old-growth fingers in the valleys. These fingers are isolated from each other—the lower ends of the valleys and lower mountain slopes where the forests would connect have been clearcut and intensively roaded. Such remnants have already lost their integrity as forests: as islands of habitat, they are open to windthrow, catastrophic fire, and invasion by alien species along their edges, and are unable to sustain the wolverine, fisher, river otter, pileated woodpecker, spotted owl, and other species associated with old-growth.

Only a precious few ancient forest areas in the Pacific Northwest are of such a size that they can be preserved as real old-growth, can be secure as forests and not simply as collections of large trees in open-air museums. But even as the Forest Service's own researchers tell the agency that an ancient forest isn't a farm of big trees that can be cut down and regrown, that an ancient forest is an interdependent, functioning *cycle* that maintains its own climate and life-support system, the Forest Service is destroying the last large ancient forest ecosystems in Oregon, California, Washington, and southeast Alaska.

Until the last decade, Washington's wildlands on the Canadian border were joined to a chain of wilderness stretching to the Arctic Sea. With timber practices and overhunting even worse in British Columbia today than in the United States, that connection has also been severed.

We have not simply turned trees into lumber. We have destroyed a complex, stable, ancient community. In the space of a century we have wrought a holocaust in the wilderness. And we continue.

FOUR CENTURIES OF FOREST DESTRUCTION

To understand today's battles for the remnant old-growth forests of the West and for the regenerated mature forests of the East, we must walk the forest trails of past centuries. There we will find the attitudes that motivate loggers, Forest Service officers, and politicians. When we hear a grizzled logger in Forks, Washington, fervently expressing his faith that there is plenty of old-growth left, we hear echoes of the timbermen a century ago who stripped the North Woods. When we listen to a forest supervisor preaching the need to bring a wild, unroaded, natural forest under "scientific management" by building roads, clearcutting, and herbiciding, we hear a refrain from Cotton Mather. When we hear an Oregon member of Congress chanting the mantra "Jobs—Jobs—Jobs" to an unquestioning media, we experience déjà vu all over again, and hear those members of Congress at the turn of the century who tried to clip Teddy Roosevelt's wings as he used presidential powers to withdraw millions of acres of the public domain to create what is now our National Forest System.

And by walking through these cemeteries of stumps, we will also find the forest remnants that may form the cores for the ecological forest reserves that are vital for the preservation of biological diversity in North America. The discussion that follows is not comprehensive but illustrative. While I will devote some attention to all forest regions of the United States, I will focus on the Pacific Northwest and New England forests because the Northwest is the last great old-growth destruction battleground and because the Northeast is the first great old-growth recovery battleground.

More than 370 years ago the Pilgrims stepped off the *Mayflower* into "a hideous and desolate wilderness." Seeing New England as a stronghold of Satan and the indigenes as his worshippers, they launched into the conquest of the wild with all the fervor their religion could muster. Roderick Nash, in *Wilderness and the American Mind*, quotes Edward Johnson in 1654, saying that "the admirable Acts of Christ" had transformed Boston from "hideous Thickets" where "Wolfes and Beares nurst up their young" into "streets full of Girles and Boys sporting up and downe."

In those "hideous Thickets" cloaking New England, eastern white pines grew 220 feet tall. So excellent were these great conifers that the Royal Navy reserved them for use as masts for His Majesty's ships. The timber wolf, eastern panther (catamount), wolverine, and other wilderness-dependent species that "nurst up their young" in primeval New England were eradicated as ruthlessly as were the native humans.

Coming from the picked-over woodlots of England, Cotton Mather and the Puritans were terrified by the dark, forbidding forest. Mather created a theology that is still with us, one that justified the reduction of the new continent and the decimation of its native humans. This frightening land, with its dangerous inhabitants, was obviously the haunt of Satan. He had established his kingdom here, the wolfes and

beares and catamounts were his demons, and the savages his faithful flock. This theology inspired a religious crusade to conquer the wilderness, to wrest it out of the hands of Satan and deliver it to the fold of the godly.

(Despite this anti-wilderness doctrine, there was a practical blessing from the New England forest that gave the Puritans as much pleasure as they could perhaps enjoy without guilt. Warmth. Awash in a wealth of wood, the Puritans chortled that they could heat their humble homes toastier than could any English lord.)

Among the first entrepreneurs of the American colonies were lumbermen. They resented the reservation of large white pines for naval masts, and opposed any regulation or taxing of their enterprises by the king's agents. Such resistance by up-and-coming capitalists in New England set off some of the sparks that flamed into the Revolutionary War.

To the south and west of New England stretched the most diverse deciduous temperate forest on Earth. In those woods the massive crown of an American chestnut might shade a quarter of an acre, and tulip poplars reached nearly as far toward the clouds as did the white pines. The story was told until it became gospel that a squirrel could travel from the Atlantic seaboard to the Mississippi River without ever touching the ground, so vast was the forest.

Penetrating ever deeper into the great forest over the next two hundred years, the pioneers were convinced that the big woods had to be cleared—for two reasons, *utilitarian* and *spiritual*. First, it was necessary to open the forest to let in sunlight and grow crops; and second, because the trees harbored savages, wild beasts, and satanic notions, the wildwood had to be conquered in a spiritual sense as well.

After the more accessible forests of New England and New York were cut, the loggers moved into the remote backcountry of Maine and the Adirondacks. Their more swashbuckling brethren pushed the timber frontier west. Lumbermen have chased the American forest from the Atlantic to the Pacific over the millrace of these centuries, scalping it in New England, stripping it bare in Pennsylvania, Wisconsin, and Michigan. All the while they have told us not to worry, the trees are without limit.

The North Woods of Wisconsin, Michigan, and Minnesota gave the timber industry its age of heroic legend. From the 1870s on, the exploitation of the virgin white pine forests there established a new scale for rapaciousness, and a gigantic folk hero— Paul Bunyan—had to be created to equal the deed. Never before had so much forest fallen so quickly. Even some within the timber industry became alarmed. Frederick Merk, in *History of the Westward Movement*, quotes the owners of the Black River Falls sawmill as telling the Minnesota legislature, "In a few years, the wealthiest portion of the pineries will present nothing but a vast and gloomy wilderness of pine stumps."

They were correct (except for their misuse of the word *wilderness*). Paul and the Blue Ox did their work well for the timber barons. The hardwoods and Great Lakes pine forests of northern Wisconsin were chopped to smithereens.

Someone from Madison recently wrote, "I keep driving north in Wisconsin to get to the North Woods, but I never find them."

To really find the North Woods, one has to go all the way north in the U.S. Midwest, up to northern Minnesota, where glaciers scoured the southern toe of the Canadian Shield to form the Boundary Waters. Make no mistake about it, Paul did his best to turn this area into a "wilderness of stumps," too. Despite Forest Service administrative protection for the Boundary Waters beginning in 1926, Paul's successors were permitted to swing their axes in much of it. In the 1964 Wilderness Act, Congress continued the exception. It was not until 1978, after a dreadful fight, that Congress finally protected the last great remnant of the North Woods, by outlawing logging in the Boundary Waters Wilderness.

The timber frontier leapt the plains, and now we stand on the Pacific shore, shipping the last of the ancient forest to Japan.

Having listened to the chop-chop-chop of the axe, the swish of the saw, and the rhetoric of *Manifest Destiny* in the backwoods of American history, perhaps we can now better understand the bombastic words of Harry Merlo of Louisiana-Pacific Lumber Company, the religious zeal of the supervisor of the Willamette National Forest, and the rage of a logger as he punches a demonstrator in the nose.

DEFENDING FORESTS...AND WILDERNESS

The grim reality of the 1990s is that it is not enough to safeguard the remaining wildlands of the United States. This is especially true for natural forests. To understand why, it is necessary to walk another trail through American history—the trail of the wilderness preservation movement.

The nineteenth century saw the first arguments in defense of the idea of wilderness, notably from Henry Thoreau and John Muir, as well as the establishment of the first national parks and the withdrawal of the forest reserves (later to be the national forests). But not until the 1920s were actual proposals made for protecting specific regions of land as wilderness. Let us look first, though, at a forest that a state protected.

There is little to be proud of in American history for the decades following the Civil War. During this period business became the business of America, and New York City became its capital. Nonetheless, during this era and from the city of Mammon itself came one of the great chapters in American forest preservation. With the enthusiastic support of the New York City Chamber of Commerce, the governor of New York signed a bill in 1885 establishing the Adirondack Forest Preserve in the northern part of the state. In 1894, the New York State Constitutional Convention enshrined protection of the Adirondacks in that state's highest law.

However, it was not a pristine wilderness being preserved. Moose, timber wolf, panther (eastern mountain lion), lynx, and beaver were already gone or virtually so. Little virgin forest remained. Streams had been heavily damaged by logging.

But the protection afforded the land has succeeded. Moose, raven, and beaver have returned. Bald eagle, peregrine falcon, and lynx have been reintroduced. Rivers and streams are healing themselves from past watershed abuse, and the trees are growing tall. Eastern old-growth researchers working with The Wildlands Project believe there may be as much as 100,000 acres of old-growth in several large and many small stands in the Adirondacks.

Adirondack Park is a complex preserve. Some 3.7 million of its 6 million acres are privately owned. Although there are large blocks of state land, private inholdings complicate preservation for key areas. The Adirondack Park Agency, created in 1970, was instructed to develop a master plan for management of the park. The agency was given limited authority to control development on private lands through strict zoning. Because of this, the Adirondack Park Agency has been unpopular with some of the local residents, who would sit well on a stool in any Idaho mill town bar.

The Adirondack master plan involved the classification of state lands into nine categories. These include "wilderness," with regulations as strict as those for federal wilderness areas, totaling more than one million acres. Additions to the "wilderness" classification are being continually made as private lands are acquired or non-conforming uses are removed from state lands. Commercial logging is prohibited on all state-owned lands in Adirondack Park, whether designated wilderness or not. Sadly, though, all is not well in Adirondack State Park. Under heavy pressure from development interests in northern New York, Governor Cuomo essentially abandoned Adirondack preservation as part of his political agenda, in effect terminating New York's land acquisition program and thus leaving hundreds of thousands of acres of Adirondack timberlands vulnerable to purchase by developers or by cut-and-run loggers. It seems the politicians of New York one hundred years ago were more visionary and courageous than are those today.

Soon after the state of New York blazed the trail for forest protection in the Adirondacks, Congress, concerned by rapacious logging of lands in the Rocky Mountains and the Southwest, authorized the president to withdraw forested lands from future transfer to private ownership. The primary motivation was to protect watersheds in the mountains for downstream water production for agriculture, homes, and industry. Towns downstream of the mountain forests of the West were strong supporters of such protection one hundred years ago. Many conservationists, particularly John Muir, hoped that these forest reserves (later called *national forests*) would be off-limits to logging of any kind, like the state lands in the Adirondacks. But Gifford Pinchot, the soon-to-be first chief of the United States Forest Service, convinced Congress to allow logging on these reserves under the doctrine of "sustained yield" and scientific management.

In the 1920s, Aldo Leopold and Arthur Carhart, both Forest Service officials, made the first concrete proposals for the protection of wilderness areas, in New Mexico, Colorado, and Minnesota. They also began to develop the arguments justifying the withdrawal of such areas from logging, road building, and other types of development. Another Forest Service official, Bob Marshall, took up the task of explicating the arguments for wilderness preservation in the late 1920s. In the 1930s, as head of recreation for the Forest Service, he established a system of protected wilderness areas on the national forests. These wilderness areas were the only national forest areas of any size protected from logging, although national parks, under the management of the rival National Park Service, were also protected from commercial tree cutting. Of federal lands, then, only forests in national parks and in national forest wilderness areas were secure in their natural condition against industrial logging.

The rapid increase in economic activity and development during and after World War II led not only to logging and road building in vast areas of unprotected wilderness in the national forests, but also to the Forest Service declassifying areas protected by Marshall. The main impetus for such declassification was to allow logging. Since the close of World War II, the Forest Service has destroyed an average of one million acres per year of de facto wilderness (Wolke 1991).

Howard Zahniser and Olaus Murie, both former employees of the U.S. Fish & Wildlife Service, and citizen conservationist David Brower took the lead in defending threatened wilderness. They elaborated on the arguments for wilderness preservation, and campaigned for the establishment of a congressionally sanctioned National Wilderness Preservation System that would remove discretion from the Forest Service and other land managing agencies.

After the passage of the Wilderness Act in 1964, a new generation of citizen conservationists continued the cause begun largely by government employees.

The Wilderness Act mandated the systematic review of Forest Service primitive areas and of roadless areas in the national park and national wildlife refuge systems for "wilderness" recommendation to Congress by 1974. This ten-year process of wilderness study continued to build the grassroots wilderness movement launched by the 1956-64 campaign for the Wilderness Act. Over the last thirty-five years, then, the leaders and activists of the crusade for congressionally protected wilderness areas have honed the arguments for the preservation of specific wilderness areas and the overall justification for the concept of wilderness.

Concurrently, an opposing movement arose consisting of those with an economic or ideological stake in exploiting or making accessible the backcountry. It included the logging, mining, grazing, and other extractive industries; government agency personnel committed to using all public land for "resource" extraction; motor-bound recreationists like downhill skiers, snowmobilers, and off-road vehicle users; and, members of the "bumpkin proletariat"—residents of small towns and rural areas near wildlands who believed themselves economically dependent on the exploitation of such lands and who wanted the "government off their backs." This heretofore uncoordinated lobby developed arguments against wilderness preservation and for so-called multiple use of the national forests: logging, mining, energy extraction, grazing, recreational development, road building, dam construction, motorized use of wildlands, and so forth.

Most of the reasons devised by conservationists for wilderness preservation coevolved with the arguments raised by the resource extraction lobby against wilderness preservation. The conservationists' arguments have served as an effective counter to those of the exploiters, although the political power of natural resource exploitation advocates and the inherent bias of the industrial state have offset the rational strength of conservation arguments. Reasons offered by conservationists for wilderness preservation (including national parks) can be grouped in four categories: utilitarian, aesthetic, recreational, and economic.

Utilitarian arguments for wilderness say that wilderness areas and national parks protect watersheds, provide habitat for huntable game, provide controls for scientific research, act as a savings account for resources that may be needed in the future, and so on.

Aesthetic arguments focus on the inspirational power of spectacular natural scenery, the spiritually renewing power of nature, the importance of the frontier in American history, and the role of wilderness in shaping traditional American values.

Recreational arguments (a powerful motivation for many wilderness activists) defend wilderness areas as places to hike, backpack, horsepack, canoe, raft, mountain climb, hunt, fish, birdwatch, seek solitude, and otherwise recreate without motorized equipment.

Economic arguments for wilderness point out that areas proposed for protection are relatively worthless in terms of resources. To underscore their point, conservationists have habitually stripped their proposed wilderness areas and national parks of areas with valuable timber, mineral deposits, potential highway corridors, and the like. When this was not enough they have further compromised by deleting controversial areas from proposals during the study and designation process. Forest areas, especially, have been cut from wilderness and park proposals in the compromise cha-cha-cha of the political process. More recently, some conservationists have used economic analysis to support wilderness preservation as the most cost-effective alternative in many regions.

THE FAILURE OF WILDERNESS AND PARKS

The character of the now 90-million-acre National Wilderness Preservation System and of the National Park System reflects the arguments used by wilderness preservationists during this give-and-take debate. Over the last fifteen years, a growing body of conservationists has become concerned that both the prevailing concept of wilderness and the reality of the Wilderness and National Park systems are inadequate. They see, despite the increase in the number of protected areas and in the growth of the total protected acreage, that the two systems have largely failed from an ecological perspective of protecting habitat—especially forests. This conclusion is based on these observations:

1. Wilderness areas and national parks are circumscribed units not connected to other protected areas and are often surrounded by areas of intense land management; they are habitat islands.

2. Even the largest wilderness areas and national parks are too small to stand alone as functional ecosystems.

3. Wilderness areas and national parks are spectacular and well-suited to primitive forms of recreation, but most habitat areas crucial for wildlife have been left out.

4. Natural ecosystems have become fragmented.

5. Populations of and habitat for wilderness-dependent species have drastically declined.

6. Outside impacts are degrading wilderness areas.

7. Wilderness areas are preserved as static landscapes, snapshots in time, instead of as dynamic reservoirs for the processes of ecological change and evolution. (Natural disturbance regimes, especially fire cycles, have been truncated.)

In summation, despite the growth of the National Wilderness Preservation System and the National Park System in the United States, the decline of natural ecosystems and the loss of biodiversity have not been stanched; indeed, they continue to accelerate. Nowhere is this more obvious than in ancient and other natural forests—particularly low-elevation forests—in all parts of the country.

Moreover, many conservationists believe that conventional arguments for wilderness uphold the worldview and value system of those who oppose wilderness. These arguments are based on anthropocentric assumptions that wilderness has value only in terms of its worth to human beings.

ECOLOGICAL WILDERNESS AND WILDERNESS RECOVERY

As we have seen, preservation of wilderness has focused on prime recreational areas—the scenic lakes and peaks of timberline regions—at the expense of the most ecologically significant areas, ancient forests. Hiking, backpacking, kayaking, mountain climbing, and cross-country skiing are compatible uses of national parks and wilderness areas, but they are not—or should not be—the purpose for such areas. The fundamental reason for designating national parks and wilderness areas is to preserve reservoirs of native diversity, reserves for continuing evolution.

Such areas are not mere scenery or outdoor exercise yards. They are the repository of four billion years of organic evolution on Earth. Within a few decades, we will destroy that continuum of life, unless we act now.

With these realizations, conservation biologists, environmental ethicists, and grass-roots conservationists have begun to develop new arguments for wilderness areas. These ideas build on Aldo Leopold's land ethic; these conservationists defend both the wilderness concept and on-the-ground wilderness from a biocentric standpoint of recognizing the intrinsic value of wild places and species.

It is from this standpoint that we can begin to look over remnant natural forests and other wildlands, seek out once-logged, roaded, and otherwise abused areas where active restoration or natural recovery can occur, and begin to develop plans for large core wilderness reserves, surrounded by buffer zones and connected to one another by biological corridors. Conservation biologists are coming to believe that such a linked system is the only way to protect the biological diversity and evolutionary processes of North America. The Wildlands Project is working with dozens of groups throughout North America to develop such a wilderness recovery plan for the continent, from Panama to Alaska. A major task of this project in the United States is to identify both remaining natural forests and once-exploited forests that can be incorporated into such a reserve network. Here, it is important that we look not only at the ancient forests and surrounding areas of the Pacific Northwest and the Northern Rocky Mountains, but at the Northeast, South, Midwest, and Southwest as well. Protection of natural and recovering forests and restoration of vast areas around them is vital for the preservation of biological diversity in the United States and Canada.

EASTERN FOREST RECOVERY

In designing a major ecological recovery effort for forest areas east of the Great Plains, two types of areas must be considered. First, there are a few large blocks of forest already in federal or state ownership that form the logical core units for a bio-diversity recovery system. These "Greater Ecosystems" in the East are Adirondack State Park in New York, the North Woods of northern Minnesota, the Upper Peninsula of Michigan (national forests, state forests, and national parks), the southern Appalachians (Great Smoky Mountains National Park and surrounding national forests), and the Florida Everglades. Smaller blocks of federal and state land with potential as wilderness recovery core areas are Baxter State Park in Maine, White Mountain National Forest in New Hampshire, state forests in north-central Pennsylvania, Shenandoah National Park and national forests in the central Appalachians of West Virginia and Virginia, and Okefenokee National Wildlife Refuge–Osceola National Forest in Georgia and Florida. National forests and state lands in other eastern states are key as smaller core areas and as biological corridors between the larger cores.

The second type of area to consider in developing a wilderness recovery network is private land suitable for public purchase and ecological restoration. While such public acquisition is necessary in forest areas throughout the East, three regions demand special attention. They are the transition forests of northern New England and New York, southern longleaf pine forests, and Ohio Valley hardwood forests. In the first two, huge areas are owned by a few corporate interests.

Let us first consider the existing public forests in the East.

Past efforts by conservationists to establish national forests in the East—and, more recently, to protect them from destructive logging—offer precedents and instruction for a more visionary strategy. This should include complete protection for eastern

national forests as the cores for continental wildland recovery, and public acquisition and restoration of large tracts of forest currently in private ownership.

When national forests were established in the West around the turn of the century, there were few public lands left in the East from which national forests could be established (the upper Midwest was the principal exception). Nonetheless, conservationists, supported by eastern members of Congress, recognized that national forests should be created in the East. The Weeks Act, enacted by Congress in 1910, authorized the purchase of private lands for national forests. Most national forests in the East, as well as most national parks and national wildlife refuges there, are former private lands that have been purchased by federal and state governments, and by private groups. Thus, buying large tracts of private land for public conservation purposes is not unprecedented.

Eastern conservationists began to suggest possible wilderness protection for national forest areas east of the Rockies before the Wilderness Act was passed in 1964. The Forest Service argued that no areas qualified, that there was a fundamental difference between national forest lands east and west (except for Minnesota's Boundary Waters). In the West, they argued, national forests had been withdrawn from the public domain and, although some minor uses such as grazing, tie-hacking, old cabins, and such may have previously been made of wilderness areas there, those areas were essentially pristine. The eastern national forests, on the other hand, had been purchased from private owners and added to the system. They had been homesteaded, cleared, and developed at various times during their history. Even if, under Forest Service management, the forests were growing up, old roads were fading, signs of habitation were disappearing, and the appearance of wilderness was being reestablished, these areas were not wilderness in the same sense as the western wilderness. There was a qualitative difference, the Forest Service insisted. To include eastern areas in the wilderness system would tarnish the whole system and demean the pristine western areas.

There was an element of sincerity in the Forest Service argument. Some foresters honestly believed it. Others used it in a Machiavellian way to keep their managerial hands from being tied. Yes, under Forest Service protection these eastern areas were recovering from past abuse, but that didn't mean the Forest Service had no plans to abuse them again as their trees became large enough to harvest.

Nevertheless, belying their own argument, the Forest Service had established three wilderness areas (called "wild areas" because they were under 100,000 acres) in the East before the Wilderness Act. They were Linville Gorge and Shining Rock in North Carolina, and Great Gulf in New Hampshire.

Convinced that there was no other potential wilderness in the East, the Forest Service's first Roadless Area Review and Evaluation (RARE), in 1972, covered only national forests in the twelve western states (with three exceptions—one each in Florida, North Carolina, and Puerto Rico). Eastern conservationists mobilized with the support of The Wilderness Society and submitted wilderness proposals to Congress. An Eastern Wilderness bill was drafted; the Forest Service countered with a proposal for a separate, but lesser, system of eastern national forest "wild areas." After a substantial campaign, a bill was passed by Congress and signed by President Ford in January 1975, establishing sixteen full-fledged units of the National Wilderness Preservation System in eastern national forests and directing the Forest Service to study for possible "wilderness" recommendation an additional seventeen areas.

The dam had been broken. The Forest Service in the second Roadless Area Review and Evaluation (RARE II), in 1977–79, considered national forests in the East equally with national forests in the West. Statewide bills in the decade after RARE II have designated additional national forest wilderness areas in most of the eastern states with national forests.

Two factors, unfortunately, work against wilderness designation in eastern national forests. First, the land-use history of these recovered wildernesses limits their size. Only a handful of national forest roadless areas in the East exceed 100,000 acres in size; most total under 25,000 acres. The lands that have recovered are small and isolated. It will require conscious planning to restore areas of several hundred thousand acres in the East to a general condition of roadlessness and continuous forest cover. This is the first prerequisite for reestablishing ecological wilderness with the full range of native species.

Second, Forest Service managers have the same bulldozer and chainsaw mind-set in the East as they have in the West. Their job is to build roads and cut trees, not to restore and protect ecosystems, or so they believe. Areas in the eastern national forests that have recovered a degree of wildness and roadlessness are under the same threat of clearcutting and roading as are larger areas in the West. Even though eastern national forests are the logical cores for wilderness restoration, this will not be achieved with the support of the Forest Service, but by overpowering them in the same way conservationists overpowered them in 1974 on the Eastern Wilderness Act. It will be a far more difficult campaign.

The designated wilderness areas on the White Mountain National Forest, for example, were not easy to win. The 1984 New Hampshire Wilderness Act was the worst one in the East. Of 262,257 acres in RARE II (conservationists proposed 495,596 acres for wilderness and that figure is a far more accurate indicator of what was roadless), only 77,000 acres were protected in the bill. Taking a page from wilderness bills in the West, most of the protected acreage was in the higher elevations of the White Mountains, leaving the ecologically more important lower-elevation forests open to increased logging.

The Green Mountain National Forest (GMNF) in Vermont has done as well as any eastern national forest in terms of wilderness designation, but the Forest Service plans clearcutting in key unprotected wildlands vital for linking existing wilderness areas into larger old-growth recovery areas. Fortunately, Preserve Appalachian Wilderness (PAW) has recently stopped most planned timber sales on the GMNF, as well as many on other eastern national forests.

The largest block of forest in Pennsylvania is on state forests in the north-central part of the state. Closure of minor roads and prohibition of logging around the Hammersley Wild Area could create a quarter-million-acre core wilderness recovery area that would serve as a vital link between the Adirondacks of New York and the central and southern Appalachians to the south. This area could also help link the Adirondacks to the Ohio Valley recovery areas.

The Eastern Wilderness Act in 1974 and subsequent wilderness legislation was too late to give us big wilderness in the national forests of the South. Nonetheless, conservationists propose visionary wilderness recovery plans for the Jefferson, Washington, and Monongahela national forests in the central Appalachians of Virginia and West Virginia. Virginians for Wilderness has set a powerful precedent for conservation groups by convincing the George Washington National Forest to include a wilderness recovery alternative in the forest plan.

National forests and Great Smoky Mountains National Park in the southern Appalachians form the largest block of federal land east of the Mississippi River—four million acres. This is the core for a major forested wilderness recovery area that could support the whole range of native species, including wolf, eastern panther, and elk. Not surprisingly, the Forest Service has launched a blitzkrieg of logging and road building in these national forests to make up for decreasing timber extraction in Washington, Oregon, and northern California.

Farther south is the most devastated major American forest type—the longleaf pine–wiregrass landscape. Once covering 60 to 70 million acres of the Southeastern Coastal Plain from the Carolinas to the Mississippi River, less than five million acres remain, mostly in small, degraded patches. No more than 2 percent of the original longleaf pine communities are in reasonably healthy condition. Fire control, logging, and conversion to pine plantations have virtually destroyed this ecosystem and threaten the species dependent on it, like Florida panther, black bear, gopher tortoise, indigo snake, Sherman's fox squirrel, and red-cockaded woodpecker. The national forests in Florida are key parts of a visionary core wilderness-biological corridor recovery plan for that state, already developed by conservation biologists Reed Noss and Larry Harris. Despite the growing support within Florida for this landmark plan, the Forest Service remains stridently opposed and goes on cutting and roading the rare longleaf pine forests under their stewardship. A similar situation exists on lowland national forests in the Carolinas, Georgia, Mississippi, and Alabama. Conservationists need to stop all logging on the longleaf pine national forests.

In the national forests of east Texas, local Forest Service officials vie for "worst in the nation" status by conducting "noncommercial" logging operations in designated wilderness areas. This led Texas conservationist Ned Fritz to launch a national forest reform campaign, the Forest Reform Network, to outlaw clearcutting.

In the Ohio Valley national forests (Wayne in Ohio, Hoosier in Indiana, and Shawnee in Illinois), conservationists led by a new coalition called Heartwood are campaigning hard for a halt to all logging on the national forests and state forests. These national forests, with nearby state forests, are the core areas for wilderness recovery in the Ohio Valley.

Opportunities abound for wilderness recovery in the North Woods of Wisconsin, Minnesota, and Michigan on national forests, national parks, and state forests. Although the largest wilderness area in Wisconsin today is less than 20,000 acres on the Nicolet National Forest—by closing roads, by stilling the chainsaws, by encouraging timber wolf and moose—ecological wilderness could come back. Botanists at the University of Wisconsin have proposed two biodiversity preserves (100,000 acres and 40,000 acres) on the Chequamegon National Forest where native old-growth ecosystems could be reestablished. To his lasting credit, the forest supervisor supported the idea, but the regional forester overruled him. The botanists have sued over the rejection of their visionary proposal in federal court. More power to them.

In the Upper Peninsula (UP) of Michigan, where Nick Adams and his kid sister fished the Big Two Hearted River… well, Paul Bunyan got that, too. But he missed a couple of places on the UP, places that offer a glimpse of what Michigan once was. These areas of national forest and state forest offer cores for ambitious wilderness/old-growth recovery areas of a quarter of a million acres and more.

The Superior National Forest of northeastern Minnesota, nearby Voyageurs National Park, and state forest lands in the peatlands of north-central Minnesota create a block of five million acres of public land that could be combined with a similar block of five million acres in adjacent Ontario for one of the largest temperate forest reserves in the world. Although logging is proceeding apace in much of this region, the Minnesota North Woods probably hold the largest block of virgin forest in North America east of the Rockies and south of the Boreal Forest.

It is not enough, however, to restore natural forests on land already owned by the federal and state governments. Some of the wildest and most important forest areas in the East are owned by large timber and paper companies. A national crusade is needed to demand the purchase and subsequent protection of these lands by federal and state governments. The three major areas demanding large public acquisitions are the Northeast, the Southeast Coastal Plain, and the Ohio Valley.

Surprisingly, much of New England is wilder today than it was 100 years ago or even 150 years ago. Fields marked by stone walls have grown up into forest again; there are rumors of catamounts. Abandoned dirt roads in the mountains are fading.

Nowhere else in the United States are the opportunities for sweeping wilderness restoration greater than in northern New York, Vermont, New Hampshire, and Maine. The land is more resilient here than in the arid West, and the pressures for development have not been so strong until recently. With the wisdom and foresight that established Adirondack Park one hundred years ago, wilderness recovery areas of millions of acres could be put together in the Northeast today from privately owned timber lands. Paper companies own a vast, once-logged but otherwise undeveloped area near the Canadian border in Maine, New Hampshire, and Vermont, which consists of northeastern spruce/fir and northern hardwoods forests, streams, lakes, and mountains.

Indeed, some *10 million acres* in Maine are uninhabited by year-round humans, according to wilderness expert and author George Wuerthner. This is the largest uninhabited area in the lower forty-eight. The "Northeast Kingdom" of Vermont, mostly paper company land, is the wildest and least populated part of that state. Much of northern New Hampshire (in private ownership) is probably as wild as the large roadless areas in the White Mountain National Forest. Similarly, huge areas in Adirondack State Park in New York are owned by paper companies. These areas have, of course, been logged, and some dirt roads scar them, but the opportunity to restore significant wilderness is greater in northern New England and New York than anywhere else in the United States. If these areas were transferred to public ownership, and closed to logging and motorized vehicles, the forests would develop old-growth characteristics in a century. Wilderness-dependent species such as wolverine, panther, lynx, pine marten, and caribou would likely return even sooner. The fisher has already repatriated.

The opportunity for such restoration will never be better than it is today. The going price for timber company land is two hundred dollars per acre or less; all of northern Maine (10 million acres) could be purchased for under $2 billion—the price of two Stealth bombers. More than enough money is currently in the federal government's Land & Water Conservation Fund to buy several million acres in northern New England for wilderness restoration and a new national park(s). All that is lacking is enough popular demand to force the necessary political will.

Now is the time for conservationists in New England and the nation to envision real wilderness, with its full complement of native species. The opportunity currently exists for wilderness on an Alaskan scale in New England.

If conservationists do not act swiftly, however, the opportunity will be lost. Forestry is becoming harsher on corporate lands. Herbicides, larger clearcuts, shorter rotation

times, more roads, and heavier machinery are having a more devastating impact than the "lighter" logging practices of the past. Relatively natural forests are being transformed into industrial tree farms. Moreover, developers like the Patten Corporation are gobbling up paper company lands that are put on the market. If this continues, condominiums, ski areas, lodges, vacation resorts, and second homes will ring the lakes and scar the mountains; loon and wolf will lose out once again.

As big timber companies cut the last old-growth forests on the Pacific coast, they are moving their principal operations to the pine forests of the Southeast, where they hope to harvest trees like corn in planted fields. Just as in New England, it is important to identify privately owned forest tracts in the Southeast as priorities for public acquisition for old-growth recovery areas. The rapid transformation of the southeastern forest into artificial pine plantations makes that task urgent.

Ecologists are also examining the remnant mixed-deciduous forests of the Ohio Valley to identify prime old-growth forest recovery areas and to set priorities for public acquisition of key private forest tracts that could expand and connect existing state lands and national forests in Ohio, Indiana, and Illinois.

WESTERN FOREST RECOVERY

Although a greater percentage of forests in the West are in public ownership and there are more old-growth or other natural forests than in the East, far too much ancient forest has already been lost. A three-part program is called for in the West to maintain and restore native forest ecosystems. First, all remaining old-growth and other natural forests on western public lands must be completely protected from logging of any kind and from new road construction. Second, previously logged national forest areas should be encouraged to once again develop old-growth characteristics. Roads should be closed, timber cuts allowed to heal, and future logging entry halted. Research should be done to determine management techniques to allow old-growth–dependent species to disperse between isolated ancient forest patches. Third, some key private forest lands, particularly on the Pacific Coast and in the Northern Rockies, should be acquired by the federal government to fill in gaps between core wilderness recovery areas on the national forests and national parks.

Let's take a quick tour of the West to point out a few specifics.

Arizona has lost more of its virgin forest than has any other western state. The last old-growth in Arizona is on the North Rim of the Grand Canyon in the Kaibab National Forest, and in the White Mountains–Mogollon Rim country of the Apache National Forest, where Aldo Leopold shot the "green fire" wolf. In New Mexico, the significant old-growth is on the Gila National Forest in the southwestern part of the state and on the Carson and Santa Fe national forests in the north. The rake-hell Forest Service is out to log it all.

In 1991 conservation groups in the Southwest, led by Forest Guardians, filed a trailblazing lawsuit to protect old-growth and other natural forests. The suit uses the 1976 National Forest Management Act to demand management for biodiversity on the national forests of the Southwest. Conservationists are using the northern goshawk as the keystone species for old-growth forest ecosystems in Arizona and New Mexico, most of which are near collapse. The suit takes an ecosystem approach, however, rather than a single-species approach as other lawsuits have in the past. Mycorrhizal fungi, ponderosa pine, tassel-eared squirrel, and northern goshawk form a chain that ties the forest together. While 260 pairs of goshawks once nested on the North Kaibab Ranger District alone, only 122 goshawk pairs could be inventoried in all of Arizona and New Mexico in 1991—a graphic indication of the collapse of the ponderosa pine ecosystem due to logging. This suit should set the pattern for future ecosystem-based lawsuits by conservation groups throughout the country.

Colorado had the second-highest acreage of roadless areas in the Forest Service's RARE II program of any state, behind Idaho, but since then it has lost more acreage in large roadless areas than has any other state because of logging. The Forest Service loses money on timber sales in Colorado; yet they continue to clearcut right up to timberline. Conservationists are mobilizing through the Colorado Forest Mapping and Monitoring Project to identify all remaining native forests and to develop a visionary wilderness and forest recovery plan.

The forests of Montana and Idaho represent the last frontier for backcountry logging. Under "wilderness" bills proposed for Montana and Idaho RARE II lands—proposed by the congressional delegations of the two states—over 90 percent of the roadless, natural forest on the national forests would be opened to roading and clearcutting. The Alliance for the Wild Rockies is whipping up opposition to this sell-out—their comprehensive Northern Rockies Ecosystem Protection Act would protect all roadless areas and establish several wilderness recovery areas.

A wide range of efforts are under way in California to protect national forests and corporate-owned forests alike. The situation is far too complex to summarize here, but one group should be mentioned for its leadership in the development of an integrated wilderness recovery network for North America. This is the Klamath Forest Alliance, which is defending biological forest corridors between designated wilderness areas in northern California. They filed a lawsuit demanding protection of forests in such corridors.

Because of widespread support for environmental protection in Washington, members of Congress from that state generally try to portray themselves as conservationists. But they reveal their true timber industry colors in the ancient forest battle. Members of Washington's congressional delegation overwhelmingly support timber industry bills that would mandate the liquidation of old-growth, hamstring the Endangered Species Act, and prevent conservationists from challenging timber sales. A notable exception was Senator Brock Adams, retired, who introduced a good bill—the Pacific Northwest Forest Community Recovery and Ecosystem Conservation Act of 1991.

In many ways, Oregon is the center of the battle for healthy, natural forests. It is here this essay began; it is here it will end.

If Oregon didn't have a gutsy statewide wilderness group like the Oregon Natural Resources Council, if hundreds of Earth First!ers hadn't blockaded bulldozers and chainsaws with their own bodies, politicans and the Forest Service would be even more effective in their service to the timber industry. Without swift enactment of comprehensive legislation to protect all remaining natural forests, without major cuts to the Forest Service road-building budget, without prohibition of below-cost timber sales, without strengthening the Endangered Species Act—without all of this, it is highly likely that the U.S. Forest Service will consume the remaining viable native forest ecosystems before the end of this century. Wilderness protection and recovery proposals have been developed by citizen groups in Oregon. For example, the Coast Range Association commissioned ecologist Reed Noss to develop a wilderness recovery plan for the Oregon Coast Range—"A Preliminary Biodiversity Conservation Plan for the Oregon Coast Range"—that provides a state-of-the-art case study of biodiversity conservation at the scale of a bioregion: the Oregon Coast Range. This report states that "the goals for conservation at a regional scale include representation of all ecosystems across their natural range of variation; maintenance

of viable population of all evolutionary processes; and adaptability to change, both natural and human-induced. The Oregon Coast Range Bioregion is defined as the Physiographic Province extending from the Coquille River in the south, north to the Columbia River, east to the Willamette Valley, and west to the Pacific Ocean." Other citizen groups, including the Siskiyou Educational Project, have identified nearly a million acres in southwestern Oregon and northern California in the Klamath-Siskiyou region, that could form the core for a world heritage biodiversity reserve. Containing portions of designated wild and scenic rivers including portions of the Rogue, Illinois, Smith, and Clear Creek drainages, this visionary proposal could be a model for wilderness and biodiversity recovery proposals throughout the continent.

But, unless citizens throughout Canada and the U.S. wake up to the vision of living, natural forests as the key to healthy and prosperous sustainable communities, our legacy will be a wasteland of stumps. Our civilization will join civilizations and empires of the past, like those of the Middle East, Greece, Rome, and North Africa, who squandered their forest wealth for fast bucks from a quick cut.

If we wake up from greed into humility, and protect the integrity of forest ecosystems of North America, we may avoid the fate of Ozymandias.

REFERENCES

Foreman, Dave. 1991. *Confessions of an eco-warrior.* New York: Harmony Books/Crown Publishers.

Foreman, Dave, and Howie Wolke. 1992. *The Big Outside.* New York: Harmony Books/Crown Publishers.

Noss, Reed. A Preliminary Biodiversity Conservation Plan for the Oregon Coast Range, a report to the Coast Range Association. 1992. Newport, Oregon: Coast Range Association.

Wilderness Society, The. *Ancient forests of the Mt. Baker-Snoqualmie National Forest.* Washington, D.C.: The Wilderness Society.

Wolke, Howie. 1991. *Wilderness on the rocks.* Tucson: Ned Ludd Books.

"Escape"

When we get out of the glass bottles of our ego,
and when we escape like squirrels turning in the
   cages of our personality
and get into the forests again,
we shall shiver with cold and fright,
but things will happen to us
so that we don't know ourselves.

Cool, unlying life will rush in,
and passion will make our bodies taut with power,
we shall stamp our feet with new power
and old things will fall down,
we shall laugh, and institutions will curl up like
   burnt paper.
—D. H. Lawrence

Lines from "Words of the Earth"

Consider the life of trees.
Aside from the axe, what trees acquire from man is inconsiderable.
What man may acquire from trees is immeasurable.
From their mute forms there flows a poise, in silence,
    a lovely sound and motion in response to wind.
What peace comes to those aware of the voice and bearing of trees!
Trees do not scream for attention.
A tree, a rock, has no pretence, only a real growth out of itself,
    in close communion with the universal spirit.
A tree retains a deep serenity.
It establishes in the earth not only its root system but also those roots
    of its beauty and its unknown consciousness.
Sometimes one may sense a glisten of that consciousness, and with such
    perspective, feel that man is not necessarily the highest form of life.
Tree qualities, after long communion, come to reside in man.
As stillness enhances sound, so through little things
    the joy of living expands.
One is aware, lying under trees,
    of the roots and directions of one's whole being.
Perceptions drift in from earth and sky.
A vast healing begins.
—Cedric Wright

THE RECOGNITION OF INTRINSIC VALUE
IN THE WRITING OF LEGISLATION

WARWICK FOX

What are we committing ourselves to when we accept a particular criterion of intrinsic value, and hence, moral consideration? Many people seem to jump to the conclusion that if an entity is recognized as being intrinsically valuable then it is inviolable; that there is something more or less sacred about it such that it cannot be interfered with under any circumstances. Clearly this understanding would make any sort of life-based ethic—one that recognized the intrinsic value of trees and plants as well as animals—unworkable. What would those who accepted such a view eat? Fortunately for those who accept such a view—and unfortunately for those who would prefer to keep their ethics simple—this understanding is quite incorrect. Even in the human case, we readily accept that it is justifiable to harm— even kill—another human, if, for example, we are acting in self-defense. Thus, the question of whether it is wrong to harm or interfere with entities that are intrinsically valuable actually turns on the question of whether we have *sufficient justification* for our actions.

At this point, however, one might say, "Well how far has the attempt to extend the recognition of intrinsic value got us? People are going to argue just as much over what constitutes a sufficient justification for harming, say a tree, as they had argued over the question of intrinsic value in the first place." But what this objection misses is that the recognition of intrinsic value (and, hence, moral consideration) changes the context of discussions concerning the question of sufficient justification in a crucial way, namely, it reverses the *onus of justification*.

If the nonhuman world is only considered to be instrumentally valuable, then people are permitted to use and otherwise interfere with any aspect of it for whatever reasons they wish (i.e., no justification for interference is required). If anyone objects to such interference, then, within this framework of reference, the onus is clearly on the person who objects to justify why it is more useful to humans to leave that aspect of the nonhuman world alone. If, however, the nonhuman world is considered to be intrinsically valuable, then the onus shifts to the person who wants to interfere with it to justify why they should be allowed to do so: anyone who wants to interfere with any entity that is intrinsically valuable is morally obliged to be able to offer a sufficient justification for their actions. Thus, recognizing the intrinsic value of the nonhuman world to the person who wants to interfere with it—and that, in itself, represents a fundamental shift in the terms of environmental debate and decision making.

Often, of course, environmentalists and developers talk at cross-purposes because environmentalists recognize that the nonhuman world (or at least certain aspects of it) is intrinsically valuable whereas developers either explicitly or effectively deny this. Each side therefore thinks that the onus of justification lies with the other side. The beauty of recognizing intrinsic values in legislation, as New Zealand had done, for example (Environment Act 1986, Conservation Act 1987), is that it helps, at least in theory, to define the situation for the participants. I say "at least in theory" because it is important that the notion of intrinsic value be a fairly precise one if it

is to clarify rather than further complicate the situation. That is, one needs to know what kind of argument for intrinsic value and, hence, what criterion of intrinsic value lies behind the legislation (e.g., does the legislation adopt, either explicitly or implicitly, a sentience-based approach, a life-based approach, an autopoietic approach, or some other kind of approach?).

Yet, however clear or murky any particular piece of intrinsic value legislation may be, one thing is clear: if the intrinsic value of nonhuman entities or natural systems is recognized by law, then the question of the onus of justification is no longer a matter for debate. Those who wish to interfere with the integrity of these entities or systems are clearly the ones who are called upon, at least in the first instance, to provide sufficient justification for their actions. This amounts to a revolution in our treatment of the nonhuman world that is comparable to the difference for humans between a legal system that operates on a presumption of guilt until innocence is proved beyond a reasonable doubt and one that operates on a presumption of innocence until guilt is proved beyond a reasonable doubt. The question of just where the onus of justification lies can be highly significant for the parties concerned!

Trygve Steen

The goal of forest policy should be healthy forest landscapes for generations (of all living beings) to come.
The goal of forest managers should be optimal support of biodiversity even as humans make use of forests for vital needs.
And the goal of citizens, should these first two goals remain unheeded, should be to bear witness personally
to the many threats to forests, and to resist excessive, commodity-based industrial forestry practices on every hill,
in every hollow, and across entire forested landscapes.

POLICY IN THE WOODS

R. EDWARD GRUMBINE

All my life I have lived among trees but I never understood the importance of forests until faced with their demise. A student of the woods through love, and of environmental policy by profession, I cannot untangle my forty years' experience with a rich variety of North American forests from a more objective analysis of forest management. Personal experience of forests provides the basis for policy in the woods.

My childhood was spent in the dark spruce-hemlock woods of the Tongass National Forest in southeastern Alaska. The time was the early 1950s, just as the U.S. Forest Service was negotiating now infamous, fifty-year logging contracts with several Japanese- and American-owned timber corporations. There were as yet few clearcuts among the myriad islands of the Inside Passage. The forests of this mountain-and-saltwater landscape were ancient and whole.

When I returned to live in the Tongass country in 1976, the trees were falling fast. Clearcuts had ravaged entire mountainsides. Salmon streams were silted. I testified at public hearings where the Forest Service, conservationists, loggers, mill owners, and the state battled over just how much more logging would occur. Congress "resolved" the issue in 1980 by giving the Forest Service a $40 million annual subsidy to get the cut out. (A recent law eliminating the subsidy has not changed the fact that forestry in southeast Alaska continues to damage ecosystems.)

From wild Alaska my family moved to the deciduous woods of central Maryland. The ancient eastern forests had been cut down long ago by the original Euro-American settlers but second-growth stands were thriving intermixed with farm fields. With most of my ecological education still to come, I knew nothing of habitat fragmentation and its effects on biodiversity. Yet I learned two important lessons from the eastern deciduous forests that would help me understand forest policy in later years.

The first lesson was that natural forests, at least in eastern North America, are resilient. Under many circumstances the processes of ecological succession have grown thriving new stands, even after the rapacious cut-and-get-out logging practices of a century ago. The Maryland forests I encountered were no more than 125 years old, yet they harbored an amazing diversity of life—except, of course, for the extirpated large eastern mammals (elk, bison, timber wolf, mountain lion, and others).

The second lesson I learned was that biodiversity mattered little to professional foresters. For a brief month I worked for the state Forest Service doing "stand conversions." This meant that I was paid to plant loblolly pines and other commercially valuable species among the wreckage of native stands that had been burned and bulldozed to make way for pine plantations. Years later, hiking in the largest remaining refuge of primal deciduous forest in the Great Smoky Mountains, I reflected on the gap between native forests and what I had wrought in Maryland. The pines did not compare favorably.

My experience with forests deepened over several years of living on the west slope of the Cascade Mountains in Washington state in the late 1980s as the northern spotted owl controversy flared up. It was here that many of the contradictions between forest policy and ecological integrity came into focus. I rambled in watersheds through intact ancient forests in the state with more acres of protected old-growth than any other. But first I had to navigate miles of clearcuts as I drove eroded logging roads toward distant trailheads. I participated in public hearings sponsored by the Forest Service but seldom saw my comments influence decisions. I met many agency employees and noticed that the higher up in the bureaucracy they labored, the less they cared about ecological forestry. The fragmented landscape I experienced in the woods was matched by a fragmented mind-set within the agency. All across the landscape of management the results of forest laws and policies were obvious—damaged ecosystems, dysfunctional management, and human conflict over resources.

To understand how present forest policies have placed us on a path toward an unsustainable future, and to fathom the relationship between healthy forest ecosystems and meaningful policy reform, we must first look back in time to the origin of forest management.

A BRIEF HISTORY OF FOREST MANAGEMENT LAW AND POLICY

Americans today take public lands for granted. But neither national forests, parks, nor wildlife refuges existed before the latter part of the nineteenth century. In fact, there was no public domain of any kind until 1781. At that time, the obscure, overlapping, and contentious "western" land claims of the original thirteen colonies were settled in favor of national ownership. By 1867, the public domain had grown to 1.84 billion acres through a combination of outright purchase and war. Almost 80 percent of the country was now in federal ownership and raw land became the richest resource of the newly expanded nation. With no management policy and less ability to enforce one, Congress began to give land away to the new states, soldiers, and speculators to encourage investment and settlement.

The last decades of the nineteenth century were the rowdiest chapter in the history of U.S. land management. Congress passed a plethora of land disposal laws, many of which contradicted each other; none were implemented with any consistency. With lax enforcement there was little difference really between private, state, and federal ownership in the U.S. Squatters camped where they wished. Timber companies cut down forests they owned and many more they did not. Ranchers "legally" claimed gargantuan spreads and then set hordes of cattle to overgrazing. There were few fences to stop them.

Westward expansion and unfettered development made the U.S. the wealthiest country in the world. Americans mixed their labor with the land and created a high-speed economy geared toward profit. Population, production, technological innovation, and specialization all grew as the country fed its ecosystems into the mills of industrial capitalism. As the nineteenth century drew to a close, however, a few visionary Americans were beginning to see beyond the taming of the continent. The standard view is that federal land management grew out of an evolving sense of the need for land-use limitations. This trend was strengthened by an increasingly urban and leisured middle class who looked upon rapacious development and lack of federal oversight as undemocratic, inefficient, and against the national interest.

Forest policy was officially born when President Benjamin Harrison, with the consent of Congress, carved the first forest reserves out of the vast public domain of the western U.S. in 1891. Pressure had been building for lawmakers to withdraw lands to protect them from squatters and trespassers ever since the first national parks were proclaimed in the 1870s. Even so, Congress did not act decisively—the new reserves were given no *raison d'être* or funding. They were drawn on maps but no one knew what purpose they were to serve.

The majority of Americans in 1891 did not consider the forest reserves essential to the welfare of the nation. Though Congress had begun to reverse its land giveaway policies, it remained to be seen what would be done with the newly consolidated public domain. This was truly the dawn of a new era. It takes imagination for citizens of late twentieth-century America to comprehend the landscape of the last decade of the nineteenth century. Today, with 80 percent of the continental U.S. in *private* hands, ownership patterns are exactly opposite those of one hundred years ago. Westward settlement was by no means complete and there were no public land policy precedents. There was not even a Forest Service to manage the new forest reserves.

Several people, John Muir and Gifford Pinchot among them, had ideas about managing the new public lands. Muir, the foremost proponent of the national parks, preferred them set aside for preservation in the manner of Yellowstone and Yosemite. Pinchot, on the other hand, felt that the reserves should become the nation's first forestry laboratories. Fresh from France and Germany where he had studied silviculture, Pinchot was eager to plant European forest management ideas in the soil of the New World. Both men became members of the 1896 National Academy of Science commission whose purpose was to recommend a forest reserve strategy to Congress. After a summer of touring the reserves, the commission, unable to reach consensus, sidestepped the main issue and suggested that more lands be set aside. When President Grover Cleveland complied, Congress reacted strongly. With a coalition of western congressmen leading the way, the Forest Management Act of 1897 passed by a two-to-one margin. The new law authorized the Secretary of Interior, who administered the forest reserves, to sell timber and protect watersheds. The reserves were not to become preserves. Pinchot won, Muir lost, and the country had its first official forest management policy.

The argument Pinchot and Muir had over the future of the forest reserves split America's nascent conservation movement into those who followed Pinchot and favored "wise use" of nature and those who believed, with Muir, that forests should be preserved forever. That Pinchot had his way with Congress is hardly surprising. But how exactly did Pinchot, the first chief of the Forest Service, define "wise use"?

Pinchot argued his ideas with a blunt and forceful clarity: "The first great fact about conservation is that it stands for development" (Pinchot 1947). The chief forester summarized this philosophy with the slogan that conservation should provide "the greatest happiness for the greatest number over the longest period of time." That his views still form the bedrock belief of Forest Service managers some nine decades later is a tribute to Pinchot's vision and political acumen. But this vision has proved insufficient as the foundation for forestry over time.

Questioning Pinchot's famous dictum is a lesson in critical thinking. Who decided what "happiness" was to be and how much of it would be enough? Lawmakers had mentioned only timber and water in the 1897 Forest Management Act. How was "satisfaction of the greatest number" to be determined? Were certain groups automatically in a position to reap the benefits or were forest products and profits to be distributed equally among all classes of society? What about nonhuman beings' claims for "happiness" and habitat? How long was the "longest period of time"? To this, Pinchot responded that resource use should first serve the needs of "people who live here now." Some scholars have argued that Pinchot's multiple-use philosophy evolved as much from the politics of satisfying multiple groups of commodity interests as it had from European forestry. Either way, Pinchot's national forest empire had little sense of the long run.

Pinchot's neat "sustained yield" equation implied that choices over how to manage nature were technical and subject to objective economic measurement. All other values were automatically discounted, with standards of land management and ecological health based on the amount of forest products and other commodities wrested from the woods. Pinchot saw the Forest Service as an alternative to the cut-and-run tactics of the private timber companies and he wanted to use scientific forestry to solve forest management problems.

While Pinchot's European schooling taught him that forestry should be scientifically based, it did not show him that science could also contribute to the destruction of ecosystems. His brand of forestry was bolstered by several key misconceptions about working with nature. Chief among these was the illusion that forests were stable over time. In a static natural world, a forester had to worry only about the short-term replacement of a new crop of trees after harvest. This image of nature allowed Pinchot and his men to design management plans atomistically—trees were merely replaceable cogs in the machinery of nature. A manager could lay out a timber sale or prescribe a grazing plan without taking into account neighboring stands, the larger watershed, or the regional ecosystem. With nature stable and separable into management units, a forester could act with certainty: "With skillful handling and within the limitations imposed by the site itself, we can produce any combination (of uses) we want," proclaimed an early *Journal of Forestry* editorial (Anonymous, 1943).

Pinchot's brand of conservation and the 1897 Forest Management Act guided the Forest Service into the modern era. The agency was bothered little by Congress and was given the discretion to achieve its goals as it best saw fit. By the end of World War II, however, pressure to extract resources from the national forests was building. Between 1950 and 1959, the annual national forest timber cut more than doubled. Recreational visits tripled. Postwar America was booming, but these increases inevitably led to conflict.

Citizen dissatisfaction with management of the national forests led Congress to pass the Multiple-Use-Sustained-Yield Act (MUSY) in 1960. MUSY was supposed to push the Forest Service toward managing for a variety of forest values—wildlife, fish, recreation, and watershed protection were given equal footing with timber and grazing. But the congressional nudge was gentle. The law, drafted by the Forest Service, did not require a strict equity between competing management concerns. It required only "equal consideration" of multiple uses and left the determination of the appropriate balance to the agency.

Post-MUSY, the Forest Service, contrary to the spirit if not the letter of the law, increased its commitment to timber production in the national forests. The decade of the 1960s saw the cut rise by another 30 percent. The agency also increased its planning for other forest activities including wildlife and recreation. These efforts were guided by administrative rules gleaned from the Forest Service Manual, but they were not legally binding. A year after MUSY was passed, Forest Service Assistant Chief Edward Cliff echoed Pinchot when he said, "The first and probably most important fact is that trees and lesser vegetation are . . . temporary. Each has its optimum life for utilization and if not utilized, dies" (Clary 1986).

The few court challenges to the Forest Service's preference for logging were not successful—the Multiple-Use-Sustained-Yield Act was simply not prescriptive enough. Even passage of the Wilderness Act in 1964, the Wild and Scenic Rivers Act in 1968, the National Environmental Policy Act in 1970, the Clean Water Act in 1972, and other acts including the Endangered Species Act in 1973 did not divert the agency from its primary focus—timber. But this new environmental legislation augured changes in societal values that even the Forest Service could not resist forever.

In 1975 Congress was spurred to action by a West Virginia court injunction. In response to a citizen's group lawsuit, the Forest Service was enjoined by the U.S. District Court from using clearcutting. Since this was the predominant logging technique in use, the *Monongahela Decision* brought timber cutting to a screeching halt on the entire national forest system and sent the Forest Service to Congress for remedial legislation. This time, however, unlike the circumstances surrounding the Multiple-Use-Sustained-Yield Act, the agency was in no position to write its own legislative ticket. Congress had to acknowledge the prolonged public outcry that had been building over the years against clearcutting and the agency's timber-heavy agenda.

Congress enacted comprehensive reforms to Forest Service land management practices with passage of the National Forest Management Act (NFMA) in 1976 (see Wilkinson and Andersen 1987). Though the law specifically allowed clearcutting, it also set a broad array of limits on logging practices. The NFMA required inventories of all forest resources and provided for public participation in a systemwide, interdisciplinary planning process. Each national forest was required to produce a detailed forest plan for a ten-to-fifty-year period. Once completed, the plans become legally binding, and citizens have the right to sue the Forest Service if the plans are inadequate. This was a most significant provision of the NFMA because it opened up agency decisions to judicial review.

Nonetheless, Congress was not about to strip the Forest Service of all professional discretion. The main weakness of the NFMA is that it contains vague, discretionary language that is open to broad interpretation in important sections throughout the act. The NFMA, as a result, is a law awaiting judicial interpretation on so many fronts that it will take years to clarify what lawmakers could have made more plain from the beginning.

There has been no major federal forest law enacted since 1976. Yet today there exists more controversy than ever over forestry policies and practices. Three interrelated factors—endangered species, Forest Service plans, and conservation biology—have contributed to this ongoing rancorous debate.

1. The Northern Spotted Owl and Ancient Forests

The northern spotted owl has forced managers and citizens to acknowledge that forests provide habitat as well as timber and jobs; that past a certain point, wild species are at risk if resource extraction continues unabated. In principle, this straightforward observation does not conflict with multiple-use philosophy. In practice, logging has always had its way on the national forests. That the owl requires the most economically valuable forests in the world to flourish has brought into focus the long-term consequences of "liquidating" old-growth. The owl and many other old-growth–dependent species—hundreds have been identified

so far—have provided a profound lesson in the full range of values in the woods (see Ruggiero et al. 1991). And old-growth Douglas-fir forest species are not alone—there are old-growth–dependent species inhabiting every different type of ancient forest nationwide.

Though the headlines have focused on the owl, loss of old-growth habitat is the real issue. In the Pacific Northwest, over 90 percent of the ancient forests have been logged (Morrison 1991). Scientists, studying what little old-growth remains, are providing new insights into not only the biology of old-growth dependent species, but also the importance of natural forests as functional ecosystems (Hansen et al. 1991). As a result, foresters can no longer discount the effects of resource extraction on ecosystems.

2. National Forest Plans

The NFMA's planning provisions resulted in much new data describing the resource conditions and capabilities of each national forest. Citizen input into the plans was extensive. When the majority of the plans had been released in the late 1980's, they provided a glimpse of Forest Service management goals to the year 2000 and beyond. But the picture that emerged did not bode well for ecosystem integrity. A Wilderness Society report using agency data showed that, over all the national forests, the Forest Service planned to increase logging by 72 percent, build 200,000 miles of new roads, and develop 83 percent of all remaining roadless areas (The Wilderness Society 1987). In addition, few people were happy with the planning process that the Forest Service employed. Both the planning process and the plan results created a constituency of frustrated forest activists who continue to pressure the agency for reform.

3. Conservation Biology

The first round of forest management plans and the northern spotted owl–ancient forest controversy have spurred an unprecedented forest ecosystem research effort. This accumulation of new data has coincided with the rise of a new scientific field, *conservation biology*, which seeks to understand the dynamics of species extinction and habitat loss, and further, to provide a sensible, scientific basis for land management. Conservation biologists are beginning to outline the biological requirements of wild species, and their work cannot be ignored by forestry professionals.

These three factors—endangered species habitat protection, long-range forest management plans, and findings of conservation biologists—are sparking the debate over forests and forest policy. But Congress has yet to act toward reforming MUSY and the NFMA. Congressional lawmakers are reluctant to transform the status quo because of the benefits their constituents derive from exploiting forest ecosystems for wood products. Congress is directly responsible for setting the Forest Service's bloated logging and road-building budgets.

Until Congress is pressured sufficiently by citizens, the Forest Service will continue to define forestry as "the conversion of biologically complex, typically virgin forests into even-aged, single product plantations" (Behan 1991). This is the forestry that has protected a mere pittance of North America's old-growth, has severely fragmented what little native forest remains, has endangered hundreds of wild plants and animals, and that has so reduced wildfire, the single most important ecological influence at work in the continent's forests, that the agency's own scientists are describing some forests as "sick" (see Gast et al. 1991). Meanwhile, the scientific jury is still out on the sustainability of intensive forest management techniques such as planting genetic "supertrees," fertilization, herbicide use, and short-period rotations. (For two sides of the debate see Maser 1988, and Aune et al. 1992.)

The debate continues while native biodiversity is increasingly fragmented by the continued obliteration of remaining forests that still possess their native ecological integrity.

SUSTAINED YIELD AND SUSTAINABLE LANDSCAPES

The MUSY and the NFMA codified the concept of multiple use as a forest policy framework. That a single use, logging, remains preeminent to the detriment of others is beyond argument. There is much debate, however, over sustained yield.

There are two mutually exclusive versions of sustained yield upon which Forest Service management rests. Bernard Fernow, the first head of the proto–Forest Service (the Bureau of Forestry), defined sustained yield in 1886 as cutting only the annual or periodic tree growth increments of a stand or forest. Fernow envisioned timber yields following a banking metaphor—foresters would only extract the interest in the forest savings account.

This concept of sustained yield is still with us today but it has been modified since the 1930s by a second version. At that time, President Herbert Hoover appointed a special panel to study the nation's timber supply future. Influenced by forest economist David Mason, the panel redefined sustained yield policy to stand for a general plan to coordinate public/private timber supplies to keep markets stable (Steen 1976). National forest logs would be kept off the market while private lands were cut. When private lands were depleted, public timber would be sold as private lands regenerated.

Forest historian Harold Steen has pointed out the essential difference between these two kinds of sustained yield. "By shifting the emphasis from the forest to the industry, sustained yield came to mean the continuous production of timber rather than forests" (Steen 1976).

The Multiple Use-Sustained Yield Act also defined sustained yield from the standpoint of industrial production, but the law also required production to occur "in perpetuity, without impairment of the productivity of the land." Here lies a key to successfully reforming forest policy. The intention of *in perpetuity* must take precedence over the economic language of outputs of commodities and amenities.

Sustained yields of logs and recreational visitor days must be replaced by sustainable ecosystems and landscapes. Forestry is not practiced on a blank slate—forest ecosystems have their own integrity that defines the limits of human use. Only if forest landscapes are sustained may human use continue over the long run.

How does this general principle of sustainable landscapes translate into concrete forest policy? To answer this question, we first need a working definition of *ecological integrity*. Biologist Jim Karr suggests that this may be defined as "the capability of supporting and maintaining a balanced, integrated, adaptive community of organisms having a species composition and functional organization comparable to that of the natural habitat of the region" (Karr and Dudley 1981).

Note that this standard is based on what we know Nature produces, not what we desire Nature to produce for us. With ecosystem integrity so defined it is difficult to limit our focus to a single timber sale, an endangered species, an old-growth fragment, or a national forest. The big picture becomes the focus. And this leads to the radical proposition that forestry cannot succeed without considering the larger regional landscape within which clearcuts, roads, wildlife corridors, and controlled burns are placed. Working with forests to provide some level of wood, water, and wilderness requires some other portion of the landscape to remain unmanaged. Healthy national forests require healthy parks and reserves. Yet the relationship between managed and unmanaged forests has never been addressed.

Given what science is telling us about protecting biodiversity (Noss 1993, Grumbine 1992), the general standard of sustainable landscapes reveals four general ecosystem management goals for forestry:

1. Protect enough habitat for viable populations of all native species in a given landscape.

2. Manage at a regional scale large enough to accommodate natural disturbance processes (fire, wind, climate change, etc.).

3. Plan over a timeline of centuries so that species and ecosystems may continue to evolve.

4. Allow for human use and occupancy at levels that do not result in significant ecological degradation.

This is the scientific heart of solving the current crisis in forest policy. These goals, when put into practice, would act as "preemptive (ecological) constraints" on the search for human economic welfare. Until managers embrace them, there will be no sustained yield, sustainable forestry, or sustainable landscapes.

AN ECOLOGICAL FOREST POLICY PLATFORM

In the present political landscape, an ecological basis for forest policy is considered to be utopian. That may be so. But if it is, then we had better be very clear about the consequences for both the forest species and ecosystems that will soon disappear and the loss of habitability of the planet for *Homo sapiens*. The loss will be great. There are, however, alternatives if we wish to consider them. The key to a new forest policy is to go beyond old ideas of "forests" and "parks" and "preserves," to the *sustainable landscape* that protects all levels of biodiversity. Here is a working sketch of such a system as it might be applied in North America over the next hundred years (for a full explanation see Grumbine 1992).

MORATORIUM ON LOGGING ANCIENT FORESTS

There is no scientific justification for the continued cutting of ancient forest. To begin implementing ecosystem-based forest management there must be a complete moratorium on all old-growth logging on private, state, and federal lands. Roadless areas and unprotected wildlands should also be off-limits to any development activities. The timeline for this ban is now. Yet, protecting all remaining old-growth and roadless lands will not be enough. The loss of most of the continent's primary forests cannot be corrected by an eleventh-hour decision. We will need to grow back more ancient forest by allowing younger stands to reach two hundred years in age or more. While planning for this, it is prudent to cease *all* logging on federal lands.

ECOSYSTEM-BASED RESEARCH

How much ancient forest will need to be restored? What is a healthy balance of roadless versus developed lands in the U.S.? Answers to these and many other questions must be based on ecological research, much of which has yet to be initiated. Step two of implementing an ecosystem-based forest policy involves funding a major conservation biology research effort. This new initiative would not replace existing programs such as endangered species and nongame wildlife research but would augment these with studies focused specifically on protecting biodiversity at state, regional, and national scales. There is also much basic research that needs to be part of any overall ecosystem effort. At what road densities are wide-ranging carnivores driven to wilder country? What percent of a watershed can sustain logging without unacceptable erosion? Is group-selection cutting better or worse than clear-cutting? How wide do wildlife corridors need to be for elk? —deer? —bear? —cougar? The list goes on and on.

A BIODIVERSITY PROTECTION NETWORK

With a moratorium in place, research results coming in, and long-term studies underway, the third step toward ecosystem-based forest management would have a firm scientific footing. Creation of a Biodiversity Protection Network would involve expanding and connecting existing reserves, and reducing human management activities, to maintain ecosystem patterns and processes.

A more sophisticated conservation biology analysis will paint a picture of what may be lost as well as gained as various proposals are challenged by those who do not make the connection between sustainable landscapes and human welfare. This is the social heart of the forest policy crisis.

One version of a Biodiversity Protection Network would be constructed around a series of core areas—a national park, wilderness, or other protected area. These cores would be surrounded by concentric buffer zones with human use increasing outward from the core. A national network would be built from this system of biodiversity protection areas.

One important research question looms large here: How big does the core need to be in proportion to the buffer zones to retain its native diversity? Or, flip the question over to its other side: How intense can human use become in the buffers before the core is no longer protected? This model is incomplete until such a balance is addressed quantitatively through research and experience.

CONNECTING PROTECTED CORE AREAS

The next step would be to connect each part of the Biodiversity Protection Network with corridors to facilitate movement of species. In the short term, even the largest unit in the system is going to be subject to continuing stress due to already existent habitat fragmentation. After the turn of the twenty-first century the effects of increasing greenhouse gases are likely to cause massive landscape shifts and migrations for numerous plants and animals (Peters and Lovejoy 1991). Species on the move will need to have somewhere to go and the webbing of corridors that holds the Biodiversity Protection Network together will provide part of the answer.

We know next to nothing about the ecological specifics of designing biological corridors. This should come as no surprise. A society that has so far paid little attention to constructing an adequate park and forest wilderness system built around individual units cannot be expected to have explored how to connect these units together. But connect we must. Given continuing development and the political costs of enlarging the current reserve system, designation of corridors may become one of the first steps toward policy reform. This is based on the untested assumption that corridors can sustain some level of resource extraction and not require the full protection of core areas.

CREATING A NATIVE ECOFORESTRY

With a ban on logging in ancient forests and roadless lands in place, and with a Biodiversity Protection Network being stitched together, the Forest Service could begin to learn how to work with forest ecosystems instead of fiber farms. Ever since Gifford Pinchot imported European silviculture to America, forestry has focused on how to cut down and regenerate trees efficiently with little regard to ecosystem structure and function. In the Pacific Northwest, the Forest Service abandoned research on old-growth in 1958. The agency's silviculturalists had by that time learned how to produce the maximum volume of board feet from what were seen as "decadent, biological deserts." Growing a native ecoforestry that sees forests as well as trees will require sustained research and experimentation over time. Most important, however, will be the willingness of people to define human vital needs within the limits of forest ecosystems (see below).

In the early 1980s, Dr. Jerry Franklin began conceiving an alternative silviculture that has since become known as "new forestry" (Swanson and Franklin 1992). Franklin envisions new forestry at both the stand and landscape levels: foresters would pay attention to a particular site as well as the landscape context surrounding the site.

At the stand level, instead of clearcuts and slash burns, Franklin suggests retaining green trees, snags, downed logs, and other woody debris. He calls these structural elements of ancient forests *biological legacies*. New forestry pays attention to what is left on the ground as well as what is hauled away.

At the landscape level, cutover areas might be reduced, rearranged, and clustered to reduce fragmentation. Current practices spread cuts out across watersheds, which maximize edge habitat and create the checkerboard effect well known to anyone who has flown over the Pacific Northwest on a clear day. The cumulative effects of logging in any given drainage would also be considered. Before roads were built the interplay of cut and uncut stands would be studied so that biological corridors could be protected.

At the regional scale, new forestry would bring conservation biology into forestry by maintaining a "dialogue" between commercial forests and reserved areas. Franklin's alternative forestry might someday govern the ground within which the Biodiversity Protection Network is set. But there are more appropriate forest practices than new forestry being articulated. The principles embodied by the Ecoforestry Institute (see Drengson 1993) are much more far-reaching and sustainable over the long term for people, forests, and nonhuman species. Ecoforestry differs from new forestry in several important ways. First, respect for forests as equal partners is made explicit. Second, the agricultural model of forests as tree farms is rejected. Third, the human use of forests is based on satisfying vital needs that can only be defined through local and regional direct experience with forests. Ecoforestry cannot be controlled from Washington, D.C.

Ecoforestry is revolutionary. It represents a policy vision that has yet to reach Congress or even most ranger district offices. Because it represents radical change from industrial forestry, there is little applied experience with ecoforestry outside of several places in the western U.S. These experiences, however, are guiding lights to change. As ecoforestry becomes more widespread, it will likely form the basis of all forestry for the future.

RESTORING DAMAGED LANDS

The final step in initiating an ecosystem-based forest policy will be the recovery of those species and ecosystems that have already been severely damaged. Restorative management is rooted in two observations, only one of which has the authority of scientific consensus behind it. Conservation biology has made clear that there is not enough protected habitat for, at the least, most of the largest animals in North America. The ecological consequences of losing many of the continent's bears, big cats, and other top-level predators are not completely known, but predictions are grim.

Building a Biodiversity Protection Network and connecting the strands together will not likely resolve this problem. Too much habitat has been destroyed or fragmented. The only prudent scientific response is to restore some balance between what "ecological goods and services" humans appropriate from nature and what nature needs to maintain functional integrity. Long-term management requires addressing these imbalances by adopting a wildlands recovery strategy: closing and revegetating roads, allowing wildfires free play to set successional rhythms, removing settlements from sensitive areas, reintroducing grizzlies, wolves, and other extirpated species, creating polyculture agro-ecosystems, and building a restoration economy based on healing these and other wounds.

Re-creating "pristine" presettlement conditions would not be the goal of restoration; there never was such a world. Instead, management would be based on understanding how long-term natural climate change and shorter-term disturbances pattern landscapes. The specific goal would be to allow native species, ecosystems, and landscapes to evolve in response to a dynamic Earth.

Economic goals must also be woven into forest ecosystem restoration. When Congress expanded Redwood National Park in California in 1978, most of the new park lands had been heavily logged. Between 1979 and 1987 the National Park Service spent over $30 million on payroll, leases, and contracts to rehabilitate these damaged lands. On a much larger regional scale, if the Forest Service could secure funding for erosion control, retiring roads, and prescribed burning (to reduce fuel loads and mimic natural fire patterns), an entirely new restoration economy of hundreds of millions of dollars would be created.

While some of these policies may be implemented immediately, others will only bear fruit in coming decades. In time, the scientific tasks called for by this expanded view of forest management may bring us to large-scale ecological restoration—with wolves and grizzlies in northern California and Colorado, and great regional ecosystems linked together across the country. If so, we will have become a different people.

By 2090, humans will have burned through almost all of the planet's currently known reserves of fossil fuels. Douglas-firs that turn a century old in the 1990s will have settled down into the steady patterns of an ancient forest. With wounds from human exploitation healing, forest management may be expressed as sustainable changes within ecosystem constraints. Visions of ecologically diverse and sustainable forests in the future inspire hope and renewed commitment to what most certainly will be decades of difficult work. In time, we may finally begin to experience what living a deep, rich, and varied life, woven into the fabric of native diversity, may provide. We, too, could become native (Snyder 1993).

BEYOND ECOLOGICAL FORESTRY

Practicing forestry within an ecosystems-based scientific framework will not—radical as it may appear—be sufficient to create sustainable landscapes. Legal expert Robert Keiter is not the first to observe that "public lands policy simply cannot be defined solely in scientific terms. [People are] now a dominant force in nature, and human interests—economic, social, and political—must be accommodated"

(Keiter 1989). This kind of "pragmatic" statement depends on separating human interests from biodiversity concerns. But healthy human economies rely on productive ecosystems. People are not disconnected from, but are in relationship with, the natural world, strained though the bond may be. Much of this strain has to do with overpopulation of the planet by humans, a problem that goes well beyond the scope of forest policy. Keiter, however, is correct on one point. If science is ever to serve as the basis for a native forestry embedded within a Biodiversity Protection Network, the federal agencies, Congress, and citizens will be called upon to work together like they have never worked together before.

The question is, How can forest management—evolving within a historical context of human-centered values, corporate domination, bureaucratic management, and elite, technocratic decision making—become integrated into the hearts, minds, and hands of these groups?

FOREST MANAGERS

There are many ways to support ecologically enlightened forest managers. A first step would be to encourage managers to understand that forest policy is the result of complex social, economic, and political forces that go well beyond science. Many managers and scientists, according to policy analyst Tim Clark, believe that management is a strictly technical task. Yet there is much more to forest management than silviculture and firefighting. To help land managers increase their awareness of the entire range of forces that influence professional practice, Clark and his coworkers are developing a broader-based framework that acknowledges the role of authority/power relationships between individuals and agencies, bureaucratic behavior, political influences, and environmental values—as well as scientific study per se (Reading et al. 1991).

With the competitive relationships of the past no longer serviceable in today's "greenhouse" world, this holistic view is being fostered none too soon. Multiple use is based on economic rather than ecological goals: its ideology is pre-ecological and therefore inappropriate to address today's forestry problems. But what goals should a manager select?

There are conflicting legislative mandates calling for protection of endangered species habitat and "harvesting" that very same habitat. Forest Service staff often complain that there is no social consensus on protecting ecosystems. Conservation biology, however, is now making it clear that biodiversity is not just another multiple-use goal but a condition fundamental to viable ecosystems over the long term.

The Forest Service has been criticized widely for its handling of the public participation mandates of the National Environment Policy Act and the NFMA. Agency public participation efforts have been thwarted by land managers' view of themselves as a professional elite who have little need of public "opinion." This outlook has been aided and abetted by their preference for a top-down, bureaucratic brand of planning. This kind of synoptic planning is familiar to anyone who has read a forest or park plan. Responding only to information already collected (and filtered), and alternatives already "preferred," citizens are disempowered. The agencies add insult to injury by attempting to hide any explicit ethical issues behind the smokescreen of a values-neutral playing field where all participants' views will be considered equally.

I believe, along with many citizen activists, that management decisions must be decentralized. There already exist many strategies based on a local/regional watershed approach rather than the traditional national forest or park focus. For years local people in the Mattolle River watershed of Northern California have worked hard to restore salmon habitat as well as wrest control of land-use decisions from the unenlightened Forest Service and private timber companies. These grassroots activists continue to work toward establishing watershed networks that link local and regional citizens together for land-use planning. Even the state of California has made an attempt to incorporate "bioregional" and "watershed" councils into public policy for biodiversity, though these efforts have yet to substantively affect any policy outcomes.

Given present levels of conflict and lack of experience in implementing grassroots approaches to citizen participation, these new approaches may not yield immediate dividends. It took three and one-half years for one experimental program, focusing on the Bob Marshall Wilderness in Montana, to be completed (Grumbine 1985). Yet decentralized planning methods could help break down the walls that insulate managers from citizens and citizens from each other. Bruce Jennings points toward a broader, cultural view of public participation that complements what science is saying about land management (1986).

If participation were seen in a broader, more positive way, as a process which has both instrumental and intrinsic value for those taking part and for society as a whole, then there is no reason, in principle, why the exercise of participatory (or representative) democratic governance need undermine the legitimate and valuable role played by experts or professionals in the policy-making process. Democracy and elitism may be antithetical, but democracy and expertise are not.

Whatever the future holds, changing forest policy to reflect ecological reality offers fundamental challenges to the status quo in political participation, decision making, decentralization, and ownership.

The Forest Service has not yet fully realized the revolutionary implications of ecological forestry. The agency's initial response was its New Perspectives program. This experimental policy supposedly aimed to bring ecosystem planning, new forestry research, and more citizen participation to federal forestry (USDA Forest Service 1990). But New Perspectives was more of a public relations campaign than an attempt at fundamental change. No mention was made of wildlands protection, the need to reduce the allowable cut, or the exhausted condition of many forests throughout the national forests. The idea of constraints on human use of ecosystems was absent from New Perspectives.

New Perspectives has since evolved into Ecosystem Management. The Forest Service appears to be committed to Ecosystem Management but the new policy still focuses on the "balance" between human use of forest products and protection of forest ecosystem processes (USDA Forest Service 1992). In fact, no such balance exists; there should be no loss of native biodiversity to satisfy human needs (see Grumbine, Island Press).

Ecosystem Management will not contribute much to forest management if the mistakes of the past are not acknowledged, or if the Forest Service continues its old balancing act of attempting to appease all (human) interest groups. A truly "new perspective" will not emerge until managers and citizens recognize the nexus of planning as human use nestled in living ecosystems, instead of park and forest islands stranded in a sea of anthropogenic change. In fact, this expanded view is essential to avoid the democratic trap of giving equal weight to the votes of those who, for short-term self-interest, would destroy forests. The balance—between protection and use, native diversity and vital needs, public and private interests, democratic and elite decision making—will not be achieved until we "give Nature a vote" in our deliberations.

CONGRESS

Congress has yet to endorse ecological forestry or fully embrace sustainable landscapes. While Congress defeated efforts to gut the Endangered Species Act in 1990 and 1991, Congressman Jim Jontz's Ancient Forest Protection Act never received a full committee hearing. The Senate rejected Mark Hatfield's timber industry bail-out bill with its high logging levels, only to sign off on a 1992 Forest Service appropriations bill that directed the agency to explore unprecedented levels of "salvage" logging.

Congress must be willing to break ranks with business interests to afford ecosystems top priority. There are numerous models available for lawmakers to follow. The foremost example is the Endangered Species Act, although it has been ineffectively implemented. Yet there is a great difference between working with a radical law on the books since 1973 and passing new protective legislation today. The difference between the 1970s and 1990s is not in the political climate, however—politics is still about power and compromise. The distinction lies with how much more aware we are of the fundamental importance of functional ecosystems and the mounting costs of their destruction.

Congress is unlikely to act for ecosystems without first feeling political pressure. Yet no member of Congress will do anything without being provided reliable information—a job that falls upon citizens, scientists, managers—from all those who would speak for nature. Outlining an ecosystems-based bill may seem utopian but doing so would bring the message to Capitol Hill. It is, however, only the first step. The second step, as Franklin D. Roosevelt once reminded a reform delegation, is more tricky: "Okay, you've convinced me—now go out and bring pressure on me."

Ecosystems management is based in biology, not politics. This is a critical distinction—a vote against ecosystems is not a victory for one party over another; it represents another increment in the loss of life support for both sides. Supporters of sustainable landscapes must not forget that "Washington, D.C.," and "national forest" are artificial constructs, nonexistent for pine martens and white oak trees. Few species will survive in the long term under any kind of land ownership until biology pushes our values away from prohibitions and toward affirmation of all life. Because Congress is ill-prepared to offer this brand of leadership, it will have to spring from somewhere else.

CITIZEN ADVOCATES

The leadership for ecological forestry within sustainable landscapes must come from citizens who are willing to speak out for and defend their Earth household. Yet there are numerous barriers to citizen participation in public affairs in the U.S.—and they are not limited to ecosystem issues. American political life, according to many, is stunted by lack of a participatory democracy. Political philosopher Benjamin Barber believes that representative democracy, where some of the people, chosen by those who vote, govern in all public affairs all of the time, needs to be revitalized by a "strong" democracy where all of the people govern themselves in at least some public matters at least some of the time (1984).

A limited representative government, coupled with the rise of government bureaucracies as the nation has grown, has stripped citizens of civic responsibility. The political system, while providing opportunities for public participation, actually encourages widespread social ignorance, apathy, and confusion about forest issues—corporate lobbying and public relations campaigns are misleading; the debates over complex issues are dominated by experts; plain citizens have little access to policy makers; loosely written laws and overlapping jurisdictional boundaries between national, state, and local interests are confusing; participatory processes are long, drawn out, and inefficient; and the time required to keep abreast of the issues makes an active public life antithetical to a private life.

The recent history of modern U.S. environmentalism helps in understanding how far away we have strayed from participatory democracy by revealing several trends—uninvolved "direct mail" memberships, more sophisticated research into issues, an evolution toward professionalized bureaucracies, and a focus on lobbying in Washington, D.C. All of the largest groups have "mainstreamed" themselves away from local and regional chapters and clubs, and become national power players. As these groups have grown and hired corporate-style leaders from business and government, they have shown a greater reluctance to challenge the political and economic status quo. The national groups, in adopting a professional hierarchical structure, have chosen the same path as the land management agencies and there now exists a "class structure" between national and local, bureaucratic and grassroots, environmental interests. This "top-down" structure does not serve forests any better than does the Forest Service.

Nor does hierarchical structure serve grassroots activists and the local people most affected by land management policies. When citizen participation is politicized into influence groups, three "classes" emerge: those who lobby and are lobbied (Congress, the industry, and major environmental groups such as the Sierra Club, National Audubon Society, etc.); those who are listened to but discounted (grassroots environmentalists); and those who have no voice or vote (grizzly bears and Douglas-firs).

Mainstream environmental groups do not often acknowledge the inequalities between their executives, field workers, and volunteer activists with respect to knowledge of the issues, formation of policy, development of strategy, and wielding of political power. But access to information and involvement opportunities are critically important to the success of a democratic, participatory citizens' movement for ecosystem protection, for at least two reasons. First, the management goals presented here will require such massive social transformations that new alliances must be forged to swell the ranks of those who want to be part of a sustainable future. Second, regardless of the leap of faith involved, there can be no hope of breaking down the class structure of present-day environmental politics without allowing people of many persuasions a voice in setting the agenda. "Involving local activists and naturalists in scoping and ground checking ecosystem protection plans," remarks grassroots organizer Richard Grossman, "is not the same as intentionally setting out to reach people in order to learn their views and to seek their participation in framing the problems and finding solutions. . ." (Grossman 1992).

Working *within* the goal of sustainable landscapes, people must be allowed to find ways to take care of forests even as they make their living from them. There is certain risk here—how can people who don't understand ecosystems, who have participated at times in their destruction, seek to protect them? Yet I believe this hazard is balanced by another political fact of life: those who remain disenfranchised by strategies to sustain nature will not likely act in support of ecological forestry. However, if we cannot somehow (soon) learn to base policies and actions on ecocentric values, then the continuing loss of biodiversity will render political consensus meaningless.

Until the onset of the biodiversity crisis, our political system produced enough token environmental reform to satisfy most people. Compromise could almost always be reached. Now, from the northern spotted owl and ancient forests of the Pacific Northwest to the tall-grass prairies of the Midwest and the carbon-loaded atmosphere of Earth, the news is compelling: "Ecological systems have a dignity, not a price" (Sagoff 1986). The management I have outlined here offers two minimum criteria for "ecological dignity": the continued evolution of species and the functioning of ecosystems. This is nature's bottom line, and the only effect that commodity-based multiple-use management has had on it is to reduce it.

Congress, land managers, and citizens have always been able to choose between environmental policies that are essential and those that reflect public preferences. The biodiversity crisis is now showing us a world where "must" is becoming the rule of management. The rise of grassroots participation is the public's response to the substitution of "must" for "may," and "shall" for "should," and so far, a thin majority of people seem to be siding with wild nature. But it is still too early in the evolution from "wise use" toward sustainable landscapes to gauge whether the costs, and inevitable dislocations, that humans must bear to accommodate ecological dignity will overwhelm the very people who are now clamoring for reform.

PERSONAL EXPERIENCE AND FOREST POLICY

The world of forest ecosystems and forest policy is no longer as it was when I first stood at the rim of the Pacific, hidden by an old-growth Sitka spruce, and watched a bald eagle fishing. The tulip tree forests I explored in high school have been transformed into suburbia. Watersheds in the east side of the North Cascades that once grew huge ponderosa pines are still available for recreational hiking, but the pines have disappeared. When I return to visit these places they are diminished beyond the facts of species loss, habitat fragmentation, and housing developments. I, too, am diminished—I can no longer identify with those elements of the larger community of life that were once manifested in ancient trees, wild deciduous woods, and the presence of large mammals.

These losses are not limited to my personal experiences. Life is being overwhelmed by human projects across the planet: three-quarters of the world's bird species are declining; one-third of North American freshwater fish are rare; 42 percent of the planet's turtles are threatened with extinction; predictions are uniformly grim for the survival in the wild of virtually all wild carnivores and primates (Ryan 1992).

Many arguments have been advanced concerning the place of forestry in resource management, but reduction of Earth's richness and diversity has never been among them. Yet the future of native forests is uncertain. Current forest policies are still written in the language of multiple use, sustained yield, and viable populations. Our experience of forests shows us a dominant single use, resulting in ecological depletion, with the specter of extinction. If we are to establish healthy relationships with forests, we will need to go beyond political policy making. We must envision forests and forest policies as wed to a larger landscape of sustainability—stable human populations, limits to economic growth, and life support for all Earth's species.

The goal of forest policy should be healthy forest landscapes for generations (of all living beings) to come. The goal of forest managers should be optimal support of biodiversity even as humans make use of forests for vital needs. And the goal of citizens, should these first two goals remain unheeded, should be to bear witness personally to the many threats to forests and to resist excessive, commodity-based industrial forestry practices on every hill, in every hollow, and across entire forested landscapes.

REFERENCES

Anonymous. 1943. Editorial. *Journal of Forestry* 15:25–26.

Aune, P. S., et al. 1990. The redesigned forest: A scientific review. *Journal of Forestry* 88(12): 33–36.

Barber, Benjamin. 1984. *Strong democracy*. Berkeley: University of California Press.

Behan, Richard. 1991. Forests and plantations and potomo-centric statutory fixes. *Forest Perspectives* 1(1):5.

Clary, David. 1986. *Timber and the Forest Service*. Lawrence: University of Kansas Press.

De Bonis, Jeff. 1990. New perspectives: Editorial. *Inner Voice* 2(4):9.

Gast, R.W., et al. 1991. *Blue mountains forest health report*. Portland, OR: USDA Forest Service.

Grossman, Richard. 1992. Letter to author, 15 October.

Grumbine, R. Edward. 1992. *Ghost bears: Exploring the biodiversity crisis*. Washington, D.C.: Island Press.

Grumbine, Ed. 1985. Can wilderness be saved from vibram soles? *High Country News* 27 May 1985: 14–15.

Hansen, A. J., et al. 1991. Conserving biodiversity in managed forests. *BioScience* 41(6): 382–92.

Jennings, Bruce. 1986. Representation and participation in democratic governance of science and technology. In *Governing Science and Technology*, ed. M. Goggin, 237. Knoxville: University of Tennessee Press.

Karr, Jim, and D. Dudley. 1981. Ecological perspective on water quality goals. *Environmental Management* 5:55–68.

Keiter, Robert. 1989. Taking account of the ecosystem on the public domain. *University of Colorado Law Review* 60:932.

Maser, Chris. 1988. *The redesigned forest*. San Pedro: R. & E. Miles.

Mathison, S., and K. Wiedenmann. 1990. Shasta Costa. *Inner Voice* 11(4):20.

Morrison, Peter, et al. 1991. *Ancient forests of the Pacific Northwest*. Washington, D.C.: The Wilderness Society.

Peters, Robert, and Thomas Lovejoy, eds. *Biological diversity and global warming*. New Haven: Yale University Press.

Pinchot, Gifford. [1947] 1987. *Breaking new ground*. Reprint. Washington, D.C.: Island Press.

Reading, R., et al. 1991. Toward an endangered species reintroduction paradigm. *Endangered Species Update* 8(11): 1–4.

Ruggiero, L., et al. 1991. Plant and animal habitat associations in Douglas-fir forests of the Pacific Northwest: An overview. In *Wildlife and Vegetation of Unmanaged Douglas-fir Forests*, ed. L. Ruggiero, 447–62. Pacific Northwest Research Station, Portland: USDA Forest Service.

Ryan, John. 1992. Life support: Conserving biological diversity. *Worldwatch Paper No. 108*. Washington, D.C.: Worldwatch Institute.

Sagoff, Mark. 1986. Process or product?: Environmental priorities in environmental management. *Environmental Ethics* 8:136.

Steen, Harold. 1976. *The U.S. Forest Service: A history*. Seattle: University of Washington Press.

Swanson, Fred, and Jerry Franklin. 1992. New forestry principles from ecosystem analysis of Pacific Northwest forests. *Ecological Applications* 2(3):262–74.

The Wilderness Society. 1987. *Forests for the future?* Washington, D.C.: The Wilderness Society.

USDA Forest Service. 1990. *Shasta Costa: From a new perspective*. Washington, D.C.: USDA Forest Service.

Wilkinson, Charles, and M. Anderson. 1987. *Land and resource planning in the National Forests*. Washington, D.C.: Island Press.

Daniel Dancer

Ecoforestry is perennial forest use, based on respect for the wisdom of the forest.

THE ECOFORESTRY
DECLARATION OF INTERDEPENDENCE

Holistic natural selection ecoforestry is the result of applying the principles of the Deep Ecology movement to the use of forests and the practice of forestry. During the latter half of the twentieth century it has become clear that forests throughout the world are being destroyed by agriculturally based industrial forestry. Industrial agriculture itself is destroying the land and soil, as well as rural human communities. In each of its major resource activities the industrial model is having the same effects. The overall stress of industrial culture on the Earth has made it apparent that we must make fundamental changes in our philosophy, values, and life practices. If we are to change these practices in ways that are ecologically responsible, as well as morally and spiritually sound, we must begin by recognizing the intrinsic value of all beings. What does this mean for forestry, fishing, farming, or for other activities we engage in such as recreation and travel?

A new approach to agriculture is being developed by Wes Jackson at The Land Institute. Wes and his associates are developing a new agriculture, a permanent form of natural farming that works with native perennials and processes of natural selection.

In forestry two main lines of theory and practice converge to provide a comprehensive, ecologically responsible approach to the use of forests. No forest resource—based work or community is sustainable unless it practices respect for, and doesn't interfere with, the full functioning integrity of natural forest ecosystems. To achieve this, two major actions must be taken: (1) we must first zone forests, starting at the landscape level, based on the principles of landscape ecology; and (2) at the watershed level, stands from which material can be *selectively* removed must be identified, and all removals must take place with minimum impact, guided by principles of conservation biology and natural selection. (All access systems, whether roads or other types, must be designed to have minimum impact.) All removals must be from the forest's abundance, not from its biological capital. Forests are self-maintaining, evolving ecological communities. In broad perspective they provide a multitude of values and services to humans and other beings.

The Ecoforestry Institute is working to build a worldwide ecoforestry movement. We love forests and want to protect them, as we pledge in our oath. We love human beings and feel the great tragedies of the destruction of all indigenous peoples and forest-based human communities. We believe that it is ecologically and morally wrong to destroy forests to get trees, and thus we pledge not to interfere with the full functioning of forests while we satisfy our vital needs.

Ecoforestry is perennial forest use, based on respect for the wisdom of the forest. Ecoforestry assumes that Nature knows best how to grow and maintain forests; human activities in relation to forests must respect and learn from this wisdom.

Humans need forests. They do not need us. Without natural forests all of the major terrestrial communities will unravel and with them the marine communities as well.

Tree plantations are not a viable or sustainable alternative. Thus, for spiritual, moral, and practical reasons we must change our practices. In addition, the consequences of our past collective actions give us a responsibility to undo the damage we have done. This can be accomplished through the use of responsible restoration ecology practices to aid the return of fully functioning natural forest ecosystems in landscapes and watersheds where they have been degraded or destroyed by our cultural activities.

We now know that the current industrial forestry practices are wrong, and even some mainstream forestry organizations are seeing this truth.

The Ecoforestry Institute is dedicated to the training and certification of ecoforesters as well as to the certification of ecologically responsible forest use. In this way both producers and consumers of forest products can make wise choices that are ecologically responsible and thus protect and honor the many beings that make up the diverse forest communities. Through ecoforestry we can develop sustainability rather than sustaining mere production for increasing consumption. We can shift toward increasing quality of life and dwelling in states of intrinsic worth. Ecoforestry is the wisdom of dwelling in place and becoming an indigenous being.

Daniel Dancer

Nature sustains us, we do not sustain Nature.

THE ECOFORESTER'S WAY

1. We shall respect and learn from the ecological wisdom (ecosophy) of Nature's forests with their multitudes of beings.

2. We shall protect the integrity of the full functioning forest.

3. We shall not use agricultural practices in the forest.

4. We shall remove from the forest only values that are in abundance and that meet vital human needs.

5. We shall remove individual instances of values only when this removal will not interfere with a full functioning forest; when in doubt, we will let them be.

6. We shall minimize the impacts of our actions on the forest by using appropriate, low impact technology practices.

7. We shall do good work and uphold the Ecoforester's Oath as a duty and trust.

This oath contains several phrases that need explanation, including *good work*, *appropriate technology*, and *ecological wisdom*.

Good work:

1. provides for basic material needs (physical sustenance);

2. satisfies the need to work cooperatively with others to realize common values;

3. perfects and actualizes abilities and skills (intellectual and physical development);

4. realizes an increasingly extended sense of identification and commitment to larger patterns of interdependence and relationship (maturity);

5. realizes the ecological self in harmony with others and Nature.

Appropriate technology:

1. is ecologically and thermodynamically sound;

2. is suitable to the problem context;

3. is economically and socially equitable and sustainable;

4. facilitates human self-realization and improvement of quality of life, not just increasing quantities of consumption.

Principles of Ecological Wisdom:

1. Nature knows best.

2. Everything is interconnected.

3. Everything goes somewhere.

4. There is no "free lunch."

5. Community, consciousness, and intrinsic values permeate all of Nature.

6. Nature sustains us; we do not sustain Nature.

7. Nature tends toward abundance and flourishing of diversity.

Daniel Dancer

The twenty-first-century forester must be a bridge between the ecology of the forest in relation to
the dynamics of the landscape and the cultural necessities and human values of society. Tomorrow's forester is the guardian of
both the forest and the future's options, because when all is said and done, the great and only gift we can give
our children is the right of choice and something of value from which to choose.

THE TWENTY-FIRST–CENTURY FORESTER

CHRIS MASER

INTRODUCTION

Put simply, traditional forestry is exploitation of the economic value of trees. It is founded on growing and harvesting trees as rapidly as possible to maximize short-term profits and minimize capital outlay. Everything but immediate profit is ignored when forest economists assume that soil, water, air, sunlight, climate, and biodiversity are nondegradable constant values.

If the twentieth-century exploitation of forests is to be replaced by a healing of forests in the twenty-first century, forestry as a profession must be founded on documented ecological truth. Universities must have daring leaders with a vision of imaginative possibilities with which to inspire future foresters.

A professional forester is a forester because of his or her university training, which in large measure reflects the views of professors and administrators who parent the evolving student into their own concept of forestry in terms of industrial economics. Truth in training is needed if the twenty-first–century forester is to fulfill his or her role as a trustee of the forest for the good of generations to come. Only when the ecological truth about forestry is acknowledged and accepted will foresters receive the kind of professional training they must have to meet growing environmental challenges.

SOME CAUSES OF TROUBLE IN THE FORESTRY PROFESSION

Ignorance might be excused when there is no information, but to act in defiance of documented knowledge is inexcusable. The forestry profession is in trouble because of the resistance of many traditionally educated foresters to altering their thinking in terms of the world today. At least four major causes of trouble in the profession of forestry are: (1) the economic myth of forestry, (2) dogmatization of forestry, (3) limitations of science, and (4) university training.

THE ECONOMIC MYTH OF FORESTRY

The practice of forestry began with the idea that forests are perpetual producers of commodities. To capitalize on the harvest of such commodities as a way of life, there had to be a disciplined, economic rationale. The *soil-rent theory* became that rationale.

The soil-rent theory—a classic, liberal, economic theory—is a planning tool devised by Johann Christian Hundeshagen in the early nineteenth century to maximize industrial profits. Since its unfortunate adoption by foresters, it has become the overriding objective for forestry worldwide. But the soil-rent theory is based on six flawed primary assumptions: (1) that the depth and fertility of the soil in which the forest grows is an ecological constant; (2) that the quality and quantity of the precipitation reaching the forest is an ecological constant; (3) that the quality of the air

infusing the forest is an ecological constant; (4) that the amount and quality of solar energy available to the forest is an ecological constant; (5) that climatic stability is an ecological constant; and (6) that biodiversity is an ecological constant.

By falsely assuming that all ecological variables are economic constants, one is misled to think that all one must do to have an economically sustainable tree farm is calculate the species of tree, the rate of growth, and the age of harvest that will give the highest rate of economic return in the shortest time for the amount of economic capital invested in a given site—the soil-rent theory.

DOGMATIZATION OF FORESTRY

Once the soil-rent theory was set as the foundation of forestry, it had to be institutionalized if forestry were to become a controllable discipline. The Germans and the British led the way by institutionalizing the practices, which sufficed to protect the discipline for many years.

It eventually became evident that cumulative ecological damage resulted from this flawed economic basis of forest management. Ecological damage threatened not only economic interests but also reputations of the idealized founders of the profession. Yet, dogma continued to supplant new information because dogma explicitly forbids new facts from being taken seriously and old mistakes from being recognized, by making such information appear to be unsubstantiated and confusing. Defeating challenges to forestry's dogma tends to protect members of the profession from perceived ecological malfeasance and liability for embracing false assumptions.

Once the soil-rent theory was cloaked in dogma, vested interests had effectively institutionalized denial of their economic motives while simultaneously alleging scientific legitimacy. But such legitimacy can be claimed only if it is protected from questioning and from testable scrutiny. As a result, students are unknowingly trained in the dogma of the soil-rent theory, which prevents recognition of the original economic errors in the foundation of today's so-called scientific forestry. What is taught therefore perpetuates the original economic falsity. So long as students uncritically accept what they are taught, the original economic falsity will remain the foundation of today's forestry practice.

To help ensure the persistence of dogma, one is encouraged, through a system of reward and punishment, to accept proffered dogma unquestioningly. When a working forester does exhibit the courage to challenge dogma, he or she is initially met with anger and then by a wall of denial and resistance.

Criticism, rejection, and shunning are powerful motivators for keeping a person's questions within prescribed boundaries. Dogma lives on one's fear of losing approval and acceptance, both of which are expressed through losing one's affiliation with colleagues, or one's livelihood, or both. The power of fear keeps people too frightened to openly and freely voice their intuitive beliefs, even preventing them from feeling and knowing their own inner truths.

Increasingly, we hear people in the profession speak of "progressive forestry," "scientific forestry," and "new forestry." But what do they mean? Forestry based on faulty premises decades old is no more progressive, scientific, or new today than in the past. How can this be, one may ask, with all the ongoing scientific research and with all of the research information we have on hand?

LIMITATIONS OF SCIENCE

The true goal of scientific endeavor is the pursuit of pure knowledge, which, by definition, demands that the scientist be unencumbered and forever open-minded. The greatest triumphs in science are not triumphs of facts, but of new ways of seeing, thinking, perceiving, and asking questions. But on the path to scientific truth lie at least five obstacles:

1. The lure of grants seeking predetermined results, such as monies from the timber industry aimed at genetic engineering of tree seedlings for faster growth.
2. Attachment to a single hypothesis, such as the necessity of fertilization to improve soil productivity or of herbicides to control unwanted vegetation.
3. The fact that science can only disprove information, which means that the timber industry can't prove its dogma through science (however, science can be used to disprove industrial dogma).
4. The fact that science began as an endeavor seeking knowledge for curiosity's sake but too often has become a problem- and method-oriented means of determining politically correct answers to safeguard established dogma.
5. The objectifying of human participation with Nature, which denies the subjectivity with which a timber company executive might view particular ecological information versus the way an ecologist might view the same information.

The Lure of Grants

Most research institutions count on grant money to help defray the costs of operation, and their people are strongly encouraged to seek grants. Such encouragement sometimes amounts to administrative coercion in that promotions and even tenure are linked to the amount of grant money captured by an individual. Researchers therefore tend to focus on those areas within their disciplines in which they have the best chance of getting money. The questions to be asked and the answers to be derived may thus be controlled by the allocation of funds. So, too, dogma can be protected, because a researcher may be prevented from asking an unrestrained question.

Attachment to a Single Hypothesis

To keep the search for truth on a credible track, we must always remember that we tend not only to form single hypotheses but also to become so attached to them that any criticism or challenge to our methods raises our ego-defenses. The moment a person derives what seems to be an original and satisfactory explanation for a phenomenon, at that instant the attachment to his or her intellectual child springs into existence. The more this explanation grows into a definite theory, the more near and dear it becomes. Then comes the massaging, as I've often heard it called in government agencies, to make the theory fit the information and the information to fit the theory, just another way of making sure it all fits within accepted dogma (e.g., we can increase the current level of harvesting timber by 10 percent because someday we'll grow 10 percent more trees that have been genetically improved).

Science Can Only Disprove Information

The truth about scientific research is that nothing can be proven, only disproven; nothing can be known, only unknown. Thus, we can never *know* anything in terms of knowledge but only in terms of *intuition*, the knowing beyond knowledge that is not admissible as scientific evidence. Scientific truth, whatever it is, can only be intuited and approached—never caught and pinned down.

Although science can prove nothing, it can "disprove" dogma through posing questions unrestrained by economically vested interests. Hence those who resist change demand "conclusive proof" that change is necessary or even desirable.

Method-oriented vs. Problem-oriented Questions

We tend to be *method-oriented* rather than *problem-oriented* in our thinking and in many of the questions we ask. A method-oriented question might be: How can we plant trees to make them grow fastest? A problem-oriented question might be: How much organic material in the form of large woody debris must be left on site following logging to ensure continued productivity of the soil?

Method-oriented questions are invariably aimed, unconsciously perhaps, at strengthening dogma. Nevertheless, we continue to believe that through method-oriented experiments we can learn the truth about Nature, when in fact we are learning only about our methods, which are our experimental designs, our assumptions, and our expectations of the outcome.

OBJECTIFYING NATURE

Nature cannot be accurately represented through science. What is observed and interpreted in Nature is a product of the personal lens through which a scientist peers. Though, in the name of science, I can attempt to detach myself from Nature and try to become "objective," I cannot, if for no other reason than I'm part of Nature and must participate with Nature to study Nature. In addition, by the very act of observing something, I change its relationship to everything else and hence its behavior, because through observation, I establish a *new* relationship with it.

The insistence in science of neutralizing human subjectivity is an attempt to objectify Nature and thereby to deny participation with Nature in any form—an impossibility of life. Nevertheless, the attempt to objectify Nature makes our scientific theories and facts no more than social constructs. Instead of allowing the facts to reach the state of speaking for themselves, scientists come to consensus only when the political, professional, and economic costs of refuting them make further negotiation untenable.

UNIVERSITY TRAINING

A curriculum can be purposefully designed and used to liberate a student's imagination and help him or her to question ideas and to soar with new possibilities, or it can be designed and used to imprison a student's imagination in the rut of worn-out dogma or "business as usual." This is possible because power is value neutral. In the hands of any special interest, educational training can be used to liberate or to confine. Unfortunately, the selection of courses offered in most forestry curricula is academic ritualism aimed at confinement and compliance with the decades-old flawed economic dogma on which today's forestry is based.

When a student is exposed to selected information through courses both offered and required, he or she is molded in the shape of the prevailing dogma. At the same time, the opportunity to examine information opposing desired dogma is not required or may not be readily available.

As a case in point, I was a guest lecturer in a forest management class in which I discussed large woody debris, small mammals, mycorrhizal fungi, nutrient cycling, and the effects of gross habitat alterations in coniferous forests. When the class was over, a young student came straight at me so angry his fists were clenched and his face was red. "I'm a senior," he almost shouted, "and I'm going to graduate in a couple of weeks. How come this is the first time I've heard any of this? I've just spent four years in what they call forest management! You just showed me that I don't know a damn thing about how a forest works! And now I'm supposed to be a forester! What in the hell am I going to do out there?" This young man was astute enough when given opposing information to let his intuition speak and thereby penetrate dogma's armor and see the economic lie of forest management. But as far as his university training was concerned, the truth came late.

The great majority of courses required for a degree in forestry at today's universities are aimed at producing wood fiber with the economic underpinnings of rapid tree growth, genetic "improvement," economically efficient harvest, cheap transportation, and maximum utilization of wood. The prime objective is the greatest short-term profit with the least outlay of economic capital. The forest as an ever-evolving living organism is discounted as having no intrinsic economic or ecological value over the long run.

We focus so narrowly on the economics of trees that we lose sight of the forest. Colleges of forestry are training "logging technicians," "industrial tree production managers," and "plantation managers," but not foresters in the sense of informed people nurturing a forest as a whole living organism and helping to educate the general public about the wonder of it all.

Forestry is no longer just a matter of cutting trees, or even of cutting and planting trees. Forestry has progressed far beyond solely the economic—or even the ecological—aspects of forests. It has become the profession of people working with people who see and want many different values from forests. But communication skills, such as writing and public speaking, the most important tools of the trade, are all but left to chance in many forestry programs. Little or no emphasis is placed on learning the skills of interpersonal relationships, how to conduct public meetings, or about professional ethics.

FORESTERS OF YESTERDAY, TODAY, AND THE TWENTY-FIRST CENTURY

Yesterday's foresters were trained as utilitarian servants of industry. Their job was to protect the commercial value of the timber from fire and insects and to get out the maximum cut. Today's foresters, while receiving essentially the same training, are beginning to question the philosophical premises of the old school.

The twenty-first—century forester must be a bridge between the ecology of the forest in relation to the dynamics of the landscape and the cultural necessities and human values of society. Tomorrow's forester is the guardian of both the forest and the future's options, because when all is said and done, the great and only gift we can give our children is the right of choice and some things of value from which to choose.

To accomplish the kind of philosophical revolution in thinking that is needed, university colleges of forestry must be imaginative and daring. They must lead the profession of forestry toward a new vision, one that harmonizes human culture and

Nature's forest beyond the dogma of traditional forestry and the economics of commodity extraction. This can best be done by helping students realize their dreams of finding a nurturing philosophy of life within the profession, as trustees of sustainable forests.

To be equipped for the twenty-first century, the forester of the future will need to:

1. understand the parts of a forest in relation to its organic whole, and the whole in terms of its parts, by learning to sit with and in the forest and hear its voice;
2. understand the science of each forest component and subsystem, that is, be able to evaluate and openly question new information in terms of the old, old information in terms of the new, and both in terms of existing ignorance;
3. understand enough about the ecological linkages among forest components and subsystems to be able to anticipate effects of management stresses;
4. understand and work with a forest as a dynamic component of an ever-evolving, culturally-oriented landscape, while simultaneously honoring the integrity of the blueprint of Nature's processes and patterns;
5. understand that the only sustainability for which we can manage is that which ensures the ability of an ecosystem to adapt to evolutionary change, which means managing for choice—for maximum biodiversity;
6. understand how to manage for a desired condition of the landscape, and abandon the cherished, unworkable notion of sustained ever-increasing yield of natural resources;
7. understand how to manage for the connectivity of habitats to help ensure the ecological wholeness and the biological richness—biodiversity—of the patterns they create across the landscape;
8. be able to abstract, simplify, synthesize, and generalize information about complex systems so his or her *intuitive mind* can and may act as the final reality check of relevant information prior to making decisions;
9. be able to articulate ideas effectively, clearly, and correctly, both in writing and in public speaking;
10. be able to work openly and skillfully with people, with sufficient knowledge and in sufficient depth to validate their concerns, and to give them the critical understanding and trust of the professional rationale behind a decision, even if they are opposed to it.

If university colleges of forestry in North America can find the courage within the decade of the 1990s to do their jobs with the professional *integrity*—truth, openness, and excellence—foresters both deserve and need, the next one hundred years can indeed become the first century of healing forests both at home and abroad.

Garth Lenz

The practical means for implementing an ecosystem-based philosophy is a system called
wholistic forest use. Wholistic forest use respects and protects the balance inherent in forests, and
ensures that people are a part of the forest web in a soft, diverse way.

WHOLISTIC FOREST USE: AN ECOSYSTEM-BASED APPROACH TO TIMBER MANAGEMENT

HERB HAMMOND

In the face of the large-scale, accelerated clearcutting of Earth's forests, it is not enough to protest, research, and object to the plans of the timber industry. We know enough to change. We have workable methods for protecting, maintaining, and assisting Nature to restore (where necessary) fully functioning forests. We must implement these methods now. This change begins with an ecosystem-based approach rather than a human-centered approach, recognizing that we are part of the forest—what we do to the forest we do to ourselves. We must focus on needs, not on greed. Consumption must be replaced by conservation. We must act on the understanding that the forest sustains us, we do not sustain the forest.

WHAT IS AN ECOSYSTEM-BASED PHILOSOPHY?

An ecosystem-based philosophy or vision can be summarized as a way of relating to and utilizing the ecosystems we are part of in ways that ensure their continued well-being, through maintaining (and restoring) biological diversity—from the genetic and species levels to the community and landscape levels. An ecosystem-based perspective works at all scales, from the microscopic to the global, and recognizes the following ecological principles.

The Earth, from microbe to globe, is a whole system, interconnected and interdependent.

The Earth functions to sustain the whole in an equilibrium that is dynamic yet stable (in human time frames).

All ecosystem composition (the parts) and structures (the arrangement of the parts) have a function (how the parts work together). If we lose the composition and structure, we lose the function.

People are part of the Earth. What we do to the Earth we do to ourselves.

Human plans must encompass ecosystem time frames of centuries—not short-term development timetables of one to five years.

Our plans and activities in the forest, from the largest landscape to the smallest patch, must reflect the principles listed above. In practical terms, an ecosystem-based approach has two components:

1. *Ecological responsibility.* All human uses within the forest landscape must protect all parts of the forest web. Although people are unable to appreciate the subtle connections in a forest, what is done to one part of the web is done to all parts. Ecological responsibility means moving toward a way of thinking that states, "If an activity cannot be proven safe, the activity will not be carried out." This contrasts with the conventional industrial timber philosophy that states, "If an activity cannot be proven harmful, the activity shall be carried out." Ecological responsibility means adopting a conservational way of thinking, rather than taking an exploitative approach. Ecologically responsible plans and activities are guided by the requirement to maintain fully functioning forests at all levels, from small communities to large landscapes, in both the short and long term.

2. *Balanced human and nonhuman use.* Within the context of ecological responsibility, we must ensure that all forest users—human and nonhuman—have fair, legally protected land bases that are well distributed throughout the forest, sufficient to meet their needs, and adequate to ensure that their functions are maintained in the ecosystem.

An ecosystem-based philosophy in today's world must include restoration. Our "use" of Earth's forests has resulted in extensive degradation. There are no ecological quick fixes for devastated forest landscapes. But thoughtful, creative human work to help restore forests to a healthy state is both a way of understanding our mistakes and, through keen observation, a way of learning about the functioning of whole forest systems. To restore forests with human technology and process is impossible, but to work with Nature to rejuvenate and regenerate degraded parts is to be one with Earth, the beginning point for all sustainable endeavors.

WHOLISTIC FOREST USE

The practical means for implementing an ecosystem-based philosophy is a system called *wholistic forest use.* Wholistic forest use respects and protects the balance inherent in forests, and ensures that people are a *part of* the forest web in a soft, diverse way.

Wholistic forest use—which defines the forest as a diverse, interconnected web of living and nonliving parts—focuses on sustaining the whole, not on the production of any one part (e.g., timber). All parts of a forest have important purposes that are respected and protected. People, too, are a part of forests. Forests purify air and water, and they moderate climate; forests furnish homes and food for animals (including humans), plants, and microorganisms; forests provide spiritual renewal for all beings; and forests are an important part of human economies. When people change one part of the forest, all parts are affected. Thus, we must interact with forests in a careful, caring manner that protects all forest components and functions.

While wholistic forest use requires protection of all aspects of the forest ecosystem both during and after human activities in the forest, there is no "scientific proof," in the narrow sense of the words, that this is necessary. Most scientific research is controlled by industrial organizations interested in forest exploitation, not in forest protection. Furthermore, the forest system is too complex to study in its entirety and so it can never be "proven" that complete, intact ecosystems are vital for forest survival. Yet our intuition tells us that protection of the whole forest is necessary. Wholistic forest use incorporates the findings of science and accepts intuition as the link between scientific and wholistic thinking, between science and wisdom.

Wholistic forest use protects the spiritual values of forests—the sense of wonder, beauty, and sustenance that all of us have felt and seen in intact, native forests. These values are often ignored or denied during conventional timber management.

Adoption of wholistic forest use means changing our priorities—changing our thinking in a fundamental way. Indigenous cultures have provided us with the following priorities that we are applying to the concepts of wholistic forest use.

Priority One: Love the forest. Appreciate the forest. Give thanks that the forest sustains us.

Priority Two: Protect the forest and use it responsibly for vital human needs.

Priority Three: Trade or barter only the excess of forest goods that are not required for human needs.

This proposed priority of thinking for wholistic use of the forest is significantly different from, perhaps the opposite of, the priorities of modern society where short-term economics are the dominant priority.

Wholistic forest use represents a different set of ethics, values, or worldview when compared to conventional timber management. Recognizing the converging ecological crises of our time—climate change, ozone depletion, toxic waste, acid rain, desertification, overpopulation, soil depletion, habitat destruction, and species extinction—wholistic forest use adopts a conservational, cautious land ethic applied at a local level. True protection of all parts of the forest is the key aspect of a new land ethic necessary to sustain the human species.

In contrast, timber managers have been manipulating complex forest ecosystems for several hundred years, based on the arrogant assumption that they could somehow manage (manipulate) and enhance a system that they have not even tried to understand. The results have been catastrophic. Forested areas in the Sahara, the Mediterranean, parts of Asia, and some islands in the Caribbean ceased to exist long ago. In Europe, simplified plantations are succumbing to acid deposition. The vulnerability of these plantations and their stressed conditions are caused by loss of biological diversity at all levels. Because of their natural resilience and biological wealth accumulated over millennia, forests subjected to clearcutting in much of North America have only recently begun to break down.

Today's timber industry refuses to believe that parallels can be drawn between the historic decline of world forests and current practices. Timber managers continue to believe that technology will overcome biological realities. Yet timber management increasingly assumes the aura of crisis control. As forests reach the end of their resilience, the natural checks and balances of functioning ecosystems break down, to be replaced by the chaos of insect and disease infestations, unexplained forest die-off, poor growth, and regeneration failures.

These events are the signs of severely stressed ecosystems. As forests become more and more stressed in the changing global environment, we must take our lead from the forest and work within its biological limits. Wholistic forest use embodies this new way of thinking about our role in the forest.

Wholistic forest use means working to ensure, within our very limited understanding, that suitable and sufficient habitats are left for all forms of life in the forest (both macroscopic and microscopic) while we extract the wood that we need. We cannot afford to dismiss as irrelevant such events as loss of soil life-forms after clearcutting and slash burning. These soil organisms manufacture important soil nutrients that all plants require to grow; they form cooperative relationships with tree roots that enable the roots to extract water and nutrients from the soil; and they protect trees from root-decaying fungi. Wholistic forest use recognizes the interdependence of all forest life-forms and fully protects biological diversity (i.e., gene pools, species diversity, ecological communities, and sustainable landscapes) in order to maintain a healthy forest.

Ideally, wholistic forest use planning starts with a complete field-based inventory of natural, social, and economic factors. From this inventory a wholistic forest use plan is prepared. While a complete inventory is the ideal starting place, wholistic forest use can be implemented even with an incomplete inventory. We can begin today to practice wholistic forest use by making conservative interpretations of available information, and by erring in favor of forest protection. A complete inventory can be acquired as wholistic forest use progresses.

Wholistic forest use planning gives priority to the protection of natural factors, recognizing that healthy ecosystems are the basis for healthy economies and societies. Forests sustain us, we do not sustain forests. Providing a diversity of uses that do not degrade the forest will protect forests for long-term benefit. So-called integrated forest management plans—currently in vogue—which place short-term profits from timber extraction ahead of more diverse, sustainable patterns of forest use, do not meet these criteria.

Wholistic forest use advocates *zoning* of forests for a variety of activities on a watershed by watershed basis. Timber extraction is considered as one possible forest use, and it is recognized as an activity with potentially large adverse impacts on future forest functioning and on other forest uses such as indigenous culture, fish and wildlife habitat, trapping, and tourism. Wholistic forest use rejects harsh practices such as conventional clearcutting, slash burning, pesticide application, and "high-grading" (removal of only the best timber). Where timber extraction is determined to be an acceptable use of the forest, partial cutting methods are used while all parts of the forest are protected and maintained. Substantial parts of a forest, including entire watersheds, are zoned for "nontimber" uses such as the protection of cultural and spiritual places, forest reserves (wilderness or ecological reserves), water supplies, fish and wildlife needs, sensitive slopes and soils, trapping areas, and acceptable forms of recreation and tourism. Some of these uses have dollar values; others do not.

The need for meaningful work from timber extraction in forests is not ignored by wholistic forest use. Fewer trees are cut down with wholistic timber management than with conventional practices. Nevertheless, approximately the same number of timber-oriented jobs may be created in wholistic forest use through "forest-friendly," labor-intensive practices and by making more products from each tree that is cut. Other forest activities, such as tourism, recreation, water production, trapping, ranching, gathering and processing of wild foods (berries, mushrooms), and fish and wildlife harvesting—all carried out in ecologically responsible ways—result in more total sustainable employment opportunities with wholistic forest use than with conventional timber management.

Under conventional timber management, rural forest communities bear the environmental and social costs of short-term exploitation of forests for timber, while residents of the major milling centers and urban areas reap most of the benefits in the short term. Clearcutting, as practiced by the timber industry, produces revenue from a particular forest area only once in approximately 60 to 200 years, permanently damages soil and biological diversity, and forecloses on ecologically responsible forest uses such as public recreation, tourism, trapping, wholistic timber extraction, and cultural activities. In contrast, wholistic forest use means diverse, community-controlled forest use. A stable, diverse economy is developed through employment and revenue generated each year from a variety of activities that use the interest generated by the forest without disturbing the forest's essential composition, structure, and functions—its capital.

The practice of wholistic forest use requires an understanding of forest landscapes and the need for protecting large reserves and landscape networks, and application of wholistic forest-use zoning according to principles of wholistic timber management.

LANDSCAPE ECOLOGY: WHOLISTIC FOREST USE IN PRACTICE

Wholistic forest use does not begin in a stand of trees or an isolated forest patch—it begins with the forest landscape. In order to maintain fully functioning forests, the natural patterns and connections in the forest landscape must be protected and maintained, both during and following human activities. The concept of landscape used here does not refer to scenery, but rather to the matrix of ecosystem patterns and connections that exist across very large areas of land, often defined as large watersheds or drainage basins.

These patterns and connections exist in both space and time. Some of the spatial and temporal aspects of the forest landscape are difficult for humans to understand, because the scales involved are both much larger and much smaller than the scale of human life. The aspect of space is probably the easier of the two for humans to understand, since we can use maps, air photos, and satellite photos to obtain at least a second-hand appreciation of spatial patterns and connections. We need to remember, however, that a forest landscape functions at every spatial level, from the microscopic level up to the whole-watershed level and beyond.

Understanding the temporal patterns and connections in a forest landscape is a greater challenge, since some forest parts such as rocks, old trees, and old-growth patches function for 500, 1,000, 2,000 years, or more—while others, equally significant in the forest web, live for only days or hours.

Many of the most serious errors in forest use have come about from our attempt to manage the forest on a human time scale—for example, planning timber clearcutting cycles of sixty to eighty years. This is a fairly normal human life cycle, but sixty to eighty years is not a normal life cycle for most tree species. At the level of a whole forest, time cycles are often hard to identify because the forest is a continuum in time and space. Broad-scale clearcut/plantation-style timber management short-circuits the lifespan of trees and removes completely the future source of dead trees vital to forest functioning. Thus, conventional timber management fragments the forest continuum and breaks landscape connections in both time and space.

Maintaining the functioning of the forest landscape, indeed any landscape, requires establishing two kinds of protected areas: *large protected reserves*, and *protected landscape networks*. These protected areas accomplish the primary goals of connectivity in the landscape and protecting the full range of biological diversity at all scales.

LARGE PROTECTED RESERVES

Large protected reserves constitute entire drainage basins or watersheds ranging upward in size from about 5,000 hectares. These areas are the storehouses of biological diversity necessary to maintain all of the forest, including that area modified by human use. The more severe and extensive the modifications

of the landscape, the greater the need for large protected reserves.

Large protected reserves protect the temporal aspect of landscape ecology. These reserves must be large enough to withstand natural disturbances, in order to retain their resiliency and integrity as fully functioning forest landscapes. How large is large enough? Scientists suggest that protected landscapes must be 50 to 200 times the size of the largest anticipated natural disturbance.

Figure 1, Large-Scale Landscape Diagram, is a conceptual map of a landscape that includes large protected reserves (labeled "protected drainage basins").

In order to maintain healthy landscapes, large protected reserves cannot exist as islands, regardless of their size; they must be connected across the landscape as shown in the diagram. Ideal connectors include riparian ecosystems and cross-valley corridors.

Riparian ecosystems include the riparian zone (wet forest area along creeks, rivers, lakes, wetlands, and all water bodies) and the riparian zone of influence (the upland forest immediately adjacent to the riparian zone). Riparian zones are biological hotspots, concentrating the water, nutrients, and energy that drain into them and regulating their dispersal back into the landscape. Moreover, riparian ecosystems are travel corridors for animals and plants. Riparian ecosystems must be protected throughout the landscape.

Cross-valley corridors consist of broad, irregularly shaped bands of forest, from two to five kilometers in width, that provide valley-to-valley connections between large protected reserves and across ridges. Cross-valley corridors should be made up of representative ecosystems found in the landscape, and they cannot be blocked by land features such as cliffs and rock bluffs that obstruct the movement of large animals.

FIGURE 1

FIGURE 2

PROTECTED LANDSCAPE NETWORKS

In the areas between large protected reserves, ecologically responsible human modification (i.e., wholistic forest use) may occur. But it is still necessary to maintain the landscape's framework in these areas outside of large protected reserves. This is achieved through protected landscape networks.

Figure 2, Landscape Network Diagram, shows that riparian ecosystems and cross-valley corridors are also components in this level of landscape protection, along with other types of small protected areas.

The term *network* makes clear the idea of connectivity; however, we need to keep in mind that the corridors and protected clusters are not narrow strips but broad areas encompassing complete ecosystem types. The overall area, seen from above, resembles a piece of Swiss cheese, with broad corridors connecting protected ecosystems interrupted by "holes." The protected landscape network forms the framework within which (in some of the holes of the Swiss cheese) various ecologically responsible human activities may occur.

The complete set of components needed to maintain the landscape framework, and therefore included in a protected landscape network, includes:

Riparian ecosystems—the backbone of the network.

Representative ecosystems—small protected nodes of 400 hectares or more. (Smaller protected nodes are established where an ecosystem type is strategically located, rare, or endangered. Old-growth or late successional forests are particularly important to include in the protected network.)

Sensitive ecosystems—shallow soils, very wet and very dry areas, steep and/or broken terrain.

Cross-valley corridors.

WHOLISTIC FOREST USE ZONING

The combination of large protected reserves and protected landscape networks will protect the landscape ecology—the patterns and connections—of the forest. Within that framework provided by the protected landscape network, ecologically responsible and balanced human use is accomplished by establishing wholistic forest use zones.

In establishing wholistic forest use zones, the most sensitive and easily damaged human uses are accommodated before allocating areas for more aggressive human uses. In order of their establishment, typical forest use zones include:

Culture—areas that are culturally or historically important to local people

Ecologically Sensitive—small sensitive areas not identified or protected in the protected landscape network

Fish and Wildlife Habitat

Recreation-Tourism-Wilderness

Ranching and Trapping

Wholistic Timber Management

Within their respective zones, human uses must be carried out in accordance with ecologically responsible standards. Some uses, such as recreation and timber extraction, are mutually exclusive and would not occur in the same zone. While timber extraction is a particularly aggressive use of the forest, when carried out in an ecologically responsible manner, it can be compatible with some other uses.

WHOLISTIC TIMBER MANAGEMENT ZONES

Timber extraction under wholistic forest use looks different in almost every respect from conventional timber management. Specifically, ecologically responsible practices in wholistic timber management zones will:

1. maintain a diverse composition and community structure that supports a fully functioning forest (important forest structures such as large old trees, snags, and large fallen trees are maintained by allowing 20 to 30 percent of overstory trees, well distributed spatially by species, to grow old and die in all timber extraction areas);

2. use ecological rotation periods of at least 150 to 250 years;

3. utilize ecologically appropriate partial cutting methods that maintain the canopy structure, age distribution, and species mixture found in healthy natural forests in a particular ecosystem type, and prohibit clearcutting as currently practiced;

4. prohibit slash burning;

5. maintain/restore fire necessary for ecosystem functioning;

6. allow the forest to regenerate trees naturally through seeds from trees in the logged area (tree planting will generally not be required, because a diverse, fully functioning forest is always maintained);

7. maintain ecological succession to protect biological diversity (and thereby avoid the need for brush control);

8. prohibit pesticide use;

9. maintain soil productivity by avoiding use of roads (including skid roads) wherever possible and constructing narrow roads (including skid roads), when necessary, that fit into the terrain and minimize erosion;

10. protect water by: (a) protecting riparian ecosystems at all scales, (b) minimizing alterations to natural drainage patterns, and (c) deactivating old roads (including skid roads) to reestablish natural drainage patterns.

CONCLUSION

The time has come to make large protected reserves, protected landscape networks, and ecologically responsible forest use the norm. Ecologically responsible models for wholistic forest use can be implemented simultaneously with the practical and basic research we need to ensure that the change to an ecosystem-based ethic not only protects the ecosystem but also sustains human societies.

Adoption of this ecologically responsible, wholistic approach to timber management will mean that we will often have to make decisions without knowing why something occurs the way it does in an ecosystem. However, we will carry out activities that protect ecosystem composition and structures to ensure that all functions continue to occur, regardless of whether or not we understand them.

Ecologically responsible forest use can best be carried out by local communities that live in or close to a particular forest landscape. Within the constraints of ecological responsibility and balanced use, community-based groups representing the spectrum of human and nonhuman interests are best equipped to plan, administer, and evaluate human activities in forests. Meaningful work will be characterized by ecologically sensitive practices, with minimal waste, healthy local economies, and optimal recycling of Nature's products. Our jobs and economies can be based on protecting, maintaining, and restoring the forests that sustain us—working with the forest.

In embarking on an ecosystem-based approach, we are seeking ecological wisdom, through our combined knowledge and intuition—through listening to our hearts, and by following our instincts. In seeking the Earth's wisdom we are reminded that instinct is the basis of survival. We need to approach wholistic forest use with humility, and remember that our human instincts for survival are not dissimilar from the instincts of all other beings.

Let us implement wholistic forest use together. We are all part of the problem, and we must move collectively to become part of the solution. The longer we wait, the fewer the options. The longer we wait, the larger the job of restoration. Let's get on with what our minds and our hearts tell us is right. Think like the forest.

Gary Braasch

Natural selection ecoforestry is a program based solely on using Nature's indicators for determining not only which trees can be removed, but also when. No tree can be harvested before it has been naturally selected for removal.

NATURAL SELECTION ECOFORESTRY

ORVILLE CAMP

In the early 1950s, as an adult, I began comparing my parents' forestland with the way I remembered it as a child when it was covered with old-growth forest. I thought how relatively easy it was to cut those big trees and that it would be impossible to get them back in my lifetime, if ever. I kept thinking there must be a better way to approach forestry.

In 1967 I began purchasing logged-over forestland in Oregon. At first I didn't consider the possibility of making a profit from forestland. I did not know anyone who made a living off their own, relatively small parcel of forested land. I began experimenting with a method that I came to call *natural selection ecoforestry*. During the next decades I began to see timber yields increase on my land, and I began to see more aesthetically pleasing vistas on my land as well as more diversity of wildlife. Natural selection ecoforestry was producing results far superior to any conventional forest-management program.

Natural selection ecoforestry is a program based solely on using Nature's indicators for determining not only which trees can be removed, but also when. No tree can be harvested before it has been naturally selected for removal. The concepts developed on my forestland in southern Oregon are discussed in my book, *The Forest Farmer's Handbook: A Guide to Natural Selection Forest Management.*

There are ten forest ecosystem management goals of natural selection ecoforestry.

1. Develop a broad identification with forests that is in harmony with the forest.

2. Conserve forestland for forest ecosystem purposes.

3. Maintain healthy forest ecosystems that can sustain all species native to that bioregion.

4. Maintain forest climate, soil, and water.

5. Maintain habitat that can sustain all species native to the bioregion.

6. Build necessary roads with care. Not all forestlands need roads, but normally when harvesting occurs some kind of access roads will be needed. A road system that is poorly laid out and constructed is detrimental to the integrity of the land. Roads constructed on principles I have developed include the following design directives: (a) minimize ecological impacts; (b) maintain the integrity of the ecosystem; (c) reduce road width to a minimum needed to extract products, which means they often can be narrow, single-lane, one-way roads; (d) allow for annual havests; (e) be aesthetically pleasing; (f) enhance recreational values; and (g) be able to limit the number of people using the access road in order to protect wildlife.

7. Minimize equipment impact on the forestland by using small, low-impact equipment and keeping all heavy equipment on access roads. Equipment should be no larger than necessary to achieve removal of a product.

8. Maintain ecological and economic net worth.

9. Never harvest the "stronger dominant" trees until after they become the "weaker members" and are being replaced by new stronger dominants, as determined by Nature. This will maintain the best genetic base for every micro-site and allow removal of trees and other growth, such as ferns and mushrooms, that the forest is capable of producing at any given time.

Stronger dominants are individual trees that are genetically in harmony with their environment as determined by Nature. They can usually be identified by observing which trees have faster growth rates for the location. They also typically out-grow others of their own species of the same age in that location.

Weaker members are those genetically less vigorous members as determined by Nature. Weaker trees of the same species are typically smaller, slower-growing trees of the same age found in the understory of a forest structure. The stronger dominants form the top of the canopy, whereas the weaker members will increasingly be in their shade.

10. When making a decision, follow the rule: "When in doubt, don't." Removing trees at the wrong time can result in harvested areas requiring hundreds of years before they can be brought back to their original health. I ask myself, "If I remove a particular tree, what will it cost and how long will it take to restore the territory it occupied back to its ecological value?"

Our real wealth is based on the natural health of the forest. I am convinced that natural selection ecoforestry maintains the health of forestlands while sustaining the economic health of local, human communities.

AFTERWORD

DOUGLAS TOMPKINS

This book was conceived while I flew over British Columbia in my small plane on a trip back from the Queen Charlotte Islands. Doug Peacock was with me, and we both were awestruck by the extensive destruction of native forests we saw below. A few weeks earlier, Bill Devall and I had flown from Arcata, California, to British Columbia. We watched with sadness and despair the landscapes below laid waste by industrial/technological managers who had clearcut vast tracts of ancient forests. Not a moment in either of these flights, nor in the hundreds of hours I've flown over the years, have I been out of sight of clearcuts in the Pacific Northwest.

As Doug Peacock and I gazed out the windows of our small plane, we withdrew into ourselves, reflecting on how one person could help stop this madness. I thought of my mother, who knows virtually nothing about forestry, apart from her broad love of trees and woods and her special care for the forests around her community in upstate New York. On a visit to my house in California she was stopped by Daniel Dancer's now famous photo of the Olympic National Forest, hanging on my wall. In Dancer's photo, the viewer sees a long line into the distance dividing a rich, healthy, old-growth forest and crushing clearcuts. My mother was so shocked by the photo that for a moment she could not comprehend what she saw. It slowly dawned on her that she was seeing a kind of pathological mode of behavior expressed in clearcutting.

My mother isn't a person given to anger, much less venomous disgust. But I saw a kind of gestalt reaction take place. Her instincts, intuitions, and nurturing sensibilities all responded simultaneously. She could only say, "this cannot be; it just cannot be right."

And so too, Doug Peacock, Bill Devall, and I, all in our own ways, were saying, "this is not possible. This has got to stop. This is a crime against nature, against life." Recalling my mother's reaction to Daniel Dancer's photo, I thought that perhaps a thorough pictorial documentation of the tragedy of industrial forestry should be produced and widely distributed to illustrate the dead-end path of industrial forestry.

That is how we started this project. Now that the book is finished, it has been evident already how this kind of imagery—clear and uncompromising, disturbing and shocking as it is—can produce an energy for action. These images call up a "green rage" in people who understand the destruction caused by industrial behemoths. During the development of this project, people involved in the project—from photographers to writers, pilots, designers, printers, typesetters, friends or acquaintances, as well as veteran forest activists—have been shocked by what they saw portrayed here.

During the course of selecting photos for this book, we assembled the largest and most comprehensive collection of photos of clearcuts in North America. The photos in this book were carefully selected from the thousands we viewed to present regional representation of all forest types in North America. In our archives we have a very powerful graphic testimony that will serve in future campaigns. A large exhibition of color prints, selected from the book and the photo archives, is being prepared. We encourage readers to write us to obtain information on organizing a show in your region.

The production of this book began after Bill Devall and I outlined its form and content. Bill took responsibility for editing, and I took responsibility for overall art direction and production. I put together a small team of friends and colleagues. Edgar Boyles took charge of photo editing. Del Rae Roth, who worked with me for years as studio manager of the graphic design studio at Esprit, took on project coordination and graphic design. Tamotsu Yagi, a good friend and renowned graphic designer, agreed to lend his time and design studio for the graphic layout and preparation.

One of our aims was to print this book with the most advanced techniques in paper production and printing that were as environmentally friendly as possible. Some criticism may come from those who feel this book is too big or too lavish. Our intention, however, is to make this a multipurpose project. First and foremost, it is intended as a tool for activists. We hope to raise consciousness and create a momentum for radical change in forest policy and practices.

Second, the massive clearcuts exposed in this book are rarely seen by most citizens. Most of the massive clearcuts illustrated in these pages are in the backcountry, away from scrutiny of citizens who drive only along major highways. It should be remembered that what is seen in these pages is only a small sample of the massive destruction. When citizens see the extent of these clearcuts, we are convinced they will call for a radically different forest policy. The sacrifice of several trees to enlarge this message, by publishing in a large format with high-impact graphics, will then be worth the effort.

Third, this book stands as a sad testimony of the need to publish a "coffee-table"-format book. Two decades ago, exhibit-format books were published and distributed by the Sierra Club as instruments to inspire awe and wonder at Nature's beauty. David Brower, who edited and produced exhibit-format books during the 1960s, is our co-publisher with his Earth Island Press. Today our world is so brutally affected by the onslaught of the industrial growth society—what Jerry Mander calls "the juggernaut of technological forces"—that books such as this will try to inspire a resistance to the runaway train of free enterprise and commodity culture.

Fourth, I hope this book will inspire other photographers and writers to do something of this sort on the devastation caused by massive dam projects, toxic wastes, mining, urban blight, ocean pollution, desertification, introduction of exotic species, and industrial tourism. Peter Beard began this type of documentation with his book about the destruction of African wildlife, *The End of the Game* (1963). Sebastião Salgado documented the famines in Africa and the subjugation of humans by machine culture. Peter Goin, in his *Nuclear Landscapes* (1991), documents the landmarks of the Atomic Age. I hope that our book—*Clearcut*—sets a standard for contemporary landscape photography by realistically documenting the landscape behind the "beauty strip."

This book increases our understanding of the major destruction occuring in the forests of North America. Change in forest policy and practices will occur only when many people become forest activists. The front in the deep, long-range ecology movement, as philosopher Arne Naess says, is long. People with many different talents, from all social classes, all ethnic and religious affiliations, male and female, young and old can contribute in a wide variety of ways. People of various occupational skills, from computer programmers and economists, to teachers, students, truck drivers, business executives, physicians, and people retired from their occupations, have a place in the grassroots movement to reform forest policies.

Your voice, your attendance at a rally, your vote, your time, energy, intelligence, moral support, and good humor—all can support the movement to change public policy. Once you join this grassroots movement you will begin to feel yourself reconnecting to the values lying at the core of your own being. This will reward itself in countless ways, and you will begin a process of self-development and become part of the solution rather than part of the problem.

In the following pages we have provided a list of some of the organizations dedicated to both forestry reform and to broader issues concerning the root causes of deforestation.

Mark Alan Wilson

WHAT YOU CAN DO

A CALL TO ACTIVISM

Clearcut was conceived, assembled, written, edited and printed as a device to increase public awareness and education of the devastating effects of industrial forestry. In particular, we focused on the principal technique of clearcutting, in all its various forms and euphemisms. We hoped to foster a better understanding of other damaging techniques that the industrial model brings with it. These include even-age management (tree farms or plantations), use of heavy equipment, road building, pesticide application, as well as boom/bust management plans and their impacts on timber communities. Through education, we believe the general public, mostly unaware of the fallacies inherent in the underlying assumptions of the industrial model, will also acknowlege the urgent need to systemically change our techniques of using and coexisting with forests. Forests provide easy parallels with which to compare our human economy. We are likely to find both a sick forest and a sick economy. The pity and the hope of the matter is that we do not have to clearcut or follow the industrial system to provide jobs in the production and use of wood. By choosing an organic or holistic forest-harvesting model, we can have a renewable resource of our forests, resulting in abundance, richness, diversity, and long-term economic security. A number of commercially viable timber operations currently exist that prove this very point. Through public education and awareness, we can ask our policy makers to rewrite the rules upon which all of us utilize the bounty of Nature, providing long-term, enduring stability for human and nonhuman communities alike.

How can the average citizen take part in this essential debate and help create change? Many readers of this book will already be engaged, perhaps intensely involved in the forest movement, working to reform or fundamentally change the way we humans deal with the forest. To those, we ask you to read this book carefully and sharpen your arguments of the forest issue. Then help us distribute the book to increase public awareness.

To those who are partially familiar with or even new to forest issues, we advise you to carefully read *Clearcut* cover to cover. This will provide a comprehensive understanding of the forest debate. You can further your education by spending as much time as you can afford *experiencing* old-growth or even mature regrown forests directly. Learn what a fully functioning forest looks and feels like. Visit some tree plantations, make practical real-life comparisons. Seek out others who know about forests. Get their viewpoints. You don't need to be an expert, however, to recognize that clearcuts, tree farms, and extensive road systems throughout the landscape do not tend toward ecological health.

As a consumer you can begin to reduce your consumption of wood and wood-based products such as paper and packaging. Begin to ask wood suppliers whether their products are purchased from companies using truly sustainable forestry practices and certified as such.

In local communities you can work directly on and support watershed restoration projects. These may include fishery, wildlife, or soil restoration. You can question local regulatory agencies as to how they are providing adequate protection for soils, long-term forest products, wildlife habitats, water courses, and breeding grounds for fish, birds, and animals.

If you are not already affiliated, join a local environmental group that is asking for a no-compromise stand on forest regulation. Government agencies dealing with forests should be forced to deeply examine the issues of scientific and intrinsic value of forests, without being influenced by commercial interests or putting economic truths before ecological truths.

We have provided a fair-sized list to allow you to see if there is a group near you. This doesn't mean that you won't find other organizations better suited to your particular sentiments. And if you deem it necessary, don't hesitate to start your own organization. There are thousands of small and large environmental groups, all of which have been started by someone very much like you. In most cases this can be done locally, even if you live in the desert or in agricultural areas that have few forests. There are environmental groups in every nook and cranny of North America. Keep in mind that educating your local, state, and provincial representatives is an excellent way to influence how our forests are treated.

Forest defense is a vital part of our national defense and security. They are one and the same. Industrial forestry, as you have seen, is like war. Its effects on the landscape, the soils, and biomes are amazingly similar, only this has been a silent, quiet war, one that is only recently making headlines. Like all war-torn societies, the economies are wrecked along with the land. Take a stand, just as you would in an unjust war—then you will have *done* something. We all thank you in advance for joining with us to redirect forest policy and procedure toward the organic or the whole model and away from the industrial and destructive model. We know you'll feel a lot better being a part of the resistance to industrial forestry and its life-threatening practices. Thanks again! —The Editors.

Doug Radies

The following directory is of regional groups engaged in forest preservation and/or biodiversity issues. The first three are playing a leading role in the distribution of this book, and the educational campaign supporting it.

SIERRA CLUB, 730 Polk Street, San Francisco, CA 94109. Tel. 415.776.2211

RAINFOREST ACTION NETWORK, 450 Sansome Street, Suite 700, San Francisco, CA 94111. Tel. 415.398.4404

VALHALLA SOCIETY, Box 224, New Denver, British Columbia VOG180. Tel. 604.358.2333

NATIONAL GROUPS, FOREST POLICY AND REGIONAL FOREST ACTIVIST GROUPS: Americans for the Ancient Forests, 2550 M Street NW, #250, Washington, DC 20037 Federal Forest Reform, 5934 Royal Lane, #223, Dallas, TX 75230 Greenpeace, 1436 U Street NW, Washington, DC 20009 National Audubon Society, 666 Pennsylvania Avenue SE, Suite 301, Washington, DC 20003 Native Forest Council, PO Box 2171, Eugene, OR 97402 Natural Resources Defense Council, 71 Stevenson, #1825, San Francisco, CA 94105 Rainforest Action Network, 450 Sansome Street, Suite 700, San Francisco, CA 94111 Save America's Forests, 4 Library Court SE, Washington, DC 20003 SEAC (Student Environmental Action Coalition), National Office, PO Box 1168, Chapel Hill, NC 27514 Sierra Club, 408 C Street NE, Washington, DC 20002 Sierra Club, Seattle, 1516 Melrose Avenue, Seattle, WA 98122 Sierra Club Legal Defense Fund, 1531 P Street NW, Washington, DC 20005 Western Ancient Forest Campaign, 1400 16th Street NW, #294, Washington, DC The Wilderness Society, 900 17th St. NW, Washington, DC 20006 World Wildlife Fund, 1250 24th NW, Washington, DC 20037 **BIODIVERSITY AND WILDLANDS RESTORATION** Ancient Forests International, PO Box 1850, Redway, CA 95560 Association for Forest Service Employees for Environmental Ethics, PO Box 11615, Eugene, OR 97440 California Wilderness Coalition, 2655 Portage Bay East, Suite 5, Davis, CA 95616 Greater Ecosystem Alliance, PO Box 2813, Bellingham, WA 98227 Lighthawk, PO Box 8613, Santa Fe, NM 87504-8613 Oregon Natural Resources Council, 1050 Yeon Bldg., 522 Southwest Fifth Ave., Portland, OR 97204 Wild Earth, PO Box 492, Canton, NY 13617 The Wildlands Project, PO Box 5365, Tucson, AZ 85703 Wilderness Covenant, PO Box 5217, Tucson, AZ 85703
SUSTAINABLE FORESTRY Ecoforestry Institute, PO Box 12543, Portland, OR 97212

U.S.A.

ALABAMA Alabama Conservancy, 2717 7th Ave. S, Suite 207, Birmingham, AL 35233 Alabama Conservancy RAG, 1747 River Road, #301, Tuscaloosa, AL 35401 Bankhead Monitor, PO Box 117, Moulton, AL 35650 H.E.L.P., PO Box 4471, Huntsville, AL 35815 **ALASKA** Alaska PIRG, PO Box 101093, Anchorage, AK 99510 Alaska Wildlife Alliance, PO Box 202022, Anchorage, AK 99520 Chugach Forest Study Groups, PO Box 662, Girdwood, AK 99587 Green Party of Alaska, PO Box 141474, Anchorage, AK 99514 Greenpeace Alaska, PO Box 6001, Sitka, AK 99835 Kachemak Heritage Land Trust, PO Box 2400, Homer, AK 99835 Southeast Alaska Conservation, 419 Sixth St., Suite 386, Juneau, AK 99802 Tatshenshini Wild, PO Box 964, Haines, AK 99827 Wrangell Resources Council, PO Box 2073, Wrangell, AK 99929 **ARIZONA** Adopt-a-Timber Sale, 5½ W. Cottage Avenue, Flagstaff, AZ 86001 Arizona Forest Watch, Route 4, Box 886, Flagstaff, AZ 86001 Arizona Lobby for Animals, General Delivery, Kayenta, AZ 86033 Arizona Rainforest Alliance, 1700 N. Wentworth Road, Tucson, AZ 85749 Arizona Rivers Coalition, 3601 N. 7th Ave., Phoenix, AZ 85013 Border Ecology Project, PO Box 5, Naco, AZ 85620 Coastal Conservation Foundation, PO Box 3621, Tucson, AZ 85722 Drylands Institute, 2003 E. 4th St., Tucson, AZ 85719 Green Fire Project, PO Box 41822, Tucson, AZ 85717 Liberate Our Verdant Ecosystems, 10610 S. 48th St., #2102, Phoenix, AZ 85044 Mt. Graham Coalition, PO Box 15451, Phoenix, AZ 85060 North American Wilderness Recovery, PO Box 5365, Tucson, AZ 85703 Rainforest Survival Foundation, PO Box 1133, Tempe, AZ 85280 Rincon Chapter, Sierra Club, 738 N. 5th Ave., Tucson, AZ 85705 Sky-Island Alliance, 1639 E. 1st St., Tucson, AZ 85719 Sonoran Institute, 6842 E. Tanque Verde, Suite D, Tucson, AZ 85719 Rainforest Survival Foundation, PO Box 1133, Tempe, AZ 85280 Wildlife Damage Review, PO Box 85218, Tucson, AZ 85754 **ARKANSAS** Concerned Citizens of Hot Springs, 531 Windamere Terrace, Hot Springs, AR 71913 Defenders of the Ouachita Forest, PO Box 242, Mena, AR 71953 Eager Beavers, Rte. 1, 369 Pine Garfield, AR 72732 Malvern Earth Day Committee, 525 Locust, Malvern, AR 72104 Mena Nature Club, Rte. 2, Box 256BB, Mena, AR 71953 Newton County Wildlife Association, PO Box 189, Jasper, AR 72641 Ouachita Garden Club, State Route 9, Box 168, Mena, AR 71953 Scott County Organization to Protect the Environment (SCOPE), PO Box 88, Parks, AR 72950 **CALIFORNIA** Alliance for a Paving Moratorium, PO Box 4347, Arcata, CA 95521 Ancient Forest International, PO Box 1850, Redway, CA 95560 Assoc. of Sierra Club Members for Environmental Ethics, 132 E St., Ste. 2F, Davis, CA 95616 Bay Area Action, 504 Emerson Street, Palo Alto, CA 94301 Bruin RAG, 308 Westwood Plaza, PO Box 178, Los Angeles, CA 90024 California Ancient Forest Alliance, 1156 Barlock Ave., Los Angeles, CA 90049 California Environmental Project, 2032 Eden Avenue, Glendale, CA 91206 Cal Tech RAG, California Institute of Technology, M.S. 139-74, Pasadena, CA 91125 Citizens for a Better Environment, 88 1st Street, Suite 203, San Francisco, CA 94105 The College of San Mateo RAG, 34 Crippleridge Ct., San Mateo, CA 94402 East Bay Rainforest Action Group, 83 Muth Drive, Orinda, CA 94563 Earth Island Action Group, 300 Broadway, Suite 203, San Francisco, CA 94133 EarthSave, 706 Frederick St., Santa Cruz, CA 95062 Ecology Information Center, 420 Broadway, Santa Monica, CA 90401 Environmental Protection Information Center (EPIC), PO Box 397, Garberville, CA 95440 Forests Forever, PO Box 1488, Redway, CA 95560 Friends of the Earth Club, 16607 Crenshaw Blvd., Torrance, CA 90506 Friends of the Foothills, PO Box 0005, Altadena, CA 91003 Friends of Lomas Barbudal, 691 Colusa Ave., Berkeley, CA 94707 Friends of the River, 909 12th Street, Suite 207, Sacramento, CA 95814 Golden Gate Rag, 1242 2nd Avenue, San Francisco, CA 94122 Humboldt RAIN, Box 4654, Arcata, CA 95521 International Society for the Preservation of Tropical Rainforests, 3931 Camino De La Cumbre, Sherman Oaks, CA 91423 Institute for Sustainable Forestry, PO Box 1580, Redway, CA 95560 Klamath Forest Alliance, PO Box 802, Etna, CA 96027 L.A.R.A.P. (Los Angeles Rainforest Action Project), 1422 N. Sweetzer Ave., #401, Los Angeles, CA 90069-1528 Lifeweb, PO Box 20803, San Jose, CA 95160 Living Jungle Alliance, 14095 Arnold Drive, Glen Ellen, CA 95442 Mendocino Environmental Center, 106 W. Standley Street, Ukiah, CA 95482 Northcoast Environmental Center, 879 9th Street, Arcata, CA 95521 Planetary Survival Alliance, PO Box 4844, San Luis Obispo, CA 93403 Rainforest Action Group Etc. (RAGE), 12617 Rubens, Los Angeles, CA 90066 Rainforest Action Project, PO Box 5219, Salton City, CA 92275 Redwood Coast Watersheds Alliance, PO Box 209, Comptche, CA 95427 Redwood Coast Environmental Law Center, PO Box 32, Mendocino, CA 95460 Rocklin RAG, 3646 Amethyst Drive, Rocklin, CA 95677 Santa Barbara RAG, 327 Loma Vista, #D, Santa Barbara, CA 93101 Silicon Valley RF Action Coalition, 985 McKendrie St., San Jose, CA 95126 Trees Foundation, PO Box 2202, Redway, CA 95560 Turlock Rainforest Action Group, 1700 N. Tully, Apt. F-145, Turlock, CA 95380 UCSC RAG/The Jungle Slugs, UCSC, Kresge #688, Santa Cruz, CA 95064 Volcan Mountain Preserve Foundation, Box 1625, Julian, CA 92036 Yuba Watershed Institute, 17790 Tyler-Foote Road, Nevada City, CA 95959 **COLORADO** Ancient Forest Rescue, PO Box 3204, Durango, CO 81302 Biodiversity Legal Foundation, PO Box 18327, Boulder, CO 80308 Boulder RAG, Campus Box 207, Univ. of Colorado, Boulder, CO 80309 Colorado Environmental Coalition, 777 Grant St., #606, Denver, CO 80203 Colorado State University RAG, Box 603, Lory Student Center, CSU, Ft. Collins, CO 80524 Earth Resource Association, PO Box 66, Manitou Springs, CO 80829 Forest Conservation Council, 863 W. Geddes Ave., Littleton, CO 80120 Global Response, PO Box 7490, Boulder, CO 80306 High Country Foundation, 124 Grand Ave., Paonia, CO 81428 Institute for Resource Management, 1410 Grant Street, Suite C107, Denver, CO 80203 Land & Water Fund of the Rockies, 2260 Baseline Road, Ste. 200, Boulder, CO 80302 Lighthawk (RMtn. Field Office), PO Box 3736, Aspen, CO 81612 Mission Wolf, PO Box 211, Silver Cliff, CO 81249 People for Eldorado Mountain, PO Box 305, Eldorado Springs, CO 80025 Sinapu, 1900 Allison St., Lakewood, CO 80215 Society for Human Ecology, 4512 McMurray Dr., Fort Collins, CO 80525 Ways of the Mountain Center, PO Box 542, Silverton, CO 81433 Western Colorado Congress, PO Box 63, Telluride, CO 81435 Western Eye Press, PO Box 66, Norwood, CO 81423 **CONNECTICUT** Connecticut RAG, Box 3614, Connecticut College, New London, CT 06320 Mattatuck RAG, 29 Windmill Road, Harwinton, CT 06791 **DELAWARE** SEAC—University of Delaware, 301 Student Center, Newark, DE 19716 **DISTRICT OF COLUMBIA** Carrying Capacity Network, 1325 G. Street, NW, Suite 1003, Washington, DC 20005 Friends of Animals, 1623 Connecticut Avenue, NW, Washington, DC 20009 Friends of the Earth, 218 D Street, SE, 2nd Floor, Washington, DC 20003 George Washington University Students Environmental Action, 800 21st Street, NW, Washington, DC 20052 New Forests Project, 731 8th Street, SE, Washington, DC 20003 People for the Ethical Treatment of Animals, PO Box 42516, Washington, DC 20015 Western Ancient Forest Campaign, 1400 16th St. NW, Suite 294, Washington, DC 20036 **FLORIDA** Coastal Plains Institute, 1313 N. Duval St., Tallahassee, FL 32303 Environmental Design, PO Box 6A, Archer, FL 32618 Escambia County Greens, 2343 Wyatt Street, Pensacola, FL 32514-7761 Gulf Specimen Marine Laboratory, PO Box 237, Panacea, FL 32346 Key West RAG, 624 Whitehead Street, Key West, FL 33040 Kissimmee Valley Audubon Society, PO Box 709, Intercession City, FL 33848 T.R.E.E.S., 145 Wisteria Drive, Longwood, FL 32779 **GEORGIA** Friends of the Mountain, PO Box 368, Clayton, GA 30525 Georgia Earth Alliance, PO Box 1025, Riverdale, GA 30274 Rabun County Coalition to Save America's Forests, PO Box 129, Lakemont, GA 30552 The Wilderness Society/Southeast Office, 1447 Peachtree St. NE, Ste. 812, Atlanta, GA 30309 **HAWAII** Big Island RAG, PO Box 341, Big Island, HI 967760 Oahu Rainforest Action Group (ORAG), EWC Box 1363, 1777 East-West Road, Honolulu, HI 96848 Pele Defense Fund, PO Box 404, Volcano, HI 96785 **IDAHO** Ancient Forest Bus Brigade, Rte. 1, Box 14C, Lenore, ID 83541 Committee for Idaho's High Desert, PO Box 2863, Boise, ID 83701 Environmental Resource Center, 411 E. 6th, PO Box 819, Ketchum, ID 83340 Idaho Conservation League, PO Box 2671, Ketchum, ID 83340 Idaho Sportsman's Coalition, PO Box 4264, Boise, ID 83711 Sandpoint Forest Watch, PO Box 1203, Sandpoint, ID 83864 Wolf Recovery Foundation, PO Box 793, Boise, ID 83701 **ILLINOIS** Chicago RAG, Biological Sci.-Hogan Hall, 2-160 Northwestern Univ., Chicago, IL 60208 Justice and Peace Network, PO Box 667, Wheaton, IL 60189 Normal Environmental Action Coalition, 503 N. School Street, Normal, IL 61761 Northwestern RAG, 1927 Orrington Ave., #3106, Evanston, IL 60201-2978 Regional Association of Concerned Environmentalists, Pomona General Store, Pomona, IL 62975 Shawnee Defense Fund, Rte. 1, Box 313, Brookport, IL 62910 University of Chicago RAG, 626 Emerson Street, Rm. 27, Chicago, IL 60201 University of Illinois RAG, 408 E. White, #10, Champaign, IL 61820 Whitmore's Recycle/Reuse, 726 W. 26th St., Chicago, IL 60616 **INDIANA** Bloomington RAG, PO Box 31, Bloomington, IN 47404 Groundwork, Rt. 1, Box 154-A, Ramsey, IN 47166 Heartwood, Rt. 3, Box 402, Paoli, IN 47454 Hoosier Environmental Council, 1002 E. Washington St., #300, Indianapolis, IN 46202 Jacob's Ladder, Frey Road, Evansville, IN 47712 Save the Dunes Council, 444 Barker Road, Michigan City, IN 46360 Trashforce, 4204 Winwood Ct., Floyd's Knob, IN 47119 **IOWA** Tallgrass Prairie Deep Ecology Group, 722 Westwinds Drive, #3, Iowa City, IA 52246 **KANSAS** ecol-o-kids, 3146 Shadow Lane, Topeka, KS 66604 Foresight Institute, 10108 Hemlock Drive, Overland Park, KS 66212 Heartland All Species, 201 Westport Road, Kansas City, KS 64111 KSU Rainforest Action Group, UFM Bldg., 1221 Thurston Ave., Manhattan, KS 66506 **KENTUCKY** Appalachia Science in the Public Interest, PO Box 298, Livingston, KY 40445 Heartwood, 1661 Coldspring Road, Anchorage, KY 40223 Help Alert Western Kentucky, PO Box 1225, Eddyville, KY 42038 Kentucky Resources Council, PO Box 1070, Frankfort, KY 40602 Kentucky Conservation Com., 1206 Paula Drive, Richmond, KY 40475 Louisville Hiking Club, 3315 Terrier Lane, Louisville, KY 40218 University of Kentucky S.A.V.E., Room 106, Student Center, Lexington, KY 40506 **LOUISIANA** Louisiana Environmental Action Network, PO Box 66323, Baton Rouge, LA 70896 RAG of Baton Rouge, 1023 Leycester Dr., Baton Rouge, LA 70808-5742 **MAINE** SEAC/University of Maine/Forest Committee, 6 Charles Place, Orono, ME 04473 SEAC, Memorial Union, University of Maine, Orono, ME 04469 **MARYLAND** Allemong Wilderness Group, 240 Manor Circle, Apt. 5, Takoma Park, MD 20912 Alley Cat Allies, PO Box 397, Mt. Ranier, MD 20712 Anacostia Watershed Society, 9706 52nd Avenue, College Park, MD 20740 Artists Protecting Earth, Maryland Institute of Art, 1300 Mt. Royal Avenue, Baltimore, MD 21217 Common Ground, USA, 2000 Century Plaza, Suite 238, Colulmbia, MD 21044 Continental Divide Trail Society, Box 30002, Bethesda, MD 20814 Ecological Community Outreach Services, PO Box 5438, Takoma Park, MD 20913 First Presbyterian Eco-Justice Committee, 6135 Camelback Lane, Columbia, MD 21045 Fund for Animals, 850 Sligo Ave., #112, Silver Spring, MD 20910 Goddard Conservation Club, 6968 Ducketts Lane, Elkridge, MD 21227 Grassroots Coalition for Environmental & Economic Justice, PO Box 1319, Clarksville, MD 21029 Maryland Advocates for Public Lands, 17936 Golf View Drive, Hagerstown, MD 21740 Mary PIRG, 2060 St. Paul St., Ste. 26, Baltimore, MD 21218 Rainforest Action of Maryland (RAM), 2413 Cool Springs Road, Bel Air, MD 21014 Shomrei Adamah, 706 Erie Ave., Takoma Park, MD 20912 **MASSACHUSETTS** Boston RAG, 649 Watertown Street, Newton, MA 01886 Boston Area RAG, 6 Monadnock Drive, Westford, MA 01886 Earthworks Action, 100 Broadway, Apt. 6, Arlington, MA 02174 Friends of the Boston Harbor, PO Box 9025, Boston, MA 02114 Gaia Institute, PO Box 852, South Lynnfield, MA 01940 Global Action Network, Lincoln Filene Center, Tufts, Medford, MA 02155 Green Earth Movement, WPI, 100 Institute Rd, Box 1336, Worcester, MA 01609 Green Sangha, Harvard Divinity School, 45 Francis Avenue, Cambridge, MA 02138 Manomet Bird Observatory, PO Box 1170, Manomet, MA 02345 National Toxics Campaign, 1168 Commonwealth Avenue, Boston, MA 02134 Neponset River Water Association, 2468A Washington Street, Canton, MA 02021 Northshore RAG, PO Box 730, Rockport, MA 01966 Rainforest Action Group, 25 Wilbur St., Taunton, MA 02780 Restore: The North Woods, PO Box 440, Concord, MA 07142 Thoreau Country Conservation Alliance, 191 Sudbury Rd., Concord, MA 01742 **MICHIGAN** Friends of Northern Rockies, 5301 Updyke Road, Grass Lake, MI 49240 FOCUS, PO Box 133, Ontonagon, MI 49953 North Woods Conservancy, 73 Third Street, Suite 11. Larium, MI 49913 Northwoods Wilderness Recovery, PO Box 107, Houghton, MI 49931 Rainforest Action Movement, School of Natural Resources, 430 E. University, Ann Arbor, MI 48109 Shakedown Street, 670 Leonard NW, Grand Rapids, MI 49504 Timber Watch, 365 Plaza Blvd., Apt. 305, Rochester Hills, MI 48307 Tropical Forest Action Committee, Dept. of Botany-MSU, East Lansing, MI 48824 **MINNESOTA** Friends/Boundary Waters Wild, 1313 Fifth St. SE, Ste. 329, Minneapolis, MN 55414 Minnesota Public Interest Research Group, 2512 Delaware Street SE, Minneapolis, MN 55414 Minnesota RAG, PO Box 580895, Minneapolis, MN 55458-0895 Preserve Our Land, Inc., PO Box 456, Little Falls, MN 56345 **MISSISSIPPI** ECO-MS, Box 31292, Jackson, MS 39286 **MISSOURI** Citizens for a Lead Free Environment, Riverton Rural Branch, Alton, MO 65606 Coalition for the Environment, 6267 Delmar, St. Louis, MO 63130 EarthWave, 7838 Big Bend, St. Louis, MO 63119 Gateway Green Alliance, 4509-A Idaho Ave., St. Louis, MO 63111 Heartland All Species Project, 3517 Virginia, Kansas City, MO 64109 Heartwood of Mid-Missouri, 2510 Brookside Ct., Columbia, MO 65201 Kansas City Rainforest Alliance, 11022 Stark Ave., Kansas City, MO 64134 Natural Streams Campaign, 1005 A South Big Bend, St. Louis, MO 63117 Sierra Club, Osage Group, 1407 Santa Fe Trail, Boonville, MO 65233 St. Louis RF Alliance, 4646 Shenandoah, St. Louis, MO 63110 **MONTANA** Alliance for the Wild Rockies, PO Box 8731, Missoula, MT 59807 American Wildlands, 40 E. Main, Suite 2, Bozeman, MT 59715 AFSEEE Lolo Chapter, 2161 South 10th West, Missoula, MT 59801 Americans/Wilderness Coalition, Box 4784, Missoula, MT 59806 Badger Chapter, Box 8374, Missoula, MT 59807 Beaverhead NF Concerned Citizens, Box 3724, Butte, MT 59701 Cabinet Resource Group, 160 Fox Lane, Trout Creek, MT 59874 Cold Mountain, Cold Rivers, PO Box 7941, Missoula, MT 59807 Deerlodge Forest Defense Fund, PO Box 780, Boulder, MT 59632 Ecology Center, 101 E. Broadway, #602, Missoula, MT 59802 FREE, 502 S. 19th, #2, Bozeman, MT 59715 Friends of the Bitterroot, PO Box 145, Victor, MT 59875 Friends of the Rattlesnake, 717 Cherry Street, Missoula, MT 59802 Friends of the Wild Swan, 127 W. Main, #F, Bozeman, MT 59715 Glacier-Two Medicine Alliance, Box 181, East Glacier, MT 59434 Great Bear Foundation, PO Box 2699, Missoula, MT 59806 Great Burn Study Group, 1434 Jackson, Missoula, MT 59802 Greater Yellowstone Coalition, PO Box 1874, Bozeman, MT 59771 Montana PIRG, 360 Corbin Hall, Missoula, MT 59812 Montana Wilderness Association, PO Box 635, Helena, MT 59624 Native Forest Network, PO Box 6151, Bozeman, MT 59771 Northern Rockies Action Group, 9 Placer, Helena, MT 59601 Predator Project, PO Box 6733, Bozeman, MT 59771 Protect Glacier Canyon Coalition, PO Box 422, Hungry Horse, MT 59919 Protect the Yaak Committee, Box 7436, Missoula, MT 59807 Swan View Coalition, Box 1901, Kalispell, MT 59901 Wild Allan Mountain, PO Box 585, Conner, MT 59827 Wilderness Watch, PO Box 127, Miltown, MT 59851 Wolf Action Group, PO Box 9286, Missoula, MT 59807 **NEBRASKA** Ecology Now, 1612 7th Ave., Kearny, NB 68847 Ecology Now-UNO, Office of Student Activities, 60th and Dodge, Omaha, NB 68182 **NEVADA** American Wildlands, 16575 Callahan Ranch Road, Reno, NV 89511 Nevada Outdoor Recreation Assoc. Inc., PO Box 1245, Carson City, NV 89702 Southern Nevada RAG, 5184 Sun Valley Drive, Las Vegas, NV 89122 **NEW HAMPSHIRE** Act for Earth, 1 Laker Lane, Meredith, NH 03253 The Northern Forest Forum, PO Box 6, Lancaster, NH 03584 WOLF, 81 Middle Street, Lancaster, NH 03584 **NEW JERSEY** Bushwackers Hiking Club, 1512 Bergenline Avenue, Union City, NJ 07087 Clean Ocean Action, PO Box 505, Sandy Hook, NJ 07732 FUTURE, 1302 Sheridan Blvd., Brigantine, NJ 08203 Kearny RAG, 226 Devon St., Kearny, NJ 07032 MAMS Environmental Club, Matawan Avenue, Cliffwood, NJ 07721 Midatlantic Wilderness Defenders, PO Box 506, Bloomfield, NJ 07003 Montclair State College Conservation Club, Montclair State College, Upper Montclair, NJ 07043 Rainforest Relief, PO Box 281, Red Bank, NJ 07701 S.A.V.E., Stockton State College, Ponoma, NJ 08240 S.T.O.P., Toms River H. S. North, Old Freehold Rd., Toms River, NJ 08753 Students for Environmental Awareness, College Center, PO Box 3300, Summerville, NJ 08876 Whippany High School SEEK, 165 Whippany Road, Whippany, NJ 07981 **NEW MEXICO** Carson Forest Watch, PO Box 15, Llano, NM 87543 Carson Watch, Box 9505, Ranchos de Taos, NM 87557 Cibola Forest Watch, 1820 Gold SE, Albuquerque, NM 87106 Forest Guardians, 612 Old Santa Fe Trail, Suite B, Sante Fe, NM 87501 Forest Trust, PO Box 519, Santa Fe, NM 87501 Forest Trust, PO Box 9226, Santa Fe, NM 87504 Friends of the Gila River, PO Box 211, Gila, NM 88038 Friends of the Owls, PO Box 37, Luna, NM 87824 Gila Watch, PO Box 309, Silver City, NM 88062 Greater Gila Biodiversity Project, PO Box 742, Silver City, NM 88062 Greenfeather Ensemble, Route 14, Box 717, Santa Fe, NM 87501 Hawkwatch International, PO Box 35706, Albuquerque, NM 87176 Jemez Action Group, PO Box 40445, Albuquerque, NM 87196 La Comunidad, PO Box 15, Llano, NM 87543 Lighthawk (Main Office), PO Box 8163, Santa Fe, NM, 87504-8163 NM PIRG Fund, PO Box 40173, Albuquerque, NM 87196 NM Wilderness Study Comm., 1391 Santa Rosa Dr., Santa Fe, NM 87501 Public Forestry Foundation, PO Box 701, Sante Fe, NM 87504 Public Lands Action Network, PO Box 712, Placitas, NM 87043 Santa Fe Mountain Center, PO Box 701, Santa Fe, NM 87504 Santa Fe National Forest Watch, Rt. 4, Box 269D, Sante Fe, NM 87501 Santa Fe Rainforest Action Group, 104 La Placita Circle, Sante Fe, NM 87501 Save the Jemez, PO Box 4067, Albuquerque, NM 87196 Upper Pecos Association, Rt. 1, Box 7, Glorieta, NM 87535 Watershed Ecosystems, PO Box 9226, Santa Fe, NM 87504 **NEW YORK** B.A.R.K/RAG (Bing. Animal Rights Koal.), Hinman 09723, PO Box 6009, Binghamton, NY 13902-6009 Brockport Environmental Action Network, Seymour College Union, SUNY, Brockport, NY 14420 Citizens Planning Board, PO Box 1454, Mt. Saini, NY 11766 Cornell Greens, PO Box 82, Will. Straight, Cornell, Ithaca, NY 14853 Delaware-Otsego Audubon Society, PO Box 544, Oneonta, NY 13820 Eco-Action, 44 Butler Place, Apt. 2A, Brooklyn, NY 11238 Environmental Action Club, 304 Norton Avenue, Endwell, NY 13760 Finger Lakes Wild!, PO Box 4542, Ithaca, NY 14850 FLAG, 68 Kewanee Rd., New Rochelle, NY 10804 Herkimer County Environmental Action, PO Box 14, Herkimer, NY 13416 Huntington Audubon Society, PO Box 735, Huntington, NY 11743 Jamestown Community College Earth Awareness Environmental Club, 525 Falconer Street, PO Box 20, Jamestown, NY 14702 Nassau/Suffolk Neighborhood Network, 511 Central Ave., Massapequa, NY 11758 North Fork Environmental Council, PO Box 799, Mattituck, NY 11952 Orange RAG, 25 Howe St., Warwick, NY 10990 Prevention of Cruelty to Animals and Plants, 97-38 42nd Avenue, Corona, NY 11368 R.A.C.E. (RF Action Comm. for our Envir.), 45 St. Mark's Lane, Islip, NY 11751 RAG for Indigenous People, 15 Upland Road, New Rochelle, NY 10804 Rainforest Action Group, SUNY-B, Hinman 9742, Binghamton, NY 13902 Rebels With A Cause, 349 Lakeville Road, Great Neck, NY 11020 Solar Coalition, 230 E. 50th Street, New York, NY 10022 Wetlands Rainforest Action Group (WRAG), 161 Hudson, New York, NY 10013 **NORTH CAROLINA** Appalachian State University, S.A.V.E., PO Box 18065, ASU Boone, NC 28607 C.A.R.E.—A.G., 824 Ideal Way, Charlotte, NC 28203 Carnivore Preservation Trust, PO Box 127, Route 1 Pittsboro, NC 27312 Center for Reflection on the Second Law, 8420 Camellia Drive, Raleigh, NC 27613 Divers Alert Network, PO Box 3823, Duke Medical Center, Durham, NC 27710 Duke RAG, Duke Station, PO Box 10554, Durham, NC 27706 Haw River Assembly, PO Box 187, Bynum, NC 27228 Katuah Journal, PO Box 638, Leicester, NC 28748 Pisgah Rivers/Infiniti Rafting Co., 233 Riverside Drive, Asheville, NC 28801 SEAC/RAG, C.B. #5115, YMCA Building, Rm. 102, University of North Carolina, Chapel Hill, NC 27599-5115 S.E.A.D., Environmental Awareness Fnd.—UNCG, PO Box 3, EUC UNCG, Greensboro, NC 27412-5001 SouthPAW, PO Box 2193, Asheville, NC 28802 Student Environmental Action Coalition, PO Box 1168, Chapel Hill, NC 27514 Triangle Land Conservancy, PO Box 13031, Research Triangle Pa., NC 27709 Western North Carolina Alliance, 70 Woodfin Place, Suite 03, Asheville, NC 28801 **OHIO** American Mother Earth Network, PO Box 223, Athens, OH 47501 Central Ohio RAG, 1519 Aberdeen Ave., Columbus, OH 43211 Cleveland RAG, Dept. of Anthropology, Cleveland State University, Cleveland, OH 44115 College of Wooster RAG, Box C-1927, College of Wooster, Wooster, OH 44691 Friends of the Wetlands, 730 S. Chillicothe Road, Aurora, OH 44202 Green Power, 3906 Little York Road, Dayton, OH 45414 Ohio RAG, 2128 Halcyon Rd., Beachwood, OH 44122 The Rainforest Conservation Group, 109-B W. Winter St., Delaware, OH 43015 Save Our Forests Campaign, 5107 Olentangy River Road, Columbus, OH 43235 Save Our Shawnee, R 5, Box 217, Portsmouth, OH 45662 Waynesville Ecology Club, 5506 Corwin Road, Waynesville, OH 45068 Western Reserve RAG, 7179 Selworthy Lane, Solon, OH 44139 Westerville Social Action, 816 Coss Circle, Westerville, OH 43081 **OKLAHOMA** Eco Law Institute Inc., PO Box 2132, Tahlequah, OK 74465 Native Americans for a Clean Environment, PO Box 1671, Tahlequah, OK 74465 Ouachita Watch League, Route 2, Box 83A, Sulphur, OK 73086 **OREGON** Ancient Forest Hikes, 16 NW Kansas Avenue, Bend, OR 97701 Assoc. of Forest Service Employees for General Support of Environmental Ethics, PO Box 11615, Eugene, OR 97440 Blue Mountain Native Forest Alliance, 2319 Balm Street, Baker City, OR 97814 Blue Mountain Biodiversity Project, HCR-82, Fossil, OR 97830 Blue Mountain Environmental Council, 2319 Balm Street, Baker City, OR 97814 Central Oregon Forest Issues Committee, 1399 NW Saginaw, Bend, OR 97701 Citizens Interested in Bull Run, Inc., PO Box 3426, Gresham, OR 97030 Coast Range Association, PO Box 148, Newport, OR 97365 Concerned Friends of Winema, 3333 Hwy. 422, Chiloquin, OR 97624 Deep Ecology Education Project, 1430 Willamette, Suite 367, Eugene, OR 97401 Earth First! Journal, PO Box 1415 Eugene, OR 97440 Ecoforestry Institute, 2100 Thompson Creek Road, Selma, OR 97538 ECOTRUST, 1200 NW Front Ave., Ste. 470, Portland, OR 97209 Forest Conservation Council, 142 Southwest Woods, Eugene, OR 97401 Friends of Elk River, PO Box 891, Port Orford, OR 97465 Friends of the Coquille River, PO Box 714, Myrtle Point, OR 97458 Headwaters, PO Box 729, Ashland, OR 97520 Hells Canyon Preservation Council, PO Box 908, Joseph, OR 97846 Kalmiopsis Audubon, PO Box 1349, Port Orford, OR 97465 League of Wilderness Defenders, 454 Williamette, Eugene, OR 97401 Marys Peak Alliance, 2020½ SW 45th St., Corvallis, OR 97333 Native Forest Council, PO Box 2171, Eugene, OR 97402 Oregon Natural Deserts Association, 16 NW Kansas, Bend, OR 97701 Oregon Natural Resources Council, Yeon Bldg., Suite 1050, 522 SW 5th Ave., Portland, OR 97204 Pacific Rivers Council, 921 SW Morrison, Suite 531, Portland, OR 97205 Pacific Rivers Council, PO Box 309, Eugene, OR 97440 PEER, PO Box 428, Eugene, OR 97440 Rest the West, PO Box 10065, Portland, OR 97210 Rogue Institute for Ecology and Economy, 1099 Corp Ranch Road, Ashland, OR 97520 Save the West, Inc., 1705 SW Clay Street, Portland, OR 97201 Siskiyou Action Project, PO Box 1310, Cave Junction, OR 97523 Siskiyou Regional Education Project, PO Box 220, Cave Junction, OR 97523 Tenmile Creek Association, PO Box 496, Yachats, OR 97498 The Survival Center, Suite 1, Erb Memorial Union, Eugene, OR 97403 Tropical Forests Forever, PO Box 69583, Portland, OR 97231 Umpqua Audubon, PO Box 658, Roseburg, OR 97479 Western Environmental Law Clinic, University of Oregon Law School, NRC, Eugene, OR 97403 **PENNSYLVANIA** Citizen's Environmental Organization of Bedford County, RD 1, Box 266 A, Buffalo Mills, PA 15534 Delaware Valley RAG, 3900 Ford Road, Apt. 14K, Philadelphia, PA 19131 Earth 2000, 18 Grouse Point Circle, Reading PA 19607 Earthlust, 400 Walnut Street, Swarthmore, PA 19081 Eco-Action RAG, 10 Vairo Blvd., Box 171, State College, PA 16803 Eye Openers, 3210 Chestnut Street, Philadelphia, PA 19104 Kittatinny Raptor Corridor Project, 629 Green St., Allentown, PA 18102 Lafayette College Environmental Awareness and Protection, Easton, PA 18042 Lehigh Valley RAG, Muhlenburg College, Box 1631, Allentown, PA 18104 NEPA RAG, Rural Route #2, Box 153, Hunlock Creek, PA 18621 Palisades ECO Club, Palisades High School, Box 15, Road 2, Kinthersville, PA 18930 Pennsylvania Rainforest Action Committee, 413 Buckthorn St., Harrisburg, PA 17104 Pittsburgh RAG, PO Box 81825, Pittsburgh, PA 15217 School of Living, Road 1, Box 185-A, Cochranville, PA 19330 SEAC of Carnegie Mellon University, PO Box 2012, 1060 Morewood, Pittsburgh, PA 15213 Student Earth Action League, 602 Second Street, California, PA 15419 Student Environmental Team, Road 2, Lot 271, Chesapeake East, Thomasville, PA 17364 Susquehanna University SEAC, Susquehanna University, Susquehanna, PA 17870 Ursinus SEAC, Ursinus College, Collegeville, PA 19426 West Branch Bioregional Project, PO Box 432, Millheim, PA 16854 **RHODE ISLAND** Providence Journal, 75 Fountain Street, Providence, RI 02902 **SOUTH CAROLINA** AFSEEE-Andrew Pickens Chapter, Rte. 1, Box 103, Mountain Rest, SC 29664 Furman University EAG, Box 28764, Furman University, Greenville, SC 29613 The Rainforest Emancipation Effort (TREE), 1027 Oakland Ave., Old Towne Bldg. 3, Rock Hill, SC 29732 South Carolina Coastal Conservation League, PO Box 1765, Charleston, SC 29402 South Carolina Forest Watch, 137 Forrester Circle, Long Creek, SC 29658 **TENNESSEE** Americans for a Clean Environment, Route One, Del Riod, TN 37727 BURNT, 1500 Acklen Ave., Nashville, TN 37212 Center for Global Sustainability, PO Box 1101, Knoxville, TN 37901 Cherokee Forest Coalition, 3200 Haggard Dr., Knoxville, TN 37917 Forest Protection Project, PO Box 1101, Knoxville, TN 37901 Highlander Center/STP School, Rt. 3, Box 370, New Market, TN 37820 RAG of Middle Tennessee, PO Box 50623, Nashville, TN 37205 Shaconage Greens/Center for Global Sustainability, PO Box 1101, Knoxville, TN 37901 South PAW, PO Box 1101, Knoxville, TN 37901 T.A.G.E.R. (Tennesseans, Alabamans and Georgians for Environmental Responsibility), PO Box 764, South Pittsburg, TN 37380 Tennessee Valley Energy Coalition, PO Box 27245, Knoxville, TN 37927 **TEXAS** Austin RAG, 2430 Cromwell Circle, #418, Austin, TX 78741 Central Distance Riders, PO Box 224, Canton, TX 75103 Federal Forest Reform, 4414 Cochran Chapel Rd., Dallas, TX 75209 Forest Reform Network, 5934 Royal Lane, Suite 223, Dallas, TX 75230 The Mexican Wolf Coalition of Texas, PO Box 1526, Spring, TX 77383 Texas Committee on Natural Resources, 5934 Royal Lane, Suite 223, Dallas, TX 75230 Texas Environmental Action Coalition, 1208 B Westridge Circle, Bryan, TX 77801 Texas RAG, 5002 Morningside, Ste. 204, Houston, TX 77005 **UTAH** Friends of Dixie NF, PO Box 1057, Duck Creek, UT 84072 Great Old Broads for Wilderness, PO Box 520307, Salt Lake City, UT 84152 RAG of Utah, 7762 Douglas Dr., Park City, UT 84060 Round River Conservation Studies, PO Box 6159, Salt Lake City, UT 84106 Southern Utah Wilderness Alliance, PO Box 518, 15 South, 300 West, Salt Lake City, UT 84105 Utah Wilderness Association, 177 East 900 South, Salt Lake City, UT 84111 **VERMONT** ALARM/Biodiversity Liberation Front, PO Box 804, Burlington, VT 05402 Arctic to Amazonia Alliance, PO Box 73 Strafford, VT 05072 P3 Magazine, PO Box 52, Montgomery, VT 05470 Preserve Appalachian Wilderness, PO Box 52A, Bondville, VT 05301 Twin State RAG (Underneath Arctic to Amazonia Alliance), PO Box 73, Stratford, VT 05072 Vermont Student Environmental Program, Billings Student Center, U of V, Burlington, VT 05405 **VIRGINIA** Dolphin Rescue Brigade, 12213 Avery Road, Fairfax, VA 22033 Earth Training Systems, 1612 N. Randolph Street, Arlington, VA 22207 Green Coalition, 5218 Dunleigh Drive, Burke, VA 22015 Northern Virginia RAG, 9538 Helenwood Drive, Fairfax Northern Virginia Greens, 4201 Lee Highway, #506, Arlington, VA 22207 Rappahanock RAG, Rt. #1, Box 3010, Washington, VA 22747 Student Environmental Action Coalition, 613 Belmont Avenue, Charlottesville, VA 22903 Tree-Action, PO Box 1306, Herndon, VA 22070 University of Richmond RAG, PO Box 1277, 28 Westhampton Way, Richmond, VA 23173-1277 University of Virginia Greens, 125 4th Street, NW, Charlottesville, VA 22901 Virginians for Wilderness, Route 1, Box 250, Staunton, VA 24401 Voices for Animals, PO Box 1324, Charlottesville, VA 22902 Wakefield School Environmental Club, Rt. 1, Box 292-D, Fauquier County, VA 22746 **WASHINGTON** Ancient Forest Chautauqua, 5031 University Way NE, Seattle, WA 98105 Bellingham RAG, 2330 Park St., Bellingham, WA 98225 Blue Heron Environmental Center, PO Box 155, White Salmon, WA 98672 Federal Land Action Group, 6708 8th NE, Seattle, WA 98115 Friends of the Trees Society, PO Box 1064, Tonasket, WA 98855 Greater Ecosystem Alliance, 1909 I Street, PO Box 2813, Bellingham, WA 98227 Inland Empire Public Lands Council, W. 315 Mission, Spokane, WA 99201 Lighthawk (NW Field Office), 340 15th Avenue East, Ste. 300, Seattle, WA 98112 North Cascades Audubon Society, PO Box 5805, Bellingham, WA 98227 North Central Audubon Society, 212 S. Iowa, East Wenatchee, WA 98802 Okanogan RAG, PO Box 93, Oroville, WA 98844 Pilchuck Audubon Society, 3123 153rd Avenue, SE, Snohomish, WA 98290 Pilchuck Audubon Society, 72007 Lakewood Road, Stanwood, WA 98292 Rainier Audubon Society, 1701 Utah Court, Mitton, WA 98354 Seattle RAG, PO Box 95967, Seattle, WA 98145 Skagit Audubon Society, Box 21, La Conner, WA 98257 Tahoma Audubon Society, 34607 S.R. 706, Ashford, WA 98304 Tonasket Forestwatch, 106 W. Lost Lake Rd., Tonasket, WA 98855 Yakima Valley Audubon Society, 703 Beacon, Yakima, WA 98901 **WEST VIRGINIA** American Chestnut Foundation, PO Box 6057, WV University, Morgantown, WV 26506 Earth First! Biodiversity Project, 2365 Willard Road, Parkersburg, WV 26101 National Sacrifice Zone, PO Box 65, Myra, WV 25544 Stump Creek Radio, PO Box 127, Cass, WV 24927 West Virginia Greens, PO Box 144, Pullman, WV 26421 **WISCONSIN** Crusade 2000, PO Box 26, Shebaygan Falls, WI 53085 Legislative Action Network, 121 N. Jefferson St., Whitewater, WI 53190 Oshkosh SEAC, Reeve Union, 748 Algoma Blvd., Oshkosh, WI 54901 Save Our Vanishing Kingdom, 2702 Fryklund Drive, #2, Menomonie, WI 54751 Society for Ecological Restoration, 1207 Seminole Highway, Madison, WI 53711 SWAN, c/o Biology Dept., Univ. of Wisconsin, Oshkosh, WI 54901 Wisconsin Greens, PO Box 341, West Bend, WI 53095 **WYOMING** Friends of the Bow, PO Box 6032, Laramie, WY 82070 Jackson Hole Alliance for Responsible Planning, PO Box 2728, Jackson, WY 83001 Medicine Wheel Alliance, PO Box 542, Powell, WY 82453 National Outdoor Leadership School, PO Box AA, Lander, WY 82520

CANADA

ALBERTA Alberta Forest Caucus, 9211-72 St., Edmonton, AB T6B 1Y6 Alberta Wilderness Association, Box 6398, Stn. D, Calgary, AB T2P 2E1 Banff Recycling Society, Box 2056, Banff, AB T0L 0C0 Bow Valley Naturalists, Box 1693, Banff, AB T0L 0C0 Calgary Eco Centre, 1019 4th Ave. SW, Calgary, AB T2P 0K8 Calgary Rainforest Action Group, 204 15th Ave. NW, Calgary, AB T2N 2A7 Calgary Student Environment Society, 233 10th Street NW, Calgary, AB T2N 1V5 Canadian Parks and Wilderness Society, Box 608, Sub PO 91, Calgary, AB T2N 1N4 Canadian Parks and Wilderness Society, Alberta Chapter, 7403 105A Street, Edmonton, AB T6E 4V2 Canadians for Responsible Northern Development, 11911 University Ave, Edmonton, AB T6G 1Z6 Castle Crown Wilderness Coalition, PO Box 2621, Pincher Creek, AB T0K 1W0 Edmonton Friends of the North, Environmental Society, 451932A Ave., Edmonton, AB T6L 4K7 Fort Assiniboine Environmental Action Association, Fort Assiniboine, AB T0G 1A0 Friends of the Athabasca Environmental Association, Box 1351, Athabasca, AB T0G 0B0 Friends of the North, Rm. 212, 8631 109 St., Edmonton, AB T6G 1E8 Friends of the Oldman River, 455 12th St. NW, Calgary, AB T2N 1Y9 Friends of the Peace, 9606 86th Ave., Peace River, AB T8S 1G4 Friends of the Slave, Box 269, High Prairie, AB T0G 1E0 Friends of the South Country, Box 2, Rocky Mountain House, AB T0M 1T0 Green Party of Canada, Rocky Mountain Region, 2004 10th Ave. SW, Calgary, AB T3C 0J8 Greenpeace—Alberta, 10920 88th Ave., Edmonton, AB T6G 0Z1 Hinton Environmental Association, Box 6120, Hinton AB T7V 1X5 Lubicon Lake Indian Nation, 3536 106th St., Edmonton, AB T6J 1A4 Mother Earth Healing Society, Suite 211, 8631 109th St., Edmonton, AB T6G 1E8 North Country Community Association, Box 269, High Prairie, AB T0G 1E0 Northern Light, Suite 210, 924 17th Ave. SW, Calgary, AB T2T 0A2 Peace River Environmental Society, Box 2333, Peace River, AB T0H 2X0 Rainforest Action Group of Edmonton, 51222 Range Road 224 Sherwood Park, AB T8C 1H3 Social Justice Commission, 10765 98th St., Edmonton, AB T5H 2P2 South Peace Environmental Association, Box 565, Grande Prairie, AB T8V 3A7 World Wildlife Fund—Canada, 855 General Services Bldg. U, Edmonton, AB T6G 2H1 **BRITISH COLUMBIA** Aboriginal Council of B.C., 204, 990 Homer St., Vancouver, BC V6B 2W7 Alberni Environmental Coalition, Box 1087, Port Alberni, BC V9Y 7L9 All About Us/Nous Autres, Box 1120, Ladysmith, BC V0R 2E0 Alouette Field Naturalist, 1239 Gray St., Maple Ridge, BC V2Z 5T9 Anawim Community Centre For Justice & Peace, 3821 Lister St., Burnaby, BC V5G 2B9 Arrow Lakes Environmental Alliance, Box 574, Nakusp, BC V0G 1R0 Arrowsmith Ecology Association, Box 179, Errington, BC V0R 1T0 AWARE, Box 3093, Courtenay, BC V9N 5N3 British Columbia Forest Caucus, RR 1, Site 10, Chase, BC V0E 1M0 British Columbia Watershed Protection Alliance, Box 9, Slocan Park, BC V0G 2E0 British Columbia Public Interest Research Group, TC 304 SFU, BurnabyBC V7G 1T8 Blewett Watershed Committee, RR 2, Blewett Road, Nelson, BC V1L 5P5 Blueberry Creek Irrigation District, 202 West 102nd St., Castlegar, BC V1N 3E2 Boundary Conservor Society, Box 2605, Grand Forks, BC V0H 1H0 Box Lake Watershed Alliannce, RR 1, S12-C16, Nakusp, BC V0G 1R0 Canada's Future Forest Alliance, Box 224, New Denver, BC V0G 1S0 Canadian Earthcare Society, Box 1810, Kelowna, BC V1Y 8P2 Canadian Parks And Wilderness Society—Victoria, Box 6007, Victoria, BC V8P 5LA Cariboo Environmental Committee, Box 2066, 100 Mile House, BC V0K2E0 Cariboo Horse Loggers Association, Box 4321, Quesnel, BC V2J 3J3 Cariboo Residents Against Pesticides and Pollution, Box 1, Likely, BC V0L 1N0 Cariboo Tribal Council, 303-383 Oliver Street, Williams Lake, BC V2G 2V4 Carmanah Forestry Society, Box 5283, Victoria, BC V8R 6N4 Carrier-Sekani Tribal Council, 1460 6th Ave., Prince George, BC V2L 3N2 Cheslatta Band, Box 909, Burns Lake, BC V0J 1E0 Chetwynd & Area Recycling & Environmental Society, Box 2023, Chetwynd, BC V0C 1J0 Chetwynd Environmental Society, Box 2049, Chetwynd, BC V0C 1J0 Chilcotin Information Network, Box 3419, Anahim Lake, BC V0L 1C0 Christina Lake Watershed Alliance, Box 574, Christina Lake, BC V0H 1E0 Citizens Responding Against Awful Policies, Box 5, Riondel, BC V0B 2B0 Coalition for Pulpwood Accountability, Box 368, New Denver, BC V0G 1S0 Committee For A Clean Kettle Valley, Box 94, Rock Creek, BC V0H 1Y0 Concerned Citizens of Deadman's Creek, Box 219, Savona, BC V0K 2J0 Concerned Residents of Johnson's Landing, Box 23, Johnson's Landing, BC V0G 1M0 Cortes Islands Forest Committee, Box 177, Manson's Island, BC V0P 1K0 Council for International Right and Care for Life on Earth (CIRCLE), Box 394, Tofino, BC V0R 2Z0 Council of the Haida Nation, Box 589, Masset, Haida Gwaii, BC V0T 1M0 Dawson Creek Recycling Association, 202-10504 10th Street, Dawson Creek, BC The Driftwood Foundation, RR 2, S57-C19, Smithers, BC V0J 2N0 Earth Embassy, 362 E. 6th Ave., Vancouver, BC V5T 1K3 Earthcare Society, Box

1810, Kelowna, BC V1Y 8P2 Earthlife Canada, Box 592, Queen Charlotte City, BC, V0T 1S0 East Cariboo Environmental Group, General Delivery, Big Lake Ranch, BC V0L 1G0 East Kootenay Environmental Society, Elkford Branch, Box 340, Elkford, BC V0B 1H0 East Kootenay Environmental Society, Golden Branch, Box 1946, Golden, BC V0A 1H0 East Kootenay Environmental Society, Invermere Branch, Box 2741, Invermere, BC V0A 1K0 East Kootenay Environmental Society, Sparwood Branch, RR1, Sparwood, BC V0B 2G0 East Shore Environmental Alliance, Box 40, Kootenay Bay, BC V0B 1X0 East Shore Forest Council, Box 20, Crawford Bay, BC V0B 1E0 Elk Valley Conservation Society, Box 208, Fernie, BC V08 1M0 Elliot, Anderson Watershed Ctte., RR 1, Winlaw, BC V0G 2J0 Environmental Savings Plan, Box 122, Wells, BC V0K 2R0 Environmental Youth Alliance, 102 West 40th Ave., Vancouver, BC, V5Y 2R2 First Nations, Island Tribal Council, Box 62, Mill Bay, BC V0R 2P0 Foothills Woodlot Association, Box 1401, Chetwynd, BC V0C 1J0 Forest Planning Canada, Box 6234, Stn. C, Victoria, BC V8P 5L5 Forest Protection Allies, Box 4321, Quesnel, BC V2J 3J3 Friends of Clayoquot Sound, Box 489, Tofino, BC V0R 2Z0 Friends of Strathcona Park, Box 3404, Courtenay, BC V9N 5N5 Friends of the Tsitika, 479, 4th Street, Courtney, BC V9N 1G9 Friends of Wells Grey Province Park, 6009 Dallas Dr., Kamloops, BC V2C 5Z9 Fructova Environmental Resource Centre, Radon Study, Box 1706, Grand Forks, BC V0H 1H0 Gitksan Wet'Suwet'En Tribal Association, Box 229, Hazelton, BC V0J 1Y0 Grand Forks Coalition for Alternatives to Pesticides, Box 2073, Grand Forks, BC V0H 1H0 Grand Forks Watershed Coalition, Box 1706, Grand Forks, BC V0H 1H0 Greater Victoria Ecological Network, 59 Moss Street, Victoria, BC V8S 5K2 Green Islands, Box 254, Ganges, BC V0S 1E0 Greenpeace, 1726 Commercial Drive, Vancouver, BC V5N 4A3 Guiding Hands Rec. Soc., Box 23, Grey Creek, BC V0B 1S0 Harrop/Proctor Community Watershed Protection Committee, Sunshine Bay, Nelson, BC V1L 5P6 Heritage Forests Society, Box 34293, Vancouver, BC V6J 4N8 Hutchison Creek Wilderness Group, 3417 5th Avenue, Castlegar, BC V1N 2V8 Institute For New Economics, Box 2687, Vancouver, BC V6R 1J5 Islands Protection Society, Box 558, Masset, BC V0T 1M0 Kianuko Drainage Coalition, Box 2756, Creston, BC V0B 1G0 Kitamaat Village Council, Haisla, PO Box 1101, Kitamaat Village, BC V0T 2B0 Kootenay Citizens for Alternatives to Pesticides, Box 1234, Kaslo, BC V0G, 1M0 Kootenay Planned Land Use Society, Box 902, Nelson, BC V1L 6A5 Kootenay Society for a Sustainable Future, 911 Carbonate Street, Nelson, BC V1L 4R3 Kyoquot Economic Environmental Protection Society, Kyoquot, BC V0P 1J0 Ladysmith Citizens Association, Box 1594, Ladysmith, BC V0R 2E0 Lake District Friends of the Environment, RR2, Burns Lake, BC V0J 1E0 Lochart Creek Heritage Committee, Box 20, Crawford, BC V0B 1E0 Mowachaht Band Council, Box 459, Gold River, BC V0P 1G0 NBC Steelhead Guides Association, Box 3873, Smithers, BC V0J 2N0 Nak'azdli Band Council, Box 1329, Fort St. James, BC V2L 4T3 Nechako Environmental Coalition, 1780 Hart Hwy, Prince George, BC V2K 3B3 Nelson & Area Watershed Committee, 707 2nd Street, Nelson, BC V1L 2M1 North Peace Nature Club, Box 6724, Fort St. John, BC V1J 4J2 Northern Environmental Action Team, Box 6355, Fort St. John, BC V1J 4H6 PPWC Local 26, Box 3675, Castlegar, BC V1N 3W4 Pro Terra, Box 9, Argenta, BC V0G 1B0 Procter/Harrop Watershed Protection Group, Box 8, Procter, BC V0G 1V0 Project North, 307 Vancouver St., Victoria, BC V8V 3T2 Project North BC, 2176 27th Ave., Vancouver, BC V2N 2W9 Quadra Island Conservancy, Box 202, Heriot Bay, BC V0P 2H0 Rainforest Action Society, 2150 Maple Street, Vancouver, BC V6J 3T3 Red Mountain Residents Association, Box 208, New Denver, BC V0G 1S0 Revelstoke Environmental Action, Box 1764, Revelstoke, BC V0E 2S0 Save the Cedar League, General Delivery, Crescent Spur, BC V0J 3E0 Shuswap Environmental Action Society, Box 1021, Salmon Arm, BC V1E 4P2 Shuswap Nation Tribal Council—Forestry, 345 Yellowhead Hwy., Kamloops, BC V2H 1H1 Sierra Club—Salt Spring, Box 5, Salt Spring Island, BC V0S 1E0 Sierra Club of Western Canada, Box 10, Victoria, BC V8X 4M6 Sierra Club of Western Canada—Cowichan Group, Box 222, Malahat, BC V0R 2L0 Sierra Club of Western Canada—Lower Mainland Group, 1367 West Broadway, Vancouver, BC V6H 4A9 Sierra Club—Victoria Group, 106, 560 Johnson St., Victoria, BC V8W 3C6 Sierra Legal Defense Fund, Suite 601, 207 West Hastings, Vancouver, BC V6B 1H6 Slocan Lake Recycling Association, Box 465, New Denver, BC V0G 1S0 Slocan Valley Watershed Alliance, Box 139 Winlaw, BC V0G 2J0 South Slocan Commission of Management, Box 47, Slocan, BC V0G 2C0 Southern Chilcotin Mountains Wilderness Society, General Delivery, Gold Bridge, BC V0K 1P0 Sproule Creek Watershed Committee, 6115 Sproule Creek Road, Nelson, BC V1L 5P5 Stellaquo Band, Box 760, Fraser Lake, BC V0J 1S0 Surge Narrows Citizens for Sensible Logging Practices, General Delivery, Surge Narrows, BC V0P 1W0 Surge Narrows Community Association, Box 52, Surge Narrows, BC V0P 1W0 Tatshenshini Wild, 843-810 West Broadway, Vancouver, BC V5Z 4C9 Thompson Watershed Coalition, Box 1053, Kamloops, BC V2C 6H2 Treaty 8 Tribal Association, 207-10139 100th Street, Fort St. John, BC V1J 3Y6 Union of British Columbian Indian Chiefs, 200-73 Water Street, Vancouver, BC V6B 1A1 Valhalla Society, Box 224, New Denver, BC V0G 1S0 West Arm Watershed Alliance, Box 787, Nelson, BC V1L 5S9 West Coast Environmental Law Association, 1001-207 West Hastings St., Vancouver, BC V6B 1H7 Weestern Canada Wilderness Committee, 20 Water Street, Vancouver, BC V6B 1A4 Western Canada Wilderness Committee—Victoria Branch, 101-1002 Wharf Street, Victoria, BC V8W 1T4 Western Canada Wilderness Committee, West Kootenay Branch, Box 186, Nelson, BC V1L 5P9 **MANITOBA** Brandon Natural History Society, Box 57, Brandon, Man. R7A 5Y3 Canadian Parks and Wilderness Association, 25 St. Pierre Street, Winnipeg, Man. R3V 1J5 Concerned Citizens of Manitoba, 763 Dowker Ave., Winnipeg, Man. R3T 1R5 Crossroads Resource Group, Box 1061, Winnipeg, Man. R3C 2X4 Defenders of Nopoming, Box 644, Winnipeg, Man. R3C 2K3 Greenpeace, 51 Osborne Street South, Winnipeg, Man. R3L 1Y2 Manitoba Environmentalists Inc., 49 Brisbane Ave., Winnipeg, Man. R3T 0T1 Manitoba Naturalists Society, 302-128 James Avenue, Winnipeg, Man. R3B 0N8 Recycling Council of Man., 1329 Niakwa Rd. E, Winnipeg, Man. R2J 3J4 Sierra Club of Manitoba, Box 631, Brandon, Man. R7A 5Z7 TREE, 25 St. Pierre, Winnipeg, Man. R3V 1T5 TREE/Friends of Nopoming, Box 3125, Winnipeg, Man. R3C 4E6 University of Manitoba Students Acting for the Environment, University of Manitoba, Winnipeg, Man., Westman Wilderness Club, Box 1413, Brandon, Man. R7A 6N2 **NEW BRUNSWICK** Atlantic Youth Coalition for Environment and Development, 14 Hamilton Cres., Riverview, NB E1B 3C3 Charlotte County Recyclers, RR 2, St. Andrews, NB E0G 2X0 Conservation Council of New Brunswick, 180 St. John St., Fredericton, NB E3B 4A9 Contact Women's Centre, RR 4, Sussex, NB E0E 1P0 EcoAction, RR 3, Port Elgin, NB E0A 2K0 Endangered Spaces Campaign, RR 9, Penniac, NB E3B 4X9 Fundy Environmental Action Group, RR 1, Albert, NB E0A 1A0 GOS Environmental Society, PO Box 208, Pokemouche, NB E0B 2J0 Local Youth for the Environment, 56 West Lane, Moncton, NB E1C 6T7 Miramachi Envirnomental Society, Box 23, Nelson—Miramachi, NB E1V 3M5 Quispamsis Beautification and Environment Ctte., 1602 Rothesay Road, Saint John, NB E2H 2J1 Student Environmental Society, 172 Eastwood St., Hanwell Cres., Fredericton, NB E3B 6M7 Students Aware of the World, RR 1, Fredericton, NB E3B 4X2 Washademoak Environmentalists, Cambridge Narrows, NB E0E 1B0 **NEWFOUNDLAND**Mr. Jamie Cillingham, Box 25, Seal Cove, Nfld. A0K 5E0 Action Environment, Box 2549, St. John's, Nfld. A1C 6K1 Conne River Indian Band Council, Conne River Reserve, Bay D'Espoir, Nfld. A0H 1JO Extension Community Development, Cooperative Society, Box 5054, St. John's, Nfld. A1C 5V3 Foxeye Environmental Coalition, 6 Garden Drive, Stephenville, Nfld., A2N 1K2Friends and Lobbyists of Waterford River, 350 Topsail Road, St. John's, Nfld. A1C 5M5 Green Party of Newfoundland and Labrador, 122 University Ave., St. John's, Nfld. A1B 1Z5 Humber Environmental Society, 45 Brookfield Ave., Corner Brook, Nfld. A2H 2R4 Humber Environment Action Group, Box 70, Cornerbrook, Nfld. A2H 2L1 Innu Nation, Box 119, Sheshatshiu, Labrador, Nfld., A0P 1M0 Manuels River Natural History Society, Box 1156, Manuels, Nfld. A1W 1NS Newfoundland and Labrador Wildlife Federation, Box 13399, Stn. A, St. John's, Nfld., A1E 4S1 Newfoundland Wilderness Society, 38 Tobin Cres., St. John's, Nfld. A1A 2J3 Newfoundland and Labrador Environment Network, Box 944, Cornerbrook, Nfld. A2H 6J2 Newfoundland and Labrador Rural Dev't Council, Box 306, Gander, Nfld. A1V 1W7 Newfoundland Canoeing Association, 32 Ennis Ave., St. John's, Nfld. A1A 1Y8 Pippy Park Conservation Society, 75 Fox Ave., St. John's, Nfld. A1B 2J1 Protected Areas Association of Newfoundland and Labrador, Box 1027, St. John's, Nfld. A1C 5M5 Quidi Vidi/Rennies Riv. Dev., Box 7332, St. John's, Nfld. A1E 3Y5 RC Social Action Commission, Box 986, St. John's, Nfld. A1C 5M3 Salmon Preservation Association, Box 924, Corner Brook, Nfld. A2H 6J2 Save Our Forest Group, Box 299, Jamestown, Nfld. A0C 1V0 Tuckamore Wilderness Club, Box 1, Site 12, Corner Brook, Nfld, A2H 6B9 **NORTHWEST TERRITORIES** Dene Nation, Box 2338, Yellowknife, NWT X1A 2P7 Ecology North, Box 2888, Yellowknife, NWT X1A 2R2 Social Justice Ministry, Diocese of Mackenzie, Box 8900, Yellowknife, NWT X1A 2R3 **NOVA SCOTIA** Ecology Action Centre, 5661 Victoria Road, Halifax, NS B3H 1M9 Forest Caucus Nova Scotia, RR1, Baddeck, NS B0L 1B0 Friends of Nature, Box 281, Chester, NS B0K 1J0 Green Web, RR 3, Saltsprings, Pictou County, NS B0K 1P0 Margaree Environmental Protection Association, Box 617, Margaree Forks, NS B0E 2A0 Nova Scotia Coalition for Alternatives to Pesticides, Box 643, Baddeck, NS B0L 1B0 Nova Scotia Coalition for Alternatives to Pesticides, RR #1, Baddeck, NS B0E 1B0 Tusket River Environmental Protection Association, Box 103, Tusket, NS B0W 3M0 **ONTARIO** Aboriginal Rights Coalition, 151 Laurier East, Ottawa, Ont. K1N 6N8 Algonquins du lac Barriere, 408 Queen Street, Ottawa, Ont. K1N 5A7 Botany Conservation Group, Botany Dept., U of T, Toronto, Ont. M5S 5A7 Brazil North, 256 Brown Street, Sault Ste. Marie, Ont. P6A 1N9 Canadian Forest Caucus, 121 Banning Street, Thunder Bay, Ont., P7B 3S1 Canadian Parks & Wilderness Society Forest Guardians, Suite 1150, 160 Bloor Street E, Toronto, Ont. M4W 1B9 Conservation International Canada, 174 Spadina Ave., Ste. 508, Ont. M5T 2C2 Earthroots, 401 Richmond St. W, Suite 251, Toronto, Ont. M5V 3A8 Environment North, 119 N. Cumberland St., Thunder Bay, Ont., P7A 4M3 Environment Probe, 225 Brunswick Avenue, Toronto, Ont. M5S 2M6 Federation Canadienne de la Faune, 1673 Carling, Ottawa, Ont. K2A 3Z1 Federation of Ontario Naturalists, Environmental Director, 355 Lesmill Rd., Don Mills, Ont. M3B 2W8 Forest Action Committee for Tomorrow, Goulais River, Ont. P0S 1E0 Forests for Tomorrow, c/o CELA, Suite 401, 517 College St, Toronto, Ont. M6G 4A2 Friends of the Earth, 53 Queen Street, Ottawa, Ont. K1P 5C5 Friends of the Forest, Box 2093, Thunder Bay, Ont. P7B 5E7 Friends of the Rainforest, Box 4612, Ottawa, Ont. K1S 5H8 Future Forests, Box 1054, London, Ont. N6A 5K2 Grassroots-Woodstock, RR 2, Tavistock, Ont. N0B 2R0 Greenfyre, Box 236, Ottawa, Ont. K1N 8V2 Greenpeace, 578 Bloor Street, Toronto, Ont. M6G 1K1 Guideposts For A Sustainable Future, Box 374, Merrickville, Ont. K0G 1N0 Native Trappers Association, Box 793, Red Lake, Ont. P0V 2M0 Northwatch, Box 36, Haileybury, Ont. P0J 1K0 Ontario Forest Caucus, 121 Banning Street, Thunder Bay, Ont., R3T 1R5 Ontario Metis & Aboriginal Association, 156 Saskville Rd., Sault Ste. Marie, Ont. P6B 2E3 OPIRG—Provincial, Rm. 201, 455 Spadina Ave., Toronto, Ont., M5S 2G8 Peace and Environment Resource Centre, Box 4075, Ottawa, Ont. K1S 5B1 Probe International, 6th Fl.—100 College St., Toronto, Ont., M5R 2S1 Probe Post, 12 Madison Ave., Toronto, Ont. M5R 2S1 Sierra Club of Canada, Suite 421, 1 Nicholas St., Ottawa, Ont. K1N 7B7 Sierra Club of Eastern Canada, 2316 Queen Street East, Toronto, Ont. M4E 1G8 Student Action for a Viable Earth, #3, 103 4th St., Ottawa, Ont. K1S 2L1 Taskforce on the Churches and Corporate Responsibility, 129 St. Clair Ave. W, Toronto, Ont. M4Y 1P4 Temagami Tall Pines Project, 902-135 Isabella Street, Toronto, Ont. M4Y1P4 Temagami Wilderness Society, Suite 307, 19 Mercer Street, Toronto, Ont, M5V 1H2 Temiskaming Environmental Action Committee, General Delivery, New Liskeard, Ont. P0J 1P0 Thames Region Eco Association, 14 Regina St., London, Ont. N5Y 3B7 Union of Ontario Indians (Health & Environment), 27 Queen Street East, Toronto, Ont. M5C 1R5 Wilderness Committee OttawaBox 175, Ottawa, Ont. K1N 8V2 Wildlands League, 902-135 Isabella Street, Toronto, Ont. M4Y 1P4 World Wildlife Fund Canada, Ste. 504, 90 Eglinton Avenue East, Toronto, Ont. M4P 2Z7 **PRINCE EDWARD ISLAND** Eastern Woodlands Association, Cardigan, PEI C0A 1G0 Environmental Coalition of PEI, RR #2, Cardigan, PEI C0A 1G0 Environmental Coalition of PEI, 126 Richmond, Charlottetown, PEI C1A 1H9 Island Nature Trust, Box 265, Charlottetown, PEI, C1A 7K4 **PROVINCE OF QUEBEC** Algonquins of Barriere Lake, Rapid Lake Indian Reserve, PQ J0W 2C0 Amies de la Terre, Succ. Place d'Armes, CP 804, Montreal, PQ H2Y 3J2 APEHL, 455 rue Coursol, Mont-Laurier, PQ J9L 1A6 AQLPA, CP658, Joliette, PQ J6E 7N3 Centre local d'ecologie des Basses-Laurentides (CLE), 190 rue St-Eustache, St-Eustache, PQ J7R 2L7 Club ornithologique de la Mauricie, Secteur la Tuque, CP 144, La Tuque, PQ G9X 3P1 Comité de l'Environment de Chicoutimi, CP 816, Chicoutimi, PQ G7H 5E8 Comité de recherche et intervention environmentale Grande Portage, 58 Ch. Bellevue, St-Louis du Haha, PQ G0L 3S5 Comité pour la protection de la sante et de l'environment de Gaspe, CP 9, Douglastown, PQ G0C 1M0 Conseil Atikamekw, CP 848, La Tuque, PQ G9X 1K9 Conseil Atikamekw-Montagnais, 390 Charest est, Quebec, PQ G1K 3H4 Conseil de bande de Sept-Iles (SADFAM), 670 rue Giasson, Sept-Iles, PQ G4R 1M4 Conseil regional en environnement, CP 658, Joliette, PQ J6E 7N3 Cooperative d'information et de recherche en environnement du Quebec, 7214 Saint-Denis, Montreal, PQ H2R 2S2 Corporation amelioration protection de l'environnement de Sept-Iles, CP 340, Sept-Iles, PQ G4R 4K6 CPAPE, CP 937, Amos, PQ J9T 3X5 CREDO, 207 Notre-Dame, Hull, PQ J8X 3T5 CREEQ, 263 Arthur Buies Ouest, Rimouski, PQ G5L 5C5 CREEQ et Environnement Vert Plus, 394 ch. Petite Riviere du Lo, Pointe-a-la-Croix, PQ G0C 1L0 Ecolo-Vallée, CP 3178, Amzui, PQ G0J 1B0 Environnement Vert-Plus, CP 1427, Maria, PQ G0C 1Y0 Greenpeace, 1444 Notre-Dame Ouest, Montreal, PQ H3J 1N5 Journal Sans Reserve, CP 635, Succ. C, Montreal, PQ H2L 4L5 Le Reve, CP 605, Val d'or, PQ J9P 4P6 Mouvement Vert Haut St-Mauricie, CP 546, La Turque, PQ G9X 3P4 Mouvement Vert Mauricie, CP 5, St-Matthieu du Parc, PQ G0X 1N0 Quebec Forest Caucus, CP 605, Val d'Or, PQ J9P 4P6 Régroupement pour un Quebec vert, CP 10066, Ste-Foy, PQ G1N 4C6 SAIDSB, 6623 Casgrain, Montreal, PQ H2S 2Z4 Societe d'analyse et d'intervention pour le dev des sc biologiq, 4216 St- Andre, Montreal, PQ H2J 2Z2 Uni-Vert-Matane, CP 631, Matane, PQ G4W 3T6 Urgence rurale, 284 rue Potvin, Rimouski, PQ G5L 7P5 **SASKATCHEWAN** Big River Citizens for Energy Alternatives, Box 536, Debden, Sask. S0J 0S0 Briar Patch Magazine, 2138 McIntyre, Regina, Sask. S4P 2R7 Canadian Parks and Wilderness Society Prairie Chapter, Box 914, Saskatoon, Sask. S7K 3M4 CUSO, 813 Broadway Ave., Saskatoon, Sask. S7N 1B5 CUSO Environmental Working Group, 1602 13th Ave., Regina, Sask. S4P 0L6 Gaia Group, 2256 Rae Street, Regina, Sask. S4T 2E9 Humbolt Wildlife Federation, Box 503, Humboldt, Sask. S0K 2A0 One Sky, 136 Ave. F South, Saskatoon, Sask. S7M 1S8 Protectors of Mother Earth, 824 Broadway Avenue, Saskatoon, Sask. S7N 1B6 Saskatchewan Forest Conservation Network, c/o Box 1372, Saskatoon, Sask. S7K 3N9 Saskatchewan Forest Conservation Network, Big River, Sask. S7K 3N9 Sask. Nat. Historical Society, 1027 King Cres., Saskatoon, Sask. S7K 0N9 Saskatchewan Action Foundation for the Environment, Box 70, Radville, Sask. S0C 2G0 Saskatoon Indigenous Coalition, 824 Broadway Ave., Saskatoon, Sask. S7N 1B6 Saskatoon Natural Historical Society, Box 448, Saskatoon, Sask. S7N 0W0 Treeplanters Association of Sask., Box 751, Big River, Sask. S0J 0E0 Village of Green Lake, Green Lake, Sask. S0M 1B0 **YUKON** Yukon Conservation Society, Box 4163, Whitehorse, Yukon Y1A 3S9

FOREST INDUSTRIES

ALABAMA Southern Pressure Treaters Association, PO Box 2389, Gulf Shores, AL 36547 **CALIFORNIA** California Forestry Association, 1311 I Street, Ste. 100, Sacramento, CA 95814 California Redwood Association, 405 Enfrente Dr., Ste. 200, Novato, CA 94949 Redwood Region Logging Conference, PO Box 174, Garberville, CA 95440 **FLORIDA** Southern Pine Inspection Bureau, 4709 Scenic Hwy., Pensacola, FL 32504 **GEORGIA** American Wood Preservers Bureau, 4 E. Washington St., Newnan, GA 30263 Forest Farmers Association, PO Box 95385, Atlanta, GA 30347 **IDAHO** Intermountain Forest Industry Association, 703 Lakeside Ave., Coeur d'Alene, ID 83814 **ILLINOIS** North American Wholesale Lumber Association, 3601 Algonquin Road, Ste. 400, Rolling Meadows, IL 60008 **INDIANA** Fine Hardwood Veneer Association / American Walnut Manufacturers Association, 5603 W. Raymond St., Ste. O, Indianapolis, IN 46241 **LOUISIANA** Southern Forest Products Association, PO Box 52468, New Orleans, LA 70152 **MAINE** National Council of Forestry Association Executives, 146 State St., Augusta, ME 04332 Northeastern Lumber Manufacturers Association, 272 Tuttle Road, Box 87A, Cumberland Center, ME 04021 **MARYLAND** American Lumber Standards Committee, PO Box 210, Germantown, MD 20875 Association of Consulting Foresters, 5410 Grosvenor Lane, Suite 205, Bethesda, MD 20814-2194 National Particleboard Association, 18928 Premiere Court, Gaithersburg, MD 20879 Society of American Foresters, 5400 Grosvenor Lane, Bethesda, MD 20814 **MASSACHUSETTS** Wood Products Manufacturers Association, 52 Racette Avenue, Gardner, MA 01440 **MINNESOTA** Northwestern Lumber Association, 1405 N. Lilac Dr., Ste. 130, Golden Valley, MN 55422 Western Red Cedar Association, PO Box 12786, New Brighton, MN 55112 **NEW YORK** American Paper Institute, 260 Madison Ave., New York, NY 10016 National Council of the Paper Industry for Air and Stream Improvement, 260 Madison Ave., New York, NY 10016 Northeastern Loggers Association, PO Box 69, Old Forge, NY 13420 Northeastern Retail Lumber Association, 339 East Ave., Rochester, NY 14604 **NORTH CAROLINA** Appalachian Hardwood Manufacturers, Inc., PO Box 427, High Point, NC 27261 Aromatic Red Cedar Closet Lining Manufacturers Association, PO Box 100, Greensboro, NC 27402 **OREGON** Cascade Holistic Economic Consultants, 14417 SE Laurie Avenue, Oak Grove, OR 97207 Northwest Forestry Association, 1500 SW 1st Ave., Ste. 770, Portland, OR 97201 Pacific Logging Congress, 2300SW 6th Avenue, Ste. 200, Portland, OR 97201 Timber Operators Council, 6825 SW Sandburg St., Tigard, OR 97223 West Coast Lumber Inspection Bureau, PO Box 23145, Portland, OR 97223 Western Forest Industries Association, 1500 SW Taylor, Portland, OR 97205 Western Forestry and Conservation Association, 4033 SW Canyon Road, Portland, OR 97221 Western Hardwood Association, 133 Second Ave. SW, Ste. 450, Portland, OR 97204 Western Red Cedar Lumber Association, Yeon Bldg., 522 SW 5th Avenue, Portland, OR 97204-2122 Western Wood Products Association, Yeon Bldg., 522 SW 5th Avenue, Portland, OR 97204-2122 **PENNSYLVANIA** Hardwood Manufacturers Association, 400 Penn Center Blvd., Pittsburg, PA 15235 **TENNESSEE** Hardwood Distributors Association, 1279 N. McLean St., PO Box 12802, Memphis, TN 38182 National Hardwood Lumber Association, PO Box 34518, Memphis, TN 38184-0518 **VIRGINIA** American Wood Preservers Institute, 1945 Old Gallows Road, Ste. 550, Vienna, VA 22182 Hardwood Plywood Manufacturers Association, 1825 Michael Faraday Dr., PO Box 2789, Reston, VA 22090 National Bark and Soil Producers Association, 13542 Union Village Circle Clifton, VA 22024 National Woodland Owners Association, 374 Maple Ave. E, Ste. 210, Vienna, VA 22180 **WASHINGTON** American Plywood Association, PO Box 11700, Tacoma, WA 98411 American Wood Chip Export Association, 4128½ California Avenue SW, No. 171, Seattle, WA 98116 American Institute of Timber Construction, 11818 SE Mill Plain Blvd., Ste. 425, Vancouver, WA 98684 Cedar Shake and Shingle Bureau, 515 116th Ave. NE, Ste. 275, Bellevue, WA 98004 Plywood Research Foundation, PO Box 11700, Tacoma, WA 98411 Timber Products Manufacturers, 951 E. Third Ave., Spokane, WA 99202 Washington Forest Protection Association, 711 Capitol Way, Evergreen Plaza Bldg., Ste. 608, Olympia, WA 98501 Western Building Material Association, PO Box 1699, Olympia, WA 98507 **WASHINGTON, DC** American Forest Council, 1250 Connecticut Ave. NW, Ste. 320, Washington, DC 20036 American Pulpwood Association, 1025 Vermont Ave. NW, Ste. 1020, Washington, DC 20036 Forest Industries Council, 1250 Connecticut Ave. NW, Ste. 230, Washington, DC 20036 National Association of State Foresters, Hall of States, 444 N. Capitol Street NW, Ste. 526, Washington, DC 20001 National Council on Private Forest, c/o American Forestry Association, PO Box 2000, Washington, DC 20013 National Forest Products Association, 1250 Connecticut Ave. NW, Ste. 200, Washington, DC 20036 National Lumber and Building Material Dealers Association, 40 Ivy Street SE, Washington, DC 20003

SPECIAL THANKS

We most gratefully thank the essayists for their generous contributions to *Clearcut*. These writers took precious time from busy lives to tailor essays specifically for this book. They consider themselves environmental activists as well as specialists in their own fields.

DAVE FOREMAN

worked during the 1970s as Southwest Regional Representative for the Wilderness Society and later as their lobbying coordinator in Washington, D.C. He left D.C. in 1980 to co-found a more militant preservation group—Earth First! From 1981 to 1988 he was editor and publisher of *The Earth First! Journal*. During his tenure as editor many revealing and newsworthy articles appeared in that journal. Some of these were collected in *The Earth First! Reader: Ten Years of Radical Environmentalism* (1991), edited by John Davis.

Foreman is director of the North American Wilderness Recovery Project and editor-in-chief of *Wild Earth*, a periodical on deep ecology.

ORVILLE CAMP

developed ecoforestry from his experience in the forests of southern Oregon. He teaches ecoforestry through the Ecoforestry Institute, Canada, and Ecoforestry Institute, USA. He consults with public agencies and designs ecoforestry for private landowners.

His book, *The Forest Farmer's Handbook: A Guide to Natural Selection Forest Management*, has been widely acclaimed as one of the most clear-viewed alternatives to the present industrial harvest models.

He lives near Selma, Oregon.

WARWICK FOX

is a ecophilosopher working at the Environmental Studies Centre, University of Tasmania. His book, *Toward a Transpersonal Ecology*, is a definitive history of the emergence of the deep, long-range ecology movement and a statement of an ecopsychological approach to deep ecology. Fox has written numerous articles on ecophilosophy and is currently writing on the relationship between science and ecophilosophy.

JIM COOPERMAN

is editor of the British Columbia Environmental Report. He spent his childhood in Minnesota and attended college at the University of California, Berkeley, during the turbulent sixties. He moved to Canada to join the "back to the land" movement. "Working in the bush opened my eyes to destructive forest practices and overcutting in the backcountry."

He currently works full-time for the environment, editing the British Columbia Environmental Report, coordinating the BCEN forest caucus, attending countless meetings and conferences, networking, and lobbying.

R. EDWARD GRUMBINE

belongs to a long line of naturalists who acknowledge the deepening crisis of biodiversity but refuse to relinquish the possibility of an ecologically wholesome future.

Grumbine has worked as a park naturalist, taught field courses on ecology and ecophilosophy, and for the past decade has been director of the Sierra Institute, part of University of California Extension, Santa Cruz. He has written several articles on principles of public policy that could protect biodiversity and a book, *Ghost Bears: Exploring the Biodiversity Crisis* (1992), which looks at the implications of this crisis and why our species-centered approach will ultimately fail to protect ecosystems and diversity.

ALAN DRENGSON

is professor of environmental philosophy at the University of Victoria. He is editor of *The Trumpeter: Journal of Ecosophy* and author of *Beyond Environmental Crisis* (1989).

He has published numerous articles on ecophilosophy and on aikido, a Japanese martial art, which he has studied for 16 years.

He founded the Ecoforestry Institute and the Ecoforestry Foundation. After studying with Orville Camp, Drengson came to the conclusion that natural selection ecoforestry offers the best approach to sustainable natural forests and diversified, sound, rural community economics.

HERB HAMMOND

is a registered professional forester, forest ecologist, and citizen activist known throughout Canada for his vision of a new forestry that will sustain the environment, the economy, and the community. For the past 20 years he has worked in applied research in soil and water degradation, as an industry forester, an instructor of silviculture and forest ecology, and as a consulting forester working with First Nations, environmental groups, and communities.

He presented his ideas on wholistic forest use in his book *Seeing the Forest Among the Trees: The Case for Wholistic Forest Use* (1991).

Hammond lives in British Columbia.

BILL DEVALL

taught environmental studies at Humboldt State University, Arcata, California, for over two decades. His books include *Deep Ecology: Living as if Nature Mattered* (1985), co-authored, with George Sessions, *Simple in Means, Rich in Ends: Practicing Deep Ecology* (1988), and *Living Richly in an Age of Limits* (1993).

He has worked on numerous campaigns to protect forest ecosystems of the Pacific Northwest including the campaign to enlarge Redwood National Park, the designation of wilderness areas in national forests, and the protection of the sacred "high country" of the Siskiyou mountains of northwestern California.

He lives on the north coast of California.

MITCH LANSKY

was drenched with pesticides in his own backyard in Maine in 1976 by modified WWII bombers targeting the spruce budworm. He consequently founded P.E.S.T. (Protect Our Environment from Spray Toxins), an organization that investigated environmentally dangerous forestry practices. For the past decade he has investigated the practices of private logging corporations in Maine. He published the results of his research in *Beyond the Beauty Strip: Saving What's Left of Our Forests* (1992). In his book he demolishes the myths of private forest practices in New England in detail.

Lansky lives in Wytopitlock, Maine.

FELICE PACE

has lived and worked in rural communities of northern California for most of the last two decades. He has proposed alternative community development processes and effectively argued for a new approach to management of national forests. He is director of the Klamath Forest Alliance and was an invited participant at President Clinton's Forest Summit conference in Portland, Oregon, in March 1993.

CHRIS MASER

spent over 20 years as a research scientist in natural history and ecology of forests, shrub steppe, subarctic regions, high mountains, deserts, and coastal zones. Trained as a vertebrate zoologist, he was a research scientist for the U.S. Department of Interior, Bureau of Land Management, and for the EPA. He spent most of the 1980s studying the ancient forests of western Oregon.

Today he is an author, lecturer, and international consultant on sustainable forestry. He was written over 220 publications including *The Redesigned Forest* (1988), *Forest Primeval: The Natural History of an Ancient Forest* (1989), and *Global Imperative: Harmonizing Culture and Nature* (1992).

JAN WILDER-THOMAS

has been active in grassroots organizing in the Shawnee National Forest since 1985, protesting widespread herbicide use by the U.S.F.S. In 1988, she was on the founding board of the Regional Association of Concerned Environmentalists. In 1990, she co-founded Shawnee Earth First! helping to organize the 80-day Hardwood Summer vigil at the Fairview timber sale. Presently, as Director of the Shawnee Defense Fund, she focuses on public education, and photographs the Shawnee timber sales before and after logging. She is organizing a statewide campaign to achieve a special Presidential Executive designation for this tiny forest as the Shawnee Songbird National Monument.

COLLEEN McCRORY

is chairperson of the Valhalla Wilderness Society, an environmental group in southeastern British Columbia that focuses primarily on wilderness, forest, and wildlife protection. She has won three international awards for her environmental activism: the 1992 Goldman Environmental Prize for outstanding grassroots initiatives, the 1992 United Nations Global 500 Roll of Honor, and the 1988 Fred M. Packard International Parks Merit Award from the International Union for the Conservation of Nature.

In 1991, she founded Canada's Future Forest Alliance, a network of environmental, labor, and community groups interested in reforming forest policy and practices.

DOUGLAS TOMPKINS

has a varied background, having been a small time chicken and sheep farmer, mountain guide, tree feller, documentary film producer, art director, entrepreneur, antique Kelim dealer, white-water kayaker, house painter, unlicensed architect, pilot, environmental activist, ski racer, and sports fanatic. He is best known as the co-founder of ESPRIT, the apparel firm, and after retirement from that, as founder of the Foundation for Deep Ecology. He now lives on a farm in southern Chile, when not traveling on foundation projects. This book is the sixth exhibit-format book he has produced, including *Esprit: The Comprehensive Design Principle* and *Amish: The Art of the Quilt*.

REED NOSS

is a Ph.D. in Wildlife Ecology from the University of Florida and author of over 70 papers on ecology and conservation biology. He is presently editor of the journal *Conservation Biology*, science director of The Wildlands Project, and 1993 winner of a Pew Scholar award in Conservation and Environment. He lives in Corvallis, Oregon, with his wife and children.

PHOTOGRAPHERS

SPECIAL THANKS

In the process of working on this book I came into contact with the most extraordinary group of people who came from far-ranging occupations and areas of North America; they are all held together with the common bond of being outraged that our industrial society continues to destroy the natural world that our existence depends on.

I viewed thousands of images of destruction to North America's forests; what you see in this book is very distilled: just over 100 examples. I would like to thank all of the people who helped me coordinate locations, photographers, activists, and pilots. I would also like to thank all the photographers whose work was submitted but not included.

Finally, I believe a project of this scope will bring together activists from British Columbia to Tennessee and from Newfoundland to New Mexico to recognize that in each locale we are not alone in our efforts.
—Edgar Boyles

JOHN F. COOPER

is an advertising photographer who shoots with a large-format camera. Cooper is considered one of the cutting-edge photographers working in the United States today, and is featured in a book, *Take Five*, published in Tokyo in the fall of 1993.

His reason for participating in the *Clearcut* project was personal. "I was raised in rural Minnesota and developed strong feelings about wilderness and its importance. I now have a two-year-old son and want to preserve the ever-diminishing ancient forests for him and his children."

Cooper lives in New Jersey.

DANIEL DANCER

is an internationally published environmental photo-journalist, artist, and explorer. His exhibit "Sacred Ground—Sacred Sky: An Eco-Experience," sponsored by Exhibits USA, began a five-year tour in museums and galleries across the United States in early 1993. This show features the "eco-mandalas" that he creates within many of the Earth's endangered ecosystems. His organic earthworks, made from on-site natural and human-made materials, are created and left beside a polluted river, on a plowed prairie, within a forest slated to be clearcut, and other endangered places.

Dancer is writing a book about "the ecotheology long buried by our ancestors."

PERRY BEATON

was raised on a small farm in southern Quebec. After graduating from college, where he pursued interests in theater, music, and photography, he began a photography business in Lennoxville, Quebec, and worked on local newspapers. He has been a freelance photographer since 1988.

His most satisfying hobby is playing fretless bass with a small vocal group.

JACK DYKINGA

began work as a journalist in 1964 on the *Chicago Tribune*. In 1971, while working for the *Chicago Sun-Times*, he won the Pulitzer Prize for Feature Photography.

Since then he has worked as a freelance photographer. His credited photos have appeared in *Arizona Highways*, *Audubon*, *National Geographic*, and magazines published by the Nature Conservancy, among others.

His books include *Frog Mountain Blues* (1985) with Charles Bowden, *The Secret Forest* (1993), and *Sonoran Desert* (1993).

GARY BRAASCH

is a nature and landscape photographer whose work has appeared in more than 70 publications. He has photographed tropical forests of Central America, the oil spill from the Exxon Valdez in Prince William Sound, Alaska, and the forests of southern Appalachia. His concern for the temperate old-growth forests of the Pacific Northwest led to his publication, with writer David Kelly, of *Secrets of the Old Growth Forest* (1988), *Entering the Grove* (1990) with essays by Kim Stafford, and *Photographing the Patterns of Nature* (1990) with images of the recurring designs in natural processes.

Braasch lives on the north coast of Oregon.

BILL ELLZEY

has photographed many of the world's more arid regions, starting with western images from his family ranch in the Texas panhandle, and currently teaches photo workshops in the desert Southwest. Bill was one of twenty international photographers invited to Australia to create the book *Salute to Western Australia*. Bill is a writer as well as a photographer; his most recent photo/story, a feature reportage on how one *National Geographic* photographer handled an assignment on the Guatemala-Mexico border, appeared in *Photo District News* and *Outdoor Photographer*.

His photos of southeastern Texas were taken in an area that will be extremely difficult to regenerate.

EDGAR BOYLES

is photo editor of *Clearcut*. He is both a cinematographer and still photographer who has woven a passion for wild places and mountain adventure into his professional life. Honored with an Emmy award for outdoor cinematography, he has worked on projects ranging from documentaries of Greenpeace whaling protests to feature films. Edgar lives with his wife Elizabeth and their two sons in an Aspen grove on the banks of the Roaring Fork River in Colorado.

ELIZABETH FERYL

of Environmental Images, has photographed extensively in the national forests documenting forest practices and forest ecology. Her photographs have been used in testimony in Federal Court and the U.S. Congress. She designed and coordinated the publication of the Ancient Forest Alliance book *If You Think Our Forests Look Like This*. She has also been published in *Multinational Monitor, Wilderness, Wild Oregon, E: The Environmental Magazine, Inner Voice, Forest Watch, Audubon, Activist, Enviro-Action, Face Value, Earth First! Journal, Bald Mountain Bulletin, Protect Our Woods, Forest Voice, What's Happening, Headwaters, The Citizen Forester,* and *National Forests* magazine.

MARK HOBSON

is intimately familiar with and passionate about the wildlife and wilderness of the Pacific Northwest. His photos have been published in *Nature Canada, National Geographic, Outdoor Canada, Canadian Geographic,* and many other publications. His books include *The Last Wilderness* (1990), *Vancouver Island: In Search of the Dream* (1992), and *Canada's Incredible Coast* (1991).

He has been active in many campaigns to protect wilderness on Vancouver Island. "The extent of devastation," he says, "has always appalled me and left a huge sense of loss especially since many places I knew well have been turned into a wastelands as a result of clearcutting."

JENNY HAGER

is a freelance photojournalist specializing in the areas of nature, adventure travel, and sport.

Hager taught wilderness skills and nature appreciation for ten years before becoming a full-time photojournalist in 1984. She has her own business, Alpine Images, for stock and assignment photography.

Her work has appeared in *Buzzworm, Climbing, Outside, Sierra, Time,* and many other publications. She searches for bold and striking compositions so that her images lend themselves to graphic illustrations.

VICKY HUSBAND

is a writer, filmmaker, fundraiser, and untiring advocate for the temperate rainforests of the Pacific Northwest.

She is past president of the Friends of Ecological Reserves of British Columbia and chair, Sierra Club of Western Canada.

She was deeply involved in the successful struggle to save South Moresby, Queen Charlotte Islands, as a Canadian National Park Reserve.

She has worked on all aspects of temperate rainforest survival in British Columbia, from lobbying for change in forest practices to organizing educational campaigns on the ecology of ancient forests.

HENDRIK HERFST

is the founder of The Defenders of Nopiming, an environmental group dedicated to the survival of the Nopiming Forest located between the Winnipeg and Wanipigow rivers of eastern Manitoba, Canada. A professional architect, Hendrick combined his experiences as teacher, artist, photographer, and designer to plan and develop an award-winning Children's Discovery Centre in Assiniboine Park, Winnipeg.

Hendrick spends leisure time canoeing, winter camping, and backpacking in Canada's wilderness areas.

JUDY KUHA JOHNSON

is a forest activist. A second-generation Finnish/American, she was born and raised in Sebeka, Minnesota, where her father ran a sawmill for fifty years.

"Papa often lamented how he hoped it wouldn't happen again...but tragically it is happening again....We have so few of the old white pine stands left and they are still being cut. Minnesota tree farms are chilling; going from a forest of biological diversity to a forest of pure sterility. It is the Forest's diversity that drives me. In Finnish: 'Sisu,' it's tough to translate...a kind of inner fire or gritty perseverance to get things done...to help save what is left...to pass on to my grandchildren."

DAVID HISER

has spent the last three decades as a photojournalist photographing endangered forests throughout the United States, Mexico, Tasmania, and Borneo. Besides contributing to over 50 *National Geographic* publications, his work has been published by *Audubon, Geo, Outside,* and the Sierra Club.

He always enjoys teaching and has led over 30 workshops and seminars. He is co-owner of Photographers/ Aspen, a stock and assignment agency, and is represented worldwide by Tony Stone Images.

Hiser lives in Aspen, Colorado.

ROBERT GLENN KETCHUM

has used his work to focus public attention on environmental issues for 25 years. His book *The Tongass: Alaska's Vanishing Rain Forest* (1987), is credited with helping pass the Tongass Timber Reform Act of 1990, one of the most comprehensive forest reform acts in the past twenty years.

Ketchum's photographs are collected and exhibited worldwide. His books include *Overlooked in America: The Success and Failure of Federal Land Management* (1991).

Ketchum is one of only four photographers in the world to be given the United Nations Outstanding Environmental Achievement Award.

KATHRYN KOLB

is a freelance photographer living in Atlanta, Georgia. As a child she hiked with her mother in the mountains of Virginia and North Carolina. "I have always wanted to communicate what I learned, especially to my friends who have always lived in cities, of the greatness and value of unmolested nature and the tragedy and insanity of our culture's greed and destruction of the American land."

Kolb's professional work includes editorial journalism and illustration, corporate and arts photography.

BALTHAZAR KORAB

was born in Hungary and recalls avidly reading the *Leatherstocking Tales* by James Fenimore Cooper as a youth. Years later, moving to Michigan, he expected to find a wilderness deeply imbedded in his youthful imagination.

Korab dedicated himself to his photographic art as a way to expose the destruction of forests. He has photographed in the Sierra of California, the Olympic Peninsula of Washington, the Danube in central Europe, and many other places.

His work has been published in all major architecture media as well as *Time, National Geographic, Geo, Fortune, House and Garden,* and *Elle Decor.*

GARTH LENZ

is a photographer and forest activist whose photos have appeared in such publications as *The New York Times, International Wildlife,* and *Suomen Kuvaletti* (Finland). Along with fellow activist Valerie Langer, he toured Europe in 1992 giving slide shows to focus international attention on the plight of Canada's temperate and boreal forests.

Based in Clayoquot Sound, the largest intact temperate rainforest on Vancouver Island, he has not only photographed destructive logging practices around his home but has also participated in blockades of logging roads into intact valleys of Vancouver Island.

TERRY LIVINGSTONE

is best known for his images of areas in the southeastern United States including flora, fauna, and seasonal photos. His work is represented by the stock photo agency "Picturesque" (Raleigh, North Carolina). His work regularly appears in books, magazines, calendars, brochures, and advertisements.

He is the owner/director of the Willow Creek Workshops, a company that offers limited-enrollment weekend courses in natural history photography.

Livingstone lives with his wife and two sons in a log cabin nestled in the woods near Franklin, Tennessee.

SANDY LONSDALE

decided to put his photography to use as an activist tool five or six years ago as he walked across a forty-year-old clearcut of 400–500-year-old trees that had never restored itself. He now uses his photographs to raise public awareness on protecting wild public lands from abusive human uses.

His work has appeared in public shows, educational videodiscs for schools, and in *Walking Guide to Oregon's Ancient Forests.*

He now concentrates on bringing attention to Oregon's eastside forests, which he feels are being neglected by the Clinton administration's focus on the coastal and Cascade forests.

He resides near Bend, Oregon.

LORI MAC

spent her childhood in Salt Lake City where she grew to appreciate the land through spending time in the Wasatch Mountains and in the deserts of Utah. After spending eight years in urban California, she and her husband moved to Portland, Oregon, in 1990, "finally back to some semblance, or at least the possibility, of seeing wilderness."

She is a partner in and photographer for Opinari, a studio specializing in sports-related product design, photography, and illustration.

Mac's photographs have been published in *Newsweek, Industrial Design, New American Design,* and many other publications.

ALEX MACLEAN

specializes in aerial photography. During the past fifteen years his images have been featured in numerous photographic exhibits, gallery shows, and feature articles in magazines. He also has taught courses on aerial photography at Harvard University, Boston Architectural Center, and MIT. MacLean's photographic firm, Landslides, has a stock aerial photo library with over 150,000 images on file.

He lives in Boston.

DOUG RADIES

coordinated the campaign to protect the headwaters of the Quesnel River in British Columbia's central interior. The Quesnel River drains the vital heartland between Bowron Lake and Wells Gray provincial parks, located on the western slopes of the rugged Caribou mountain range.

Radies uses the power of photography to bring remote wilderness areas into the sight and mind of people who live elsewhere.

GALEN ROWELL

creates landscapes featuring the unexpected convergence of light and form, seemingly unrepeatable moments he finds by combining imagination and action. He calls these images "dynamic landscapes" and his quest for these images is documented in his book *Mountain Light: In Search of the Dynamic Landscape* (1986). His other books in large format include *The Vertical World of Yosemite* (1974), *In the Throne Room of the Mountain Gods* (1977), *High and Wild* (1979), *Many People Come, Looking, Looking* (1980), *Alaska: Images of the Country* (1981), and *My Tibet* (1990) with text by His Holiness the Dalai Lama.

LEILA STANFIELD

and her friends Don Duerr and Jeff Kessler are the backbone of Friends of the Bow, a citizen activist group in Laramie, Wyoming, working to preserve native ecosystems in the Rocky Mountains. Since 1988, the group has continued aggressive actions to stop clearcutting on the Medicine Bow National Forest. In 1989 they began an aerial survey. Stanfield is a private pilot, Duerr and Kessler are proficient in computer-imaging technologies; together they have produced vivid pictures of forest damage.

TRYGVE STEEN

is a biologist-photographer who creates images of Pacific Northwest forests, ranging from aerials to close-ups of their organisms. His aerial photography documenting logging damage to the Northwest forest resources began in collaboration with a BLM hydrologist in 1972, and his most recent work included his friends, Sky, as pilot–flight coordinator and LightHawk, for aircraft support. He has co-developed a computer and GPS-based system to record aircraft position as each photo is taken. The library of Tryg-Sky/LightHawk aerials exceeds 12,000 images and includes nearly all the national forests in the Northwest plus associated BLM and private land.

He lives in Portland, Oregon.

RANDY STOLTMANN

alerted the environmental community to the imminent logging of the Carmanah Valley on Vancouver Island, home of some of the world's tallest known Sitka spruce trees. Half of that valley is currently protected within Carmanah Pacific Provincial Park but the fate of the remainder is uncertain.

Stoltmann has served on the boards of the Heritage Forests Society and Western Canada Wilderness Committee. He was a contributing writer and photographer on *Carmanah: Artistic Visions of an Ancient Rain Forest* (1989) and is author of *Hiking Guide to the Big Trees of Southwestern British Columbia*.

BARRY TESSMAN

recently spent two years exploring and photographing ethnic peoples in Siberia and in the former Soviet Union. He now travels extensively doing outdoor and environmental photography. He is a rafting guide and Class V white-water boater with experience in Alaska, Russia, Chile, and the continental U.S.

When not traveling he makes his home in Lake Isabella, California.

DOUG THRON

has for the past year been working on getting public support to preserve Headwaters Ancient Redwood Forest by traveling throughout America giving slide shows and lectures about the forest. Doug believes that it is his obligation to use his photography in a way that allows others to see the ancient forest as he sees it—an irreplaceable ecosystem of peace and beauty that is quickly being destroyed for the corporate dollar.

"Photography is the key way to protect the last of the old-growth forest because most people have no idea of the mass destruction being caused by the giant timber corporations."

LINDE WAIDHOFER

is a landscape photographer as well as a sports-action and travel photographer. Her first love is what she calls the "non-literal landscape"—natural images that defy the common-sense expectations of everyday outdoor experience.

While she prefers photographing landscapes full of mystery and poetry, she feels that photographers have a special, if painful obligation to document the increasing destruction of wild places. Her published works include two books, *High Color: Spectacular Wildflowers of the Rockies* and *Red Rock, Blue Sky: Mysterious Landscapes of the Southwest*.

CLINTON WEBB

resigned from the British Columbia Forest Service in 1987 because he was increasingly opposed to its policy of "liquidating" all remaining unprotected old-growth forests. During the past six years he has worked full-time in the environmental movement. "I've had the privilege of working with many fine people who are dedicated to their work. I believe we are slowly winning the battle to save this beautiful planet."

Since resigning from the Forest Service, Webb has worked as a wholistic forestry consultant and a grassroots organizer.

Webb lives in southern British Columbia.

MARK ALAN WILSON

directs a nonprofit photography service for environmental groups.

His photos have appeared in *Rolling Stone, Greenpeace Journal, American Photo, Outside*, and many other magazines and newspapers.

Wilson's major shows and projects include: "Shadows in the Land," a photographic essay of eighty Superfund hazardous waste sites across the state of Montana; "Silverbow National Park"; and "The Big Open," a photo-documentary of land use and its effects on the landscape, environment, and people of Montana's arid central plateau.

Wilson lives in Great Falls, Montana.

GEORGE WUERTHNER

is a freelance writer, photographer, naturalist, and botanist. A former ranger and university instructor, Wuerthner is the author of thirteen books and hundreds of magazines articles on endangered species, fire ecology, wilderness management, and other wilderness topics. Wuerthner has traveled throughout the continent and has extensive knowledge of many different bioregions. In addition to serving on the board of The Wildlands Project, he is currently on the boards of Rest the West and Restore the North Woods, and is president of the National Wolf Growers Association.

SELECTED READING LIST ON FORESTS, BIODIVERSITY, DEEP ECOLOGY

Clary, David A. *Timber and the Forest Service.* Lawrence: University Press of Kansas, 1986.

Ehrlich, Paul and Anne. *Extinction.* New York: Ballantine, 1981.

Grumbine, Edward. *Ghost Bears: Exploring the Biodiversity Crisis.* Island Press, 1992.

Hammond, Herb. *Seeing the Forest Among the Trees: The Case for Wholistic Forest Use.* Vancouver: Pole Star Press, 1991.

Harris, Larry D. *The Fragmented Forest: Island Biogeography Theory and the Preservation of Biotic Diversity.* University of Chicago Press, 1984.

Lansky, Mitch. *Beyond the Beauty Strip: Saving What's Left of Our Forests.* Tilbury House, 1992.

McLaughlin, Andrew. *Regarding Nature: Industrialism and Deep Ecology.* Albany, NY: SUNY Press, 1993.

Manning, Richard. *Last Stand: Logging, Journalism, and the Case for Humility.* Salt Lake City: Peregrine Smith Books, 1991.

Maser, Chris. *Global Imperative: Restoring Harmony with Nature.* Stillpoint Press, 1992.

———. *The Forest Primeval.* San Francisco: Sierra Club Books, 1990.

———. *The Redesigned Forest.* San Pedro, CA: R. and E. Miles, 1988.

Mitchell, John G. *Dispatches from the Deep Woods.* University of Nebraska Press, 1991.

Norse, Elliott. *Ancient Forests of the Pacific Northwest.* Island Press, 1990.

Robinson, Gordon. *The Forest and the Trees: A Guide to Excellent Forestry.* Island Press, 1988.

Soulé, Michael E., ed. *Conservation Biology: The Science of Scarcity and Diversity.* Sinauer Associates, 1986.

Wilson, Edward O. *The Diversity of Life.* Cambridge: Harvard University Press, 1992.

BOOKS ON THE DEEP, LONG-RANGE ECOLOGY MOVEMENT

Abbey, Edward. *Desert Solitaire.* Tucson: University of Arizona Press, 1988.

Berman, Morris. *Coming to Our Senses: Body and Spirit in the Hidden History of the West.* New York: Bantam, 1989.

Devall, Bill. *Simple in Means, Rich in Ends.* Salt Lake City: Peregrine Smith Books, 1988.

———. *Living Richly in an Age of Limits.* Salt Lake City: Peregrine Smith Books, 1993.

Devall, Bill, and George Sessions. *Deep Ecology: Living as if Nature Mattered.* Salt Lake City: Peregrine Smith Books, 1985.

Drengson, Alan. *Beyond Environmental Crisis: From Technocrat to Planetary Person.* New York: Peter Lang Publishing, 1989.

Ehrenfeld, David. *Beginning Again: People and Nature in the New Millennium.* New York: Oxford University Press, 1993.

Fox, Warwick. *Toward a Transpersonal Ecology: Developing New Foundations for Environmentalism.* Boston: Shambhala, 1991.

LaChapelle, Dolores. *Sacred Land Sacred Sex: Rapture of the Deep.* Durango, CO: Kivaki Press, 1988.

Naess, Arne. *Ecology, Community, and Lifestyle: Outline of an Ecosophy,* trans. and rev. David Rothenberg. Cambridge: Cambridge University Press, 1989.

Leopold, Aldo. *A Sand County Almanac: And Sketches Here and There.* New York: Oxford University Press, 1949.

Roszak, Theodore. *The Voice of the Earth.* New York: Simon and Schuster, 1992.

Rothenberg, David, ed. *Is it Painful to Think? Conversations with Arne Naess.* Minneapolis: University of Minnesota Press, 1992.

Rothenberg, David, ed. *Wisdom of the Open Air: The Norwegian Roots of Deep Ecology.* Minneapolis: University of Minnesota Press, 1992.

Seed, John, and Joanna Macy, Pat Fleming, and Arne Naess. *Thinking Like a Mountain: Towards a Council of All Beings.* Santa Cruz: New Society Publishers, 1988.

Shepard, Paul. *Nature and Madness.* San Francisco: Sierra Club Books,.

Snyder, Gary. *The Practice of the Wild.* San Francisco: North Point Press, 1991.

———. *The Old Ways.* San Francisco: City Lights Books, 1977.

Wilson, Edward O. *Biophilia.* Cambridge: Harvard University Press, 1984.

ACKNOWLEDGMENTS & THANKS

In big projects such as a book like this involving thirty-five photographers and fifteen writers, hundreds of activists, dozens of production, design, and make-ready people, not to mention so many who lent a hand along the way, it is fitting that we spend a moment here to thank one and all. For the most part *everyone* on this project worked either pro bono or for immensely less than they normally charge for their time. This was, in all its aspects, a labor of love *and* hope. We hope that this effort might in some way stem the rising tide of deforestation taking place here in North America and perhaps influence education and awareness elsewhere, not just in North America.

THE HEAVIES
Edgar and Elizabeth Boyles, Bill Devall, Del Rae Roth

SPECIAL THANKS
The following persons made invaluable contributions to this project during various stages in its development. The editors acknowledge their good work and thank them for their help.

A.F.S.E.E.E., Burnham Arndt, Mike Bader, Steve Beckwitt, Peter Berg, Weston Boyles, Doug Brazil, Jim Brittel, David Brower, Charla Brown, Ruthie Brown, Kevin Browning, Mary Camp, Adriane Carr, Mark Chambers, Alain Charest, Yvon Chouinard, Sharon Chow, Jim Cohee, Michael Crawford, Jim Darwish, Alan Davis and Conservatree Paper Co., John Davis, Marie Davis, Bob Diamond, Rob Dryden, Jules Dufour, Rudy Engholm, Paul Fanelli, Trudy Frisk, Ned Fritz, Paul Genez, Michel Goudreau, Rod Greenough, Scott Groene, Herb Chao Gunther, Susan Hammond, Eric Hansen, Randy Hayes, Ocean Hellman, Chuck Henk, Jeff Henry, Tim Hermach, Patrick Higgins, Jeri Hise, Sam Hitt, Dan Imhoff, Tracy Katelman, Stephanie Kaza, Peggy Kiss, Tom Knudson, Myron Kozak, Jerry Kunz, Dan Lamont, Valerie Langer, Lucie Lavoie, Tim Lillebo, Laurel Hilde Lippert, Tom Lippert, Robert Locklin, Lone Wolf Circles, Joanna Macy, Dolly Mah, Andy Mahler, Elizabeth Mander, Jerry Mander, Sam Mark, Ed Marster, Kris McDivitt, Victor Menotti, Rob Messick, Stephanie Mills, James Monteith, Valerie Moore, Dennis Morgan, Danny Moses, Arne Naess, Oscar Nelder, Jay Noyes, Justin O'Cathain, David Orten, Leonard Palmer, Gary Payne, Vivian Pharis, Denise Quitiquit, Steve Rahn, Charles Restino, Sharon Risedorph, Carl Ross, Lynn Ryan, Kim Salloway, Jamie Sayen, Paul Senez, Larry Shelton, Steve Smith, Gary Snyder, Mark Spense, Rick Steiner, Tom Stibolt, Craig Stockstill and Andresen Press, Stump Central, Shozo Suzuki, Kevin Sweeney, Takuji Takato, Lito Tejada-Flores, Quincey Tompkins, Ray Travers, Sylvie Trudel, Tom Tuxill, Martin von Mirbach, Lorraine Vetch, Beth Wald, Cliff Wallis, Lorna Walsh, Phil Wasson, Wild Earth, Bill Willers, Harvey Williams, Jerry Williams, Denise Peters Wilson, Mark Winstein, Christian Wolfe, Katherine Wright, Michiko Yagi, Neil Yeszin, Alan Young, Cameron Young.

LIGHTHAWK
The editors also give special thanks to Lighthawk pilots who flew photographers, sometimes on short notice, and to students at Humboldt State University who offered critical feedback on many of the ideas and photos presented in this book during critical stages in the development of this project, to local forest activists in many bioregions of North America who graciously guided photographers to important areas where clearcutting was occurring and who answered phone calls requesting information for this book.

BIOREGIONS
Peter Berg, David Haenke, Stephanie Mills, Bioregional Project/Newburg, Mo., Planet Drum, San Francisco, Turtle Island Office, David Levine at Learning Alliance, N.Y.C.

DONORS AND CONTRIBUTORS
Andresen Graphic Services, Foundation for Deep Ecology, New Lab, Patagonia Company, Tamotsu Yagi Design

EDITORIAL ASSISTANCE & RESEARCH
Edgar and Elizabeth Boyles

GRAPHIC DESIGN
Graphic Design: Tamotsu Yagi/Del Rae Roth.   Project/Production Coordination: Del Rae Roth.
Production: Tamotsu Yagi Design; Misa Awatsuji, Giorgio Baravalle, Hiroyuki Kondo, Akira Yagi. Special thanks to Tamotsu Yagi for the donation of his studio and personnel.

PRINTING
Nissha Printing Co., LTD., Kyoto, Japan. Printing Directors: Kazuo Nakae, Mitsuo Shindo. Production Managers: Motomu Itahashi/Hiroyuki Nakao
Director of U.S. Operations: Hiroshi Kurosawa

Dust jacket: Kikurasha-White (100% cotton paper). Cover: LG Lamy Gold: (100% postconsumer waste paper)
Endpapers: Saitan-Natural (50% postconsumer waste paper)
Text pages: High-Land (50% postconsumer waste paper). Color section: Refreshland (70% postconsumer waste paper)
All paper was oxygen bleached. To the best of our knowledge, no clearcut was used in the manufacture of these papers.

From our extensive searches it appears that we have managed to use paper not from any clearcuts. However, due to the untraceability of pulp source transfers by various intermediaries it is uncertain where a small percentage of virgin fibers originate that have been mixed in with known origin fiber. We were unable to make a life cycle audit.

NATURE
designed a
forest as an
experiment in
unpredictability:
we are trying to
design a regulated
forest. Nature designed
a forest over a landscape:
we are trying to design a
forest on each hectare. Nature
designed a forest with diversity:
we are trying to design a forest with
simplistic uniformity. Nature designed
a forest of interrelated processes: we are
trying to design a forest based on isolated
products. Nature designed a forest in which
all elements are neutral: we are trying to design
a forest in which we perceive some elements to be
good and others bad. Nature designed a forest to be
a flexible, timeless continuum of species: we are
trying to design a forest to be a rigid, time-constrained
monoculture. Nature designed a forest of long-term
absolutes. Nature designed a forest to be self-sustaining and
self-repairing: we are designing a forest to require increasing
external subsidies—fertilizers, herbicides, and pesticides.
Nature designed forests of the Pacific Northwest to live 500
to 1,200 years: we are designing a forest that may live 100 years.
Nature designed Pacific Northwest forests to be unique in the
world, with twenty-five species of conifers, the longest lived and the
largest of their genera anywhere: we are designing a forest that is largely a
single-species on a short rotation. Everything we humans have been doing
to the forest is an attempt to push nature to a higher sustained yield. We
fail to recognize, however, that we must have a sustainable forest before we can
have a sustainable yield (harvest). In other words, we cannot have a sustainable
yield until we have a sustainable forest. We must have a sustainable forest to have a
sustainable yield: we must
have a sustainable yield
to have a sustainable
industry: we must have
a sustainable industry
to have a sustainable
economy: we must have a
sustainable economy to
have a sustainable society.

Chris Maser